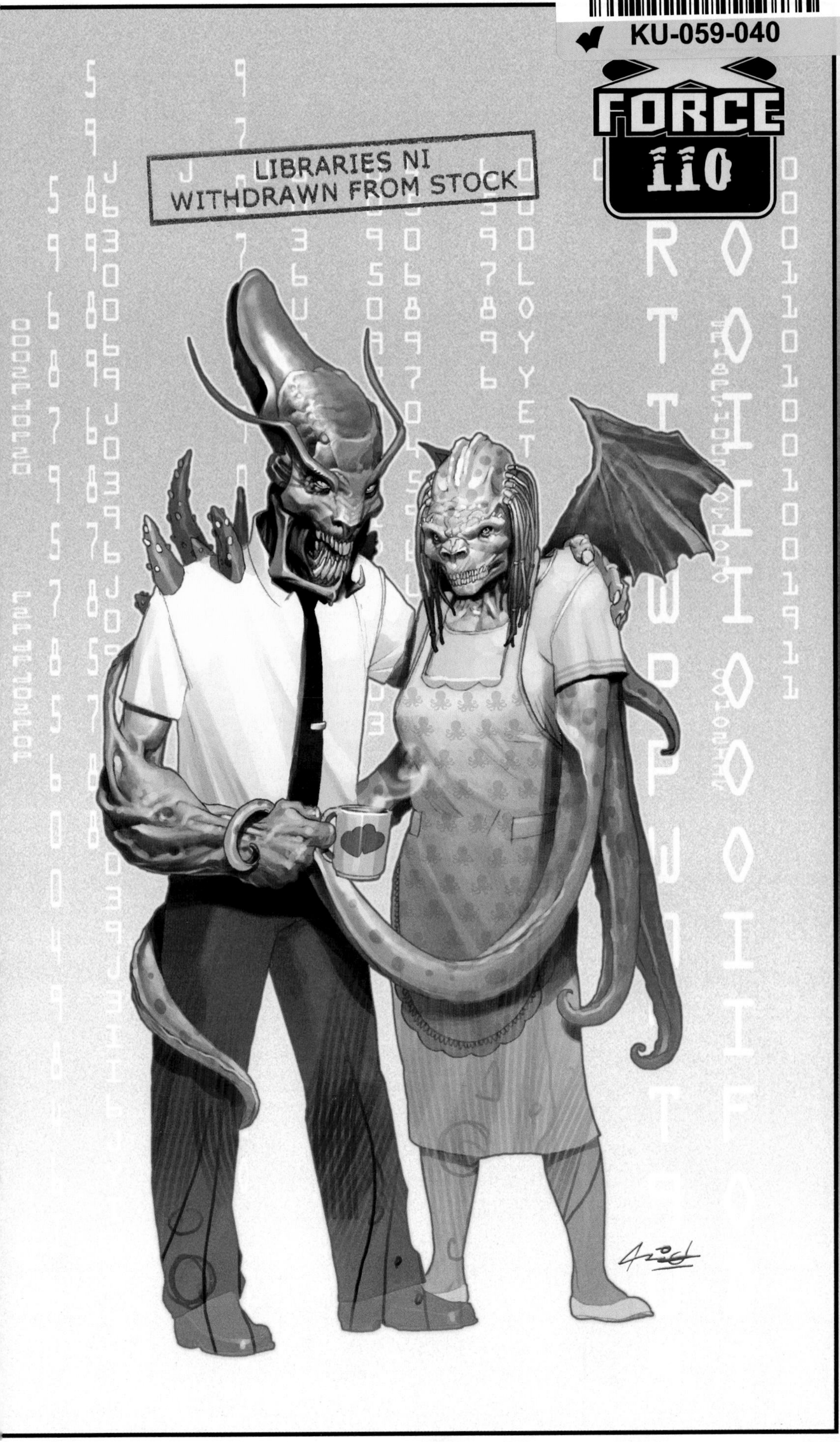
FORCE
110

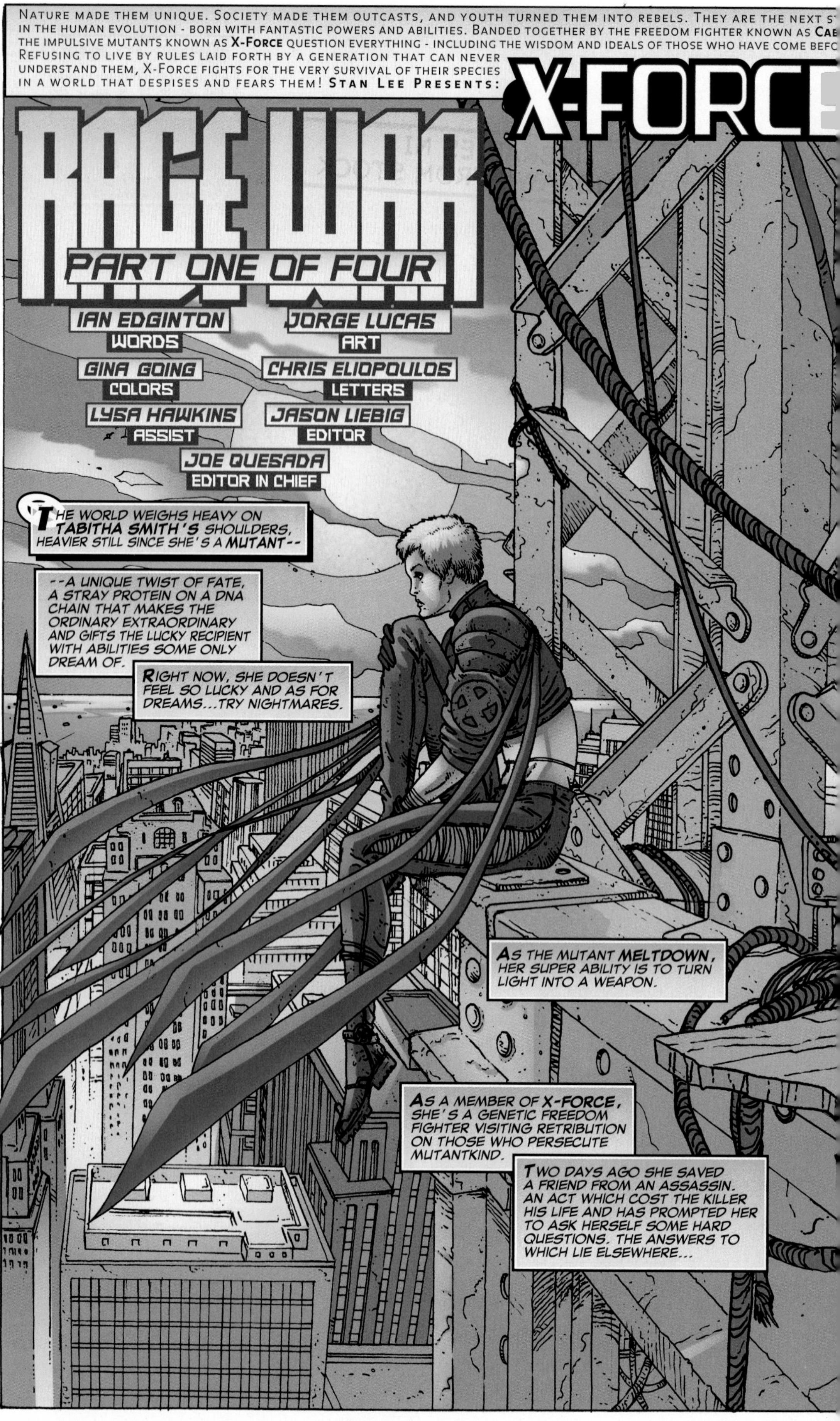
NATURE MADE THEM UNIQUE. SOCIETY MADE THEM OUTCASTS, AND YOUTH TURNED THEM INTO REBELS. THEY ARE THE NEXT
IN THE HUMAN EVOLUTION - BORN WITH FANTASTIC POWERS AND ABILITIES. BANDED TOGETHER BY THE FREEDOM FIGHTER KNOWN AS
THE IMPULSIVE MUTANTS KNOWN AS X-FORCE QUESTION EVERYTHING - INCLUDING THE WISDOM AND IDEALS OF THOSE WHO HAVE COME
REFUSING TO LIVE BY RULES LAID FORTH BY A GENERATION THAT CAN NEVER UNDERSTAND THEM, X-FORCE FIGHTS FOR THE VERY SURVIVAL OF THEIR SPECIES IN A WORLD THAT DESPISES AND FEARS THEM! STAN LEE PRESENTS:
X-FORCE
RACE WAR
PART ONE OF FOUR
IAN EDGINTON WORDS
JORGE LUCAS ART
GINA GOING COLORS
CHRIS ELIOPOULOS LETTERS
LYSA HAWKINS ASSIST
JASON LIEBIG EDITOR
JOE QUESADA EDITOR IN CHIEF
THE WORLD WEIGHS HEAVY ON TABITHA SMITH'S SHOULDERS, HEAVIER STILL SINCE SHE'S A MUTANT--
--A UNIQUE TWIST OF FATE, A STRAY PROTEIN ON A DNA CHAIN THAT MAKES THE ORDINARY EXTRAORDINARY AND GIFTS THE LUCKY RECIPIENT WITH ABILITIES SOME ONLY DREAM OF.
RIGHT NOW, SHE DOESN'T FEEL SO LUCKY AND AS FOR DREAMS...TRY NIGHTMARES.
AS THE MUTANT MELTDOWN, HER SUPER ABILITY IS TO TURN LIGHT INTO A WEAPON.
AS A MEMBER OF X-FORCE, SHE'S A GENETIC FREEDOM FIGHTER VISITING RETRIBUTION ON THOSE WHO PERSECUTE MUTANTKIND.
TWO DAYS AGO SHE SAVED A FRIEND FROM AN ASSASSIN. AN ACT WHICH COST THE KILLER HIS LIFE AND HAS PROMPTED HER TO ASK HERSELF SOME HARD QUESTIONS. THE ANSWERS TO WHICH LIE ELSEWHERE...

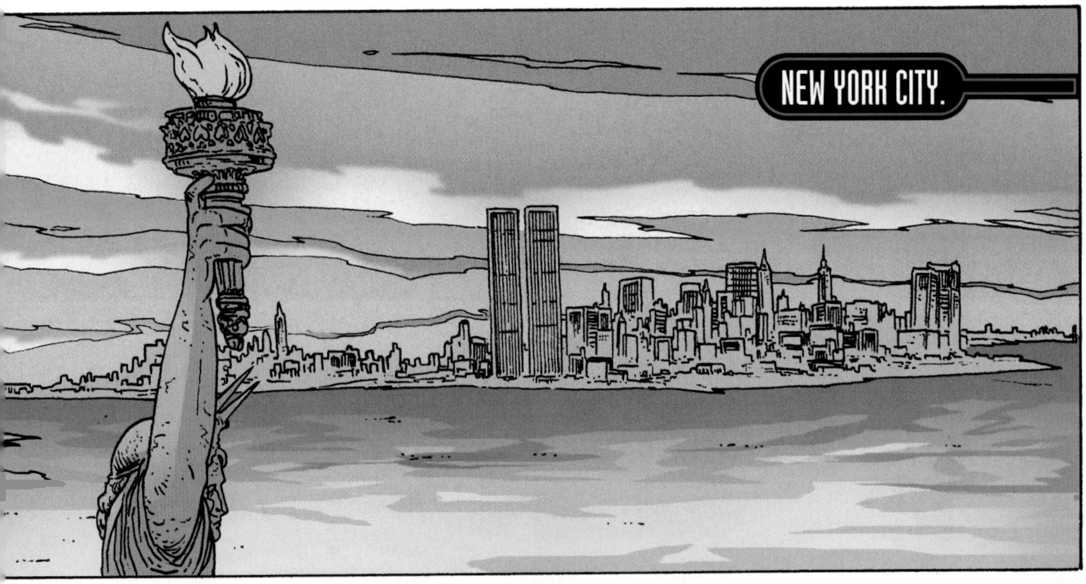
NEW YORK CITY.

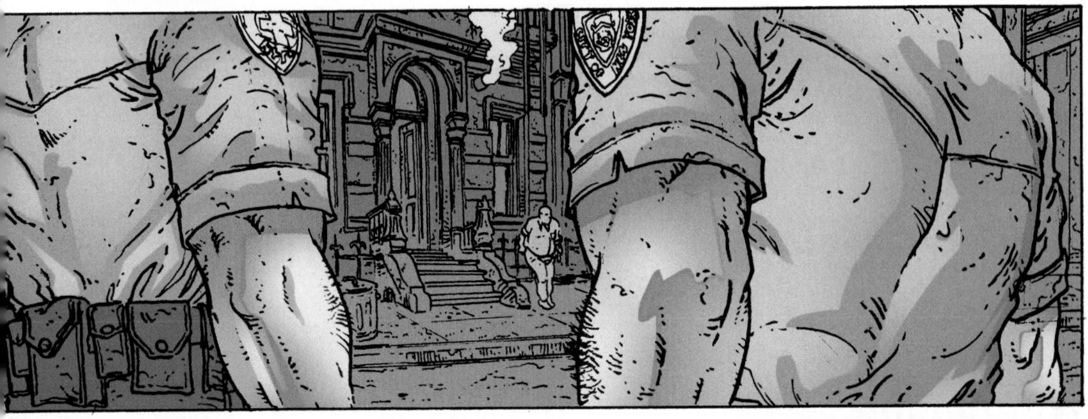

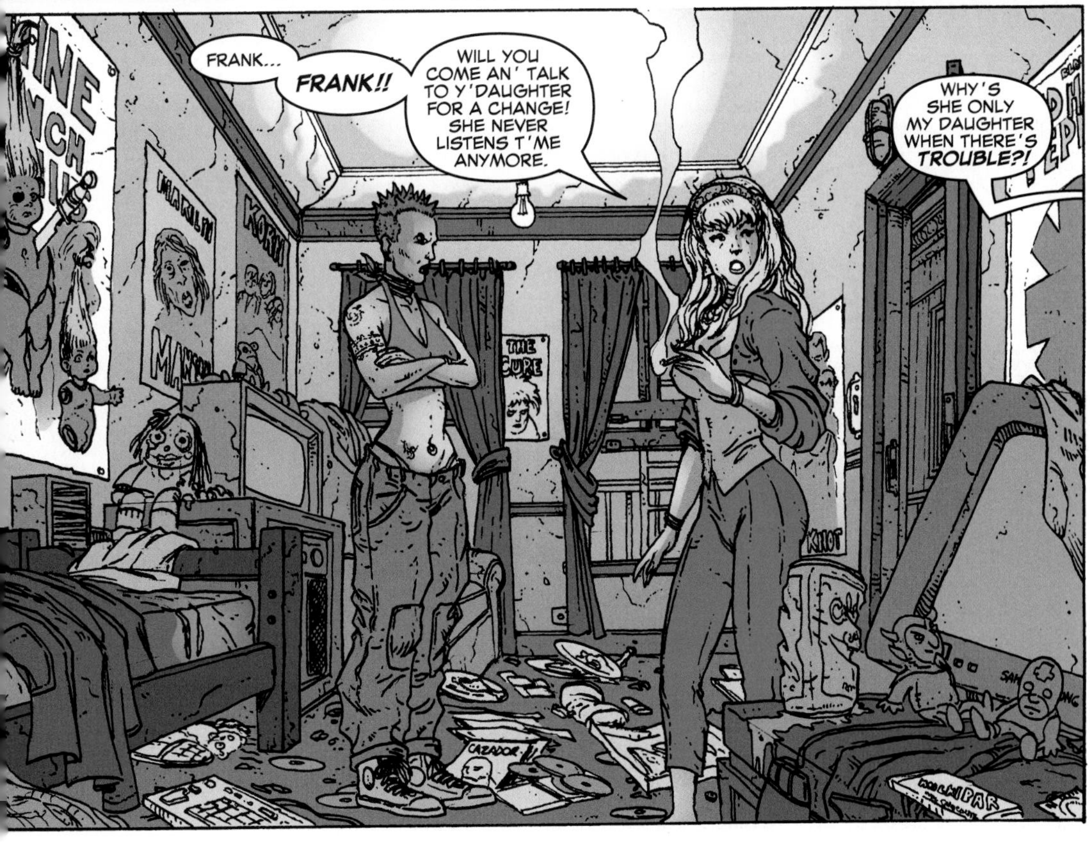
FRANK... FRANK!!
WILL YOU COME AN' TALK TO Y'DAUGHTER FOR A CHANGE! SHE NEVER LISTENS T'ME ANYMORE.
WHY'S SHE ONLY MY DAUGHTER WHEN THERE'S TROUBLE?!
THE CURE
KORN
CAZADOR

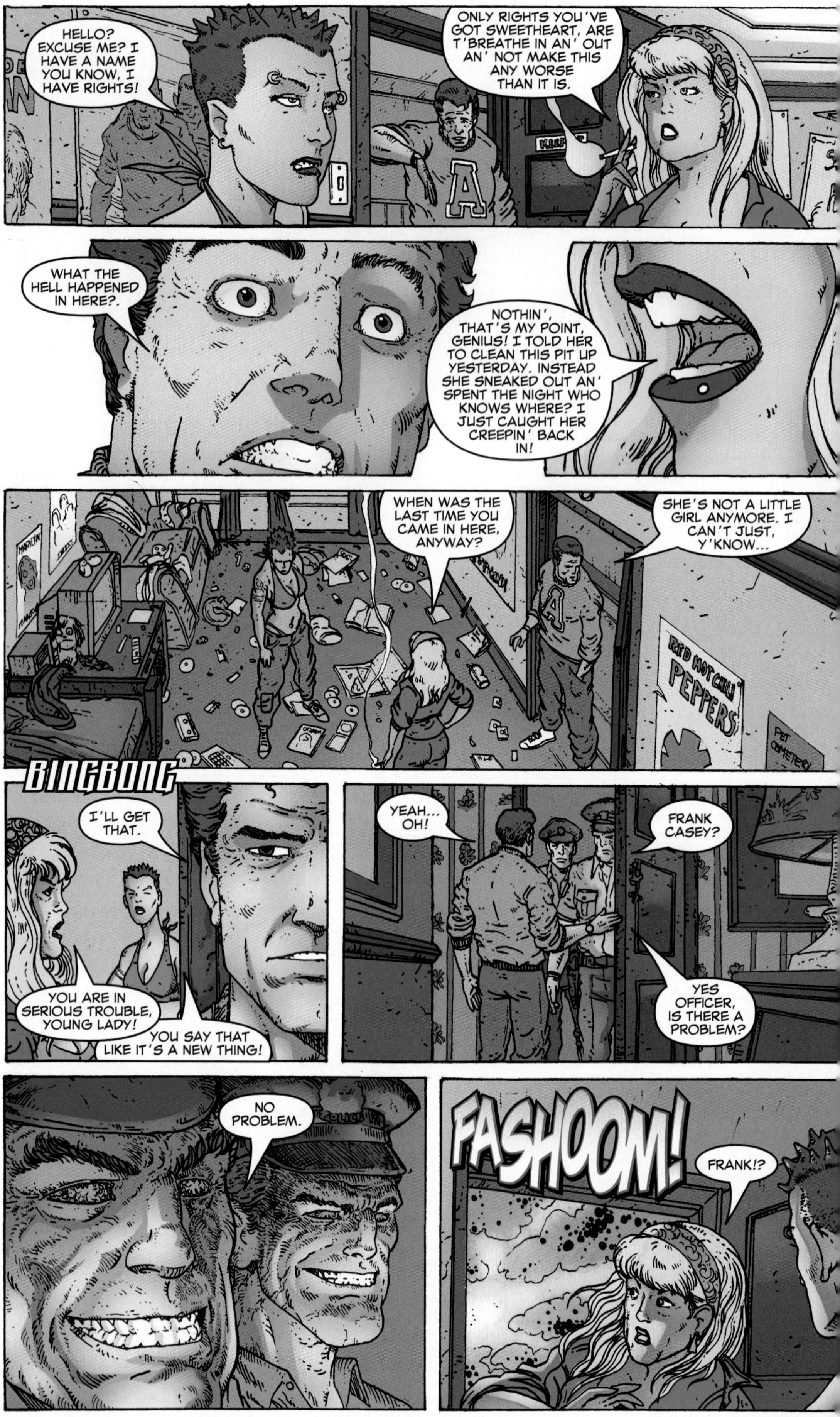
HELLO? EXCUSE ME? I HAVE A NAME YOU KNOW, I HAVE RIGHTS!
ONLY RIGHTS YOU'VE GOT SWEETHEART, ARE T'BREATHE IN AN' OUT AN' NOT MAKE THIS ANY WORSE THAN IT IS.
WHAT THE HELL HAPPENED IN HERE?.
NOTHIN', THAT'S MY POINT, GENIUS! I TOLD HER TO CLEAN THIS PIT UP YESTERDAY. INSTEAD SHE SNEAKED OUT AN' SPENT THE NIGHT WHO KNOWS WHERE? I JUST CAUGHT HER CREEPIN' BACK IN!
WHEN WAS THE LAST TIME YOU CAME IN HERE, ANYWAY?
SHE'S NOT A LITTLE GIRL ANYMORE. I CAN'T JUST, Y'KNOW...
RED HOT CHILI PEPPERS
PET CEMETERY
BINGBONG
I'LL GET THAT.
YOU ARE IN SERIOUS TROUBLE, YOUNG LADY!
YOU SAY THAT LIKE IT'S A NEW THING!
YEAH... OH!
FRANK CASEY?
YES OFFICER, IS THERE A PROBLEM?
NO PROBLEM.
FASHOOM!
FRANK!?

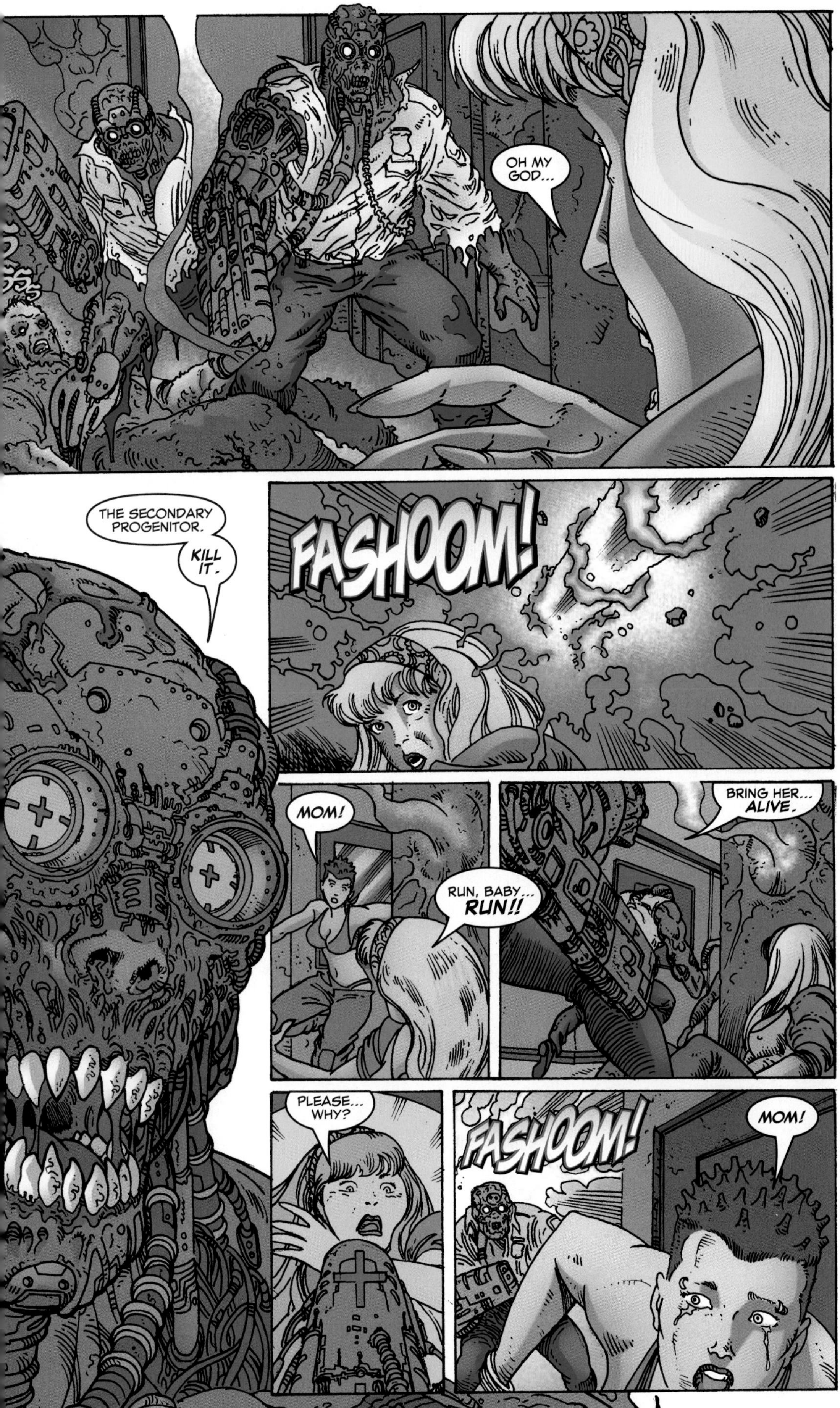
OH MY GOD...
THE SECONDARY PROGENITOR.
KILL IT.
FASHOOM!
MOM!
RUN, BABY... RUN!!
BRING HER... ALIVE.
PLEASE... WHY?
FASHOOM!
MOM!

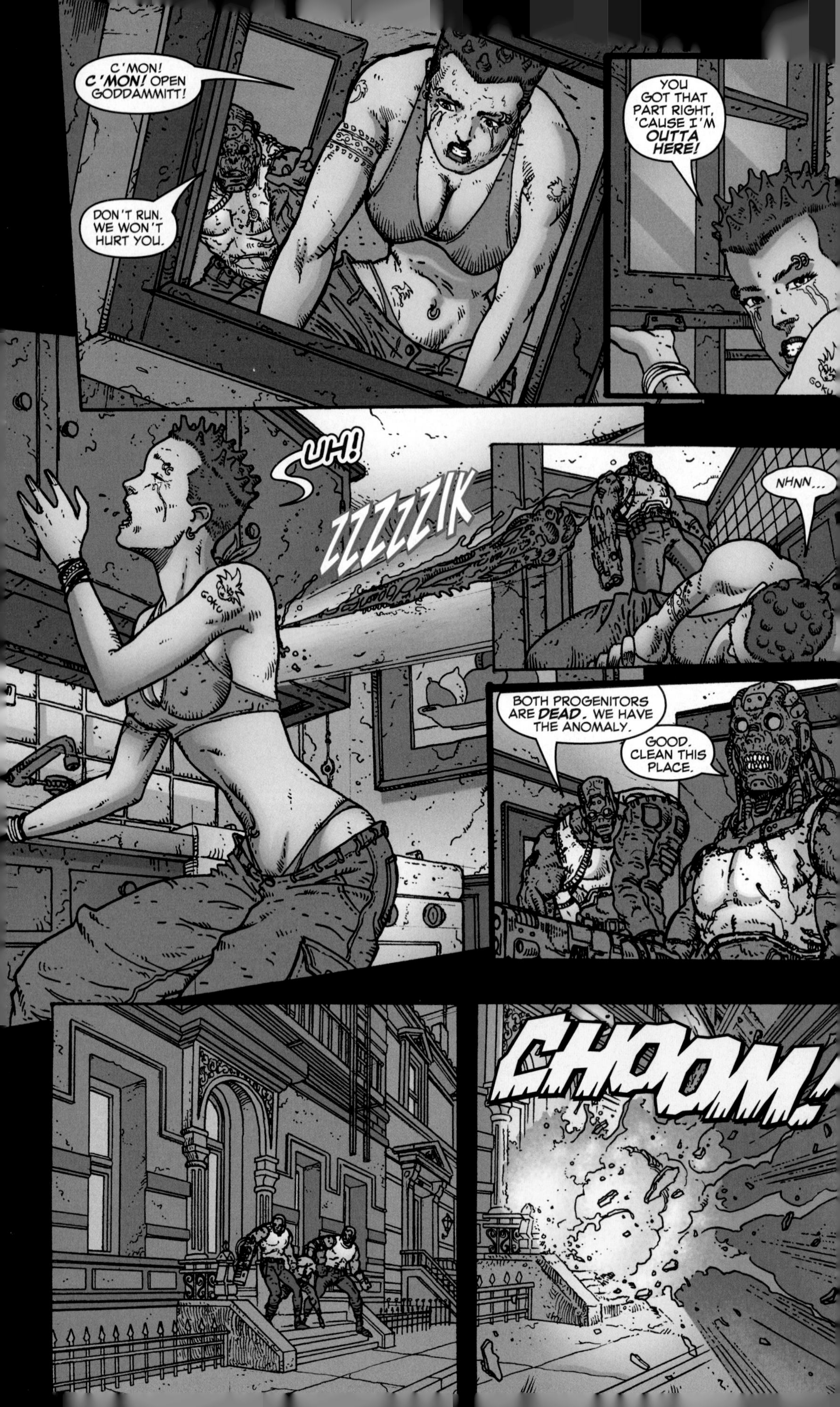
C'MON! C'MON! OPEN GODDAMMITT!
DON'T RUN. WE WON'T HURT YOU.
YOU GOT THAT PART RIGHT, 'CAUSE I'M OUTTA HERE!
GOKU
UH!
ZZZZZZIK
GOKU
NHNN...
BOTH PROGENITORS ARE DEAD. WE HAVE THE ANOMALY.
GOOD. CLEAN THIS PLACE.
CHOOM!

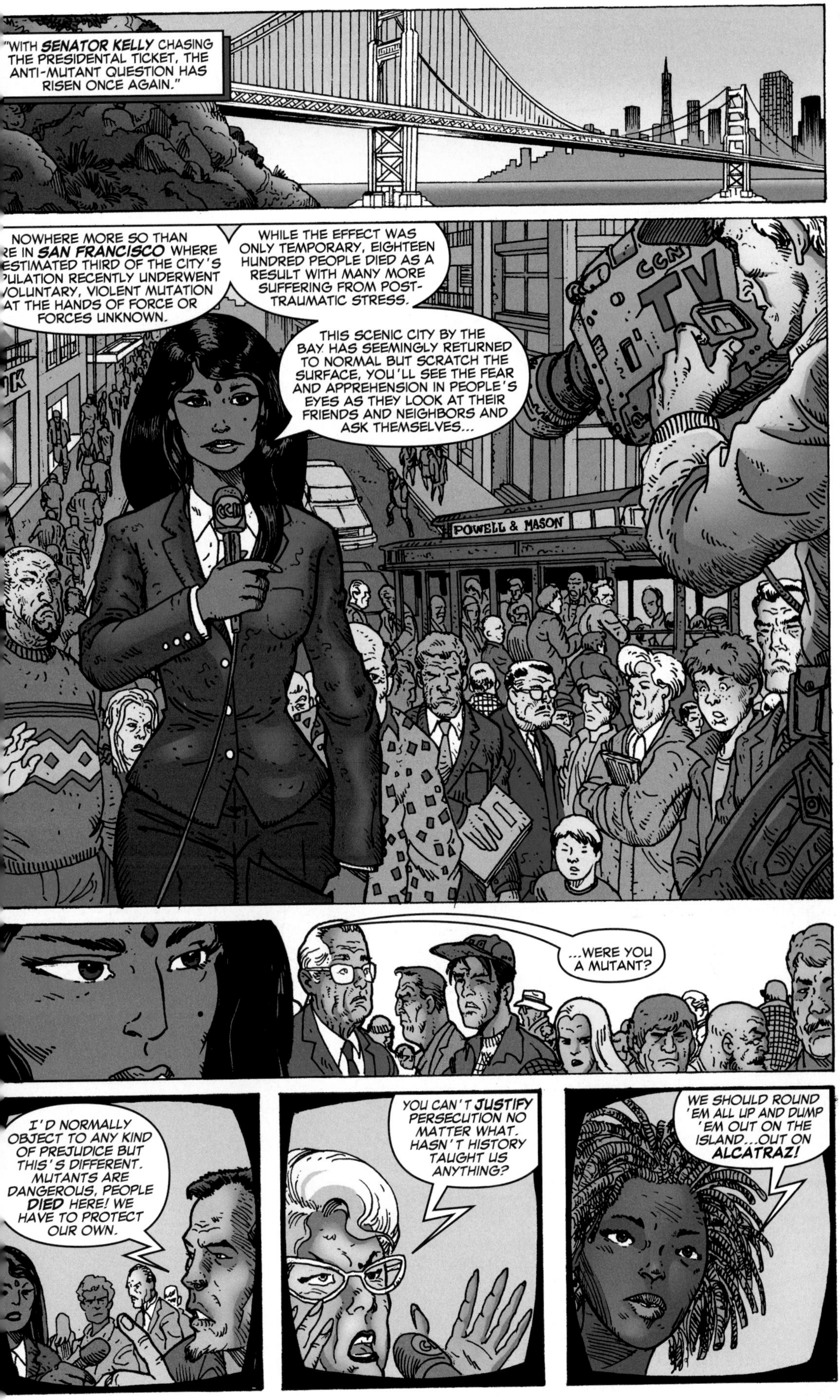
"WITH SENATOR KELLY CHASING THE PRESIDENTAL TICKET, THE ANTI-MUTANT QUESTION HAS RISEN ONCE AGAIN."
NOWHERE MORE SO THAN RE IN SAN FRANCISCO WHERE ESTIMATED THIRD OF THE CITY'S PULATION RECENTLY UNDERWENT VOLUNTARY, VIOLENT MUTATION AT THE HANDS OF FORCE OR FORCES UNKNOWN.
WHILE THE EFFECT WAS ONLY TEMPORARY, EIGHTEEN HUNDRED PEOPLE DIED AS A RESULT WITH MANY MORE SUFFERING FROM POST-TRAUMATIC STRESS.
THIS SCENIC CITY BY THE BAY HAS SEEMINGLY RETURNED TO NORMAL BUT SCRATCH THE SURFACE, YOU'LL SEE THE FEAR AND APPREHENSION IN PEOPLE'S EYES AS THEY LOOK AT THEIR FRIENDS AND NEIGHBORS AND ASK THEMSELVES...
CCN
TV
POWELL & MASON
...WERE YOU A MUTANT?
I'D NORMALLY OBJECT TO ANY KIND OF PREJUDICE BUT THIS'S DIFFERENT. MUTANTS ARE DANGEROUS, PEOPLE DIED HERE! WE HAVE TO PROTECT OUR OWN.
YOU CAN'T JUSTIFY PERSECUTION NO MATTER WHAT. HASN'T HISTORY TAUGHT US ANYTHING?
WE SHOULD ROUND 'EM ALL UP AND DUMP 'EM OUT ON THE ISLAND...OUT ON ALCATRAZ!

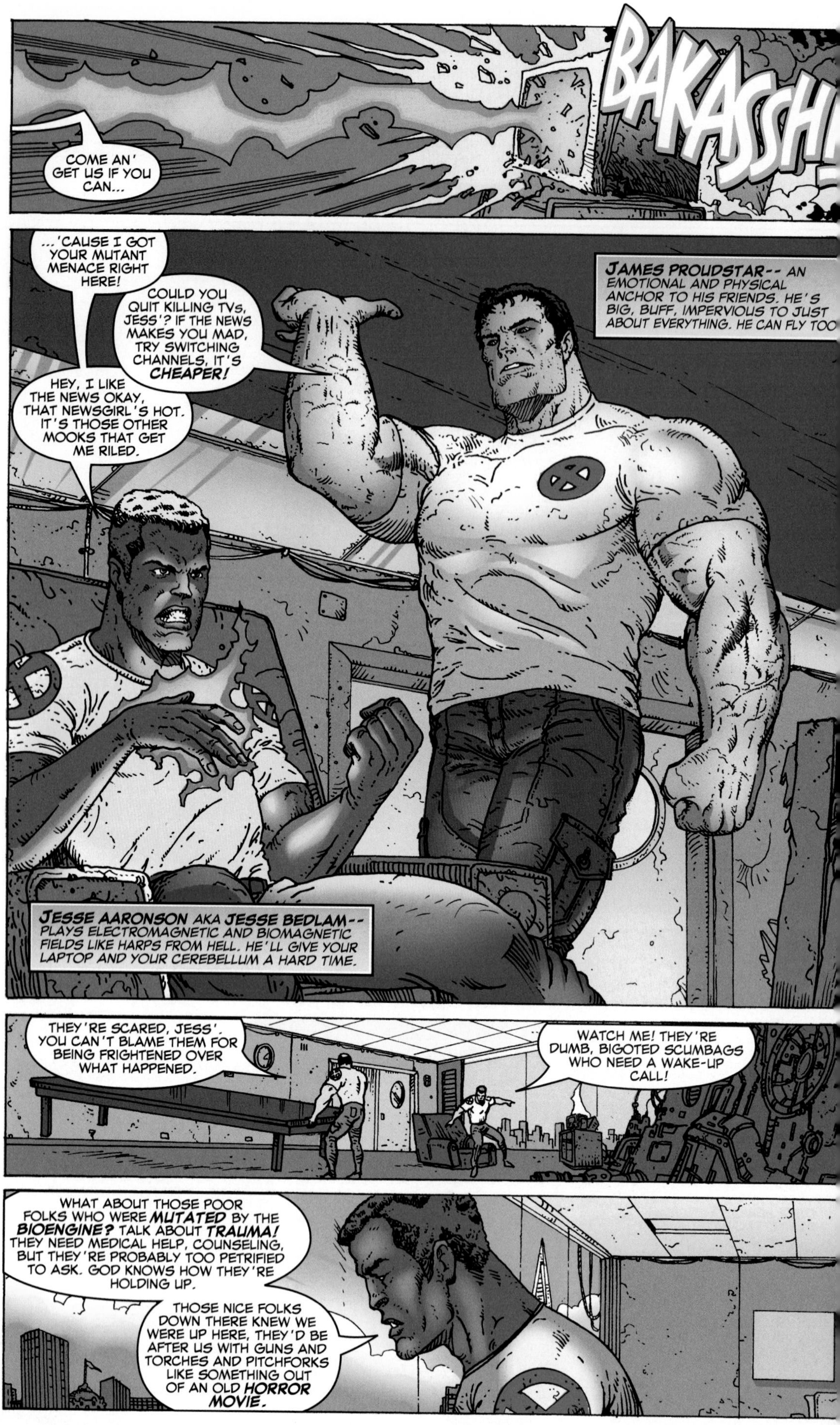
COME AN' GET US IF YOU CAN...
BAKASSH!
...'CAUSE I GOT YOUR MUTANT MENACE RIGHT HERE!
COULD YOU QUIT KILLING TVs, JESS'? IF THE NEWS MAKES YOU MAD, TRY SWITCHING CHANNELS, IT'S CHEAPER!
JAMES PROUDSTAR-- AN EMOTIONAL AND PHYSICAL ANCHOR TO HIS FRIENDS. HE'S BIG, BUFF, IMPERVIOUS TO JUST ABOUT EVERYTHING. HE CAN FLY TOO
HEY, I LIKE THE NEWS OKAY, THAT NEWSGIRL'S HOT. IT'S THOSE OTHER MOOKS THAT GET ME RILED.
JESSE AARONSON AKA JESSE BEDLAM-- PLAYS ELECTROMAGNETIC AND BIOMAGNETIC FIELDS LIKE HARPS FROM HELL. HE'LL GIVE YOUR LAPTOP AND YOUR CEREBELLUM A HARD TIME.
THEY'RE SCARED, JESS'. YOU CAN'T BLAME THEM FOR BEING FRIGHTENED OVER WHAT HAPPENED.
WATCH ME! THEY'RE DUMB, BIGOTED SCUMBAGS WHO NEED A WAKE-UP CALL!
WHAT ABOUT THOSE POOR FOLKS WHO WERE MUTATED BY THE BIOENGINE? TALK ABOUT TRAUMA! THEY NEED MEDICAL HELP, COUNSELING, BUT THEY'RE PROBABLY TOO PETRIFIED TO ASK. GOD KNOWS HOW THEY'RE HOLDING UP.
THOSE NICE FOLKS DOWN THERE KNEW WE WERE UP HERE, THEY'D BE AFTER US WITH GUNS AND TORCHES AND PITCHFORKS LIKE SOMETHING OUT OF AN OLD HORROR MOVIE.

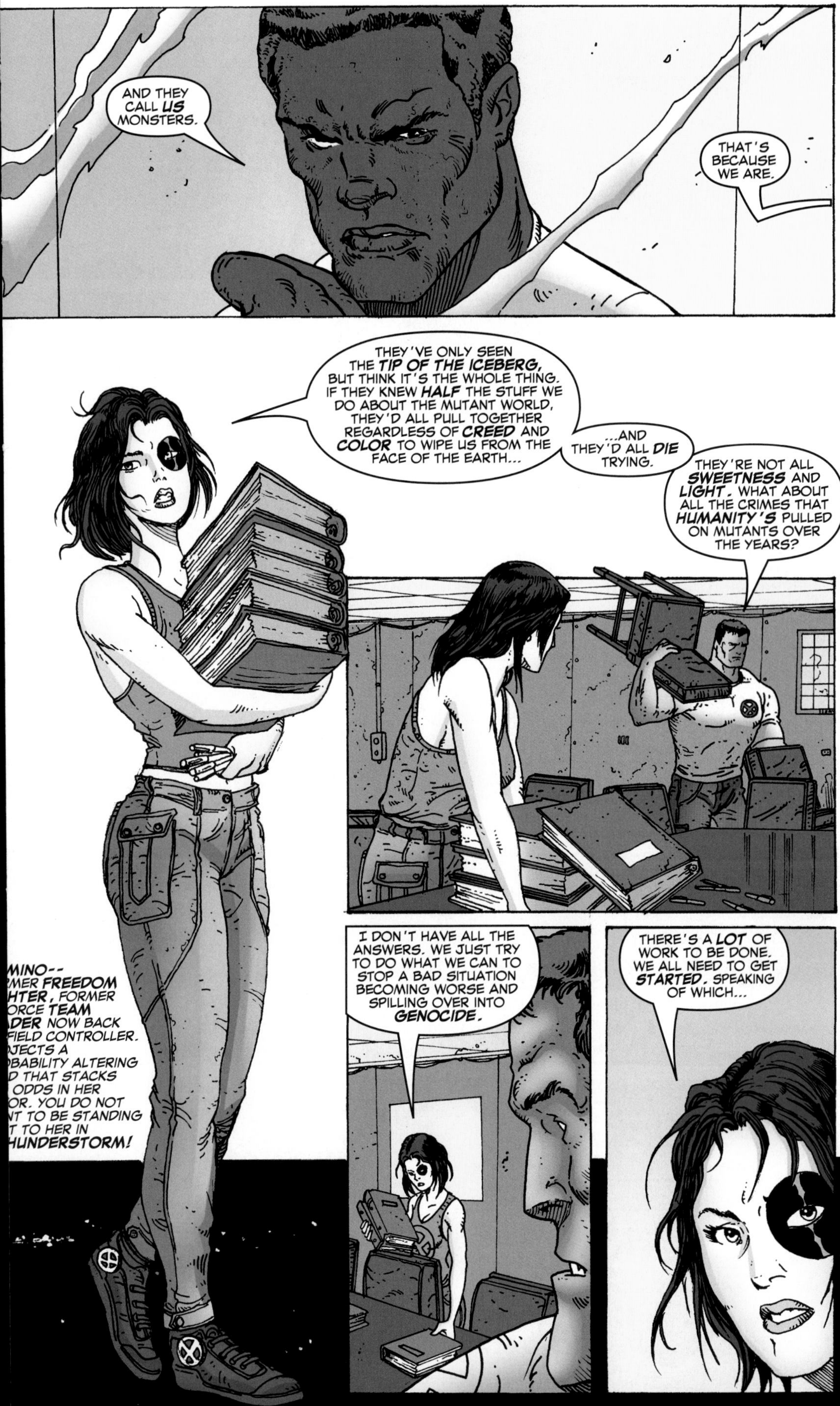

AND THEY CALL US MONSTERS.
THAT'S BECAUSE WE ARE.
THEY'VE ONLY SEEN THE TIP OF THE ICEBERG, BUT THINK IT'S THE WHOLE THING. IF THEY KNEW HALF THE STUFF WE DO ABOUT THE MUTANT WORLD, THEY'D ALL PULL TOGETHER REGARDLESS OF CREED AND COLOR TO WIPE US FROM THE FACE OF THE EARTH...
...AND THEY'D ALL DIE TRYING.
THEY'RE NOT ALL SWEETNESS AND LIGHT. WHAT ABOUT ALL THE CRIMES THAT HUMANITY'S PULLED ON MUTANTS OVER THE YEARS?
MINO-- RMER FREEDOM HTER, FORMER ORCE TEAM ADER NOW BACK FIELD CONTROLLER. OJECTS A OBABILITY ALTERING D THAT STACKS ODDS IN HER OR. YOU DO NOT NT TO BE STANDING T TO HER IN HUNDERSTORM!
I DON'T HAVE ALL THE ANSWERS. WE JUST TRY TO DO WHAT WE CAN TO STOP A BAD SITUATION BECOMING WORSE AND SPILLING OVER INTO GENOCIDE.
THERE'S A LOT OF WORK TO BE DONE. WE ALL NEED TO GET STARTED. SPEAKING OF WHICH...

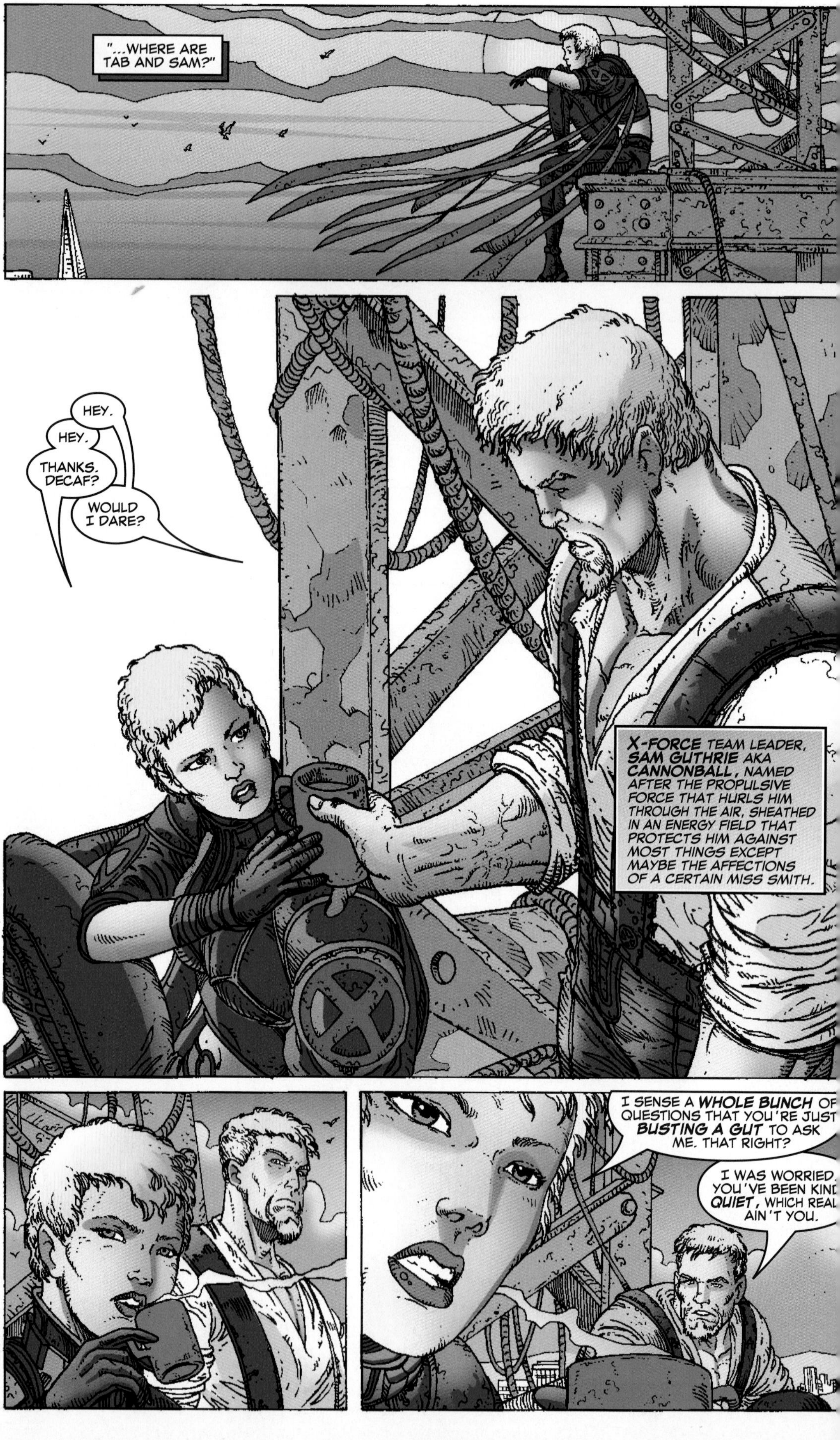
"...WHERE ARE TAB AND SAM?"
HEY.
HEY.
THANKS. DECAF?
WOULD I DARE?
X-FORCE TEAM LEADER, SAM GUTHRIE AKA CANNONBALL, NAMED AFTER THE PROPULSIVE FORCE THAT HURLS HIM THROUGH THE AIR, SHEATHED IN AN ENERGY FIELD THAT PROTECTS HIM AGAINST MOST THINGS EXCEPT MAYBE THE AFFECTIONS OF A CERTAIN MISS SMITH.
I SENSE A WHOLE BUNCH OF QUESTIONS THAT YOU'RE JUST BUSTING A GUT TO ASK ME. THAT RIGHT?
I WAS WORRIED. YOU'VE BEEN KIND QUIET, WHICH REAL AIN'T YOU.

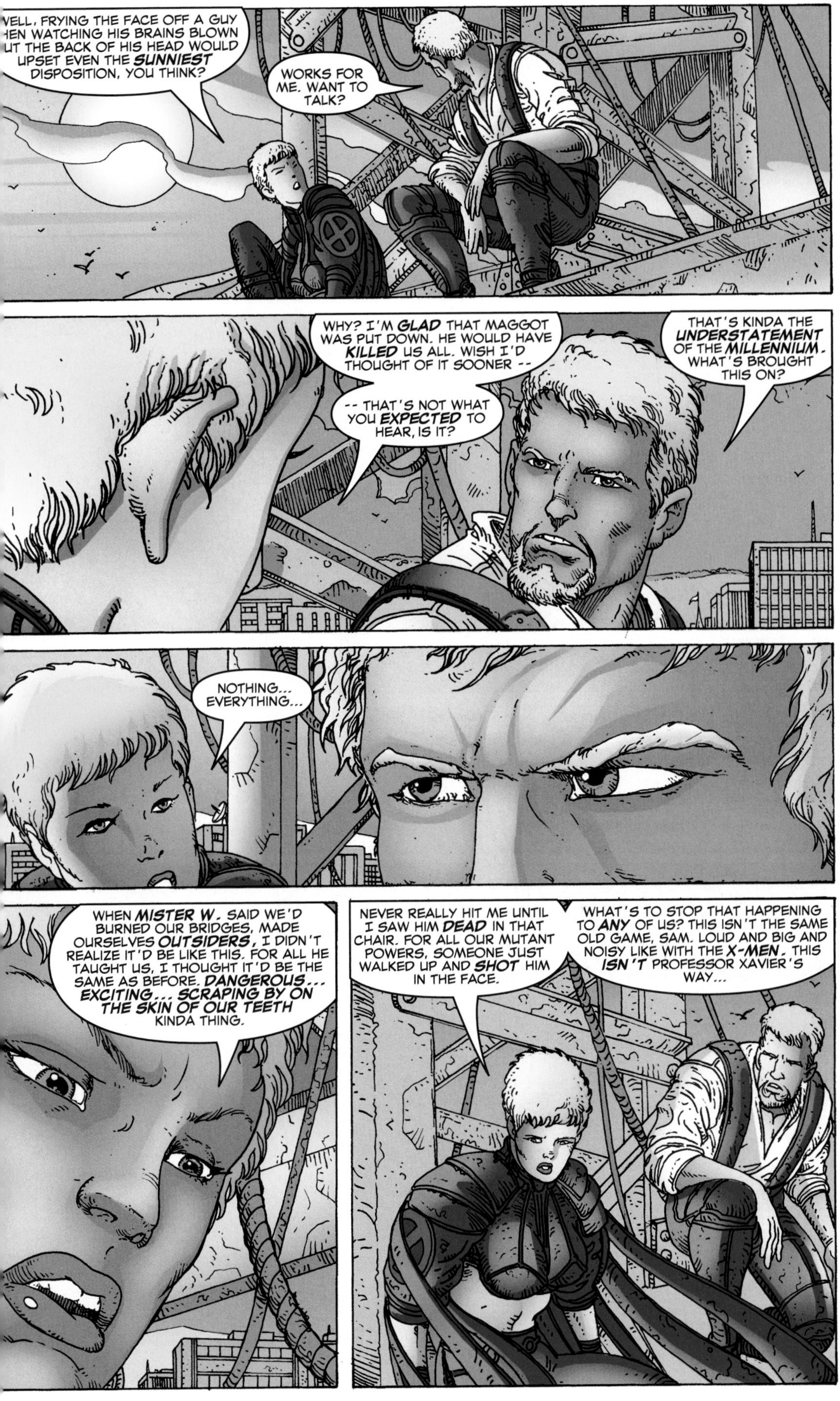
VELL, FRYING THE FACE OFF A GUY HEN WATCHING HIS BRAINS BLOWN UT THE BACK OF HIS HEAD WOULD UPSET EVEN THE SUNNIEST DISPOSITION, YOU THINK?
WORKS FOR ME. WANT TO TALK?
WHY? I'M GLAD THAT MAGGOT WAS PUT DOWN. HE WOULD HAVE KILLED US ALL. WISH I'D THOUGHT OF IT SOONER --
-- THAT'S NOT WHAT YOU EXPECTED TO HEAR, IS IT?
THAT'S KINDA THE UNDERSTATEMENT OF THE MILLENNIUM. WHAT'S BROUGHT THIS ON?
NOTHING... EVERYTHING...
WHEN MISTER W. SAID WE'D BURNED OUR BRIDGES, MADE OURSELVES OUTSIDERS, I DIDN'T REALIZE IT'D BE LIKE THIS. FOR ALL HE TAUGHT US, I THOUGHT IT'D BE THE SAME AS BEFORE. DANGEROUS... EXCITING... SCRAPING BY ON THE SKIN OF OUR TEETH KINDA THING.
NEVER REALLY HIT ME UNTIL I SAW HIM DEAD IN THAT CHAIR. FOR ALL OUR MUTANT POWERS, SOMEONE JUST WALKED UP AND SHOT HIM IN THE FACE.
WHAT'S TO STOP THAT HAPPENING TO ANY OF US? THIS ISN'T THE SAME OLD GAME, SAM. LOUD AND BIG AND NOISY LIKE WITH THE X-MEN. THIS ISN'T PROFESSOR XAVIER'S WAY...

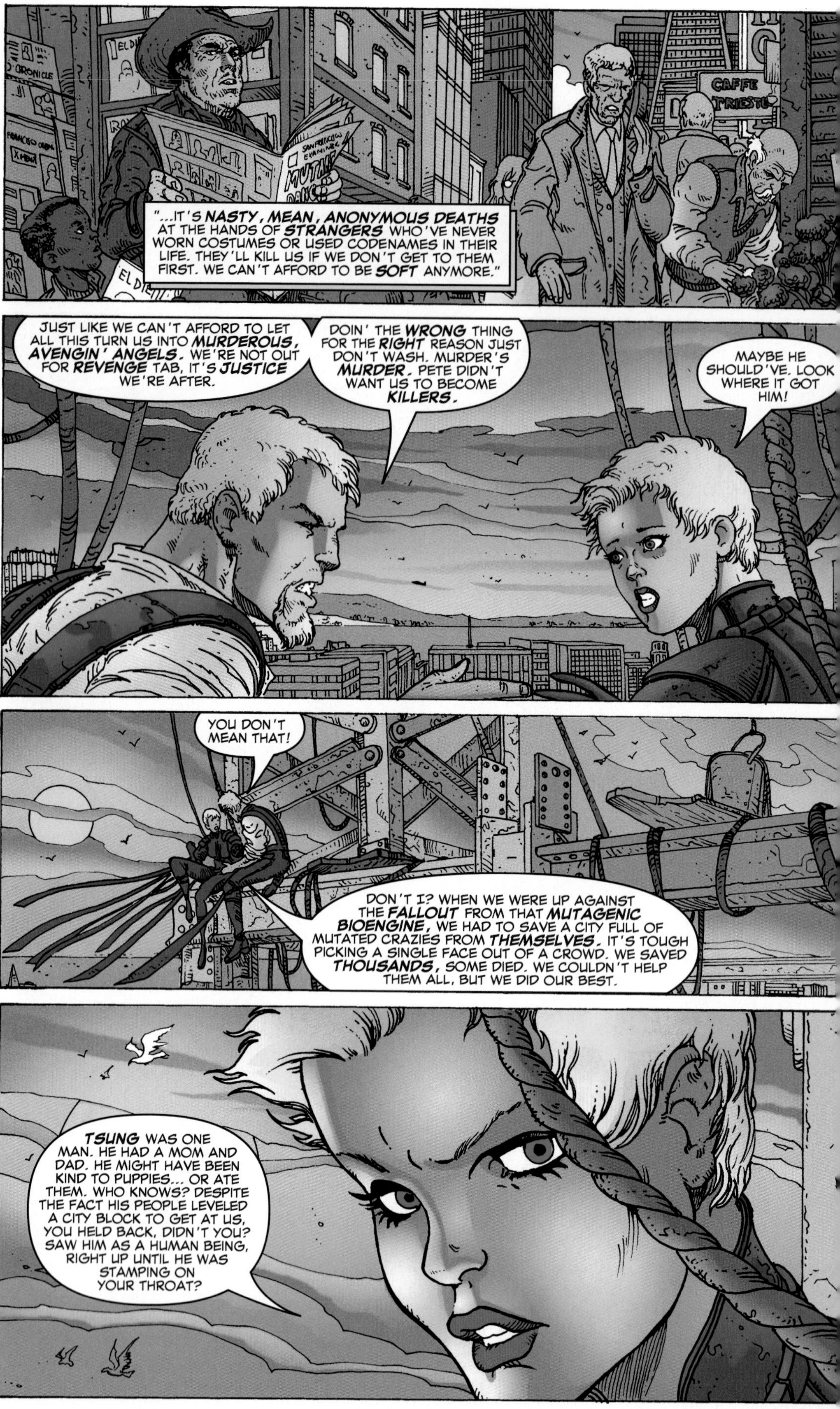
"...IT'S NASTY, MEAN, ANONYMOUS DEATHS AT THE HANDS OF STRANGERS WHO'VE NEVER WORN COSTUMES OR USED CODENAMES IN THEIR LIFE. THEY'LL KILL US IF WE DON'T GET TO THEM FIRST. WE CAN'T AFFORD TO BE SOFT ANYMORE."
CAFFE TRIESTE
JUST LIKE WE CAN'T AFFORD TO LET ALL THIS TURN US INTO MURDEROUS, AVENGIN' ANGELS. WE'RE NOT OUT FOR REVENGE TAB, IT'S JUSTICE WE'RE AFTER.
DOIN' THE WRONG THING FOR THE RIGHT REASON JUST DON'T WASH. MURDER'S MURDER. PETE DIDN'T WANT US TO BECOME KILLERS.
MAYBE HE SHOULD'VE. LOOK WHERE IT GOT HIM!
YOU DON'T MEAN THAT!
DON'T I? WHEN WE WERE UP AGAINST THE FALLOUT FROM THAT MUTAGENIC BIOENGINE, WE HAD TO SAVE A CITY FULL OF MUTATED CRAZIES FROM THEMSELVES. IT'S TOUGH PICKING A SINGLE FACE OUT OF A CROWD. WE SAVED THOUSANDS, SOME DIED. WE COULDN'T HELP THEM ALL, BUT WE DID OUR BEST.
TSUNG WAS ONE MAN. HE HAD A MOM AND DAD. HE MIGHT HAVE BEEN KIND TO PUPPIES... OR ATE THEM. WHO KNOWS? DESPITE THE FACT HIS PEOPLE LEVELED A CITY BLOCK TO GET AT US, YOU HELD BACK, DIDN'T YOU? SAW HIM AS A HUMAN BEING, RIGHT UP UNTIL HE WAS STAMPING ON YOUR THROAT?

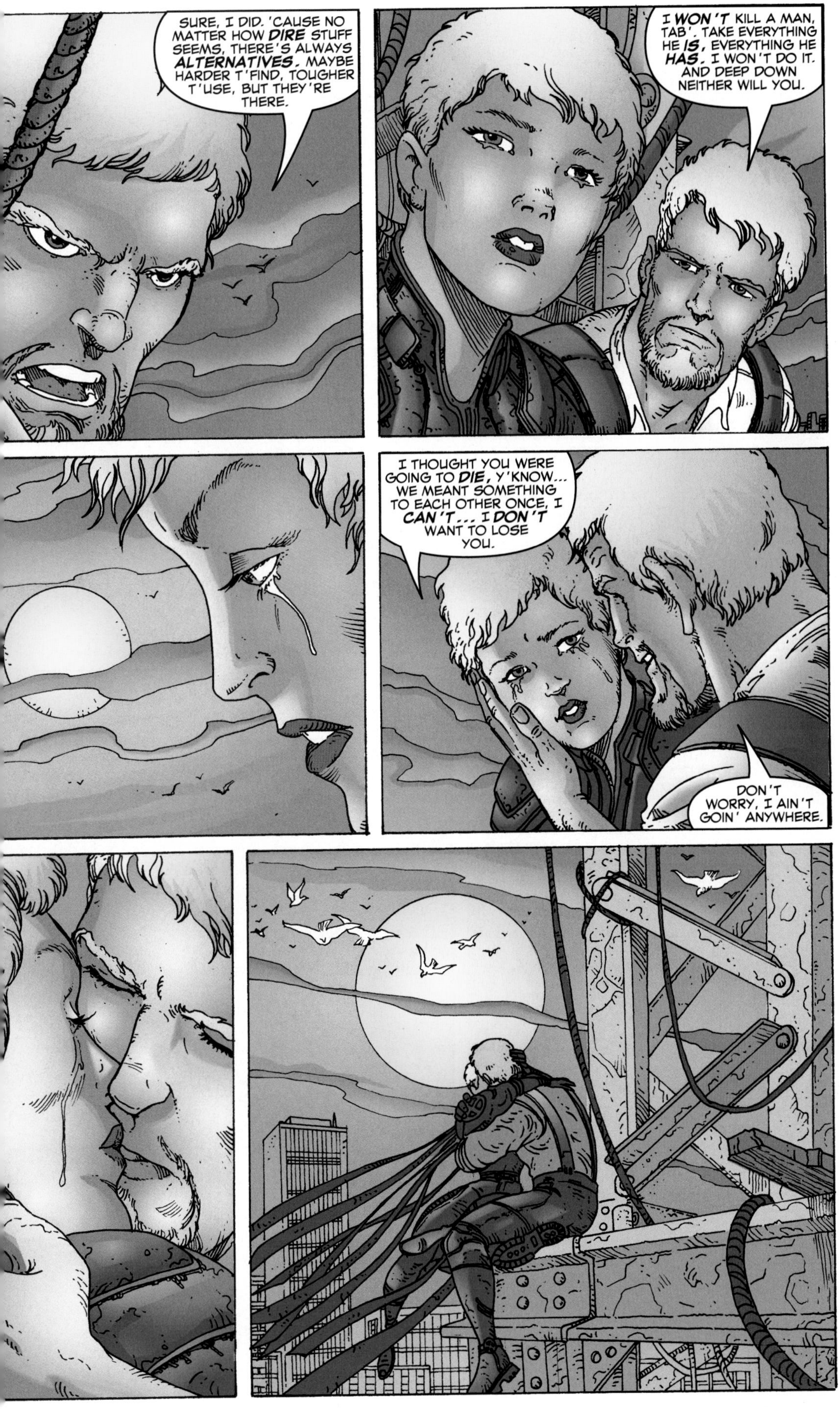
SURE, I DID. 'CAUSE NO MATTER HOW DIRE STUFF SEEMS, THERE'S ALWAYS ALTERNATIVES. MAYBE HARDER T'FIND, TOUGHER T'USE, BUT THEY'RE THERE.
I WON'T KILL A MAN, TAB'. TAKE EVERYTHING HE IS, EVERYTHING HE HAS. I WON'T DO IT. AND DEEP DOWN NEITHER WILL YOU.
I THOUGHT YOU WERE GOING TO DIE, Y'KNOW... WE MEANT SOMETHING TO EACH OTHER ONCE, I CAN'T... I DON'T WANT TO LOSE YOU.
DON'T WORRY, I AIN'T GOIN' ANYWHERE.

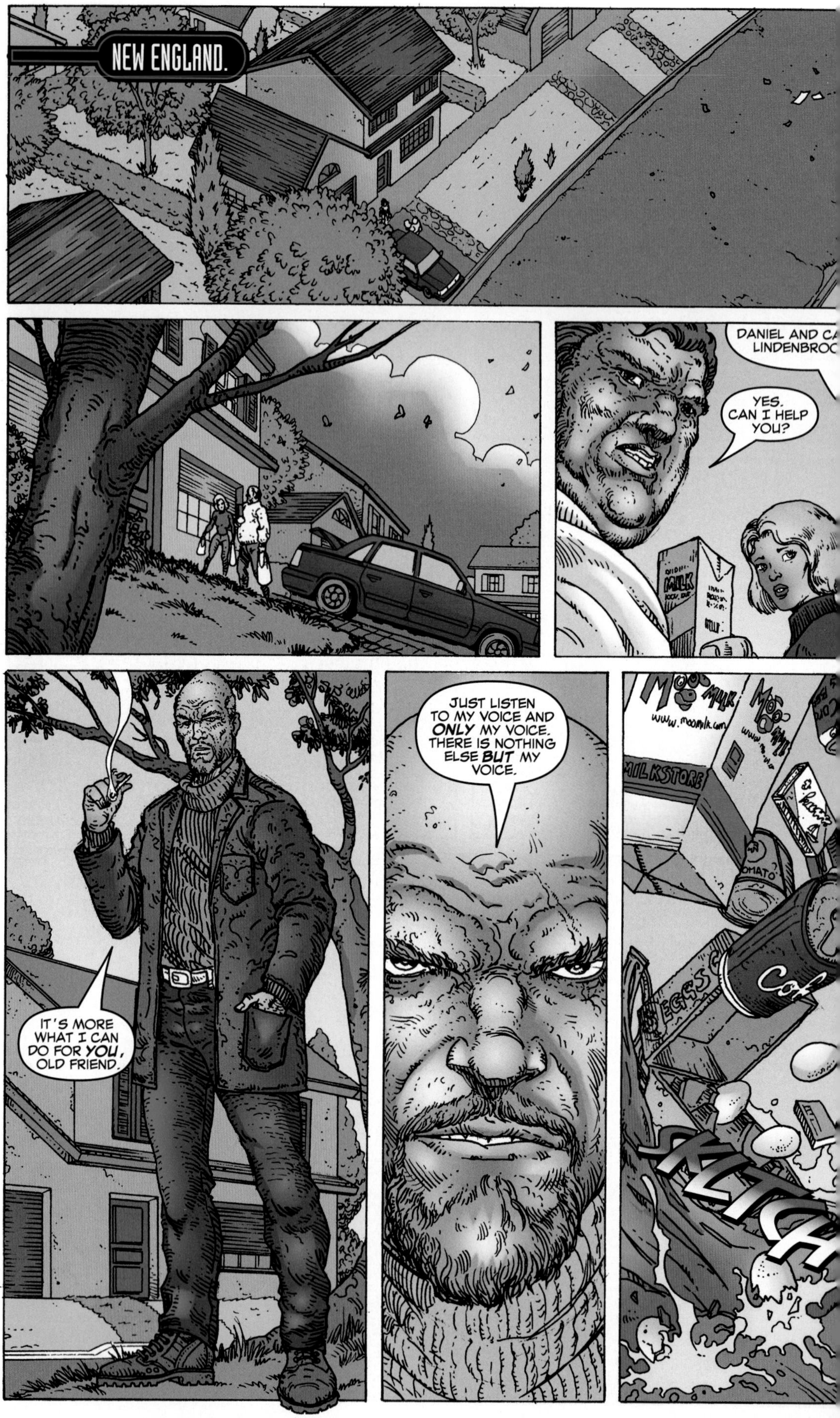
NEW ENGLAND.
DANIEL AND CA
LINDENBROC
YES. CAN I HELP YOU?
MILK
IT'S MORE WHAT I CAN DO FOR YOU, OLD FRIEND.
JUST LISTEN TO MY VOICE AND ONLY MY VOICE. THERE IS NOTHING ELSE BUT MY VOICE.
MOO MILK
www.moomilk.com
MILKSTORE
TOMATO
EGGS
Cof
SKLTCH

"THE WOODS ARE LOVELY, DARK AND DEEP AND I HAVE PROMISES TO KEEP... AND MILES TO GO BEFORE I SLEEP."

...AND MILES TO GO BEFORE I SLEEP.

REMEMBER... REMEMBER.

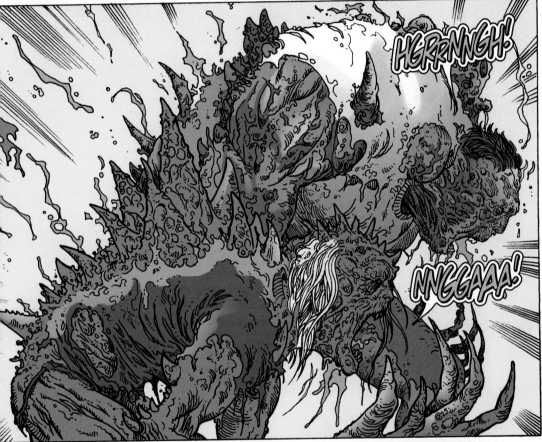

HGRRNNGH!

NNGGAAA!

GNNRR... COM... COMRADE DOCTOR?

HELLO, MAJOR. LIEUTENANT.

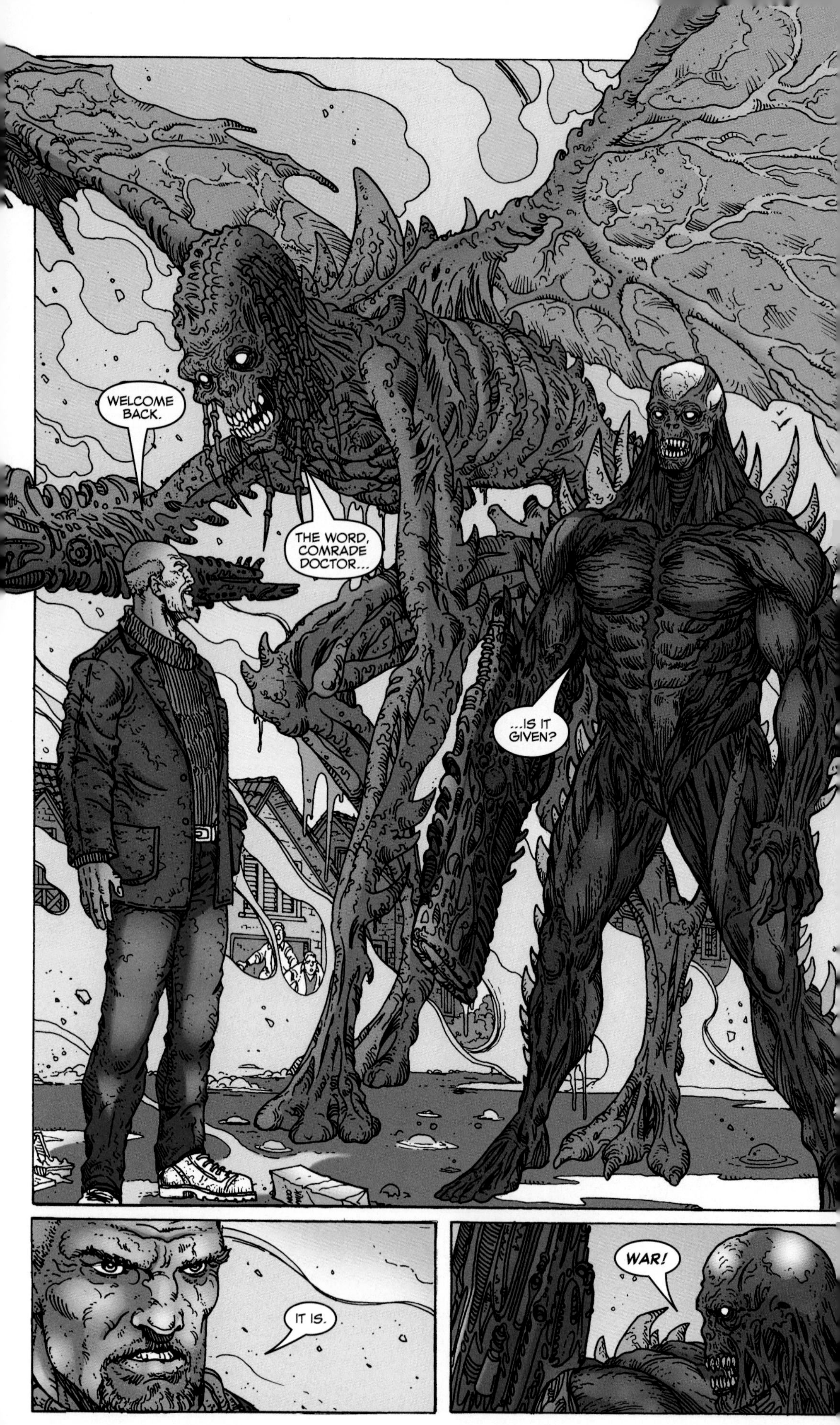
WELCOME BACK.
THE WORD, COMRADE DOCTOR...
...IS IT GIVEN?
IT IS.
WAR!

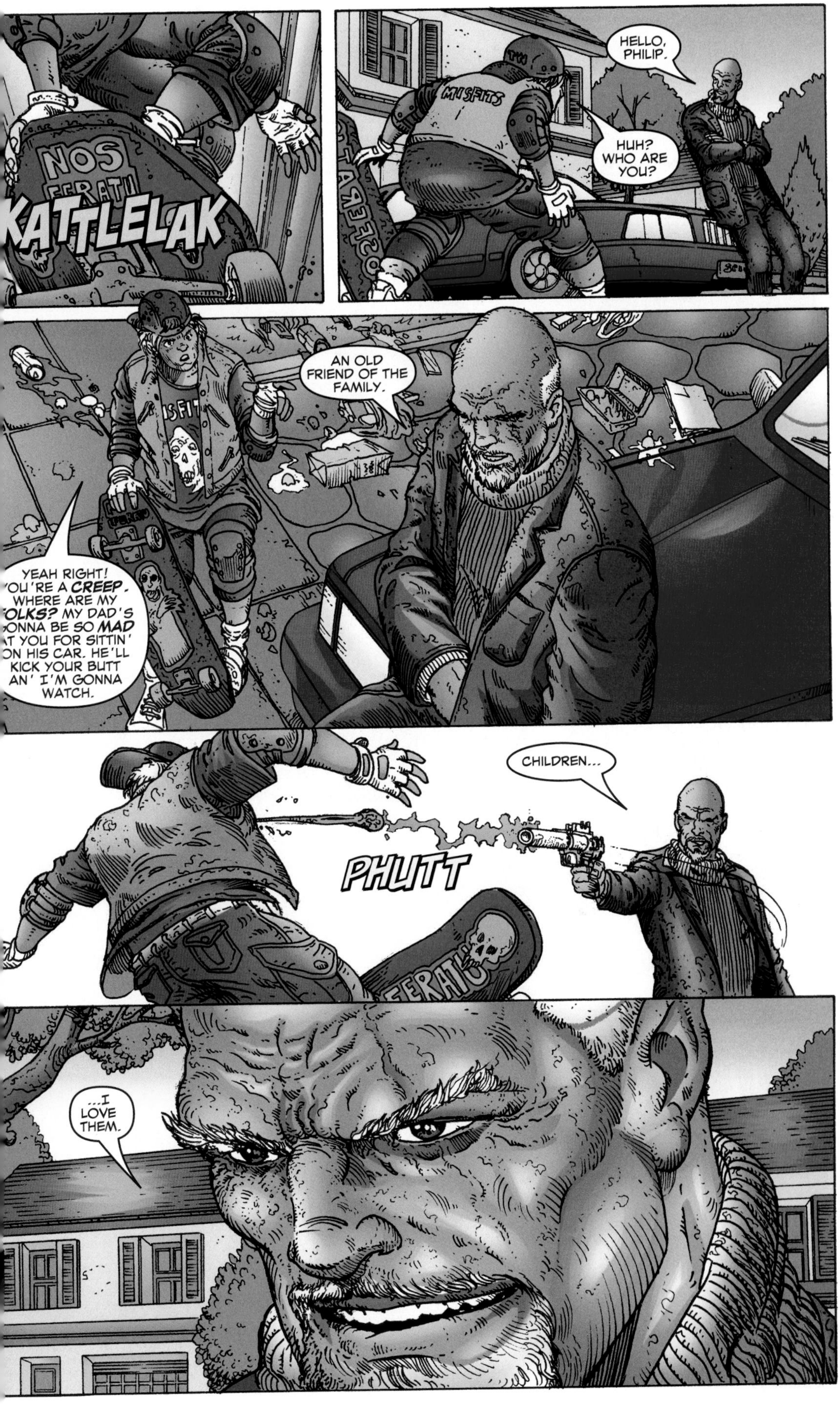
NOS FERATU
KATTLELAK
HELLO, PHILIP.
MISFITS
HUH? WHO ARE YOU?
AN OLD FRIEND OF THE FAMILY.
YEAH RIGHT! YOU'RE A CREEP. WHERE ARE MY FOLKS? MY DAD'S GONNA BE SO MAD AT YOU FOR SITTIN' ON HIS CAR. HE'LL KICK YOUR BUTT AN' I'M GONNA WATCH.
CHILDREN...
PHUTT
FERATU
...I LOVE THEM.

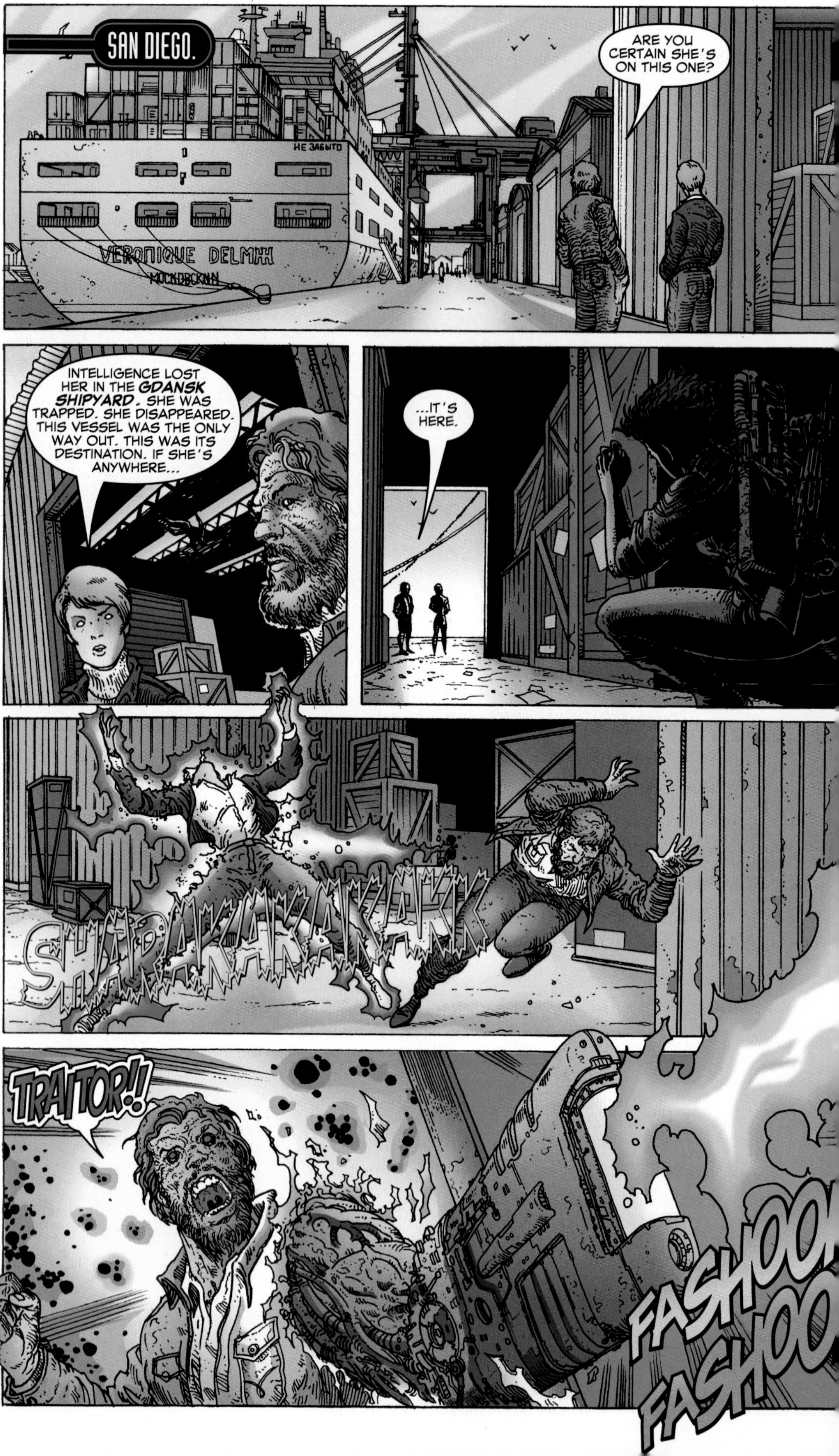
SAN DIEGO.
ARE YOU CERTAIN SHE'S ON THIS ONE?
НЕ ЗАБЫТО
VERONIQUE DELMИЖ
INTELLIGENCE LOST HER IN THE GDANSK SHIPYARD. SHE WAS TRAPPED. SHE DISAPPEARED. THIS VESSEL WAS THE ONLY WAY OUT. THIS WAS ITS DESTINATION. IF SHE'S ANYWHERE...
...IT'S HERE.
SHAAKAKAKAKAKKK
TRAITOR!!
FASHOOO
FASHOOO

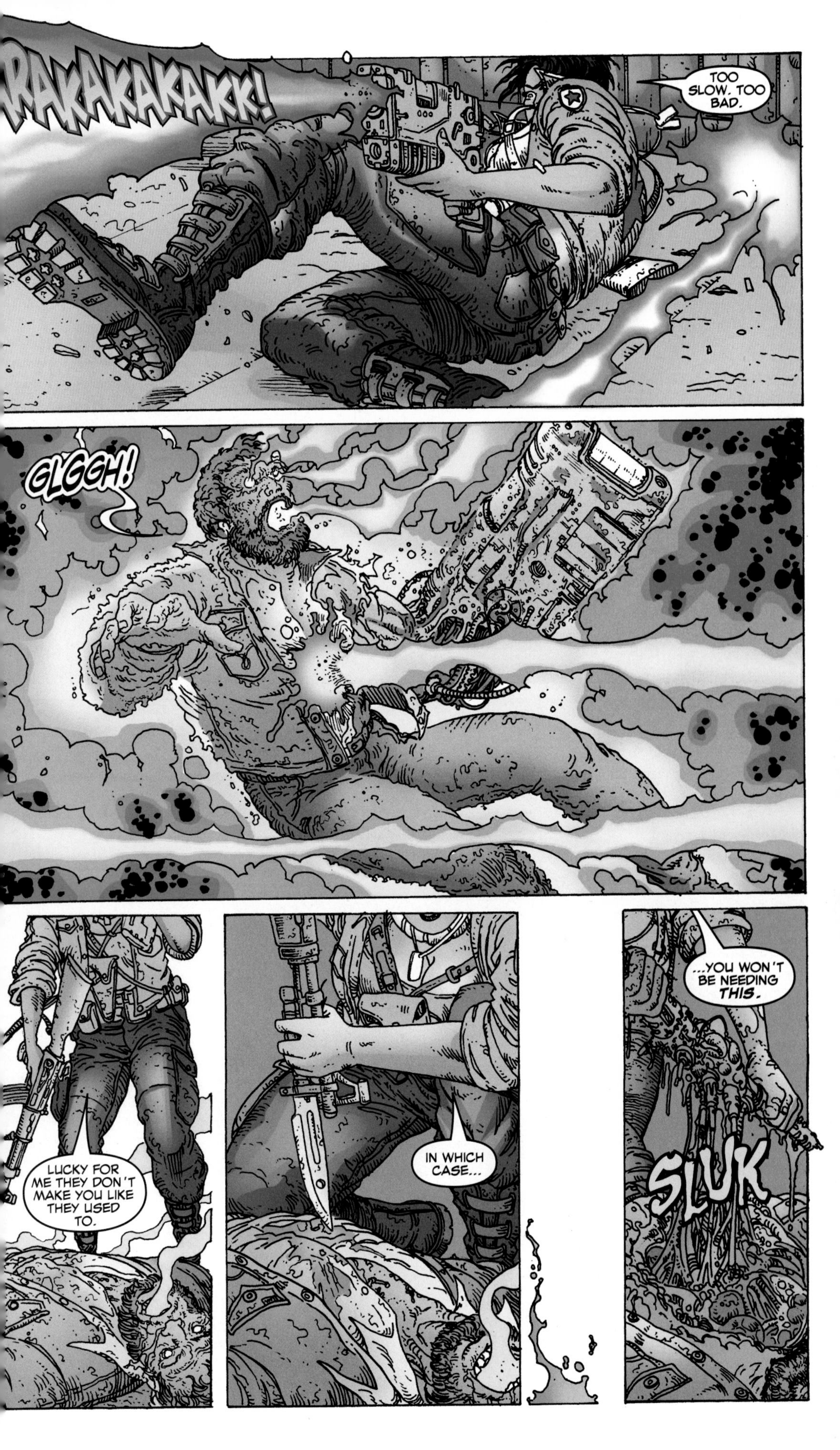

RAKAKAKAKK!
TOO SLOW. TOO BAD.
GLGGH!
LUCKY FOR ME THEY DON'T MAKE YOU LIKE THEY USED TO.
IN WHICH CASE...
...YOU WON'T BE NEEDING THIS.
SLUK

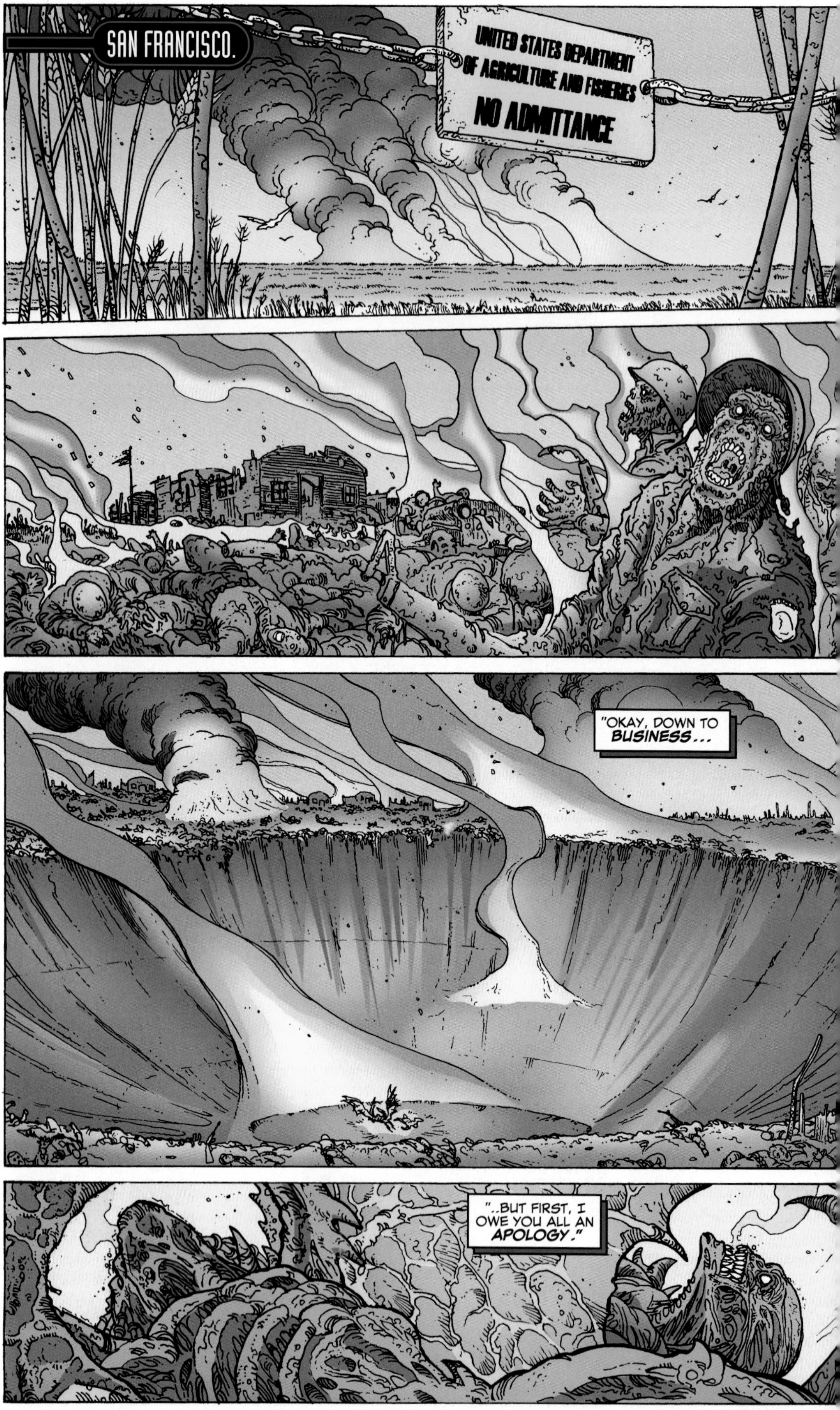
SAN FRANCISCO.
UNITED STATES DEPARTMENT OF AGRICULTURE AND FISHERIES
NO ADMITTANCE
"OKAY, DOWN TO BUSINESS...
"..BUT FIRST, I OWE YOU ALL AN APOLOGY."

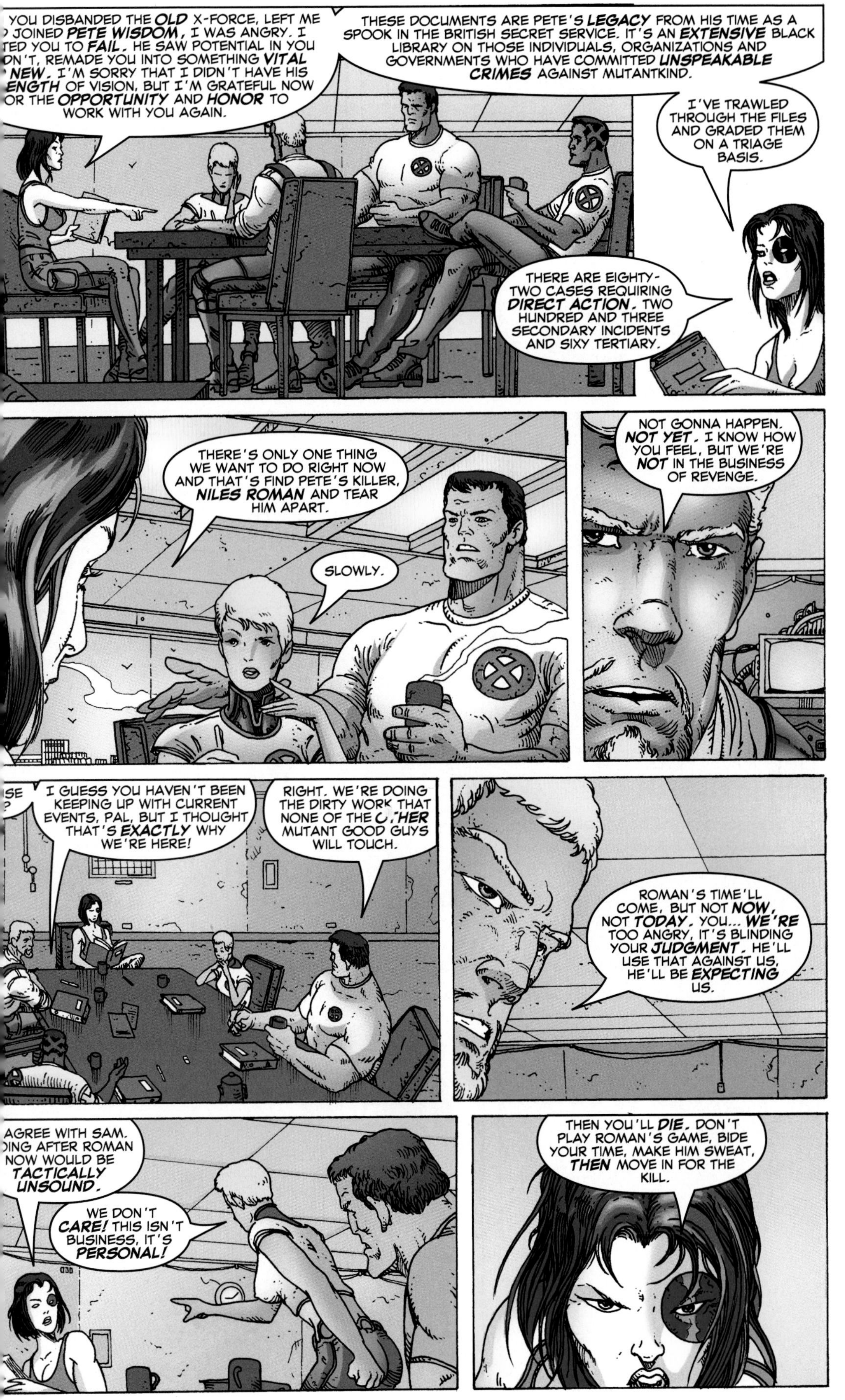
YOU DISBANDED THE OLD X-FORCE, LEFT ME D JOINED PETE WISDOM, I WAS ANGRY. I TED YOU TO FAIL. HE SAW POTENTIAL IN YOU DN'T, REMADE YOU INTO SOMETHING VITAL NEW. I'M SORRY THAT I DIDN'T HAVE HIS ENGTH OF VISION, BUT I'M GRATEFUL NOW OR THE OPPORTUNITY AND HONOR TO WORK WITH YOU AGAIN.
THESE DOCUMENTS ARE PETE'S LEGACY FROM HIS TIME AS A SPOOK IN THE BRITISH SECRET SERVICE. IT'S AN EXTENSIVE BLACK LIBRARY ON THOSE INDIVIDUALS, ORGANIZATIONS AND GOVERNMENTS WHO HAVE COMMITTED UNSPEAKABLE CRIMES AGAINST MUTANTKIND.
I'VE TRAWLED THROUGH THE FILES AND GRADED THEM ON A TRIAGE BASIS.
THERE ARE EIGHTY-TWO CASES REQUIRING DIRECT ACTION. TWO HUNDRED AND THREE SECONDARY INCIDENTS AND SIXY TERTIARY.
THERE'S ONLY ONE THING WE WANT TO DO RIGHT NOW AND THAT'S FIND PETE'S KILLER, NILES ROMAN AND TEAR HIM APART.
SLOWLY.
NOT GONNA HAPPEN. NOT YET. I KNOW HOW YOU FEEL, BUT WE'RE NOT IN THE BUSINESS OF REVENGE.
SE
I GUESS YOU HAVEN'T BEEN KEEPING UP WITH CURRENT EVENTS, PAL, BUT I THOUGHT THAT'S EXACTLY WHY WE'RE HERE!
RIGHT. WE'RE DOING THE DIRTY WORK THAT NONE OF THE OTHER MUTANT GOOD GUYS WILL TOUCH.
ROMAN'S TIME'LL COME, BUT NOT NOW, NOT TODAY. YOU... WE'RE TOO ANGRY, IT'S BLINDING YOUR JUDGMENT. HE'LL USE THAT AGAINST US, HE'LL BE EXPECTING US.
AGREE WITH SAM. DING AFTER ROMAN NOW WOULD BE TACTICALLY UNSOUND.
WE DON'T CARE! THIS ISN'T BUSINESS, IT'S PERSONAL!
THEN YOU'LL DIE. DON'T PLAY ROMAN'S GAME, BIDE YOUR TIME, MAKE HIM SWEAT, THEN MOVE IN FOR THE KILL.

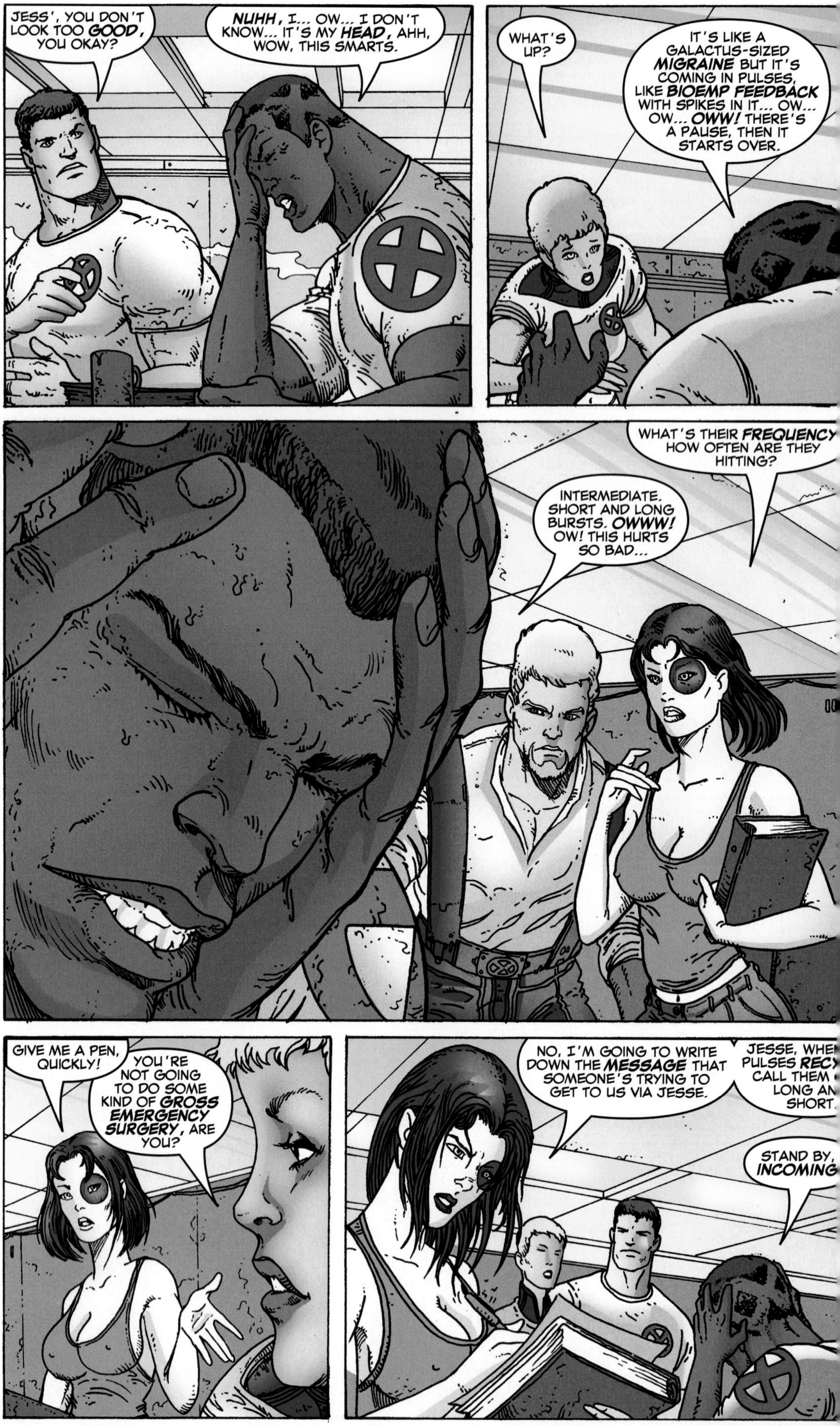
JESS', YOU DON'T LOOK TOO GOOD, YOU OKAY?
NUHH, I... OW... I DON'T KNOW... IT'S MY HEAD, AHH, WOW, THIS SMARTS.
WHAT'S UP?
IT'S LIKE A GALACTUS-SIZED MIGRAINE BUT IT'S COMING IN PULSES, LIKE BIOEMP FEEDBACK WITH SPIKES IN IT... OW... OW... OWW! THERE'S A PAUSE, THEN IT STARTS OVER.
WHAT'S THEIR FREQUENCY HOW OFTEN ARE THEY HITTING?
INTERMEDIATE. SHORT AND LONG BURSTS. OWWW! OW! THIS HURTS SO BAD...
GIVE ME A PEN, QUICKLY!
YOU'RE NOT GOING TO DO SOME KIND OF GROSS EMERGENCY SURGERY, ARE YOU?
NO, I'M GOING TO WRITE DOWN THE MESSAGE THAT SOMEONE'S TRYING TO GET TO US VIA JESSE.
JESSE, WHE PULSES REC CALL THEM LONG AN SHORT.
STAND BY, INCOMING

MESSAGE? DID I *MISS* SOMETHING?

...G AND ...T PULSES ON ...EATING CYCLE, ...D-FASHIONED ...RSE CODE.

NHH... ALL DONE FOR NOW. GET ANYTHING *USEFUL?*

I CAN'T TELL.

IT SAYS *VALENTINA* AND THEN SOME NUMBERS WHICH READ LIKE *COORDINATES.* MEAN ANYTHING TO ANYONE?

WE KNOW HER...

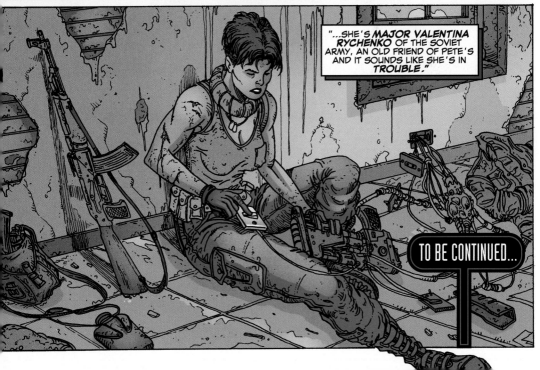

"...SHE'S *MAJOR VALENTINA RYCHENKO* OF THE SOVIET ARMY, AN OLD FRIEND OF PETE'S AND IT SOUNDS LIKE SHE'S IN *TROUBLE.*"

TO BE CONTINUED...

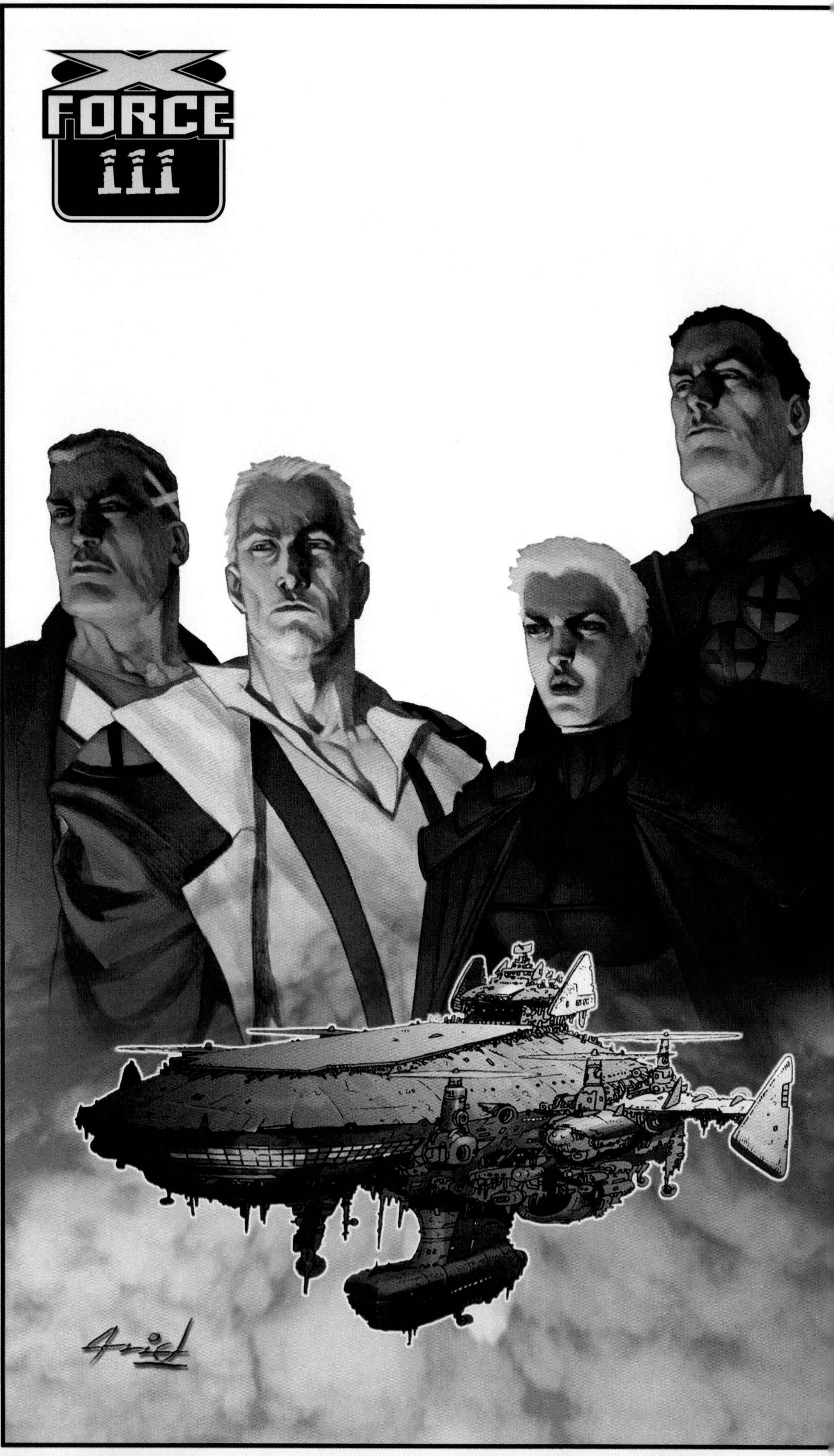
X
FORCE
111

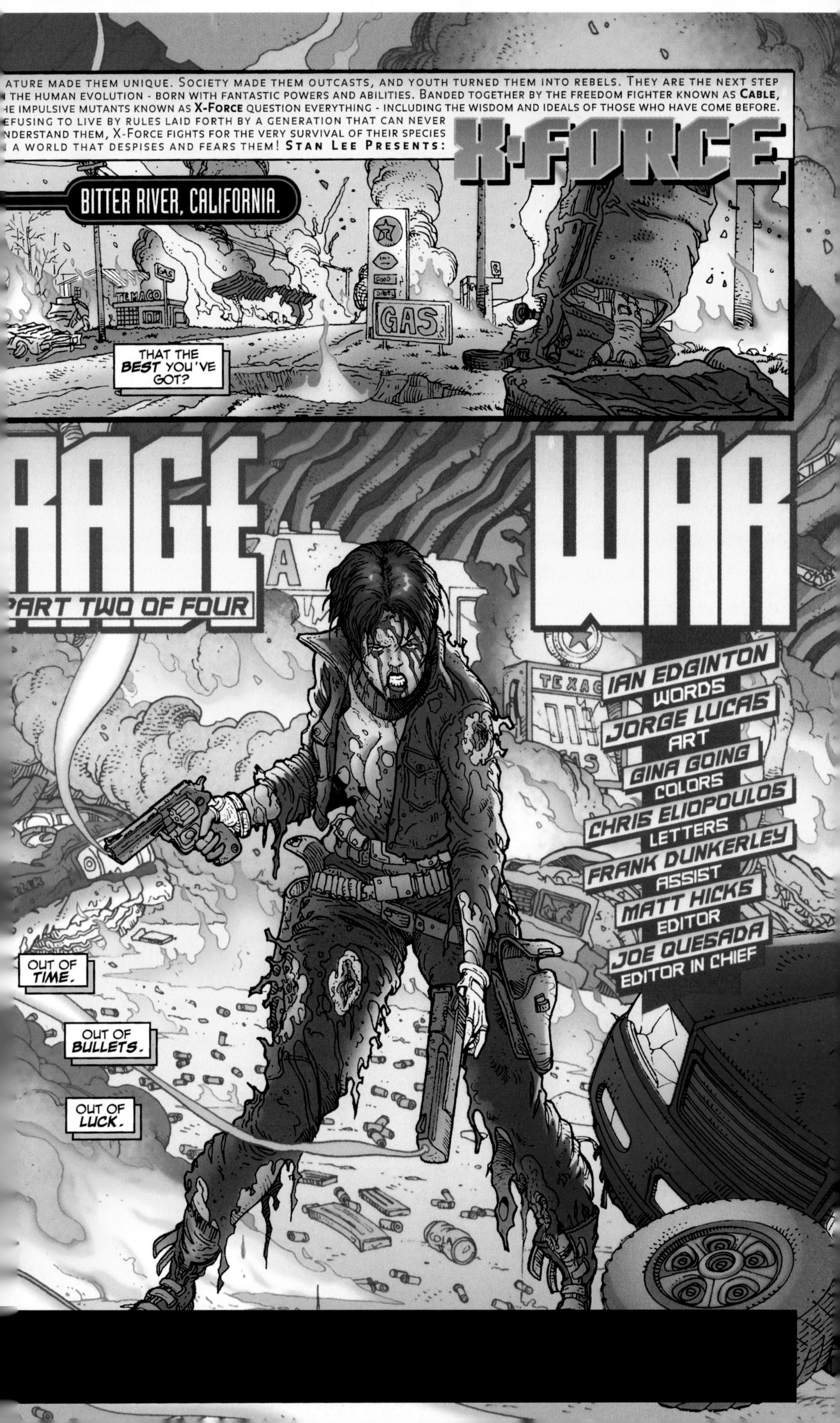

ATURE MADE THEM UNIQUE. SOCIETY MADE THEM OUTCASTS, AND YOUTH TURNED THEM INTO REBELS. THEY ARE THE NEXT STEP
THE HUMAN EVOLUTION - BORN WITH FANTASTIC POWERS AND ABILITIES. BANDED TOGETHER BY THE FREEDOM FIGHTER KNOWN AS CABLE,
HE IMPULSIVE MUTANTS KNOWN AS X-FORCE QUESTION EVERYTHING - INCLUDING THE WISDOM AND IDEALS OF THOSE WHO HAVE COME BEFORE.
EFUSING TO LIVE BY RULES LAID FORTH BY A GENERATION THAT CAN NEVER
NDERSTAND THEM, X-FORCE FIGHTS FOR THE VERY SURVIVAL OF THEIR SPECIES
A WORLD THAT DESPISES AND FEARS THEM! STAN LEE PRESENTS:
X-FORCE
BITTER RIVER, CALIFORNIA.
GAS
TEXACO
GAS
THAT THE BEST YOU'VE GOT?
RACE WAR
PART TWO OF FOUR
IAN EDGINTON WORDS
JORGE LUCAS ART
GINA GOING COLORS
CHRIS ELIOPOULOS LETTERS
FRANK DUNKERLEY ASSIST
MATT HICKS EDITOR
JOE QUESADA EDITOR IN CHIEF
OUT OF TIME.
OUT OF BULLETS.
OUT OF LUCK.
COLA

[redacted]

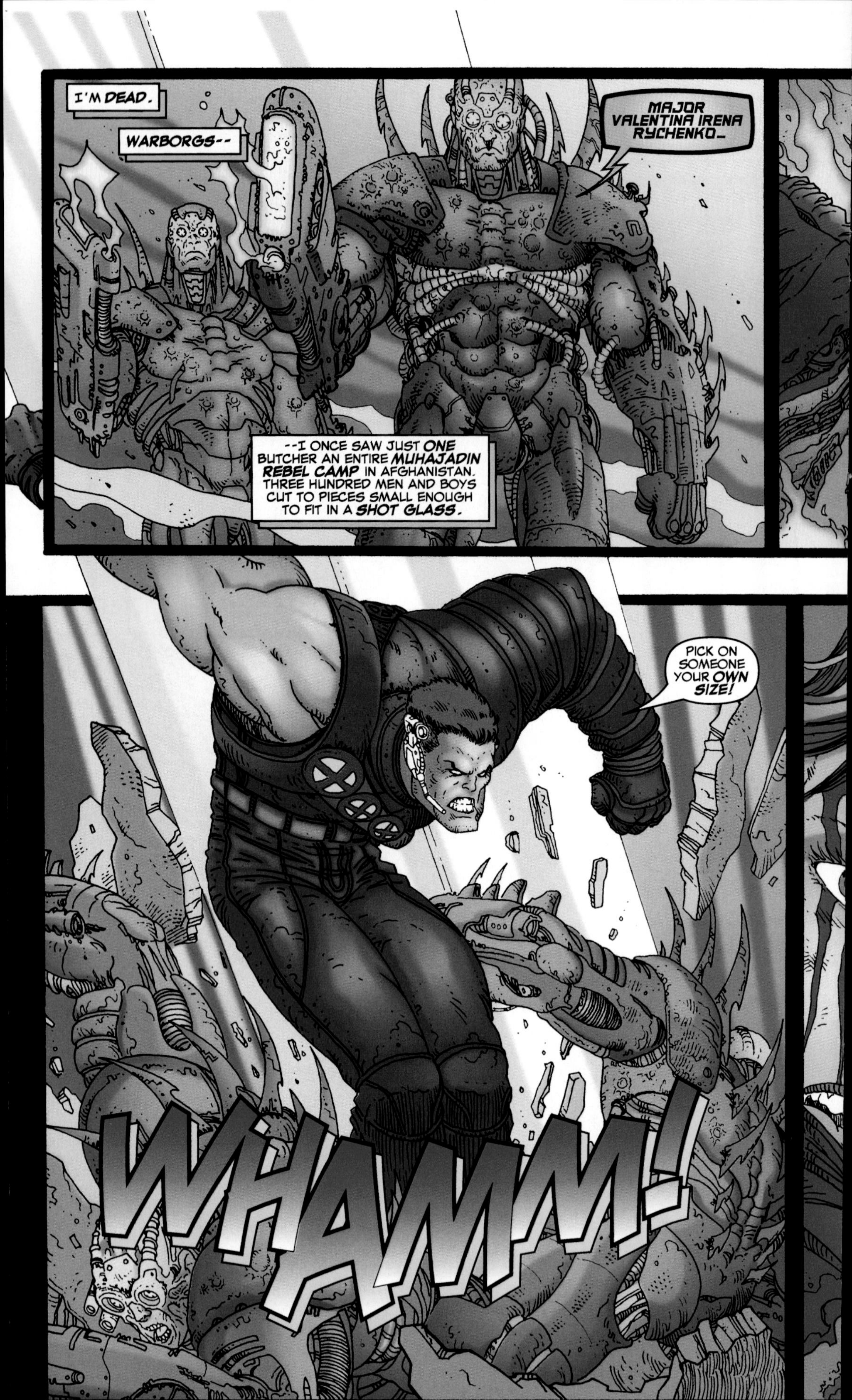

I'M DEAD.
WARBORGS--
MAJOR VALENTINA IRENA RYCHENKO--
--I ONCE SAW JUST ONE BUTCHER AN ENTIRE MUHAJADIN REBEL CAMP IN AFGHANISTAN. THREE HUNDRED MEN AND BOYS CUT TO PIECES SMALL ENOUGH TO FIT IN A SHOT GLASS.
PICK ON SOMEONE YOUR OWN SIZE!
WHAMM!

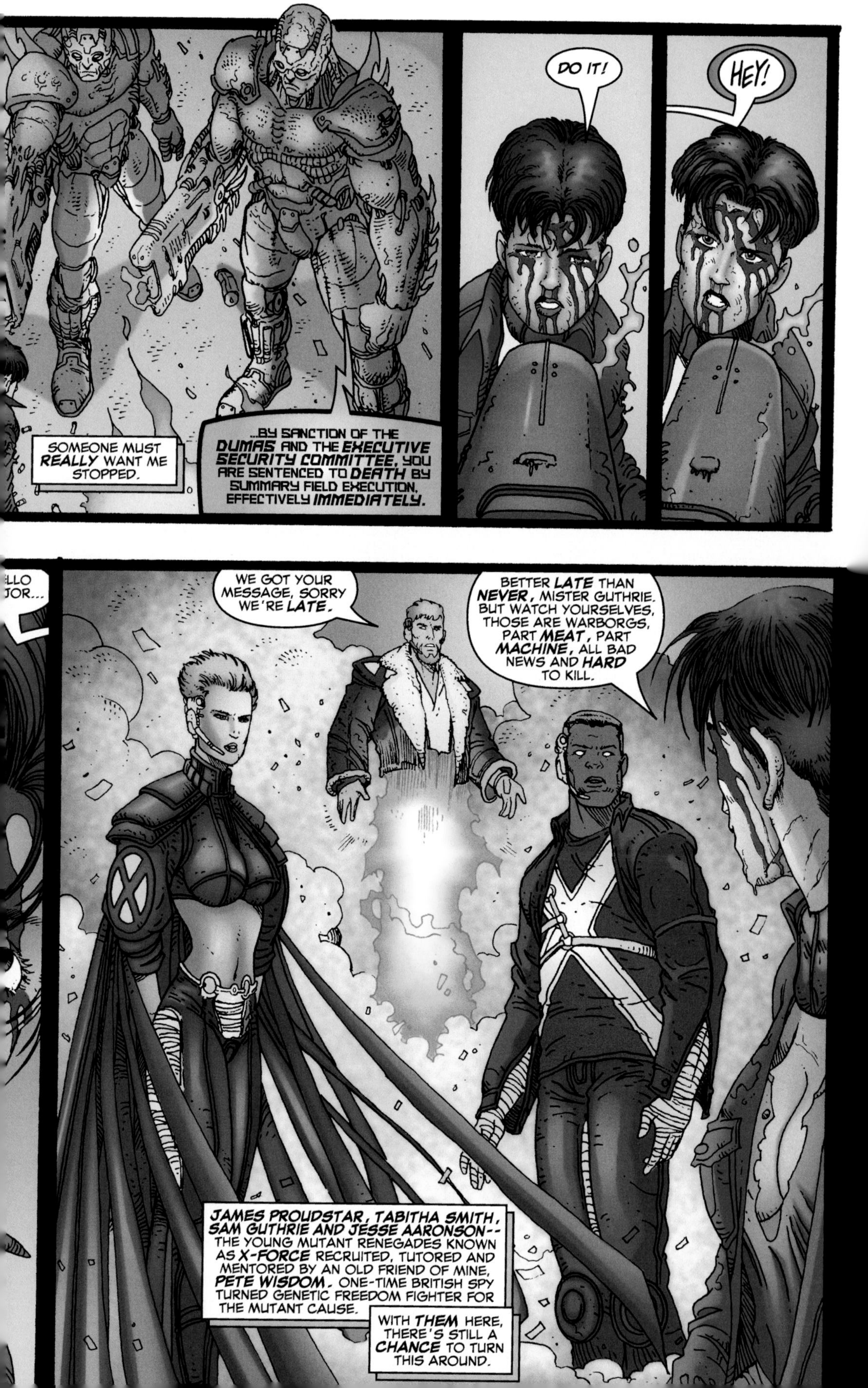

SOMEONE MUST REALLY WANT ME STOPPED.
...BY SANCTION OF THE DUMAS AND THE EXECUTIVE SECURITY COMMITTEE, YOU ARE SENTENCED TO DEATH BY SUMMARY FIELD EXECUTION, EFFECTIVELY IMMEDIATELY.
DO IT!
HEY!
WE GOT YOUR MESSAGE, SORRY WE'RE LATE.
BETTER LATE THAN NEVER, MISTER GUTHRIE. BUT WATCH YOURSELVES, THOSE ARE WARBORGS, PART MEAT, PART MACHINE, ALL BAD NEWS AND HARD TO KILL.
JAMES PROUDSTAR, TABITHA SMITH, SAM GUTHRIE AND JESSE AARONSON-- THE YOUNG MUTANT RENEGADES KNOWN AS X-FORCE RECRUITED, TUTORED AND MENTORED BY AN OLD FRIEND OF MINE, PETE WISDOM. ONE-TIME BRITISH SPY TURNED GENETIC FREEDOM FIGHTER FOR THE MUTANT CAUSE.
WITH THEM HERE, THERE'S STILL A CHANCE TO TURN THIS AROUND.

RAKKABOOM!

SEE!

NO SWEAT, WE PACK FOR *EVERY* OCCASION.

"TAB. JESSE. *YOU'RE* THE FLOOR SHOW."

COPY THAT.

"TAB, I WANT *HARD LIGHT BLADES*. KEEP 'EM *BLIND* AND *BUSY!*"

"*JESS'*. WHATEVER *TECH* THEY'RE PACKIN', COOK IT WITH AS MUCH *EMP* AS YOU CAN MUSTER."

SAM, IT'S *NOT* WORKING!

FASHOOM!

FASHOOM!

"DOMINO TO *ALL POINTS!*"

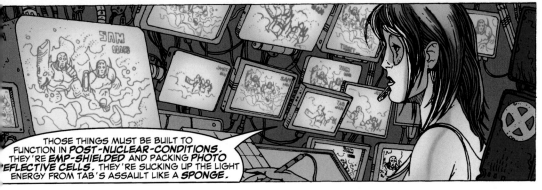

THOSE THINGS MUST BE BUILT TO FUNCTION IN *POST-NUCLEAR-CONDITIONS*. THEY'RE *EMP-SHIELDED* AND PACKING *PHOTO REFLECTIVE CELLS*. THEY'RE SUCKING UP THE LIGHT ENERGY FROM TAB'S ASSAULT LIKE A *SPONGE*.

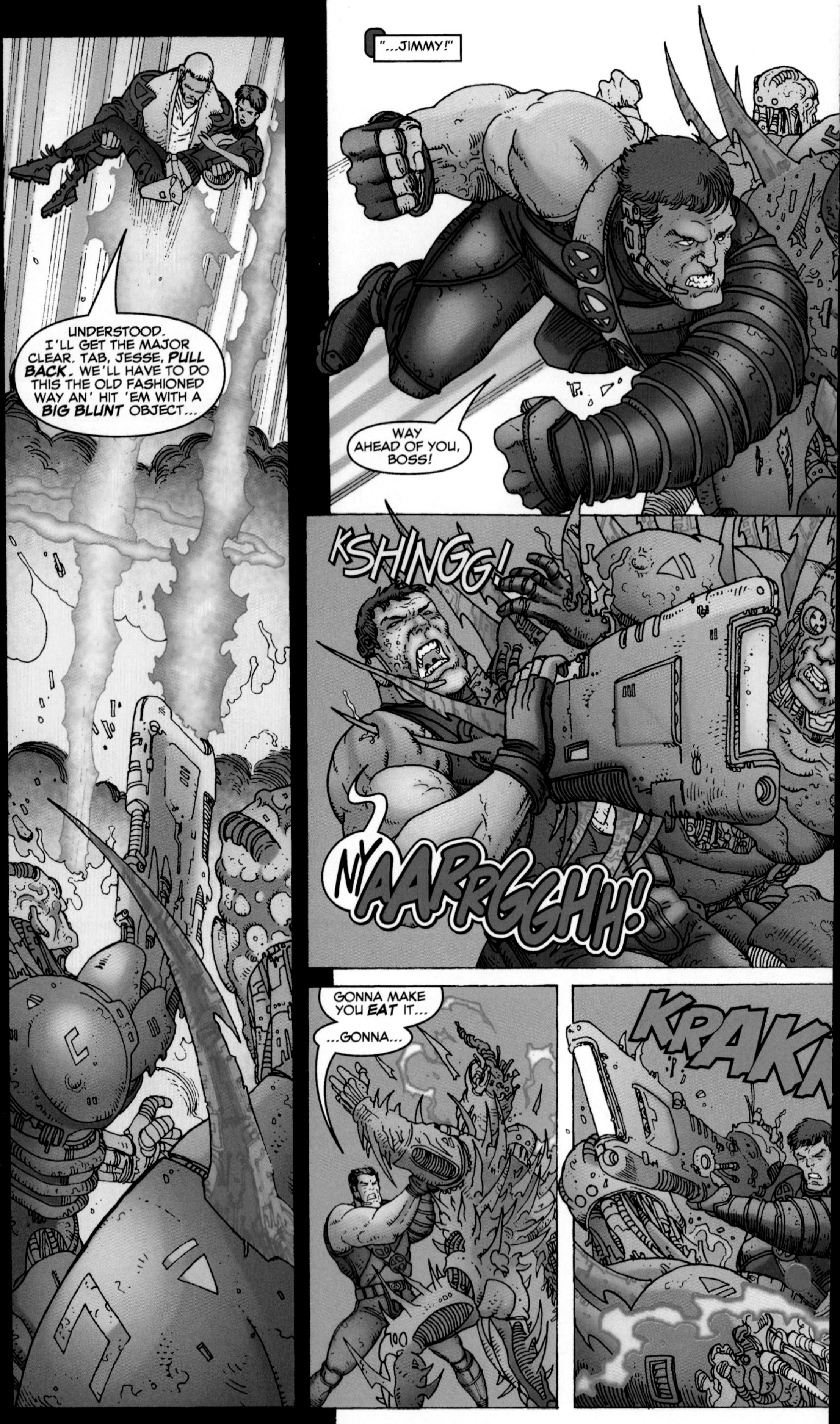
UNDERSTOOD. I'LL GET THE MAJOR CLEAR. TAB, JESSE, PULL BACK. WE'LL HAVE TO DO THIS THE OLD FASHIONED WAY AN' HIT 'EM WITH A BIG BLUNT OBJECT...
"...JIMMY!"
WAY AHEAD OF YOU, BOSS!
KSHINGG!
NYAARRGGHH!
GONNA MAKE YOU EAT IT...
...GONNA...
KRAKK

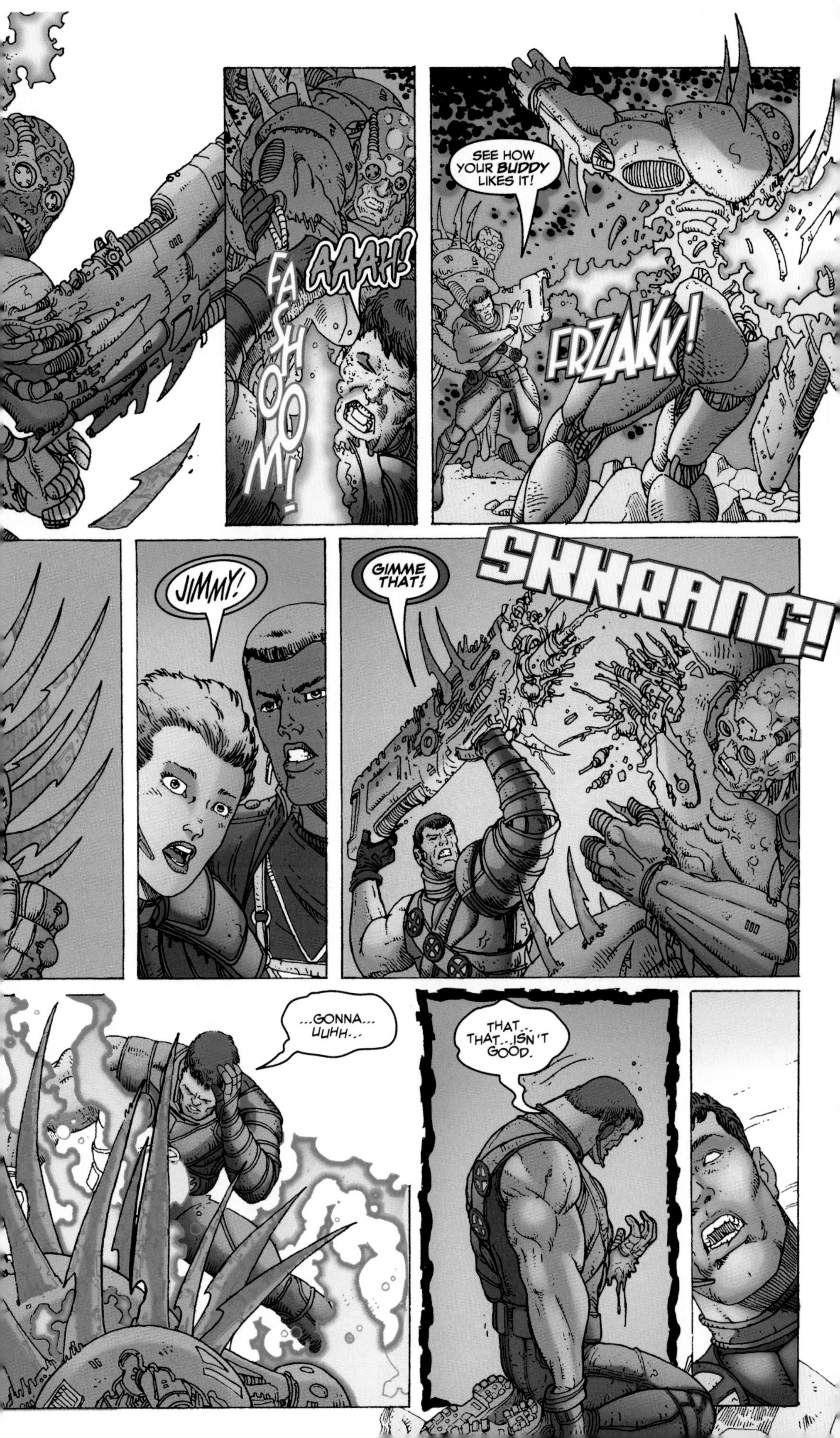
FASHOOOM!
AAAH!
SEE HOW YOUR BUDDY LIKES IT!
FRZAKK!
JIMMY!
GIMME THAT!
SKKRANG!
...GONNA... UUHH...
THAT... THAT...ISN'T GOOD.

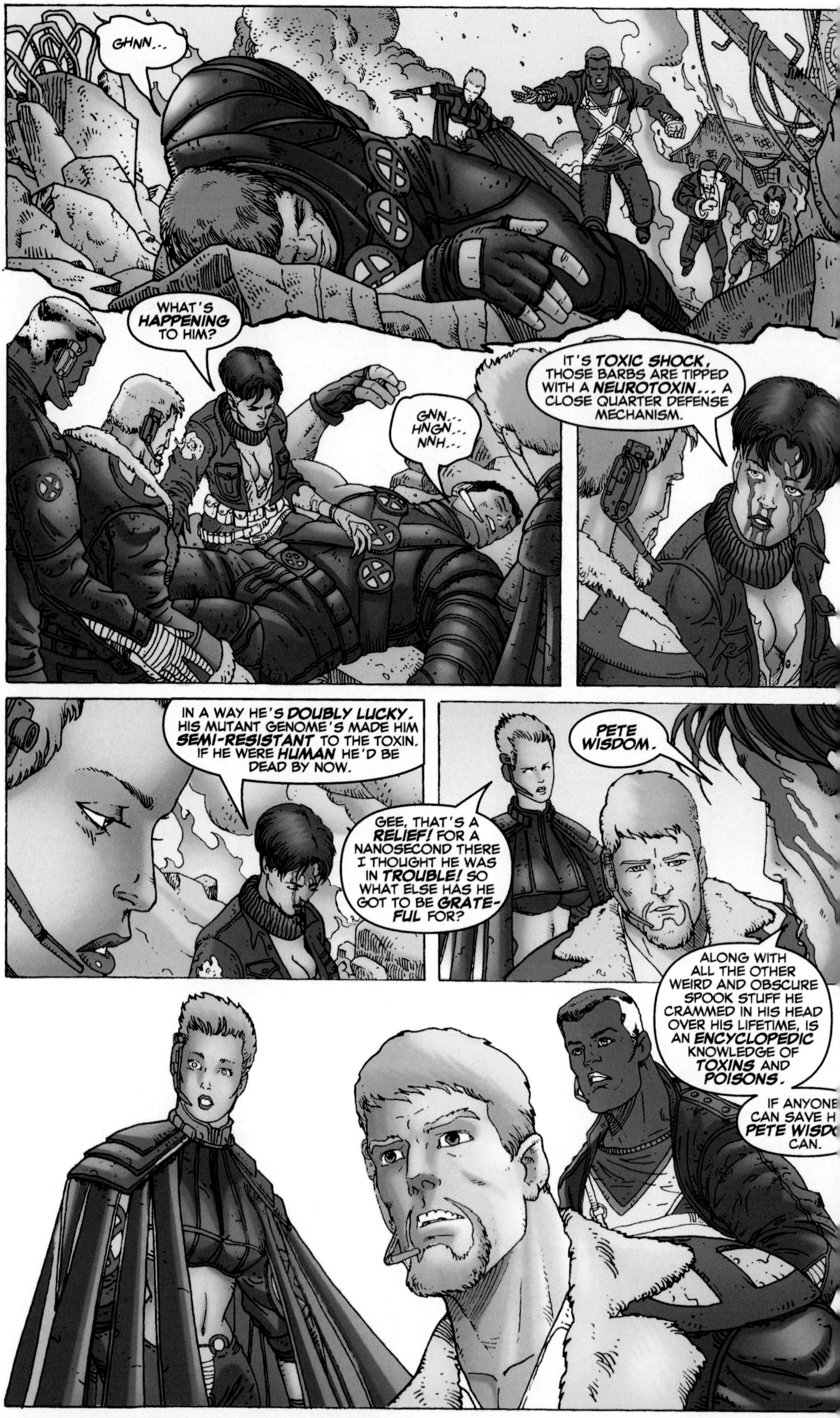
GHNN...
JIM!
WHAT'S HAPPENING TO HIM?
GNN... HNGN... NNH...
IT'S TOXIC SHOCK, THOSE BARBS ARE TIPPED WITH A NEUROTOXIN... A CLOSE QUARTER DEFENSE MECHANISM.
IN A WAY HE'S DOUBLY LUCKY. HIS MUTANT GENOME'S MADE HIM SEMI-RESISTANT TO THE TOXIN. IF HE WERE HUMAN HE'D BE DEAD BY NOW.
GEE, THAT'S A RELIEF! FOR A NANOSECOND THERE I THOUGHT HE WAS IN TROUBLE! SO WHAT ELSE HAS HE GOT TO BE GRATE-FUL FOR?
PETE WISDOM.
ALONG WITH ALL THE OTHER WEIRD AND OBSCURE SPOOK STUFF HE CRAMMED IN HIS HEAD OVER HIS LIFETIME, IS AN ENCYCLOPEDIC KNOWLEDGE OF TOXINS AND POISONS.

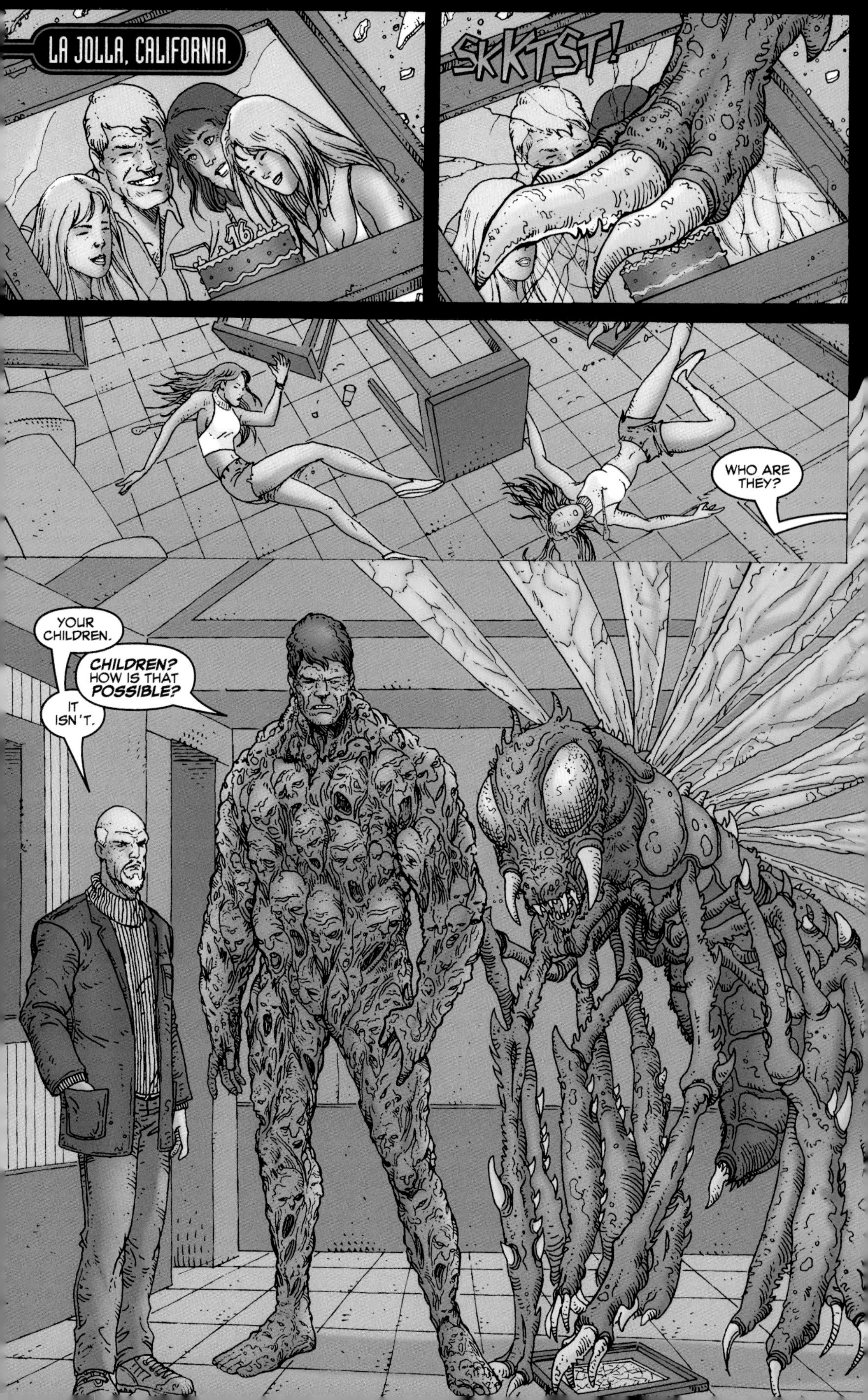
LA JOLLA, CALIFORNIA.
SKKTST!
WHO ARE THEY?
YOUR CHILDREN.
CHILDREN? HOW IS THAT POSSIBLE?
IT ISN'T.

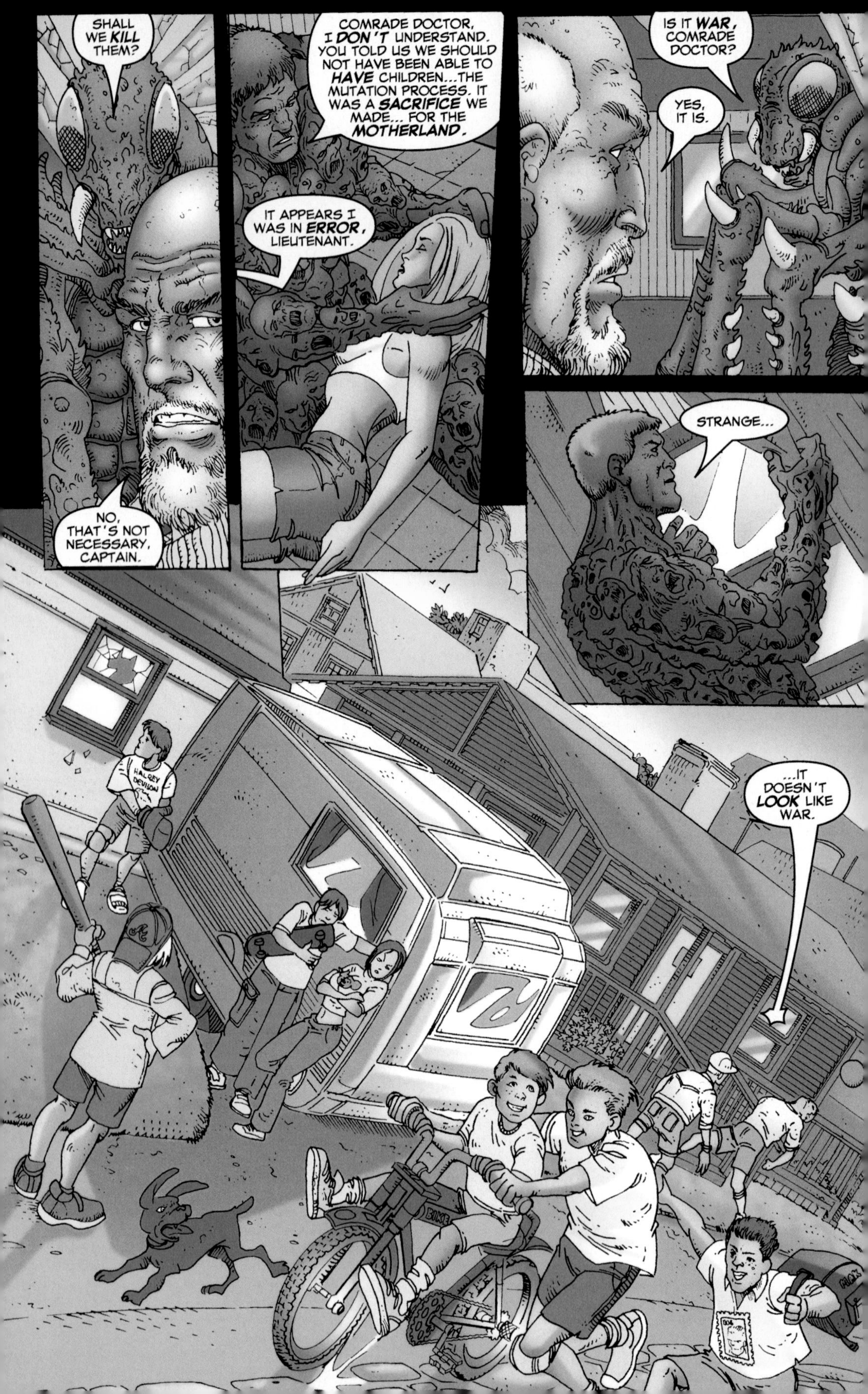

SHALL WE KILL THEM?
NO, THAT'S NOT NECESSARY, CAPTAIN.
COMRADE DOCTOR, I DON'T UNDERSTAND. YOU TOLD US WE SHOULD NOT HAVE BEEN ABLE TO HAVE CHILDREN...THE MUTATION PROCESS. IT WAS A SACRIFICE WE MADE... FOR THE MOTHERLAND.
IT APPEARS I WAS IN ERROR, LIEUTENANT.
IS IT WAR, COMRADE DOCTOR?
YES, IT IS.
STRANGE...
...IT DOESN'T LOOK LIKE WAR.

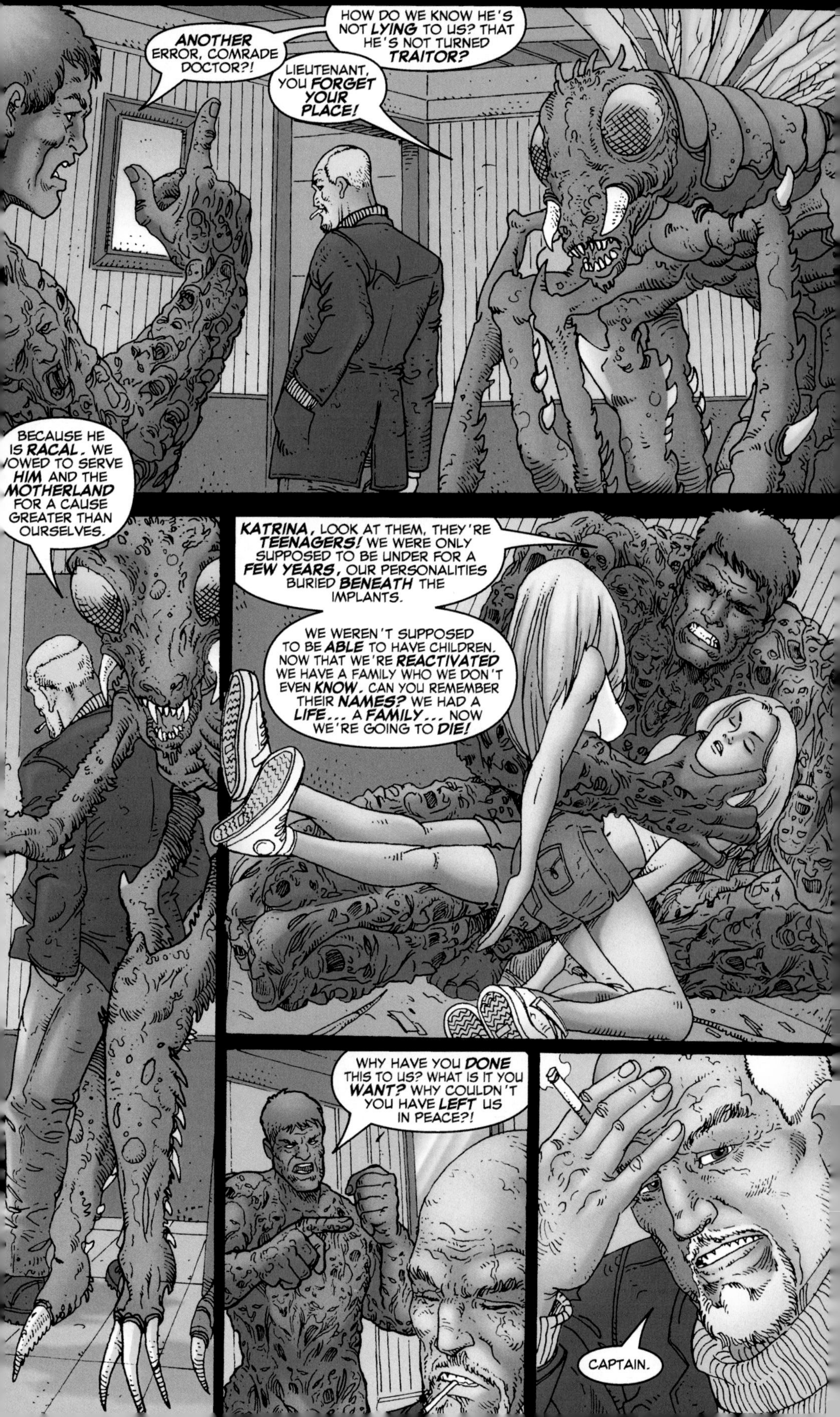
ANOTHER ERROR, COMRADE DOCTOR?!
HOW DO WE KNOW HE'S NOT LYING TO US? THAT HE'S NOT TURNED TRAITOR?
LIEUTENANT, YOU FORGET YOUR PLACE!
BECAUSE HE IS RACAL. WE VOWED TO SERVE HIM AND THE MOTHERLAND FOR A CAUSE GREATER THAN OURSELVES.
KATRINA, LOOK AT THEM, THEY'RE TEENAGERS! WE WERE ONLY SUPPOSED TO BE UNDER FOR A FEW YEARS, OUR PERSONALITIES BURIED BENEATH THE IMPLANTS.
WE WEREN'T SUPPOSED TO BE ABLE TO HAVE CHILDREN. NOW THAT WE'RE REACTIVATED WE HAVE A FAMILY WHO WE DON'T EVEN KNOW. CAN YOU REMEMBER THEIR NAMES? WE HAD A LIFE... A FAMILY... NOW WE'RE GOING TO DIE!
WHY HAVE YOU DONE THIS TO US? WHAT IS IT YOU WANT? WHY COULDN'T YOU HAVE LEFT US IN PEACE?!
CAPTAIN.

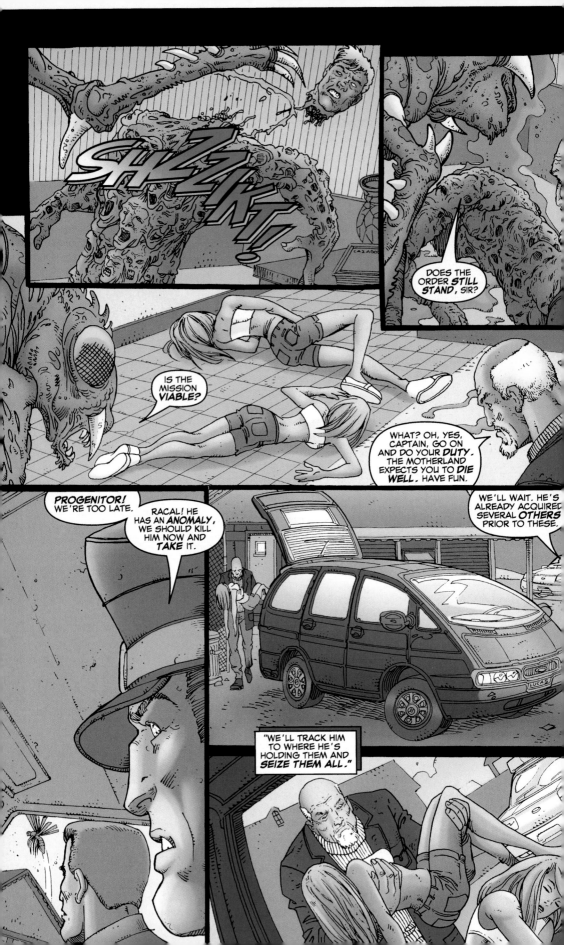

SHZZKT!

DOES THE ORDER STILL STAND, SIR?

IS THE MISSION VIABLE?

WHAT? OH, YES, CAPTAIN, GO ON AND DO YOUR DUTY. THE MOTHERLAND EXPECTS YOU TO DIE WELL. HAVE FUN.

PROGENITOR! WE'RE TOO LATE.

RACAL! HE HAS AN ANOMALY, WE SHOULD KILL HIM NOW AND TAKE IT.

WE'LL WAIT. HE'S ALREADY ACQUIRED SEVERAL OTHERS PRIOR TO THESE.

"WE'LL TRACK HIM TO WHERE HE'S HOLDING THEM AND SEIZE THEM ALL."

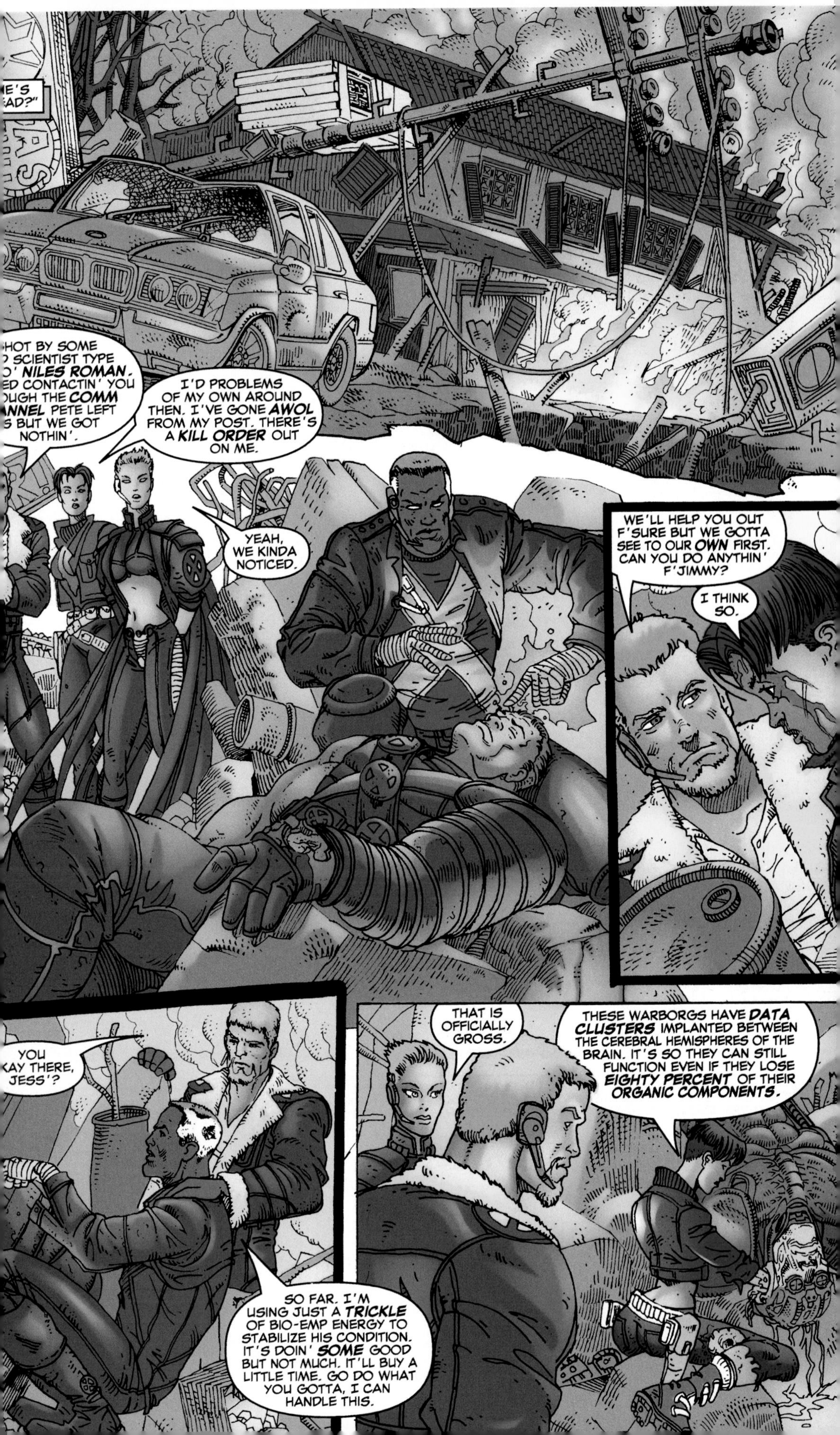

E'S
EAD?"
HOT BY SOME
D SCIENTIST TYPE
O' NILES ROMAN.
ED CONTACTIN' YOU
OUGH THE COMM
ANNEL PETE LEFT
S BUT WE GOT
NOTHIN'.
I'D PROBLEMS OF MY OWN AROUND THEN. I'VE GONE AWOL FROM MY POST. THERE'S A KILL ORDER OUT ON ME.
YEAH, WE KINDA NOTICED.
WE'LL HELP YOU OUT F'SURE BUT WE GOTTA SEE TO OUR OWN FIRST. CAN YOU DO ANYTHIN' F'JIMMY?
I THINK SO.
YOU
KAY THERE,
JESS'?
SO FAR. I'M USING JUST A TRICKLE OF BIO-EMP ENERGY TO STABILIZE HIS CONDITION. IT'S DOIN' SOME GOOD BUT NOT MUCH. IT'LL BUY A LITTLE TIME. GO DO WHAT YOU GOTTA, I CAN HANDLE THIS.
THAT IS OFFICIALLY GROSS.
THESE WARBORGS HAVE DATA CLUSTERS IMPLANTED BETWEEN THE CEREBRAL HEMISPHERES OF THE BRAIN. IT'S SO THEY CAN STILL FUNCTION EVEN IF THEY LOSE EIGHTY PERCENT OF THEIR ORGANIC COMPONENTS.

ORGANIC?

RUSSIA LOST *A LOT* OF MEN IN *AFGHANISTAN* AND *CHECHNYA*. WE DON'T LIKE TO *WASTE* RESOURCES, EVEN *DEAD* ONES. THESE MEN WERE *REANIMATED* WITH SOME KIND OF *SMART TECHNOLOGY* I'VE NEVER SEEN BEFORE.

YOU DON'T SAY. WE CAME ACROSS SOMETHING LIKE THAT NOT SO LONG AGO OURSELVES.

TAB', ANOTHER TIME.

TH

A KIND OF *HARD DRIVE*. WITH IT WE CAN ACCESS THE *SHARED MEMORY DATA* OF THE OTHER WARBORG CELLS OPERATING *STATESIDE*. THERE'S A GOOD CHANCE THEY'LL GIVE US A LEAD ON RACAL.

RACAL?

HE'S THE MAN I'M AFTER. SO ARE THE WARBORGS. THEY'RE BASED ON *HIS* DESIGNS. HE'S THE *ONLY ONE* WHO CAN SAVE JAMES.

ONLY PROBLEM IS WE NEED A *PHONE LINE* AND A *COMPUTER TERMINAL*.

OUT HER THIS PLACE WAR ZO

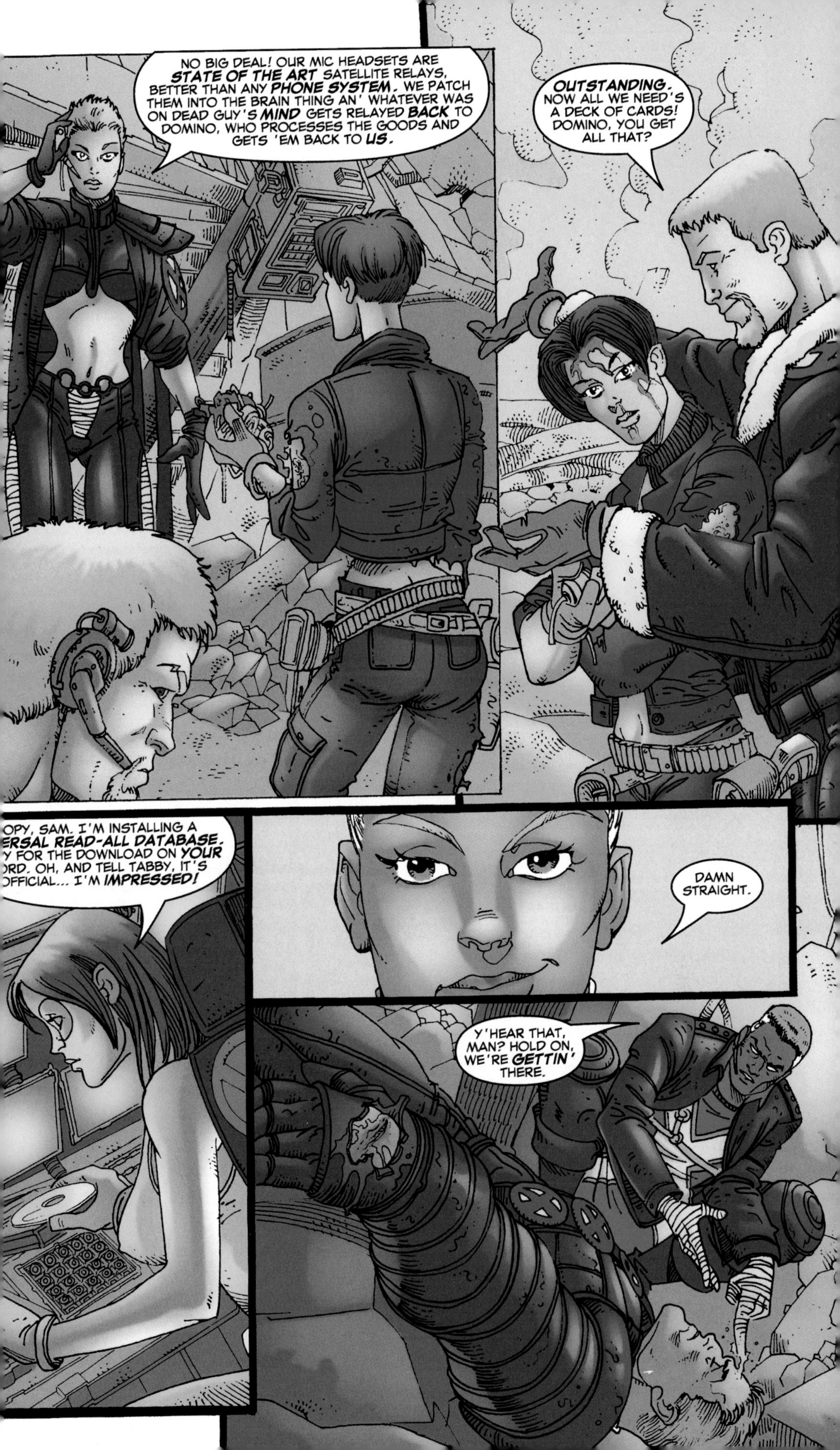
NO BIG DEAL! OUR MIC HEADSETS ARE STATE OF THE ART SATELLITE RELAYS, BETTER THAN ANY PHONE SYSTEM. WE PATCH THEM INTO THE BRAIN THING AN' WHATEVER WAS ON DEAD GUY'S MIND GETS RELAYED BACK TO DOMINO, WHO PROCESSES THE GOODS AND GETS 'EM BACK TO US.
OUTSTANDING. NOW ALL WE NEED'S A DECK OF CARDS! DOMINO, YOU GET ALL THAT?
OPY, SAM. I'M INSTALLING A ERSAL READ-ALL DATABASE. Y FOR THE DOWNLOAD ON YOUR ORD. OH, AND TELL TABBY, IT'S OFFICIAL... I'M IMPRESSED!
DAMN STRAIGHT.
Y'HEAR THAT, MAN? HOLD ON, WE'RE GETTIN' THERE.

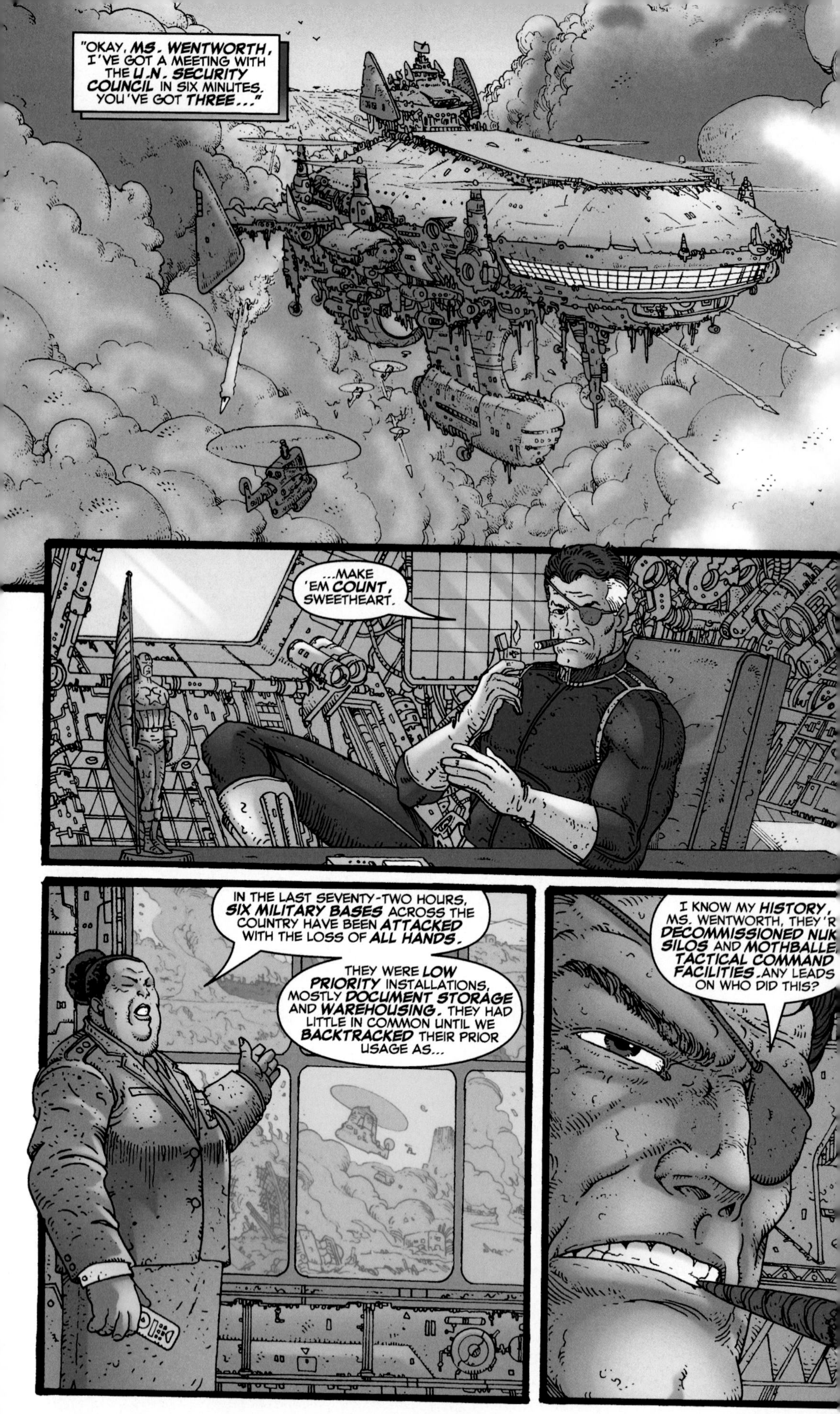

"OKAY, MS. WENTWORTH, I'VE GOT A MEETING WITH THE U.N. SECURITY COUNCIL IN SIX MINUTES. YOU'VE GOT THREE..."
...MAKE 'EM COUNT, SWEETHEART.
IN THE LAST SEVENTY-TWO HOURS, SIX MILITARY BASES ACROSS THE COUNTRY HAVE BEEN ATTACKED WITH THE LOSS OF ALL HANDS.
THEY WERE LOW PRIORITY INSTALLATIONS, MOSTLY DOCUMENT STORAGE AND WAREHOUSING. THEY HAD LITTLE IN COMMON UNTIL WE BACKTRACKED THEIR PRIOR USAGE AS...
I KNOW MY HISTORY, MS. WENTWORTH, THEY'R DECOMMISSIONED NUK SILOS AND MOTHBALLE TACTICAL COMMAND FACILITIES. ANY LEADS ON WHO DID THIS?

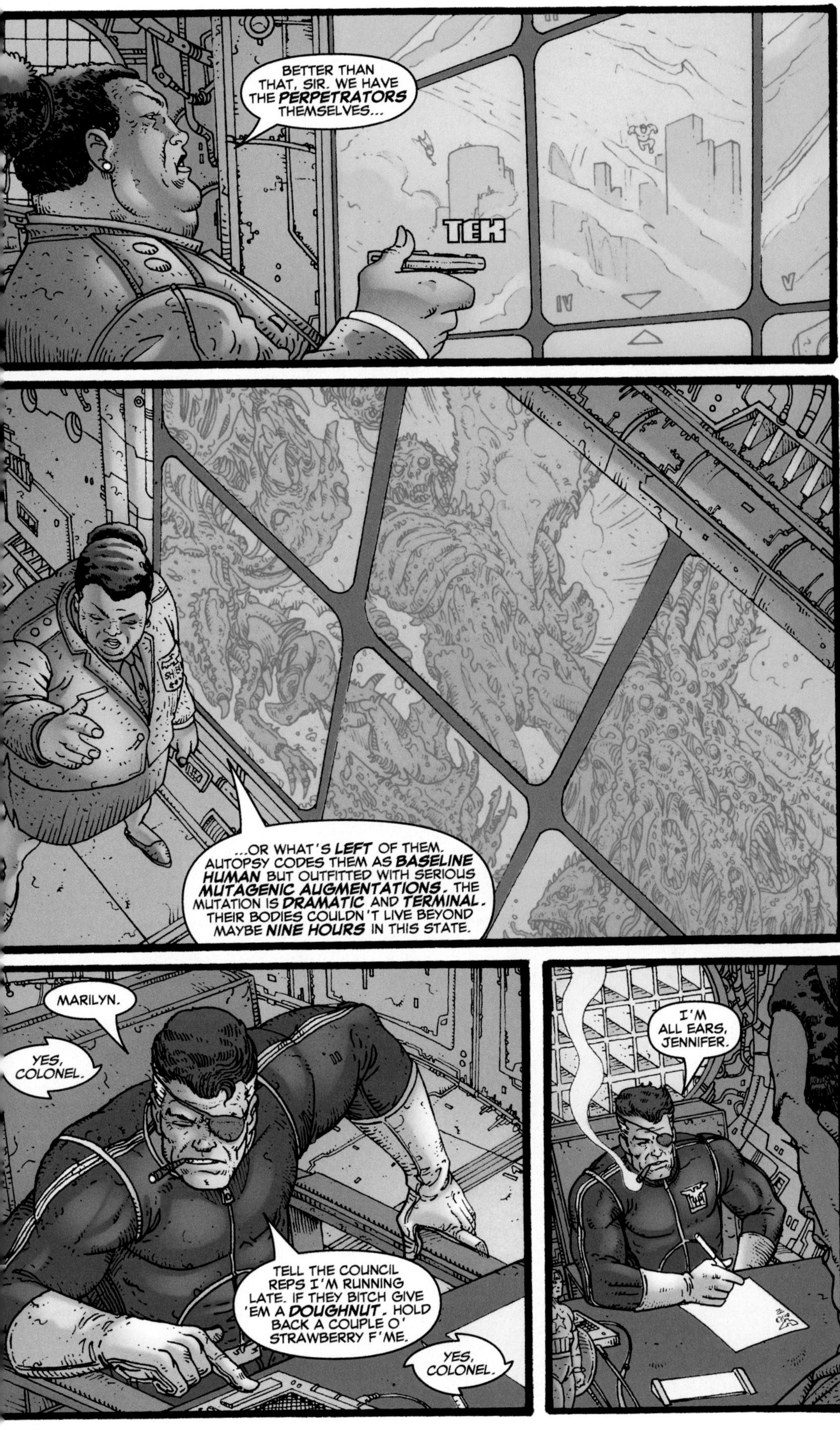
BETTER THAN THAT, SIR. WE HAVE THE PERPETRATORS THEMSELVES...
TEK
...OR WHAT'S LEFT OF THEM. AUTOPSY CODES THEM AS BASELINE HUMAN BUT OUTFITTED WITH SERIOUS MUTAGENIC AUGMENTATIONS. THE MUTATION IS DRAMATIC AND TERMINAL. THEIR BODIES COULDN'T LIVE BEYOND MAYBE NINE HOURS IN THIS STATE.
MARILYN.
YES, COLONEL.
TELL THE COUNCIL REPS I'M RUNNING LATE. IF THEY BITCH GIVE 'EM A DOUGHNUT. HOLD BACK A COUPLE O' STRAWBERRY F'ME.
YES, COLONEL.
I'M ALL EARS, JENNIFER.

EXTECHOP SAYS THE AUGMENTATIONS ARE OLD SOVIET WORK, DATES THEM AT *TWENTY YEARS PLUS*. ASIDE FROM THAT THEY'RE A *MYSTERY*.

WE'VE NOTHING ELSE ON THEM... OR AT LEAST DIDN'T HAVE *UNTIL* THIS MORNING.

CLASSIF. 10238-B MOCXY 1986

WARBORGS! WHERE?

SAN DIEGO. WE DID A GENETIC CROSS MATCH WITH THE OTHER MUTATES, THEY'RE BASICALLY THE *SAME*. THE WARBORGS ARE THIS YEAR'S MODEL, UPDATED VERSIONS.

THEIR HARD DRIVES WERE *CORRUPTED* BUT WE RESTORED SOME *PARTIAL FILES*. THEY'RE ONE OF *THREE* EXCURSION DEATH SQUADS SENT STATESIDE TO *KILL* TWO HIGH RANKING COVERT SERVICE OFFICERS GONE AWOL.

TEK

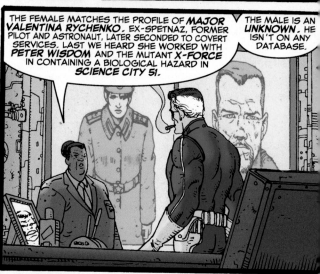

THE FEMALE MATCHES THE PROFILE OF *MAJOR VALENTINA RYCHENKO*. EX-SPETNAZ, FORMER PILOT AND ASTRONAUT, LATER SECONDED TO COVERT SERVICES. LAST WE HEARD SHE WORKED WITH *PETER WISDOM* AND THE MUTANT *X-FORCE* IN CONTAINING A BIOLOGICAL HAZARD IN *SCIENCE CITY 51*.

THE MALE IS AN *UNKNOWN*. HE ISN'T ON ANY DATABASE.

I KNOW HIS NAME...

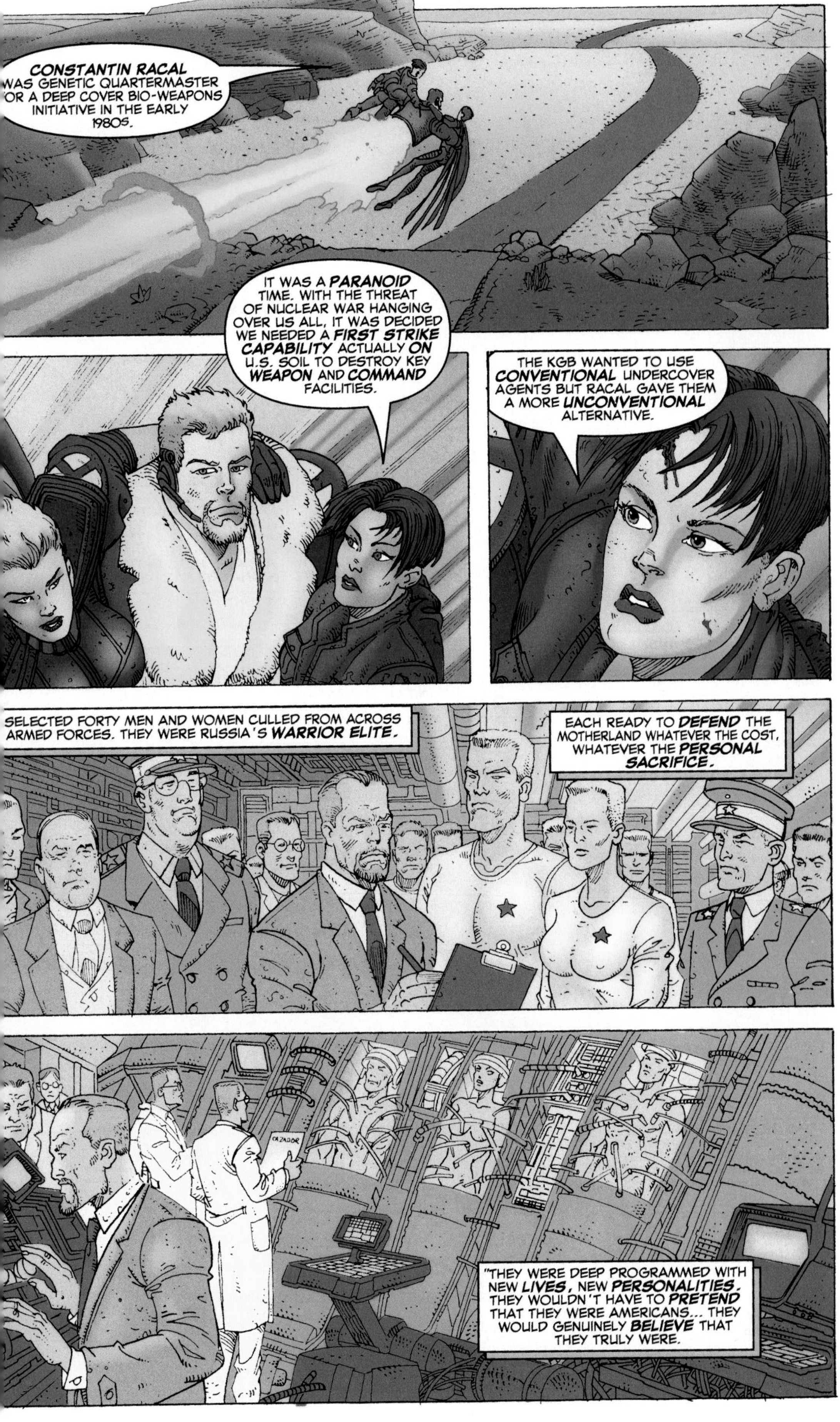
CONSTANTIN RACAL WAS GENETIC QUARTERMASTER FOR A DEEP COVER BIO-WEAPONS INITIATIVE IN THE EARLY 1980S.
IT WAS A PARANOID TIME. WITH THE THREAT OF NUCLEAR WAR HANGING OVER US ALL, IT WAS DECIDED WE NEEDED A FIRST STRIKE CAPABILITY ACTUALLY ON U.S. SOIL TO DESTROY KEY WEAPON AND COMMAND FACILITIES.
THE KGB WANTED TO USE CONVENTIONAL UNDERCOVER AGENTS BUT RACAL GAVE THEM A MORE UNCONVENTIONAL ALTERNATIVE.
SELECTED FORTY MEN AND WOMEN CULLED FROM ACROSS ARMED FORCES. THEY WERE RUSSIA'S WARRIOR ELITE.
EACH READY TO DEFEND THE MOTHERLAND WHATEVER THE COST, WHATEVER THE PERSONAL SACRIFICE.
"THEY WERE DEEP PROGRAMMED WITH NEW LIVES, NEW PERSONALITIES. THEY WOULDN'T HAVE TO PRETEND THAT THEY WERE AMERICANS... THEY WOULD GENUINELY BELIEVE THAT THEY TRULY WERE.

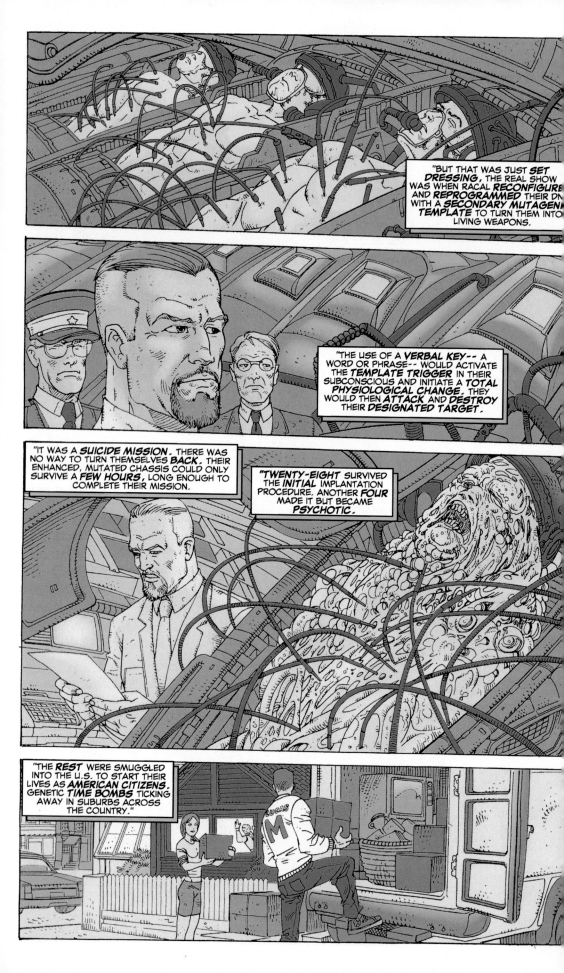

"BUT THAT WAS JUST **SET DRESSING**, THE REAL SHOW WAS WHEN RACAL **RECONFIGURE** AND **REPROGRAMMED** THEIR DN WITH A **SECONDARY MUTAGEN** **TEMPLATE** TO TURN THEM INTO LIVING WEAPONS.

"THE USE OF A **VERBAL KEY**-- A WORD OR PHRASE-- WOULD ACTIVATE THE **TEMPLATE TRIGGER** IN THEIR SUBCONSCIOUS AND INITIATE A **TOTAL PHYSIOLOGICAL CHANGE**. THEY WOULD THEN **ATTACK** AND **DESTROY** THEIR **DESIGNATED TARGET**.

"IT WAS A **SUICIDE MISSION**. THERE WAS NO WAY TO TURN THEMSELVES **BACK**. THEIR ENHANCED, MUTATED CHASSIS COULD ONLY SURVIVE A **FEW HOURS**, LONG ENOUGH TO COMPLETE THEIR MISSION.

"**TWENTY-EIGHT** SURVIVED THE **INITIAL** IMPLANTATION PROCEDURE. ANOTHER **FOUR** MADE IT BUT BECAME **PSYCHOTIC**.

"THE **REST** WERE SMUGGLED INTO THE U.S. TO START THEIR LIVES AS **AMERICAN CITIZENS**. GENETIC **TIME BOMBS** TICKING AWAY IN SUBURBS ACROSS THE COUNTRY."

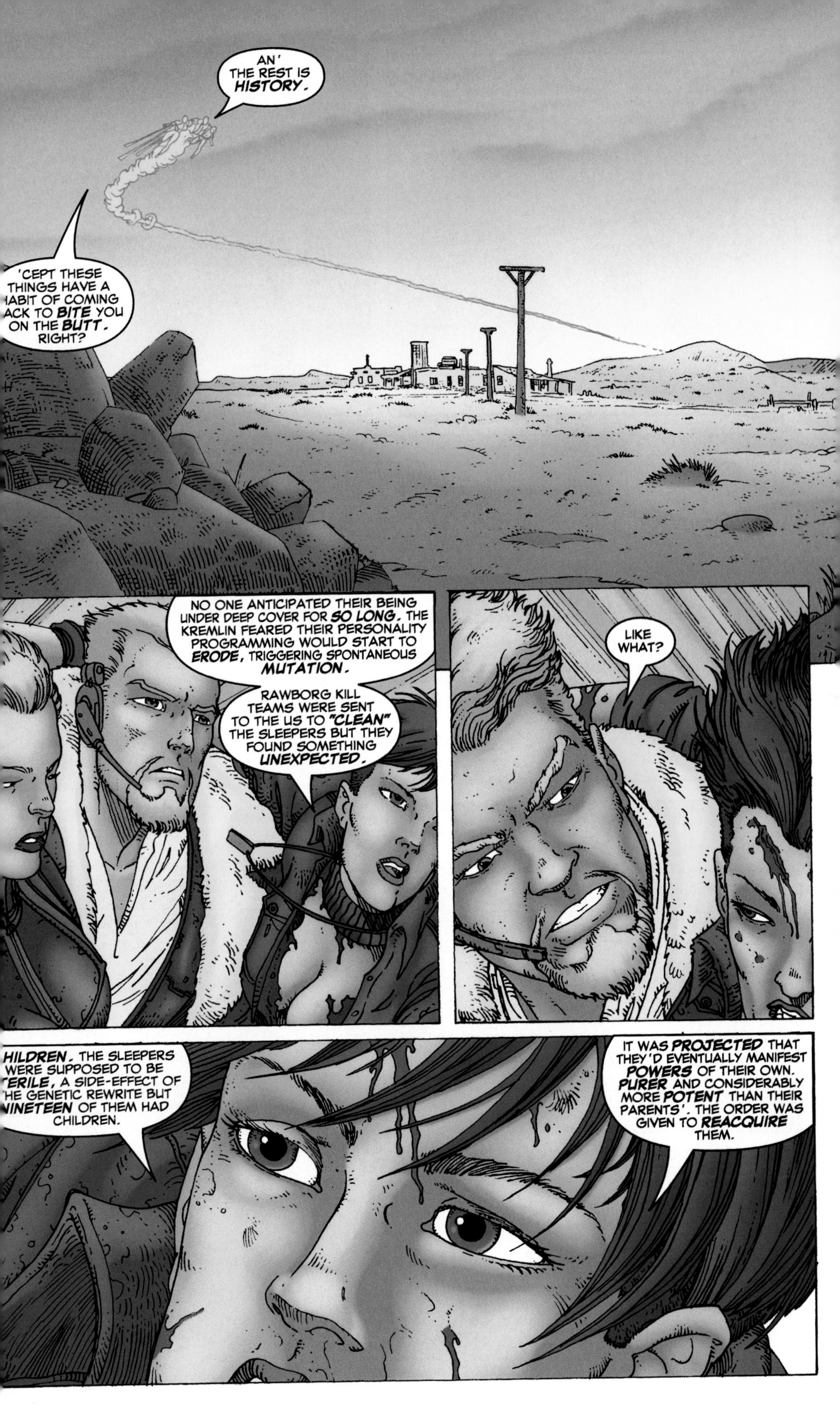
AN' THE REST IS HISTORY.
'CEPT THESE THINGS HAVE A HABIT OF COMING BACK TO BITE YOU ON THE BUTT. RIGHT?
NO ONE ANTICIPATED THEIR BEING UNDER DEEP COVER FOR SO LONG. THE KREMLIN FEARED THEIR PERSONALITY PROGRAMMING WOULD START TO ERODE, TRIGGERING SPONTANEOUS MUTATION.
RAWBORG KILL TEAMS WERE SENT TO THE US TO "CLEAN" THE SLEEPERS BUT THEY FOUND SOMETHING UNEXPECTED.
LIKE WHAT?
CHILDREN. THE SLEEPERS WERE SUPPOSED TO BE STERILE, A SIDE-EFFECT OF THE GENETIC REWRITE BUT NINETEEN OF THEM HAD CHILDREN.
IT WAS PROJECTED THAT THEY'D EVENTUALLY MANIFEST POWERS OF THEIR OWN. PURER AND CONSIDERABLY MORE POTENT THAN THEIR PARENTS'. THE ORDER WAS GIVEN TO REACQUIRE THEM.

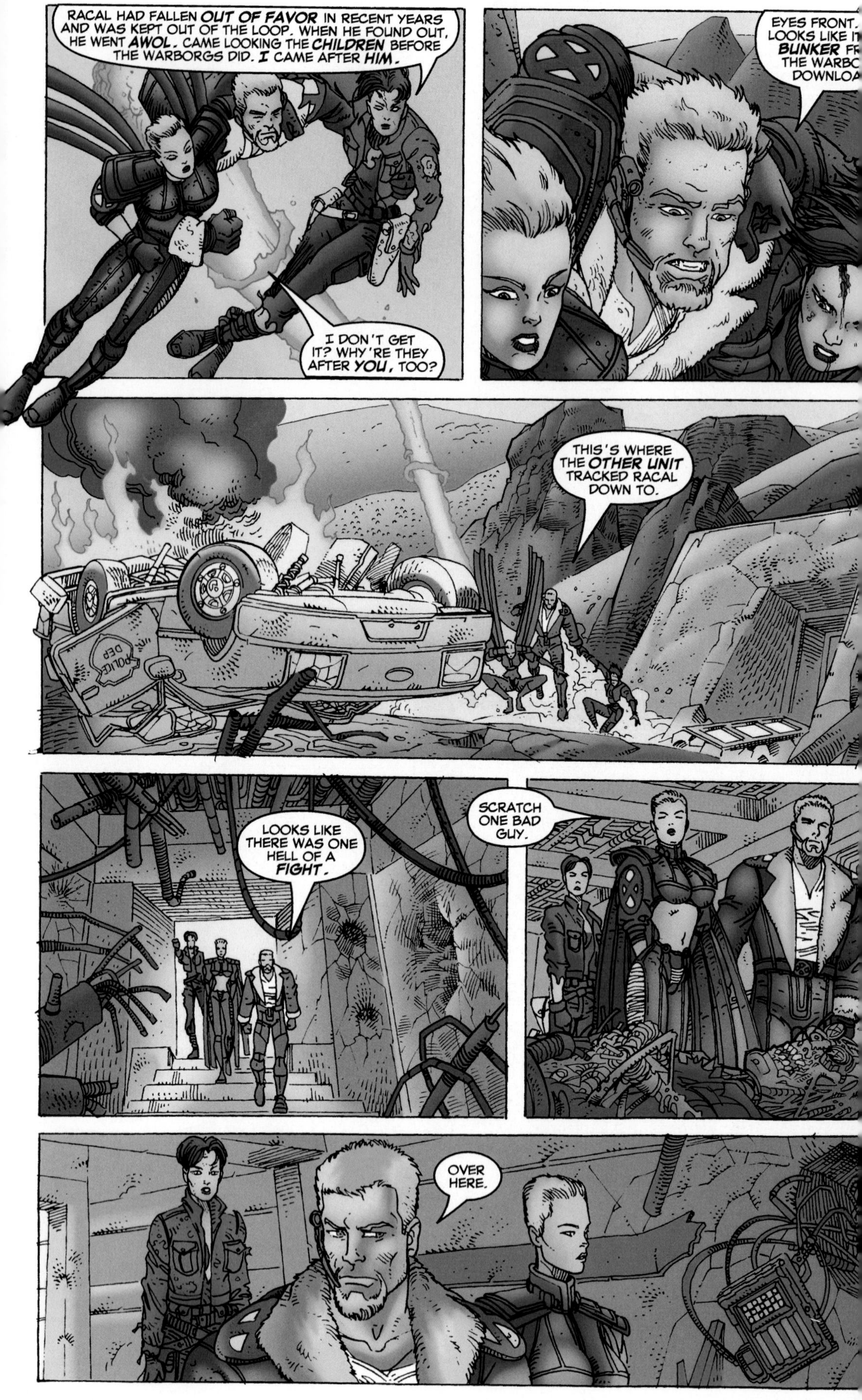
RACAL HAD FALLEN OUT OF FAVOR IN RECENT YEARS AND WAS KEPT OUT OF THE LOOP. WHEN HE FOUND OUT, HE WENT AWOL. CAME LOOKING THE CHILDREN BEFORE THE WARBORGS DID. I CAME AFTER HIM.
I DON'T GET IT? WHY'RE THEY AFTER YOU, TOO?
EYES FRONT. LOOKS LIKE IT BUNKER FR THE WARBO DOWNLOA
POLICE DEP
THIS'S WHERE THE OTHER UNIT TRACKED RACAL DOWN TO.
LOOKS LIKE THERE WAS ONE HELL OF A FIGHT.
SCRATCH ONE BAD GUY.
OVER HERE.

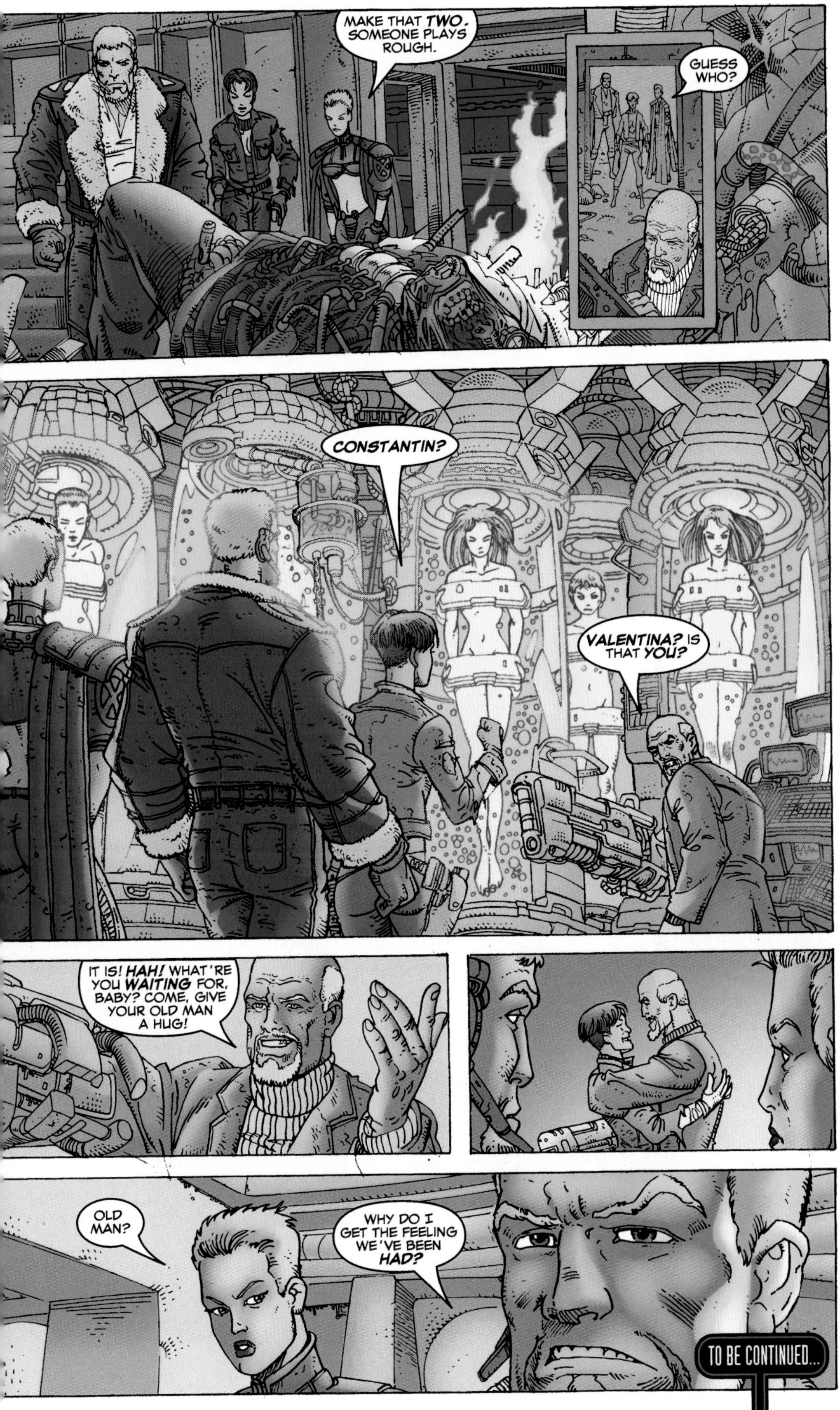
MAKE THAT TWO. SOMEONE PLAYS ROUGH.
GUESS WHO?
CONSTANTIN?
VALENTINA? IS THAT YOU?
IT IS! HAH! WHAT'RE YOU WAITING FOR, BABY? COME, GIVE YOUR OLD MAN A HUG!
OLD MAN?
WHY DO I GET THE FEELING WE'VE BEEN HAD?
TO BE CONTINUED...

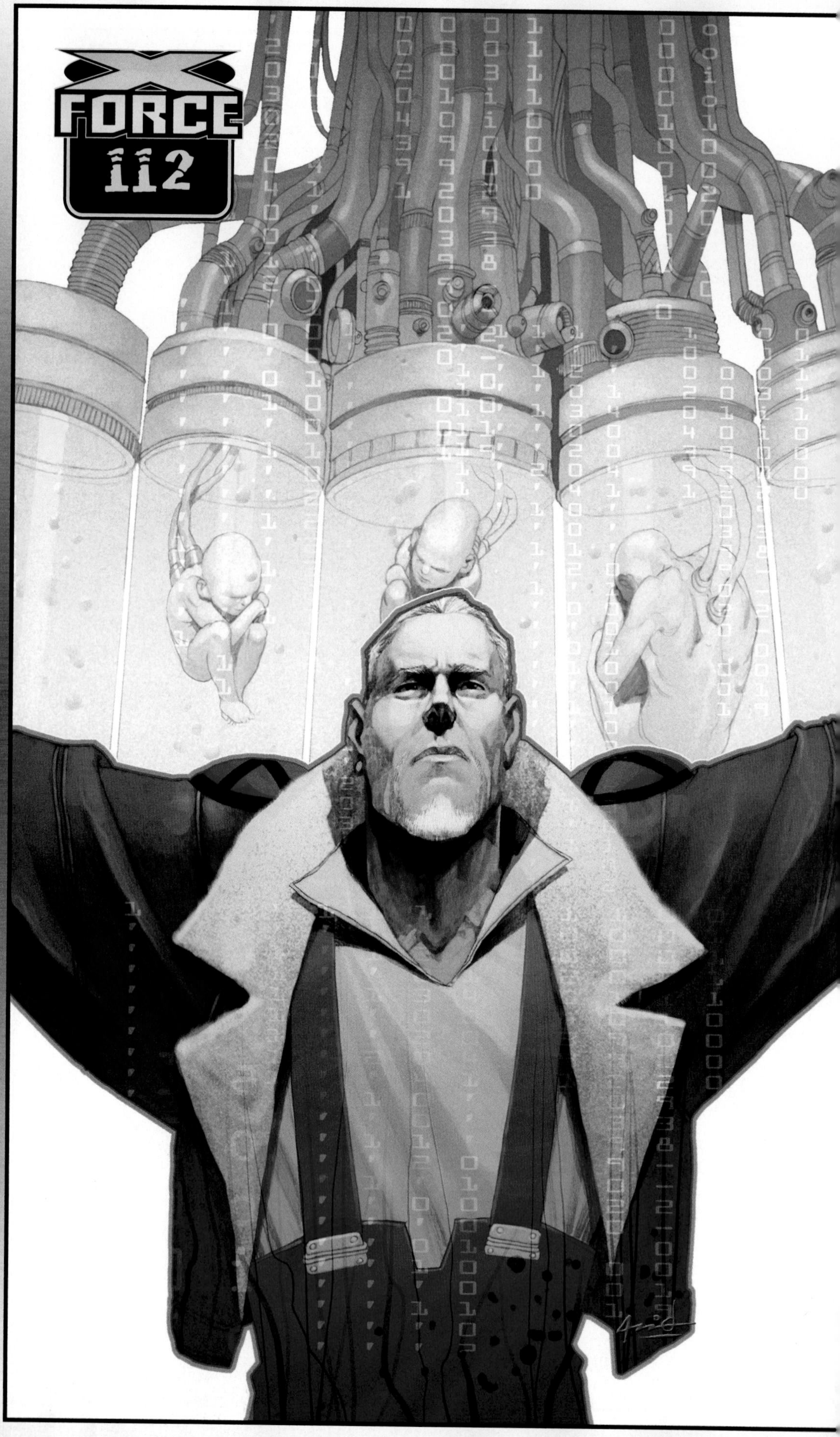
X FORCE
112

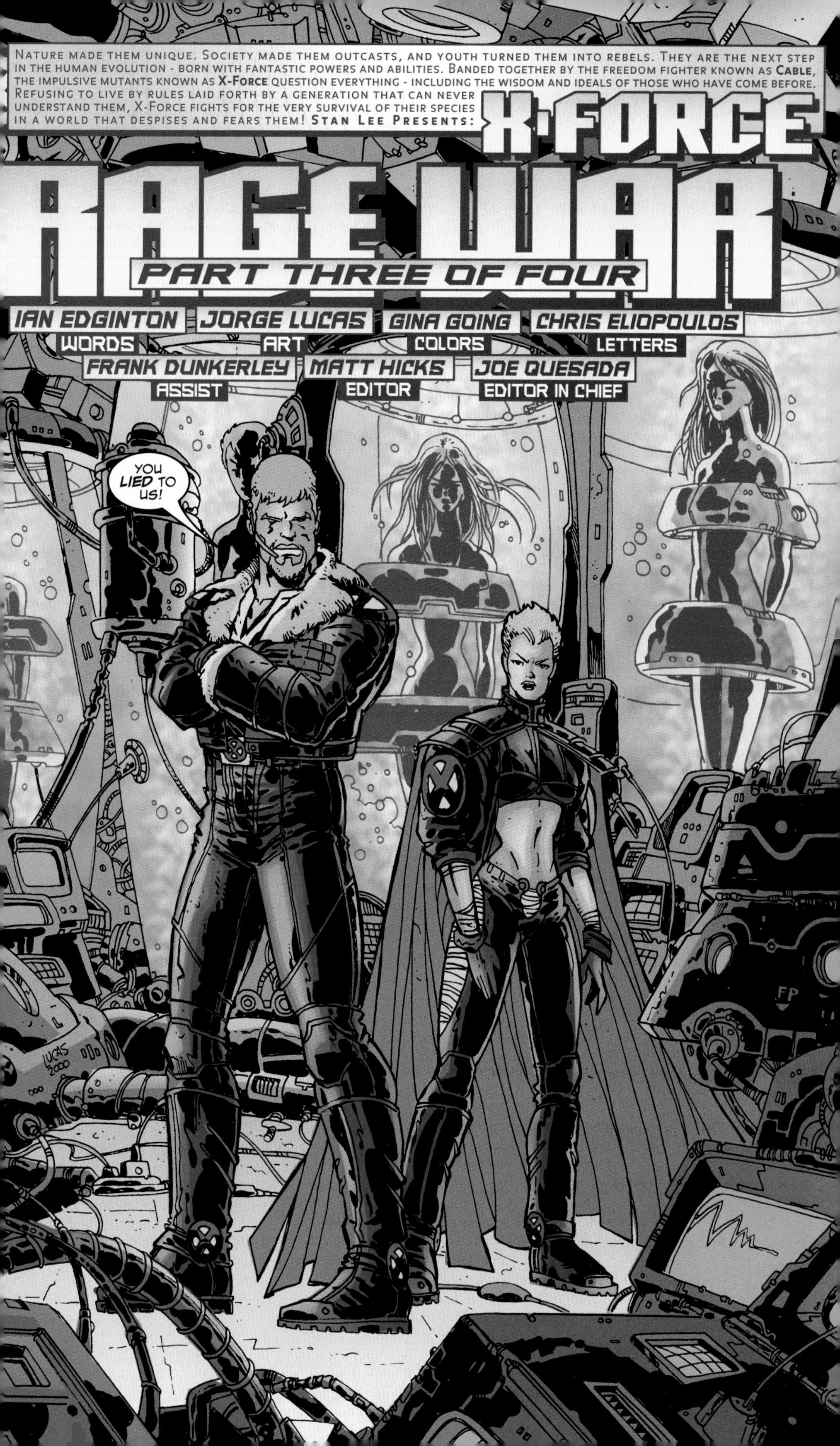

Nature made them unique. Society made them outcasts, and youth turned them into rebels. They are the next step in the human evolution - born with fantastic powers and abilities. Banded together by the freedom fighter known as Cable, the impulsive mutants known as X-Force question everything - including the wisdom and ideals of those who have come before. Refusing to live by rules laid forth by a generation that can never understand them, X-Force fights for the very survival of their species in a world that despises and fears them! Stan Lee Presents:
X-FORCE
RACE WAR
PART THREE OF FOUR
IAN EDGINTON WORDS
JORGE LUCAS ART
GINA GOING COLORS
CHRIS ELIOPOULOS LETTERS
FRANK DUNKERLEY ASSIST
MATT HICKS EDITOR
JOE QUESADA EDITOR IN CHIEF
YOU LIED TO US!
LUCAS 2000

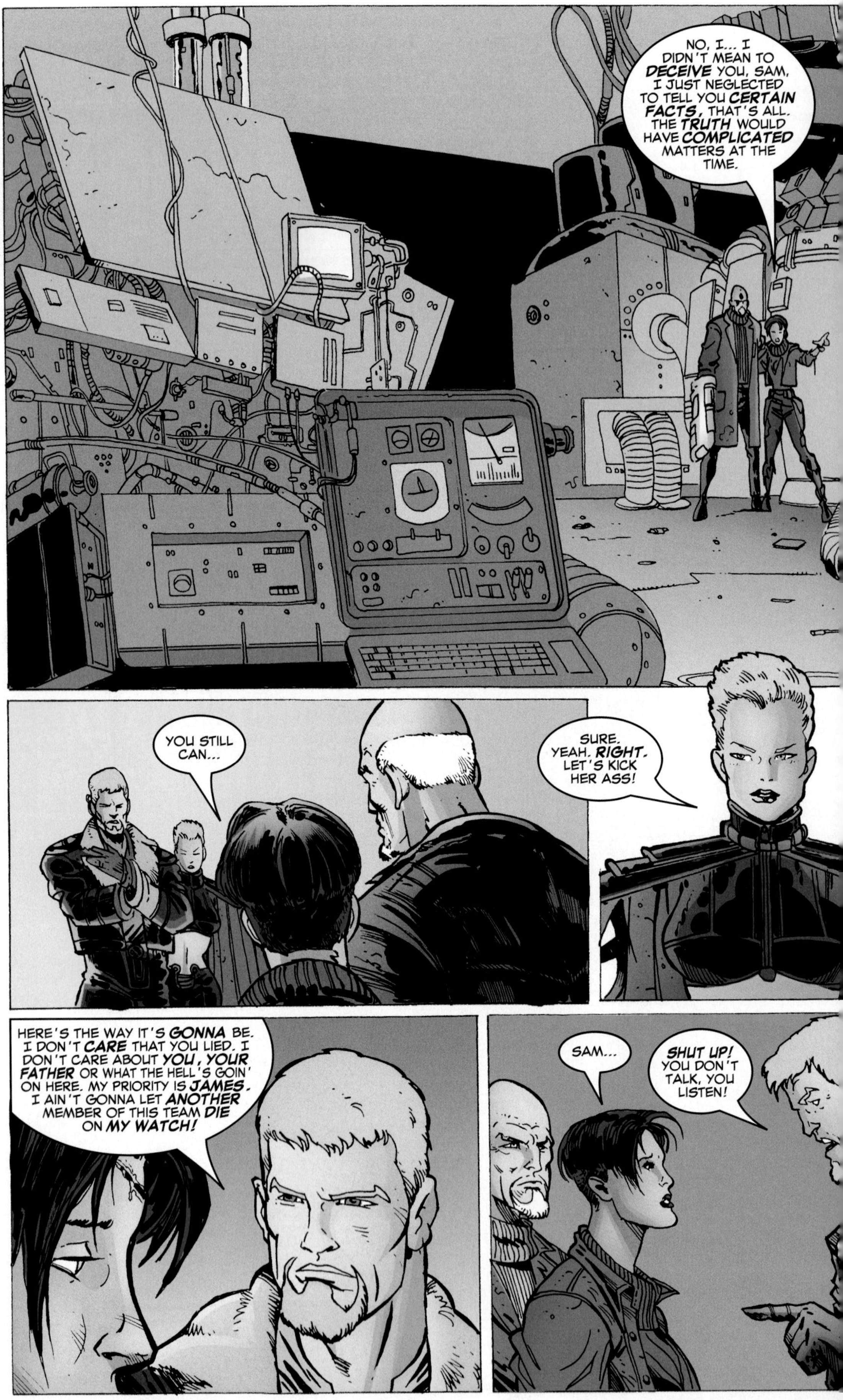
NO, I... I DIDN'T MEAN TO DECEIVE YOU, SAM, I JUST NEGLECTED TO TELL YOU CERTAIN FACTS, THAT'S ALL. THE TRUTH WOULD HAVE COMPLICATED MATTERS AT THE TIME.
YOU STILL CAN...
SURE. YEAH. RIGHT. LET'S KICK HER ASS!
HERE'S THE WAY IT'S GONNA BE. I DON'T CARE THAT YOU LIED. I DON'T CARE ABOUT YOU, YOUR FATHER OR WHAT THE HELL'S GOIN' ON HERE. MY PRIORITY IS JAMES. I AIN'T GONNA LET ANOTHER MEMBER OF THIS TEAM DIE ON MY WATCH!
SAM...
SHUT UP! YOU DON'T TALK, YOU LISTEN!

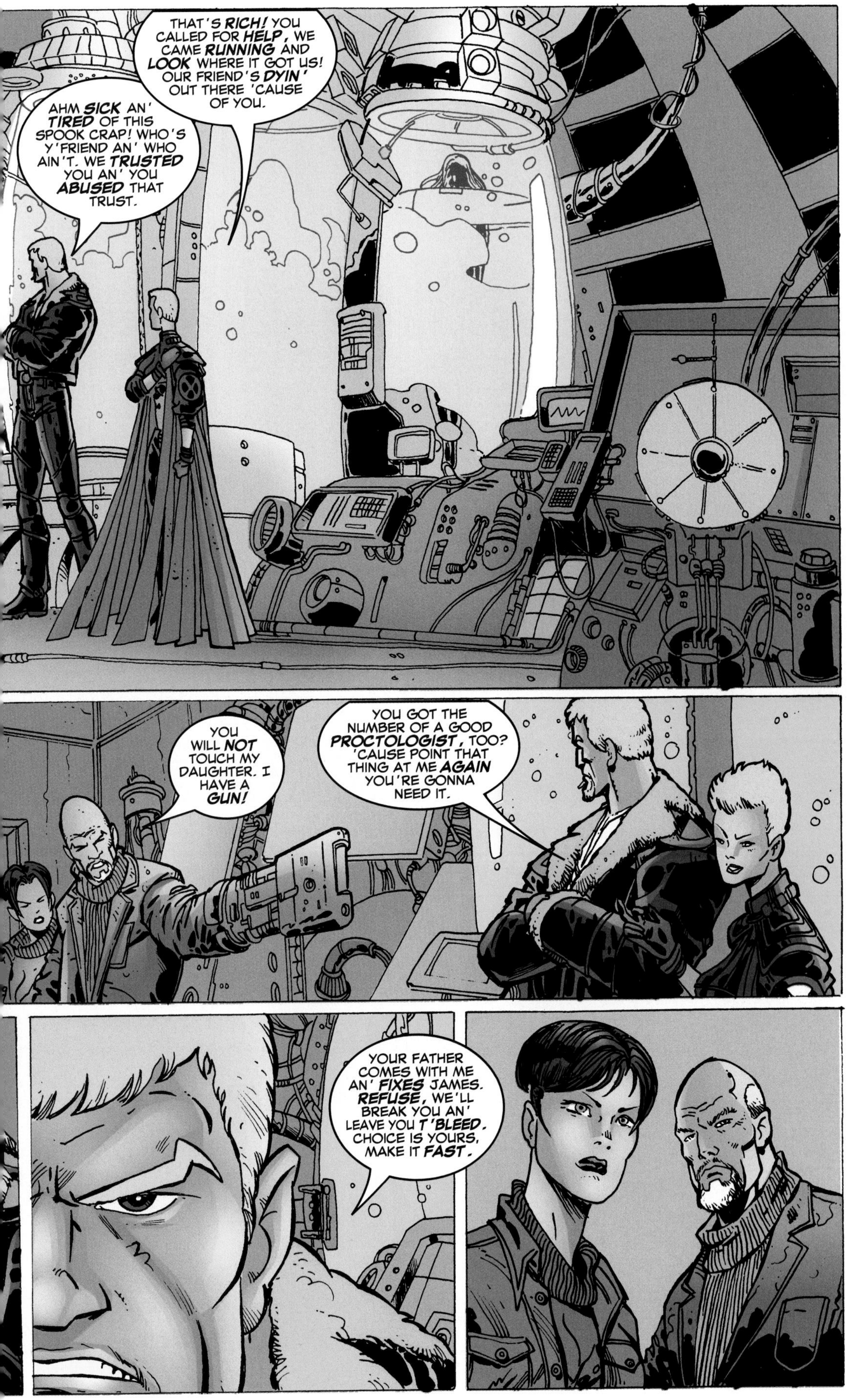
AHM SICK AN' TIRED OF THIS SPOOK CRAP! WHO'S Y'FRIEND AN' WHO AIN'T. WE TRUSTED YOU AN' YOU ABUSED THAT TRUST.
THAT'S RICH! YOU CALLED FOR HELP, WE CAME RUNNING AND LOOK WHERE IT GOT US! OUR FRIEND'S DYIN' OUT THERE 'CAUSE OF YOU.
YOU WILL NOT TOUCH MY DAUGHTER. I HAVE A GUN!
YOU GOT THE NUMBER OF A GOOD PROCTOLOGIST, TOO? 'CAUSE POINT THAT THING AT ME AGAIN YOU'RE GONNA NEED IT.
YOUR FATHER COMES WITH ME AN' FIXES JAMES. REFUSE, WE'LL BREAK YOU AN' LEAVE YOU T'BLEED. CHOICE IS YOURS. MAKE IT FAST.

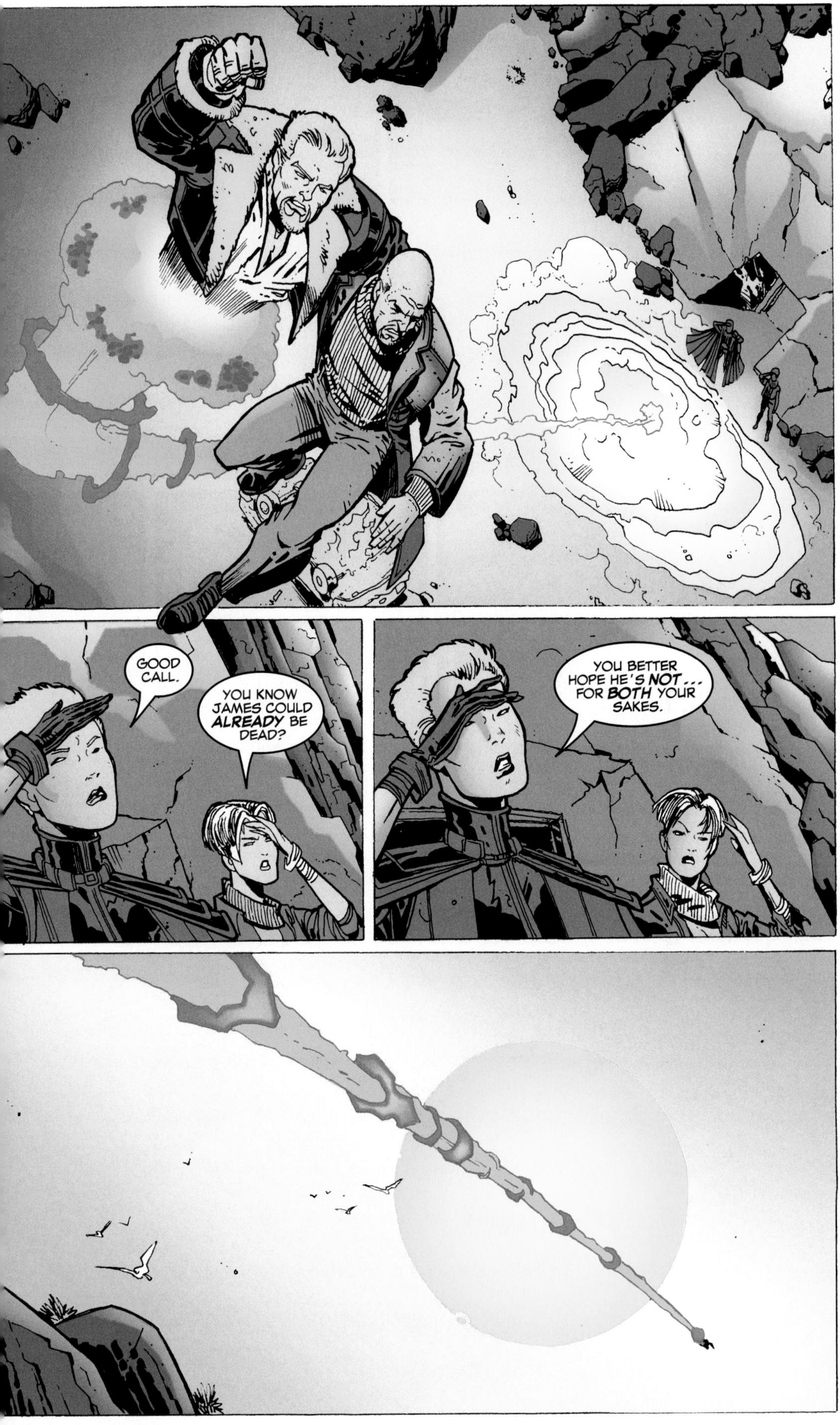
GOOD CALL.
YOU KNOW JAMES COULD ALREADY BE DEAD?
YOU BETTER HOPE HE'S NOT... FOR BOTH YOUR SAKES.

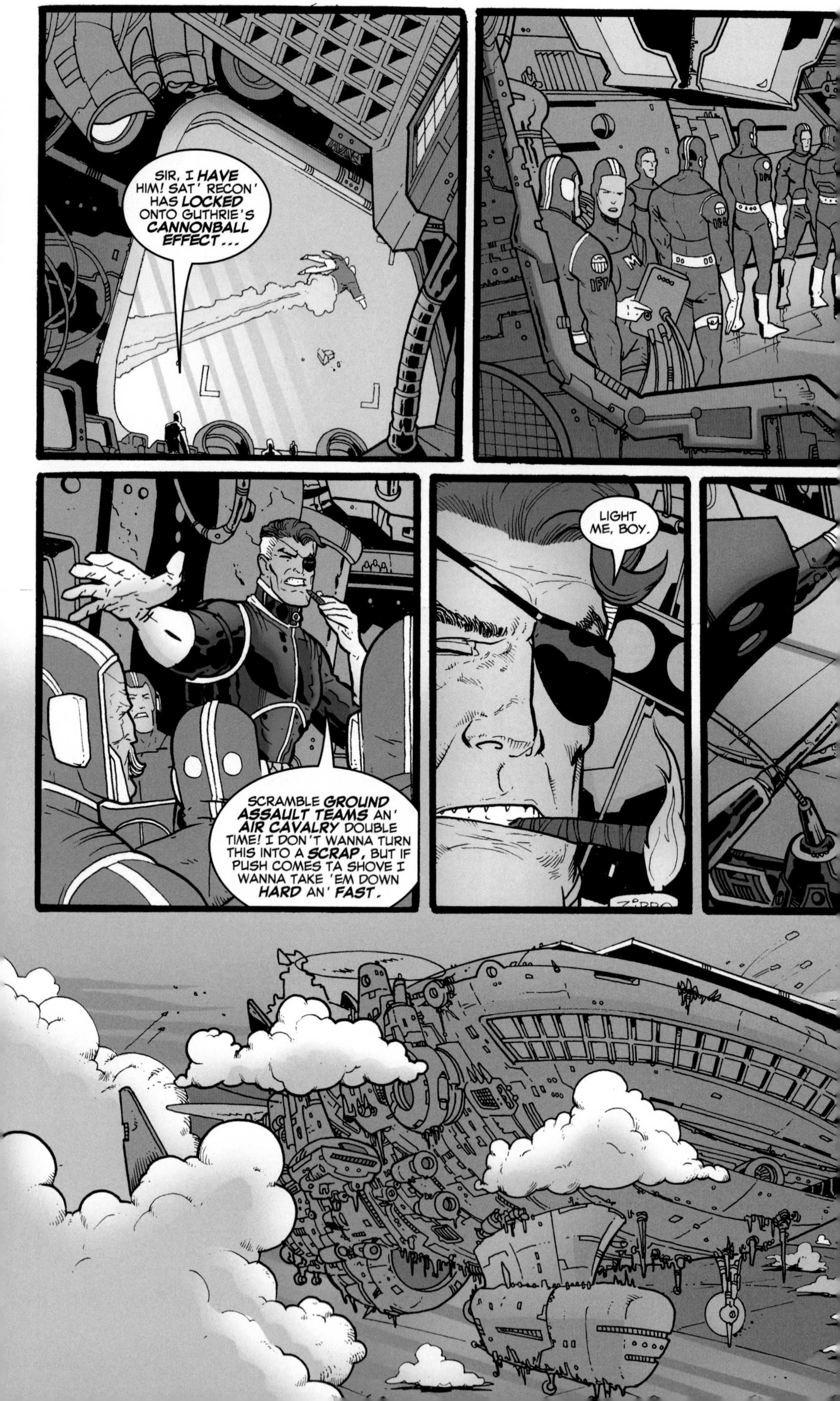
SIR, I HAVE HIM! SAT' RECON' HAS LOCKED ONTO GUTHRIE'S CANNONBALL EFFECT...
SCRAMBLE GROUND ASSAULT TEAMS AN' AIR CAVALRY DOUBLE TIME! I DON'T WANNA TURN THIS INTO A SCRAP, BUT IF PUSH COMES TA SHOVE I WANNA TAKE 'EM DOWN HARD AN' FAST.
LIGHT ME, BOY.

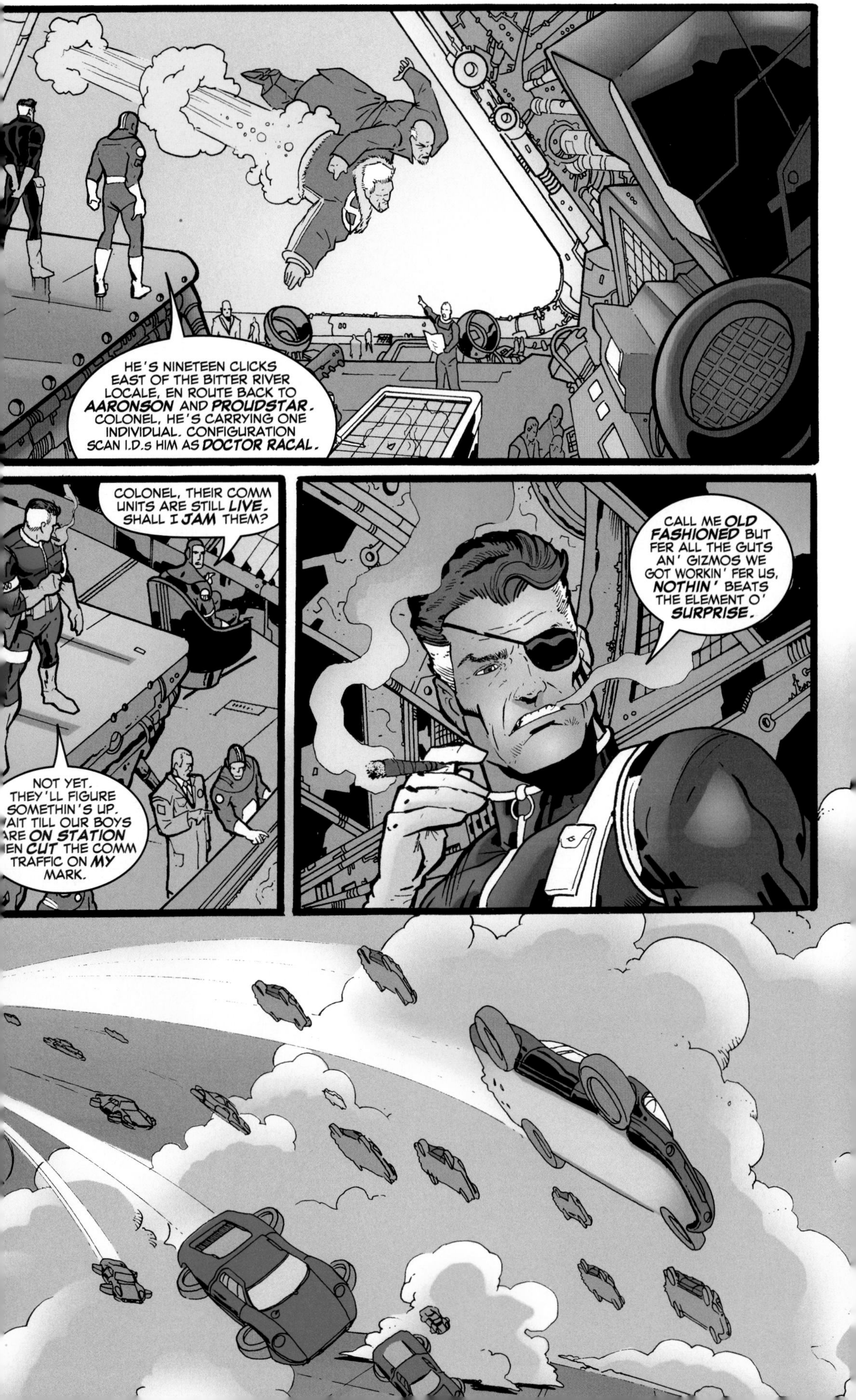
HE'S NINETEEN CLICKS EAST OF THE BITTER RIVER LOCALE, EN ROUTE BACK TO AARONSON AND PROUDSTAR. COLONEL, HE'S CARRYING ONE INDIVIDUAL. CONFIGURATION SCAN I.D.s HIM AS DOCTOR RACAL.
COLONEL, THEIR COMM UNITS ARE STILL LIVE. SHALL I JAM THEM?
NOT YET. THEY'LL FIGURE SOMETHIN'S UP. AIT TILL OUR BOYS ARE ON STATION EN CUT THE COMM TRAFFIC ON MY MARK.
CALL ME OLD FASHIONED BUT FER ALL THE GUTS AN' GIZMOS WE GOT WORKIN' FER US, NOTHIN' BEATS THE ELEMENT O' SURPRISE.

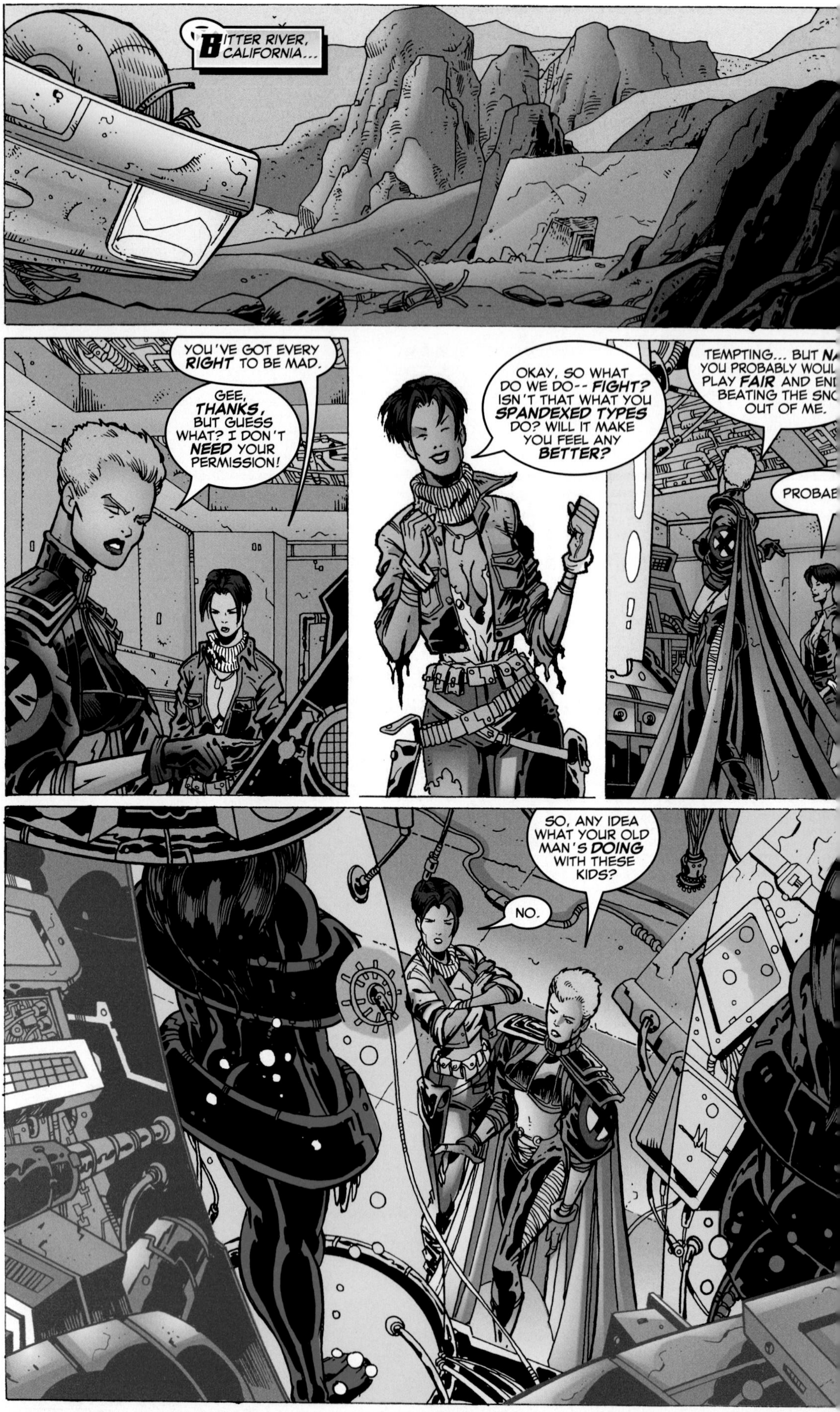
BITTER RIVER, CALIFORNIA...
YOU'VE GOT EVERY RIGHT TO BE MAD.
GEE, THANKS, BUT GUESS WHAT? I DON'T NEED YOUR PERMISSION!
OKAY, SO WHAT DO WE DO-- FIGHT? ISN'T THAT WHAT YOU SPANDEXED TYPES DO? WILL IT MAKE YOU FEEL ANY BETTER?
TEMPTING... BUT NA
YOU PROBABLY WOUL
PLAY FAIR AND END
BEATING THE SNO
OUT OF ME.
PROBAB
SO, ANY IDEA WHAT YOUR OLD MAN'S DOING WITH THESE KIDS?
NO.

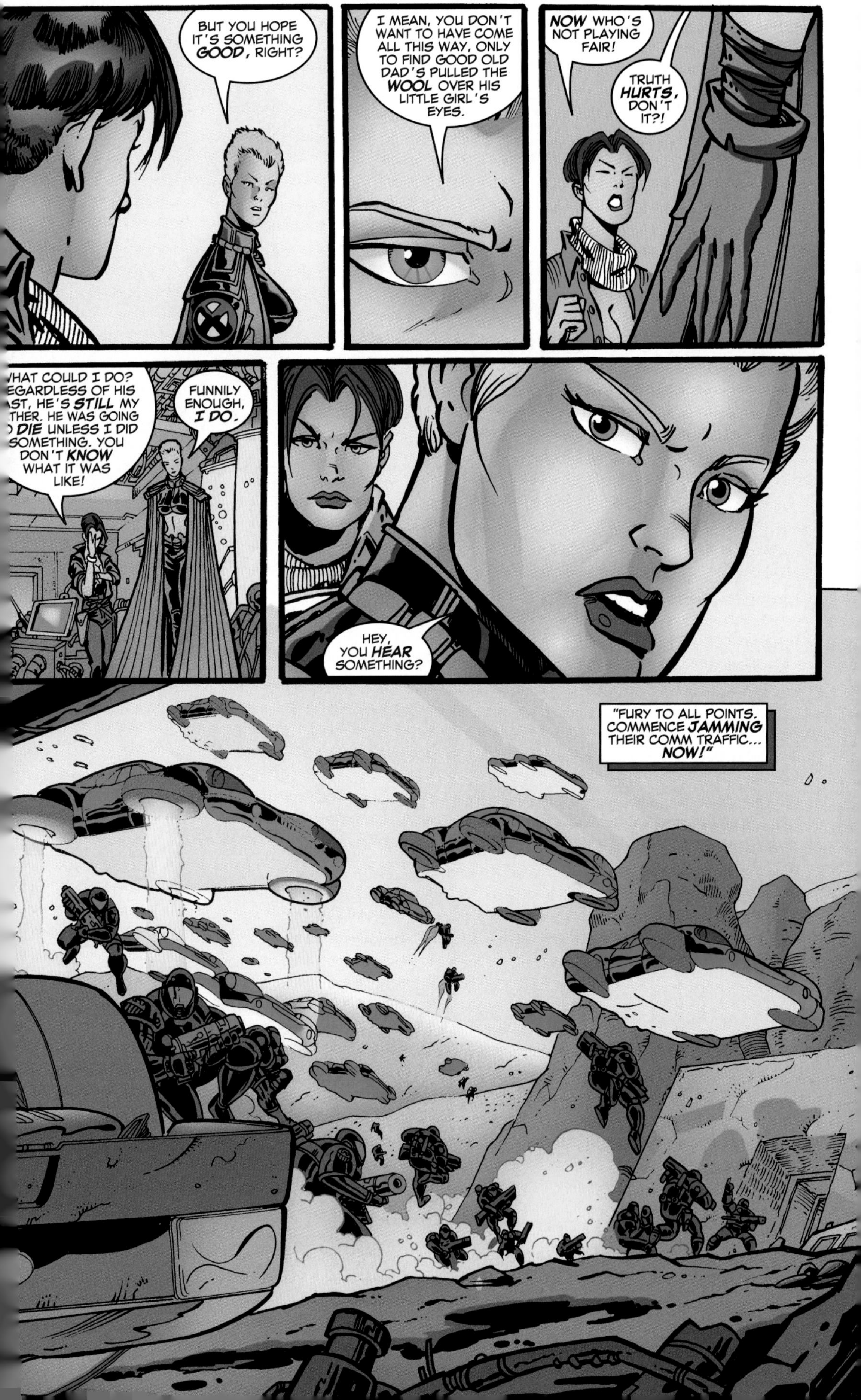

BUT YOU HOPE IT'S SOMETHING GOOD, RIGHT?
I MEAN, YOU DON'T WANT TO HAVE COME ALL THIS WAY, ONLY TO FIND GOOD OLD DAD'S PULLED THE WOOL OVER HIS LITTLE GIRL'S EYES.
NOW WHO'S NOT PLAYING FAIR!
TRUTH HURTS, DON'T IT?!
HAT COULD I DO? EGARDLESS OF HIS AST, HE'S STILL MY THER. HE WAS GOING DIE UNLESS I DID SOMETHING. YOU DON'T KNOW WHAT IT WAS LIKE!
FUNNILY ENOUGH, I DO.
HEY, YOU HEAR SOMETHING?
"FURY TO ALL POINTS. COMMENCE JAMMING THEIR COMM TRAFFIC... NOW!"

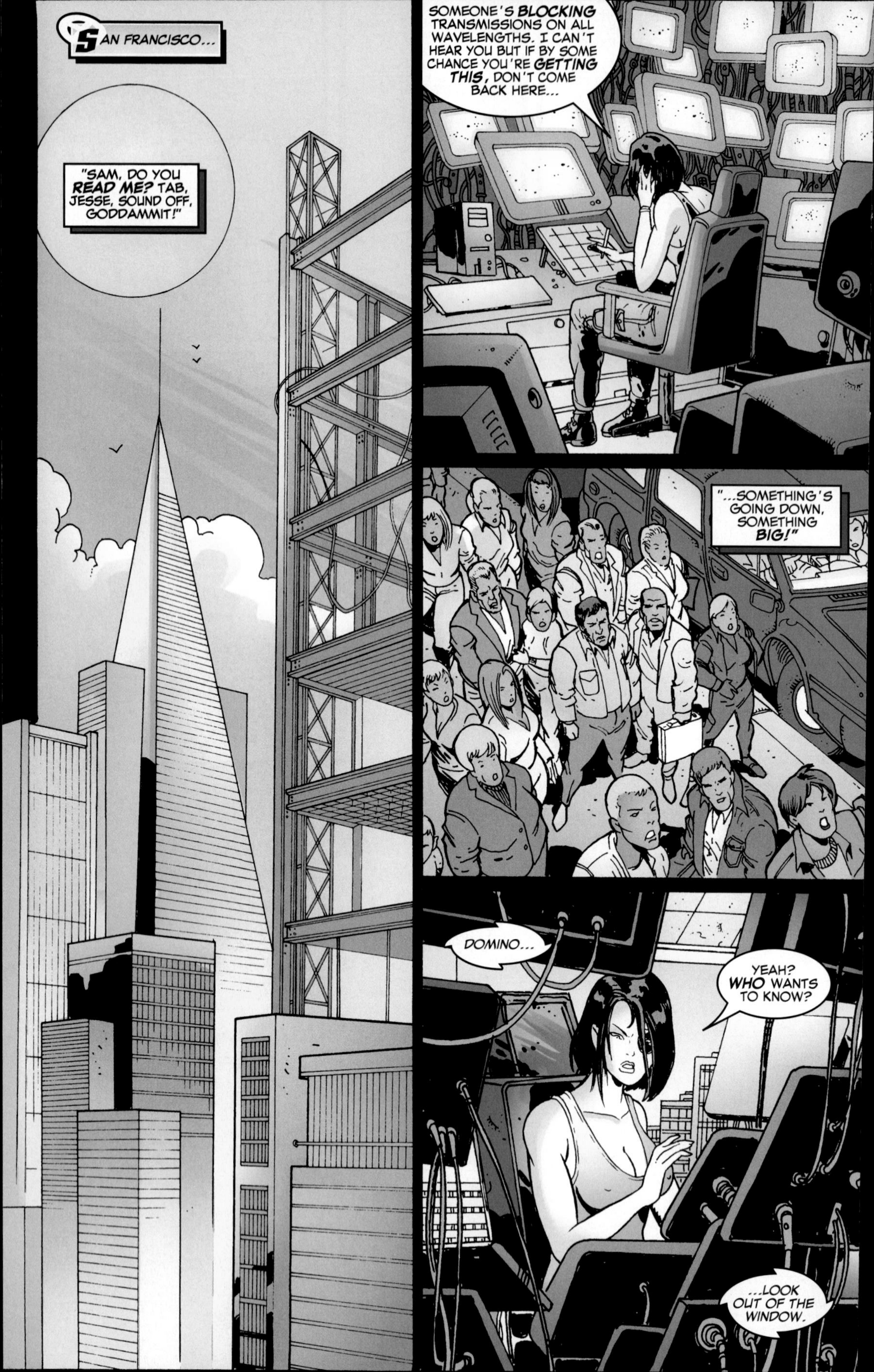
SAN FRANCISCO...
"SAM, DO YOU READ ME? TAB, JESSE, SOUND OFF, GODDAMMIT!"
SOMEONE'S BLOCKING TRANSMISSIONS ON ALL WAVELENGTHS. I CAN'T HEAR YOU BUT IF BY SOME CHANCE YOU'RE GETTING THIS, DON'T COME BACK HERE...
"...SOMETHING'S GOING DOWN, SOMETHING BIG!"
DOMINO...
YEAH? WHO WANTS TO KNOW?
...LOOK OUT OF THE WINDOW.

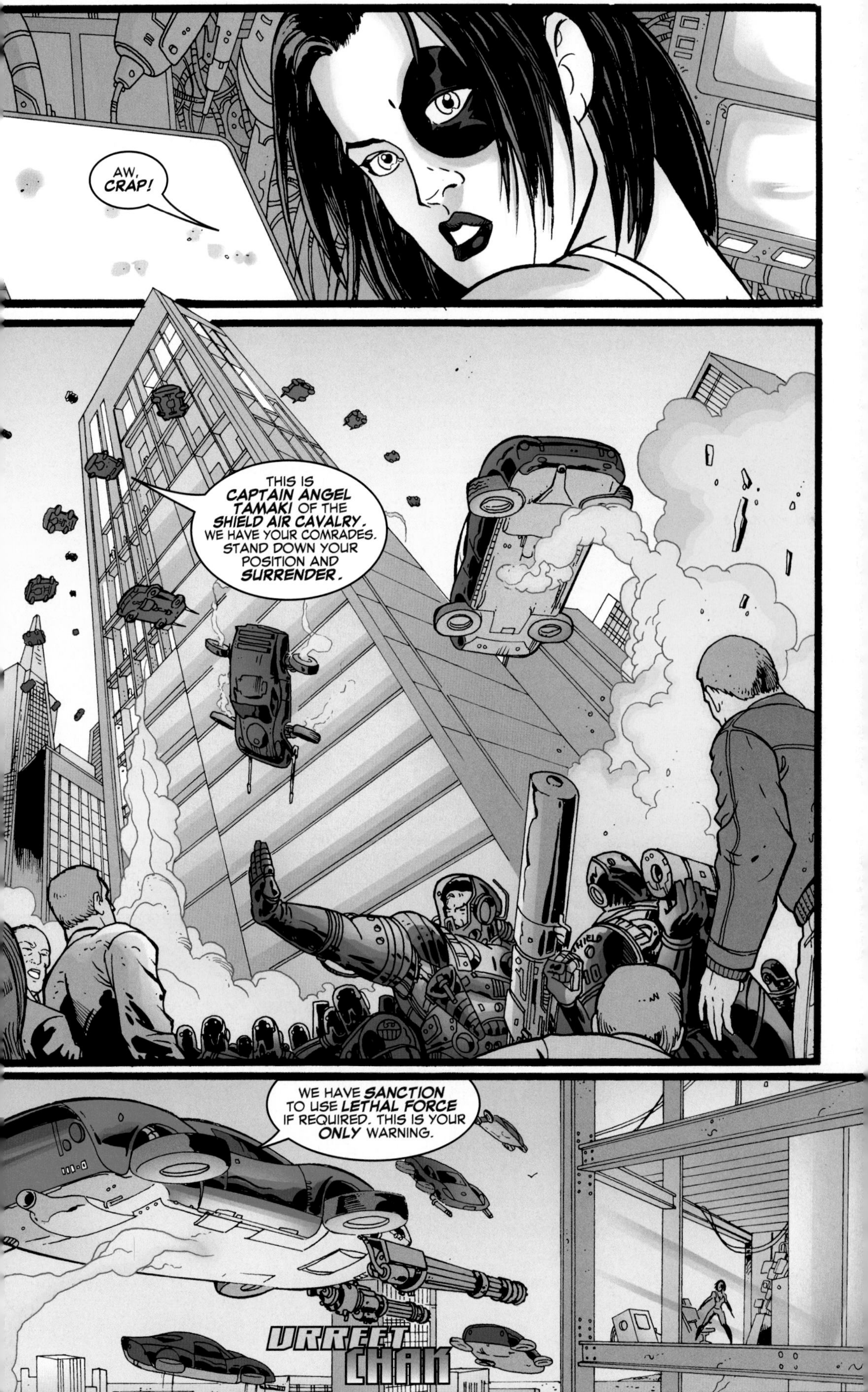
AW, CRAP!
THIS IS CAPTAIN ANGEL TAMAKI OF THE SHIELD AIR CAVALRY. WE HAVE YOUR COMRADES. STAND DOWN YOUR POSITION AND SURRENDER.
WE HAVE SANCTION TO USE LETHAL FORCE IF REQUIRED. THIS IS YOUR ONLY WARNING.
VRREET
CHAK

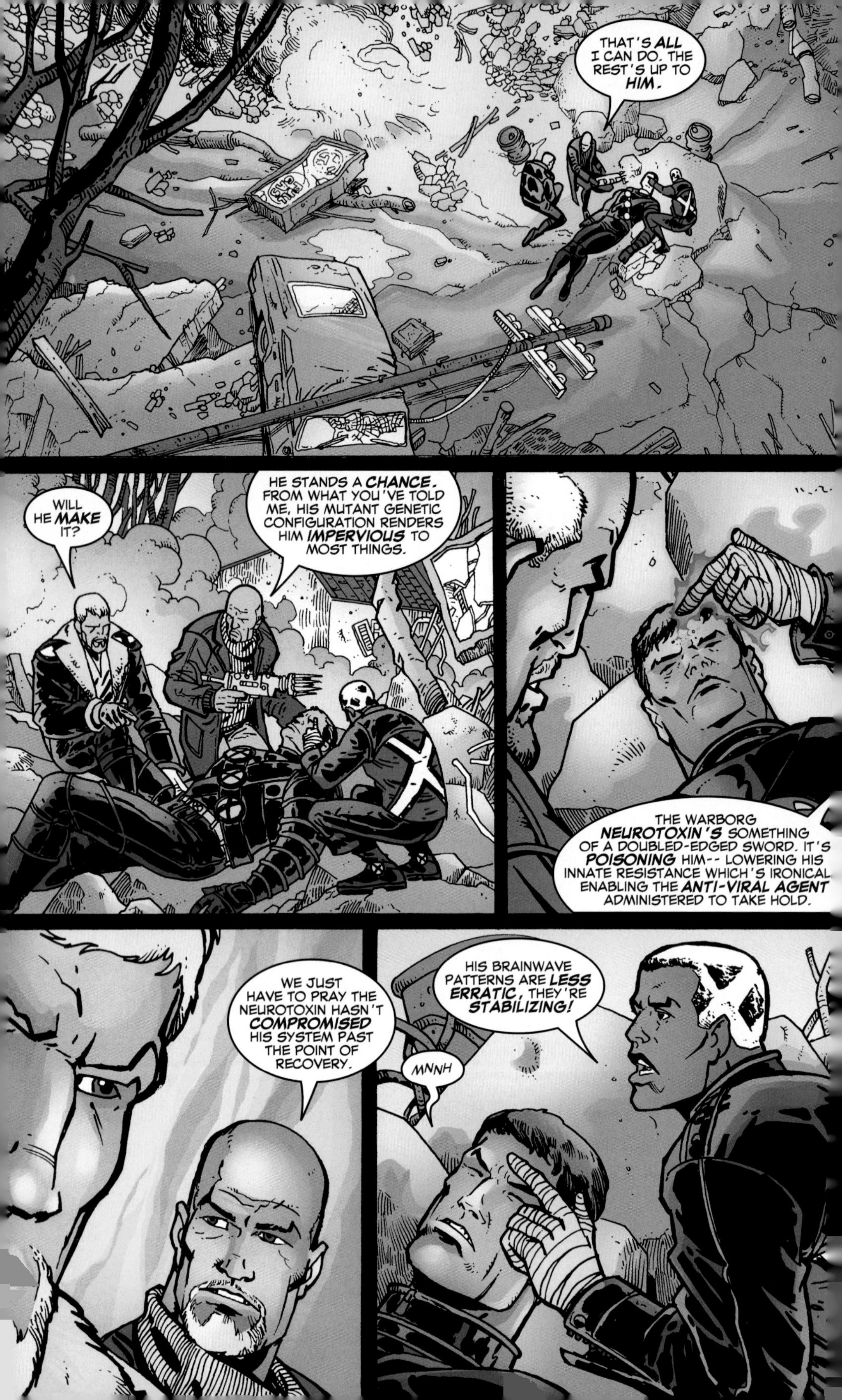

THAT'S ALL I CAN DO. THE REST'S UP TO HIM.
WILL HE MAKE IT?
HE STANDS A CHANCE. FROM WHAT YOU'VE TOLD ME, HIS MUTANT GENETIC CONFIGURATION RENDERS HIM IMPERVIOUS TO MOST THINGS.
THE WARBORG NEUROTOXIN'S SOMETHING OF A DOUBLED-EDGED SWORD. IT'S POISONING HIM-- LOWERING HIS INNATE RESISTANCE WHICH'S IRONICAL ENABLING THE ANTI-VIRAL AGENT ADMINISTERED TO TAKE HOLD.
WE JUST HAVE TO PRAY THE NEUROTOXIN HASN'T COMPROMISED HIS SYSTEM PAST THE POINT OF RECOVERY.
HIS BRAINWAVE PATTERNS ARE LESS ERRATIC, THEY'RE STABILIZING!
MNNH

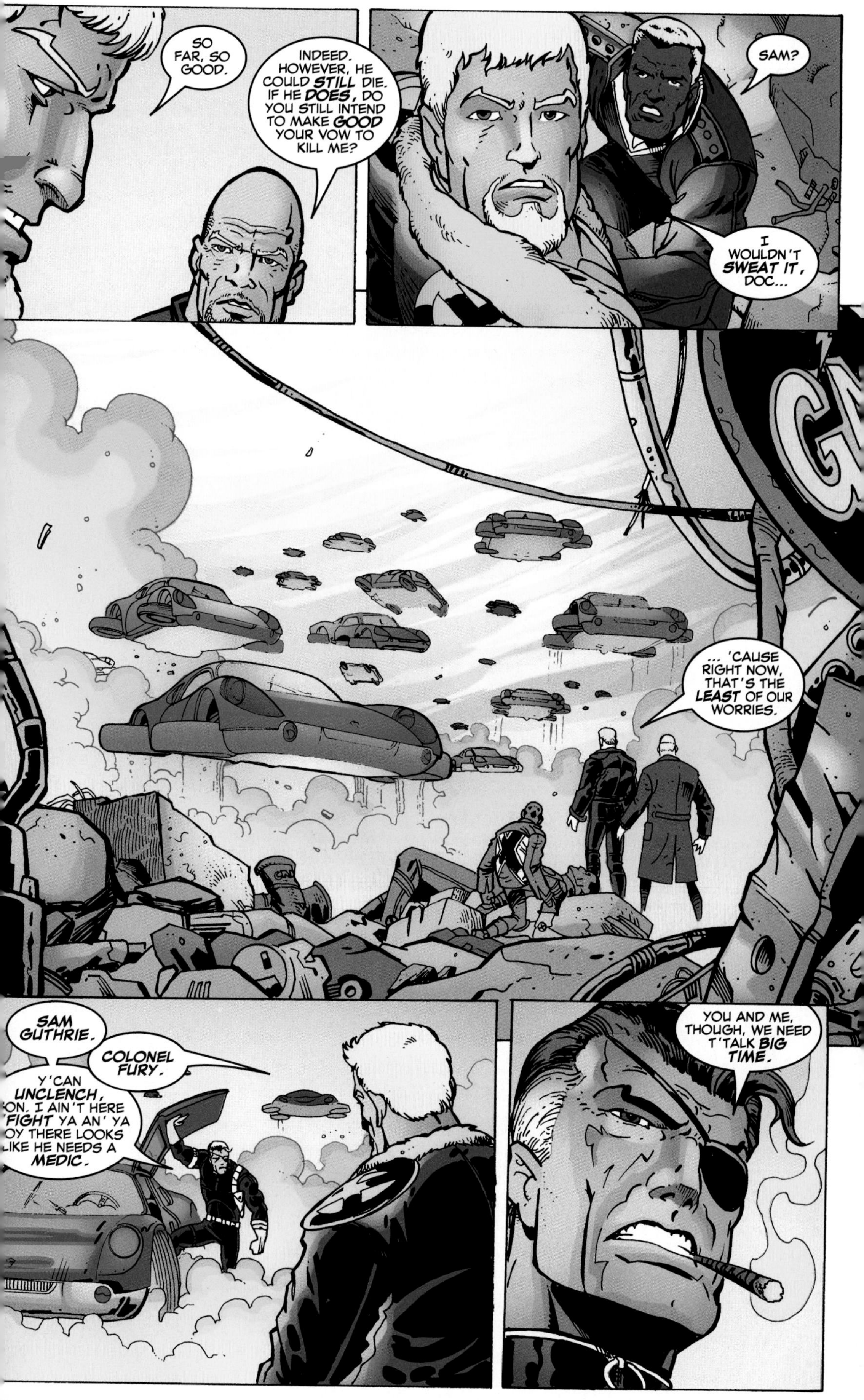
SO FAR, SO GOOD.
INDEED. HOWEVER, HE COULD STILL DIE. IF HE DOES, DO YOU STILL INTEND TO MAKE GOOD YOUR VOW TO KILL ME?
SAM?
I WOULDN'T SWEAT IT, DOC...
... 'CAUSE RIGHT NOW, THAT'S THE LEAST OF OUR WORRIES.
SAM GUTHRIE.
COLONEL FURY.
Y'CAN UNCLENCH, ON. I AIN'T HERE FIGHT YA AN' YA OY THERE LOOKS LIKE HE NEEDS A MEDIC.
YOU AND ME, THOUGH, WE NEED T'TALK BIG TIME.

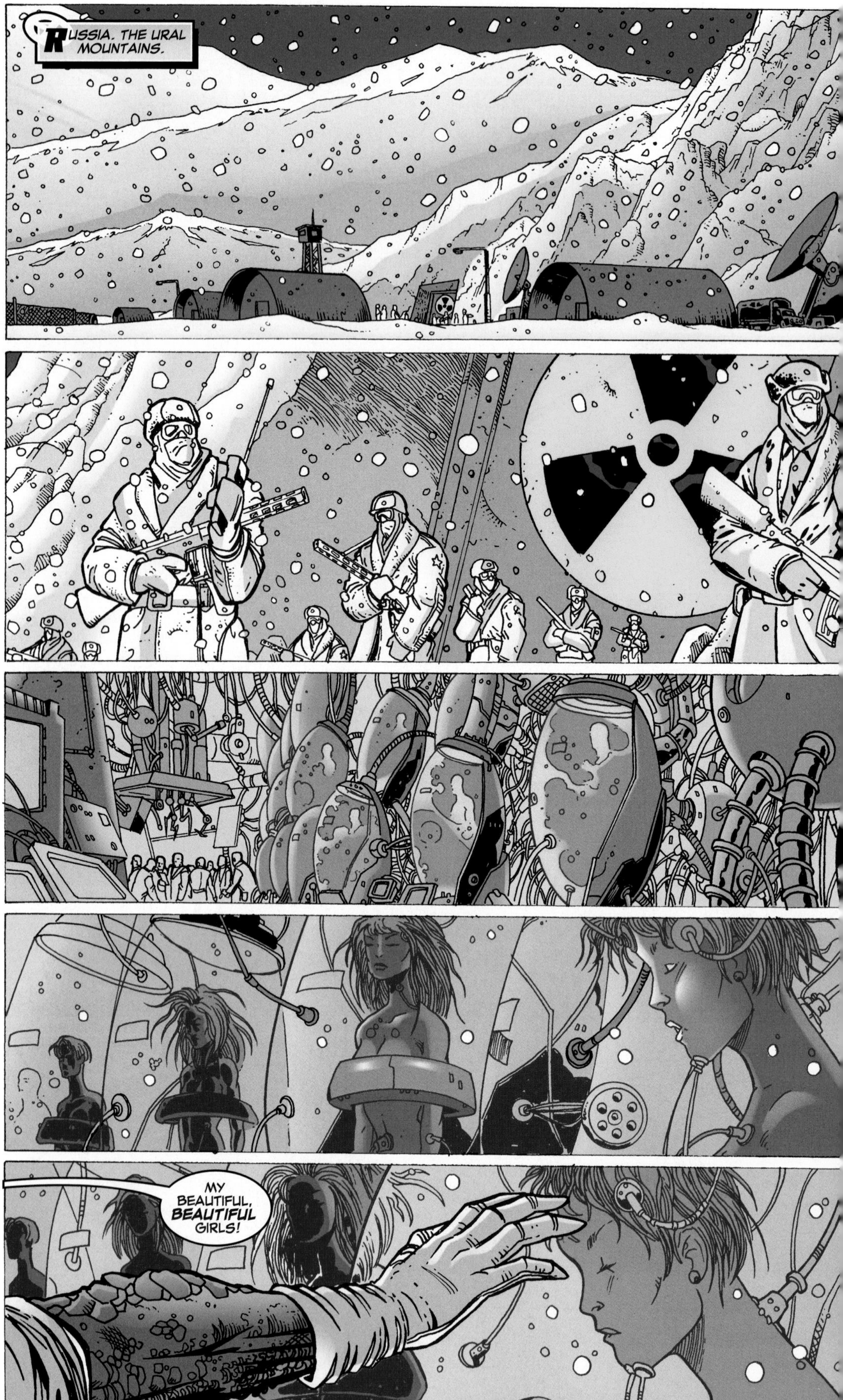
RUSSIA. THE URAL MOUNTAINS.
MY BEAUTIFUL, **BEAUTIFUL** GIRLS!

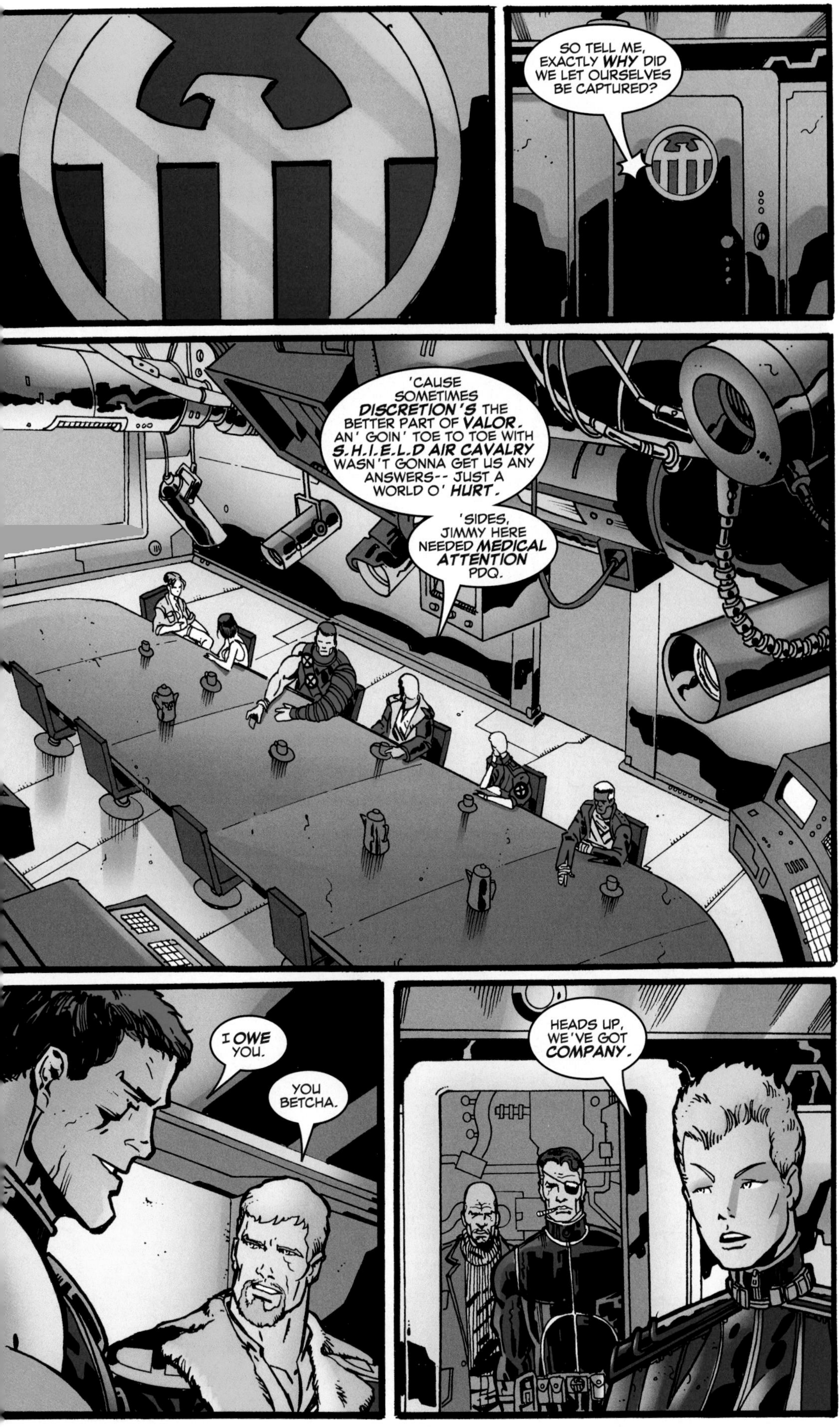
SO TELL ME, EXACTLY WHY DID WE LET OURSELVES BE CAPTURED?
'CAUSE SOMETIMES DISCRETION'S THE BETTER PART OF VALOR. AN' GOIN' TOE TO TOE WITH S.H.I.E.L.D AIR CAVALRY WASN'T GONNA GET US ANY ANSWERS-- JUST A WORLD O' HURT.
'SIDES, JIMMY HERE NEEDED MEDICAL ATTENTION PDQ.
I OWE YOU.
YOU BETCHA.
HEADS UP, WE'VE GOT COMPANY.

OKAY, GUESS YOU GOT A *MILLION QUESTIONS* BUT THEY'LL HAVETA KEEP. WE'RE ON A CLOCK AN' I DON'T HAVE *TIME* T'PLAY NICE.

HERE'S THE DEAL. I WANT YOU T'WORK FER *ME* ON A JOB S.H.I.E.L.D CAN'T TOUCH BUT AS MUTANT *LOOSE CANNONS,* YOU CAN.

WHY WOULD WE *WANT* T' DO THAT?

'CAUSE IT'LL GIVE YOU THE CHANCE TO *CATCH UP* WITH THIS GUY...

TEK

...DR. NILES *ROMAN*-- THE MAGGOT WHO MURDERED YOUR BOSS-- *PETE WISDOM.*

WE'RE LISTENING.

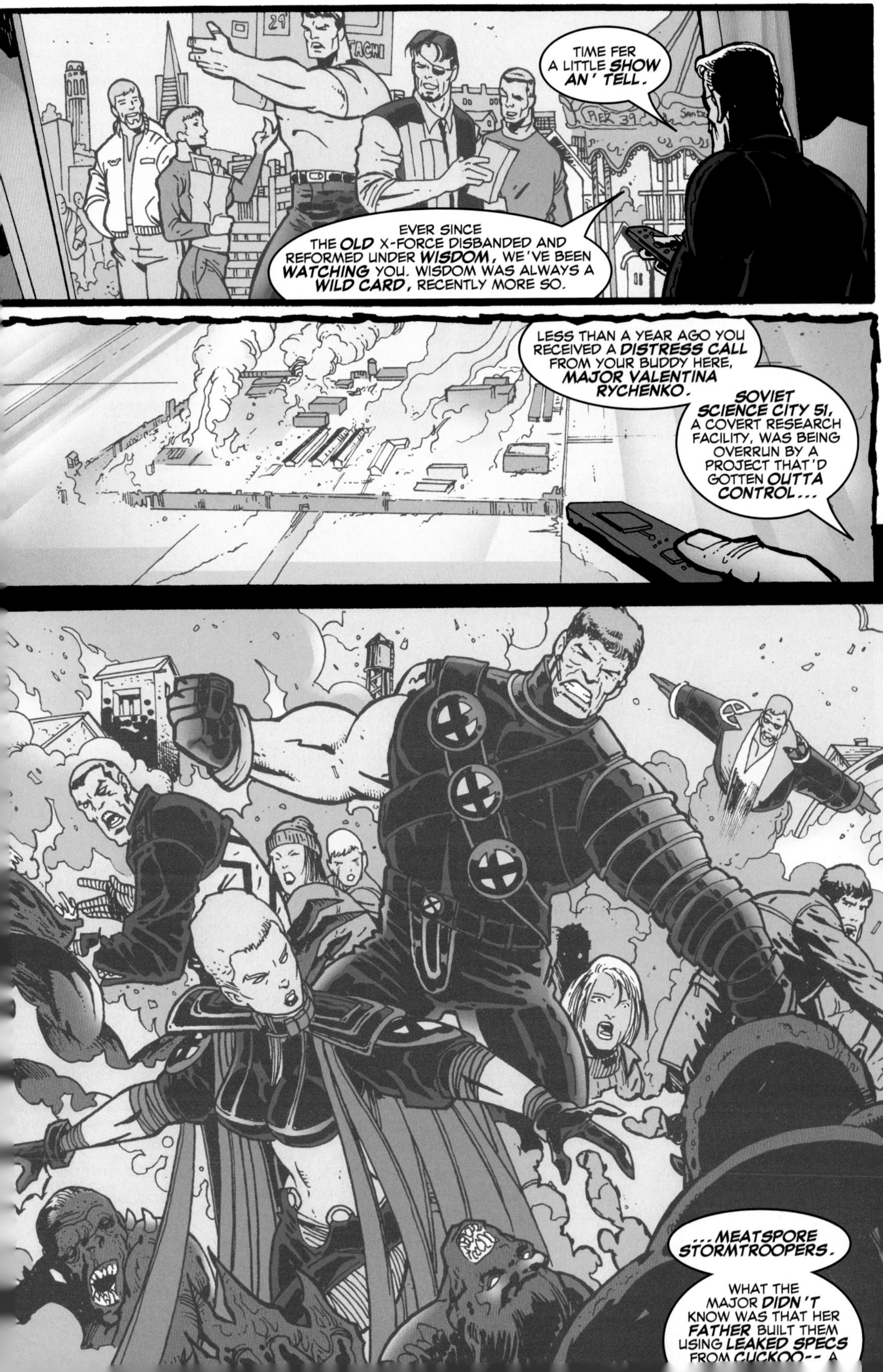
TIME FER A LITTLE SHOW AN' TELL.
EVER SINCE THE OLD X-FORCE DISBANDED AND REFORMED UNDER WISDOM, WE'VE BEEN WATCHING YOU. WISDOM WAS ALWAYS A WILD CARD, RECENTLY MORE SO.
LESS THAN A YEAR AGO YOU RECEIVED A DISTRESS CALL FROM YOUR BUDDY HERE, MAJOR VALENTINA RYCHENKO.
SOVIET SCIENCE CITY 51, A COVERT RESEARCH FACILITY, WAS BEING OVERRUN BY A PROJECT THAT'D GOTTEN OUTTA CONTROL...
...MEATSPORE STORMTROOPERS.
WHAT THE MAJOR DIDN'T KNOW WAS THAT HER FATHER BUILT THEM USING LEAKED SPECS FROM CUCKOO-- A

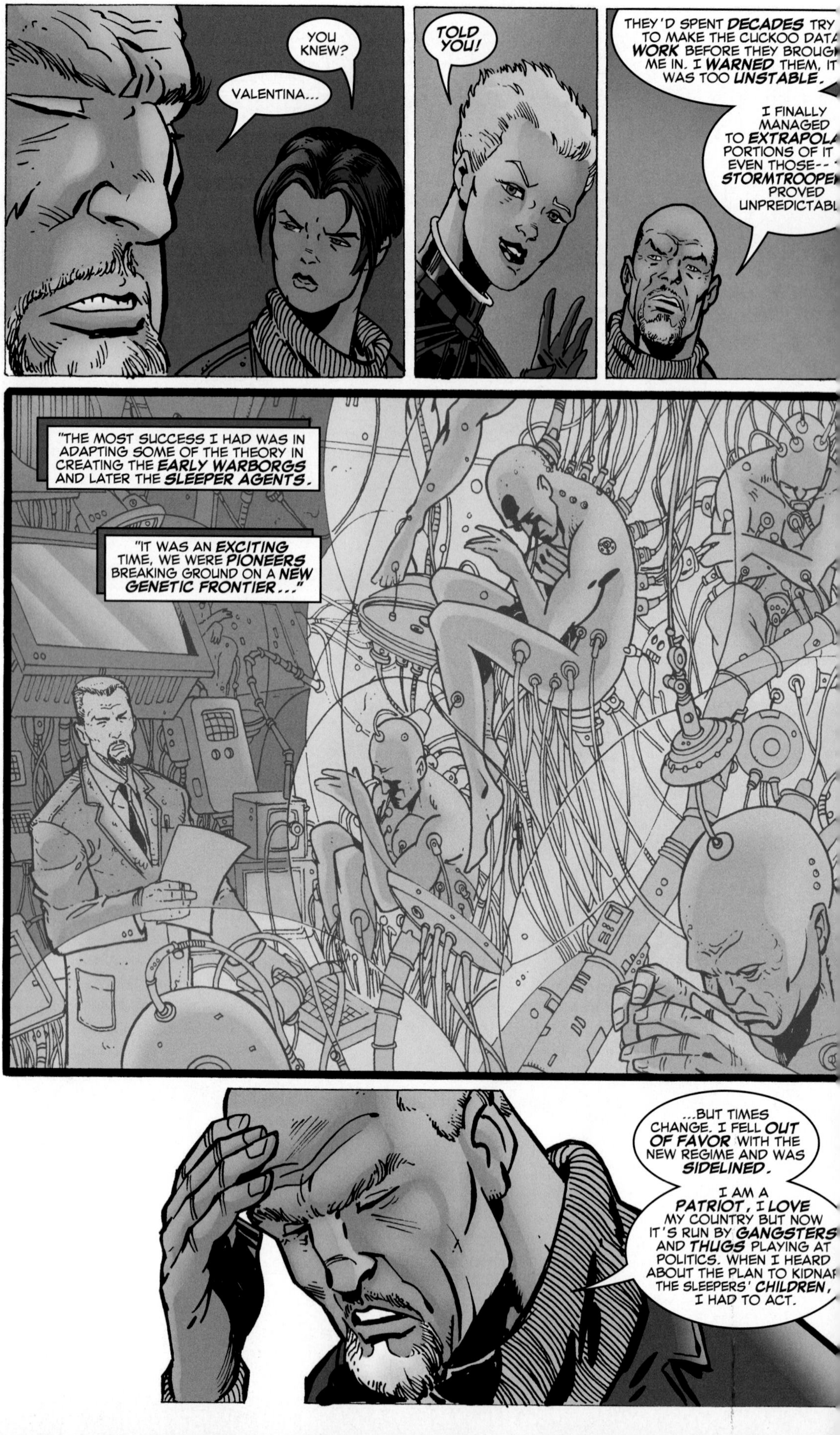
VALENTINA...
YOU KNEW?
TOLD YOU!
THEY'D SPENT DECADES TRY
TO MAKE THE CUCKOO DATA
WORK BEFORE THEY BROUG
ME IN. I WARNED THEM, IT
WAS TOO UNSTABLE.
I FINALLY MANAGED TO EXTRAPOLA
PORTIONS OF IT EVEN THOSE--
STORMTROOPE
PROVED UNPREDICTABL
"THE MOST SUCCESS I HAD WAS IN ADAPTING SOME OF THE THEORY IN CREATING THE EARLY WARBORGS AND LATER THE SLEEPER AGENTS.
"IT WAS AN EXCITING TIME, WE WERE PIONEERS BREAKING GROUND ON A NEW GENETIC FRONTIER..."
...BUT TIMES CHANGE. I FELL OUT OF FAVOR WITH THE NEW REGIME AND WAS SIDELINED.
I AM A PATRIOT, I LOVE MY COUNTRY BUT NOW IT'S RUN BY GANGSTERS AND THUGS PLAYING AT POLITICS. WHEN I HEARD ABOUT THE PLAN TO KIDNAP THE SLEEPERS' CHILDREN, I HAD TO ACT.

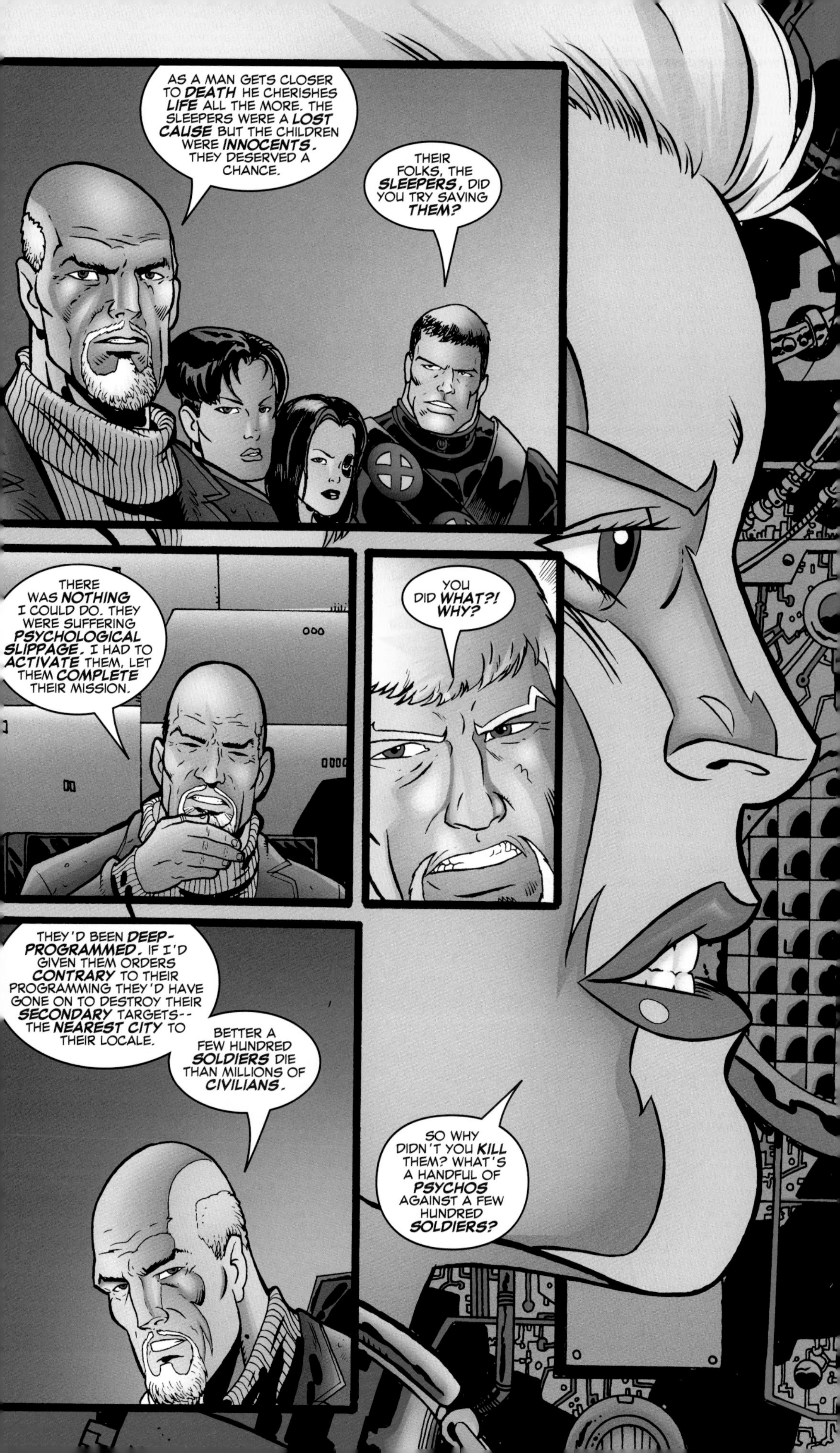

AS A MAN GETS CLOSER TO DEATH HE CHERISHES LIFE ALL THE MORE. THE SLEEPERS WERE A LOST CAUSE BUT THE CHILDREN WERE INNOCENTS. THEY DESERVED A CHANCE.
THEIR FOLKS, THE SLEEPERS, DID YOU TRY SAVING THEM?
THERE WAS NOTHING I COULD DO. THEY WERE SUFFERING PSYCHOLOGICAL SLIPPAGE. I HAD TO ACTIVATE THEM, LET THEM COMPLETE THEIR MISSION.
YOU DID WHAT?! WHY?
THEY'D BEEN DEEP-PROGRAMMED. IF I'D GIVEN THEM ORDERS CONTRARY TO THEIR PROGRAMMING THEY'D HAVE GONE ON TO DESTROY THEIR SECONDARY TARGETS-- THE NEAREST CITY TO THEIR LOCALE.
BETTER A FEW HUNDRED SOLDIERS DIE THAN MILLIONS OF CIVILIANS.
SO WHY DIDN'T YOU KILL THEM? WHAT'S A HANDFUL OF PSYCHOS AGAINST A FEW HUNDRED SOLDIERS?

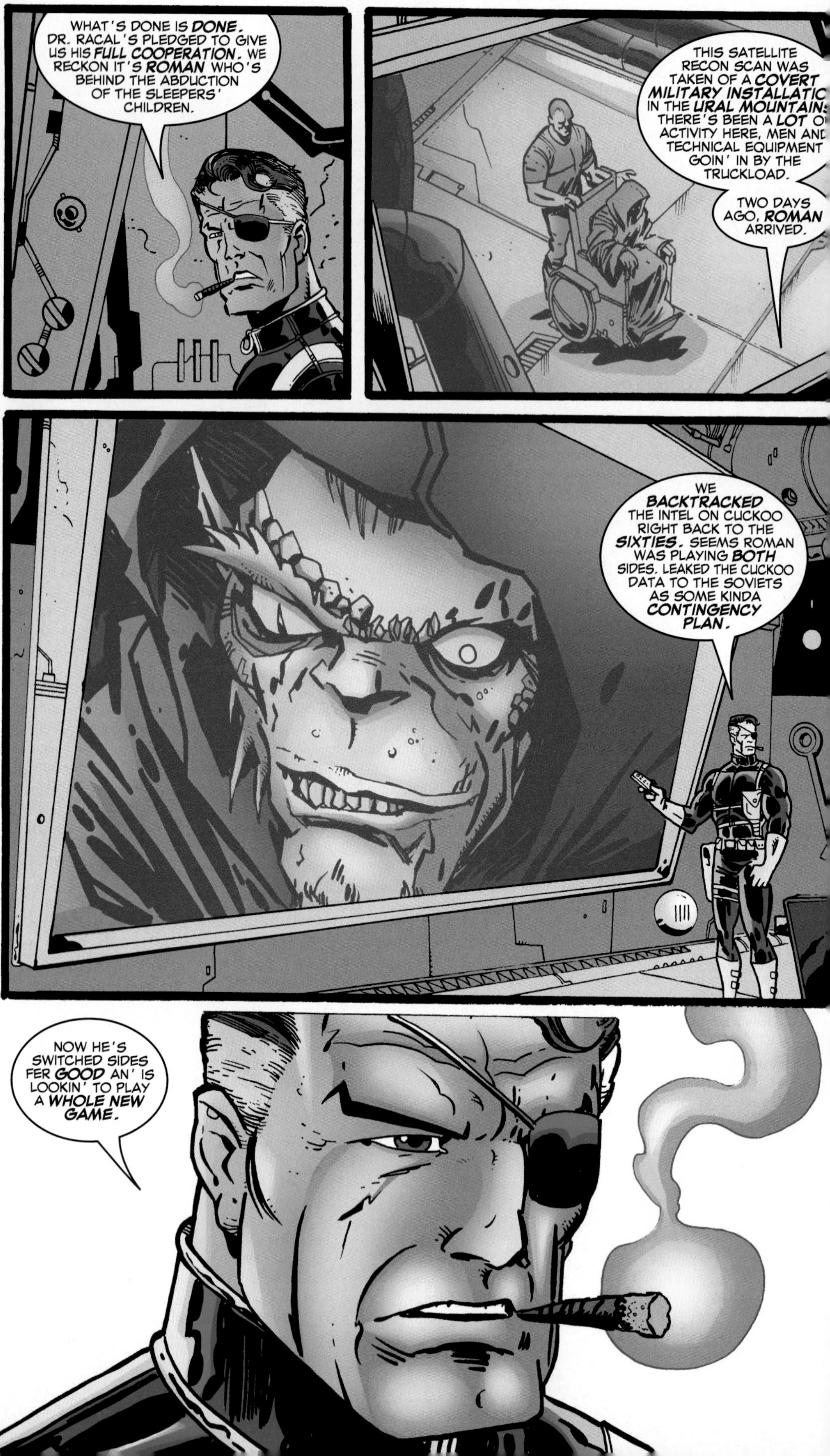

WHAT'S DONE IS DONE. DR. RACAL'S PLEDGED TO GIVE US HIS FULL COOPERATION. WE RECKON IT'S ROMAN WHO'S BEHIND THE ABDUCTION OF THE SLEEPERS' CHILDREN.
THIS SATELLITE RECON SCAN WAS TAKEN OF A COVERT MILITARY INSTALLATIC IN THE URAL MOUNTAINS THERE'S BEEN A LOT O ACTIVITY HERE, MEN AND TECHNICAL EQUIPMENT GOIN' IN BY THE TRUCKLOAD.
TWO DAYS AGO, ROMAN ARRIVED.
WE BACKTRACKED THE INTEL ON CUCKOO RIGHT BACK TO THE SIXTIES. SEEMS ROMAN WAS PLAYING BOTH SIDES. LEAKED THE CUCKOO DATA TO THE SOVIETS AS SOME KINDA CONTINGENCY PLAN.
NOW HE'S SWITCHED SIDES FER GOOD AN' IS LOOKIN' TO PLAY A WHOLE NEW GAME.

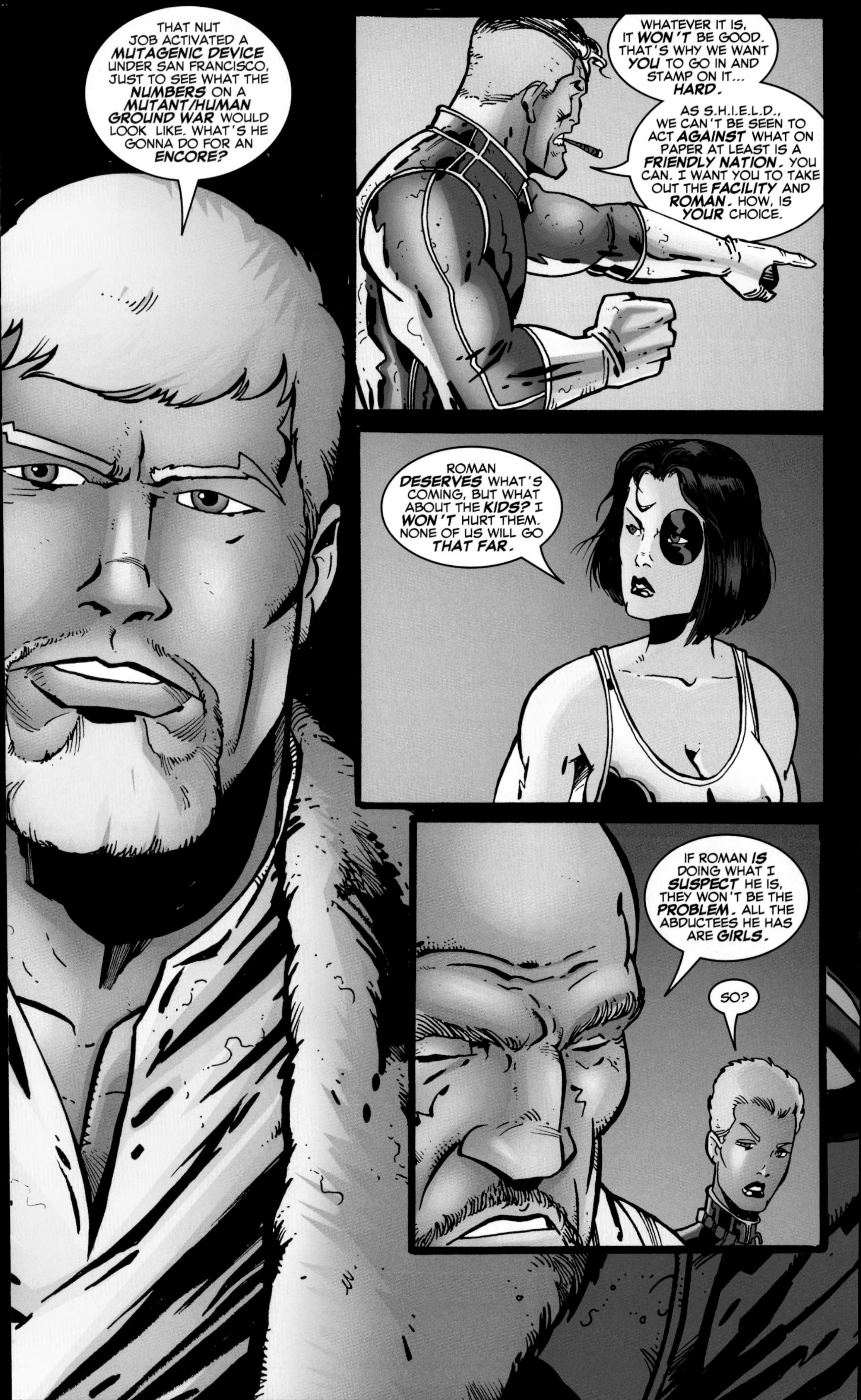
THAT NUT JOB ACTIVATED A MUTAGENIC DEVICE UNDER SAN FRANCISCO, JUST TO SEE WHAT THE NUMBERS ON A MUTANT/HUMAN GROUND WAR WOULD LOOK LIKE. WHAT'S HE GONNA DO FOR AN ENCORE?
WHATEVER IT IS, IT WON'T BE GOOD. THAT'S WHY WE WANT YOU TO GO IN AND STAMP ON IT... HARD.
AS S.H.I.E.L.D., WE CAN'T BE SEEN TO ACT AGAINST WHAT ON PAPER AT LEAST IS A FRIENDLY NATION. YOU CAN. I WANT YOU TO TAKE OUT THE FACILITY AND ROMAN. HOW, IS YOUR CHOICE.
ROMAN DESERVES WHAT'S COMING, BUT WHAT ABOUT THE KIDS? I WON'T HURT THEM. NONE OF US WILL GO THAT FAR.
IF ROMAN IS DOING WHAT I SUSPECT HE IS, THEY WON'T BE THE PROBLEM. ALL THE ABDUCTEES HE HAS ARE GIRLS.
SO?

"HUMAN FEMALES ARE BORN WITH A *LIFETIME'S SUPPLY* OF *VIABLE EGGS*-- POTENTIAL *CHILDREN* IF YOU LIKE. *HUNDREDS* OF THEM.

"ALL OF THESE POTENTIAL CHILDREN ARE *FEMALE*. IT'S ONLY *LATER*, AFTER FERTILIZATION, THAT *HORMONES* DICTATE THEIR FINAL GENDER.

"IT STANDS TO REASON THAT THE SLEEPER'S DAUGHTER'S EGGS EACH POSSESS THE *ENHANCED GENOME* OF THE ORIGINAL.

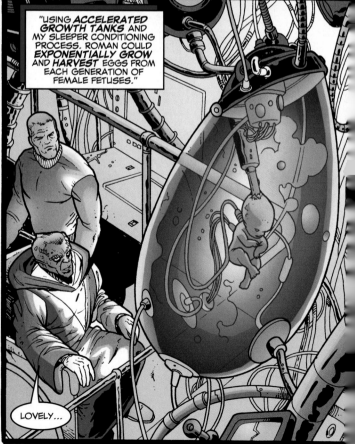

"USING *ACCELERATED GROWTH TANKS* AND MY SLEEPER CONDITIONING PROCESS, ROMAN COULD *EXPONENTIALLY GROW* AND *HARVEST* EGGS FROM EACH GENERATION OF FEMALE FETUSES."

LOVELY...

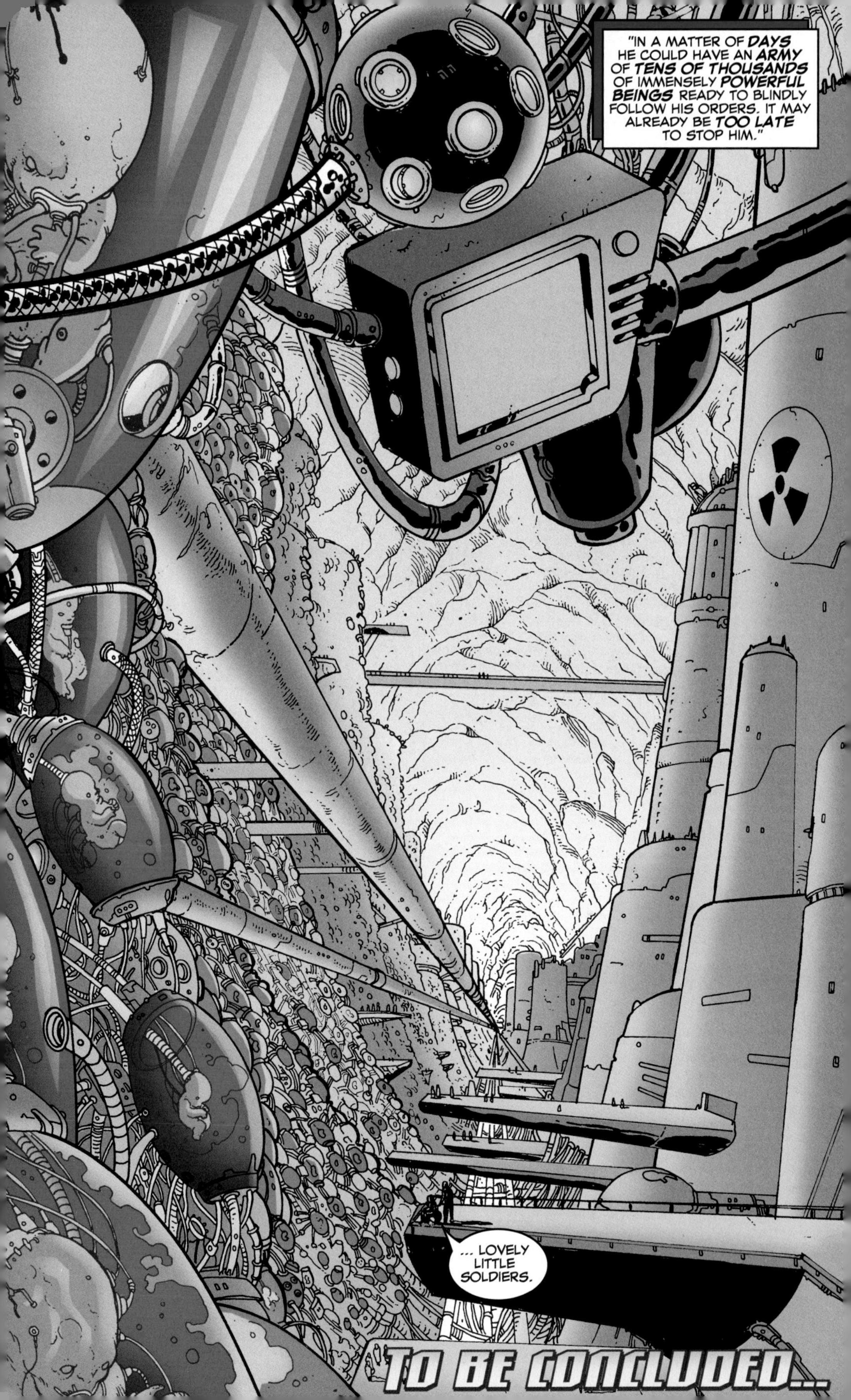
"IN A MATTER OF DAYS HE COULD HAVE AN ARMY OF TENS OF THOUSANDS OF IMMENSELY POWERFUL BEINGS READY TO BLINDLY FOLLOW HIS ORDERS. IT MAY ALREADY BE TOO LATE TO STOP HIM."
... LOVELY LITTLE SOLDIERS.
TO BE CONCLUDED...

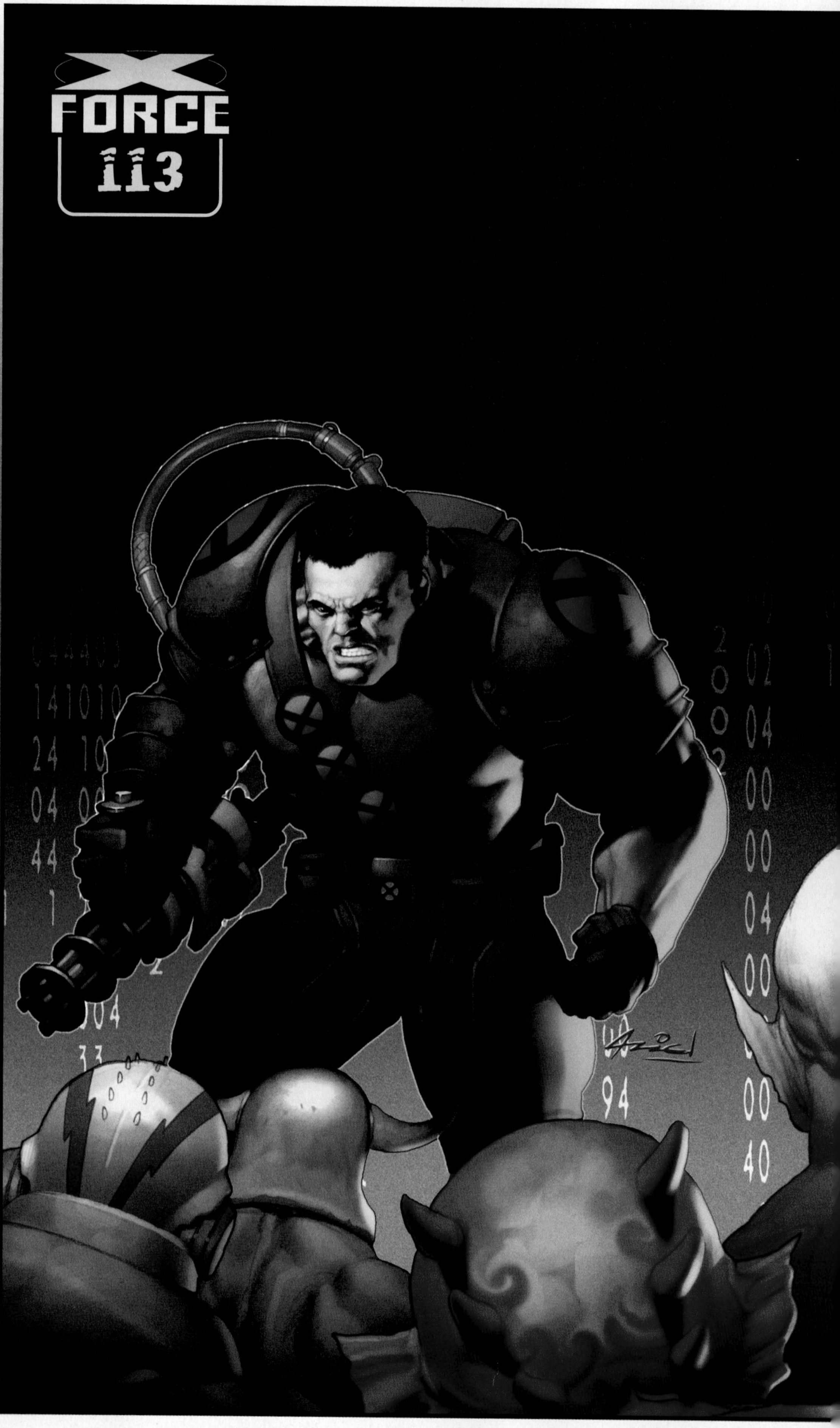
X
FORCE
113

RAGE WAR
PART FOUR OF FOUR

IAN EDGINTON	JORGE LUCAS	VLM	CHRIS ELIOPOULOS
WORDS	ART	COLORS	LETTERS

FRANK DUNKERLEY	MATT HICKS	JOE QUESADA
ASSIST	EDITOR	EDITOR IN CHIEF

"ONCE UPON A TIME, A NOBLE MAN HAD A FINE DREAM THAT THE DIFFERENT AND DISENFRANCHISED-- *MUTANTS,* LIKE HIMSELF, COULD COEXIST IN PEACE AND TOLERANCE WITH THE REST OF HUMANITY.

"HE DREW TO HIM OTHERS LIKE US WHO WOULD SHARE THAT DREAM. WE KEPT ON DREAMING IT TOO, WHILE HUMANS BURNED MUTANT HOMES, DESTROYED MUTANT BUSINESSES, DENIED US THE RIGHT TO EDUCATION, FREE SPEECH, LIBERTY, EQUALITY... *LIFE.*

"MAYBE THAT'S WHY WE WEAR THE "*X.*" NOTHING TO DO WITH GENES OR CHROMOSOMES, INSTEAD IT REMINDS US OF WHAT HUMANITY WANTS TO DO TO US...

"EXAMINE... EXCLUDE... EXTERMINATE!

"ONCE UPON A TIME, WE SHARED A NOBLE MAN'S FINE DREAM..."

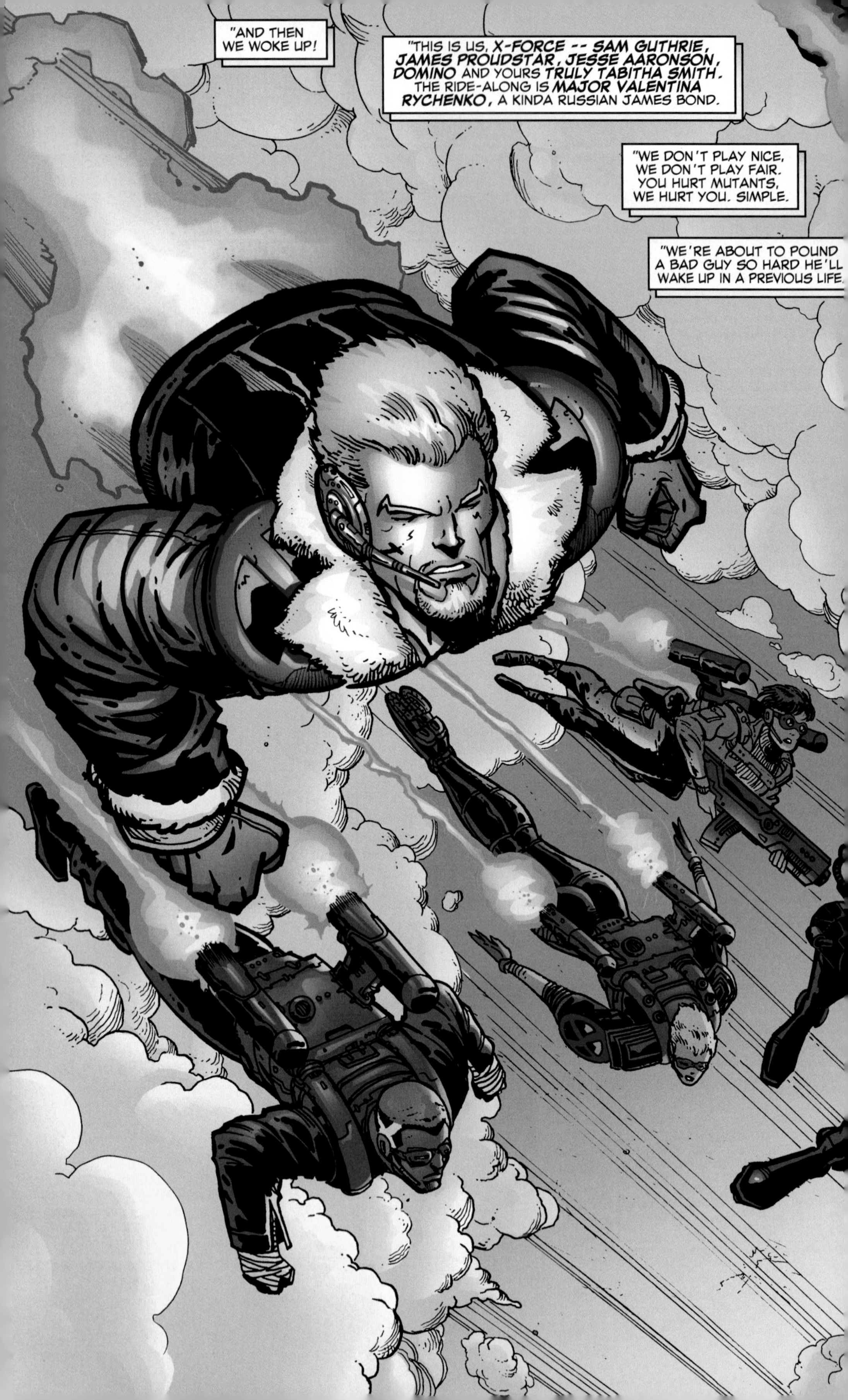
"AND THEN WE WOKE UP!
"THIS IS US, X-FORCE -- SAM GUTHRIE, JAMES PROUDSTAR, JESSE AARONSON, DOMINO AND YOURS TRULY TABITHA SMITH. THE RIDE-ALONG IS MAJOR VALENTINA RYCHENKO, A KINDA RUSSIAN JAMES BOND.
"WE DON'T PLAY NICE, WE DON'T PLAY FAIR. YOU HURT MUTANTS, WE HURT YOU. SIMPLE.
"WE'RE ABOUT TO POUND A BAD GUY SO HARD HE'LL WAKE UP IN A PREVIOUS LIFE.

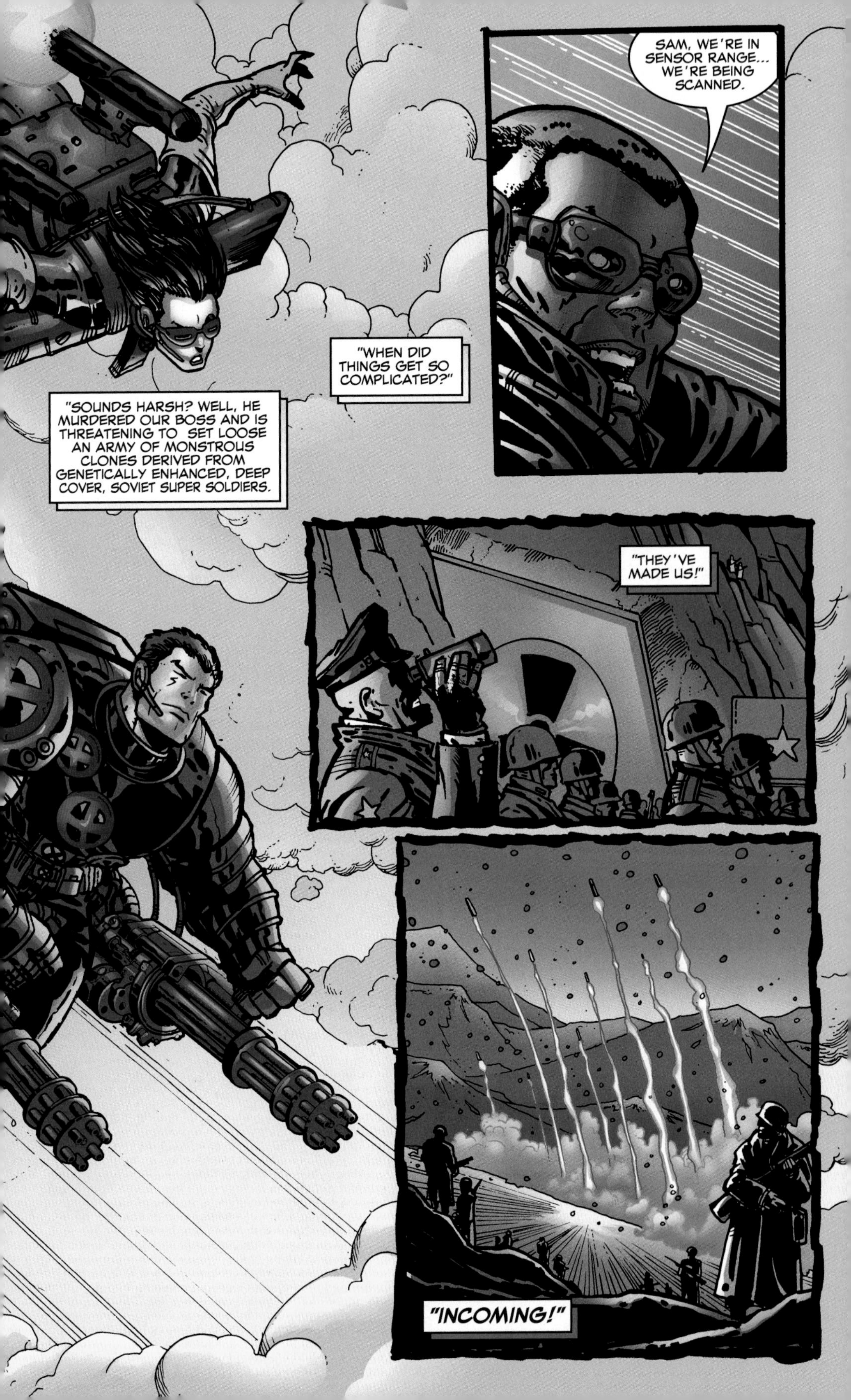
SAM, WE'RE IN SENSOR RANGE... WE'RE BEING SCANNED.
"WHEN DID THINGS GET SO COMPLICATED?"
"SOUNDS HARSH? WELL, HE MURDERED OUR BOSS AND IS THREATENING TO SET LOOSE AN ARMY OF MONSTROUS CLONES DERIVED FROM GENETICALLY ENHANCED, DEEP COVER, SOVIET SUPER SOLDIERS.
"THEY'VE MADE US!"
"INCOMING!"

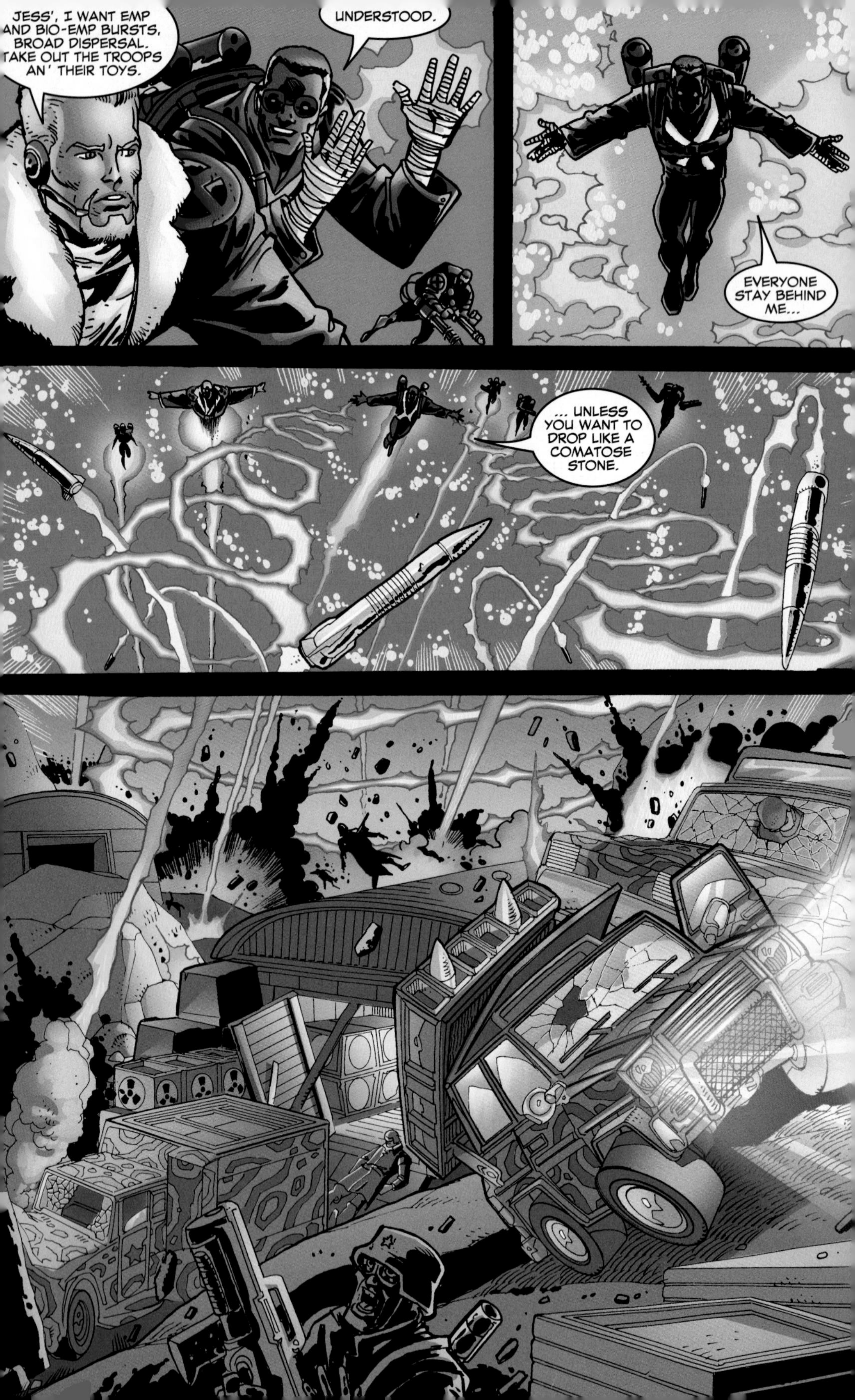
JESS', I WANT EMP AND BIO-EMP BURSTS, BROAD DISPERSAL. TAKE OUT THE TROOPS AN' THEIR TOYS.
UNDERSTOOD.
EVERYONE STAY BEHIND ME...
... UNLESS YOU WANT TO DROP LIKE A COMATOSE STONE.

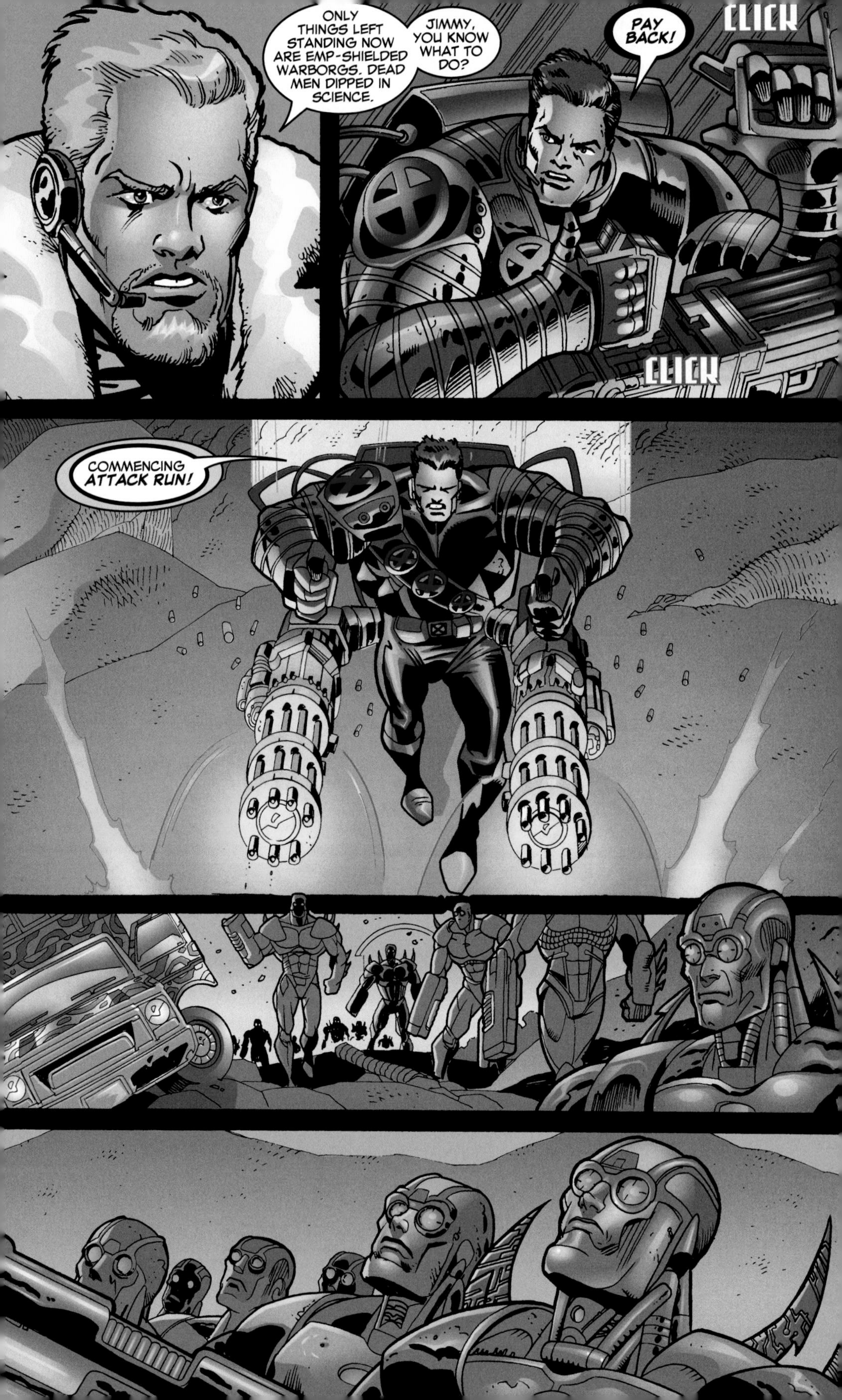
ONLY THINGS LEFT STANDING NOW ARE EMP-SHIELDED WARBORGS. DEAD MEN DIPPED IN SCIENCE.
JIMMY, YOU KNOW WHAT TO DO?
PAY BACK!
CLICK
CLICK
COMMENCING ATTACK RUN!

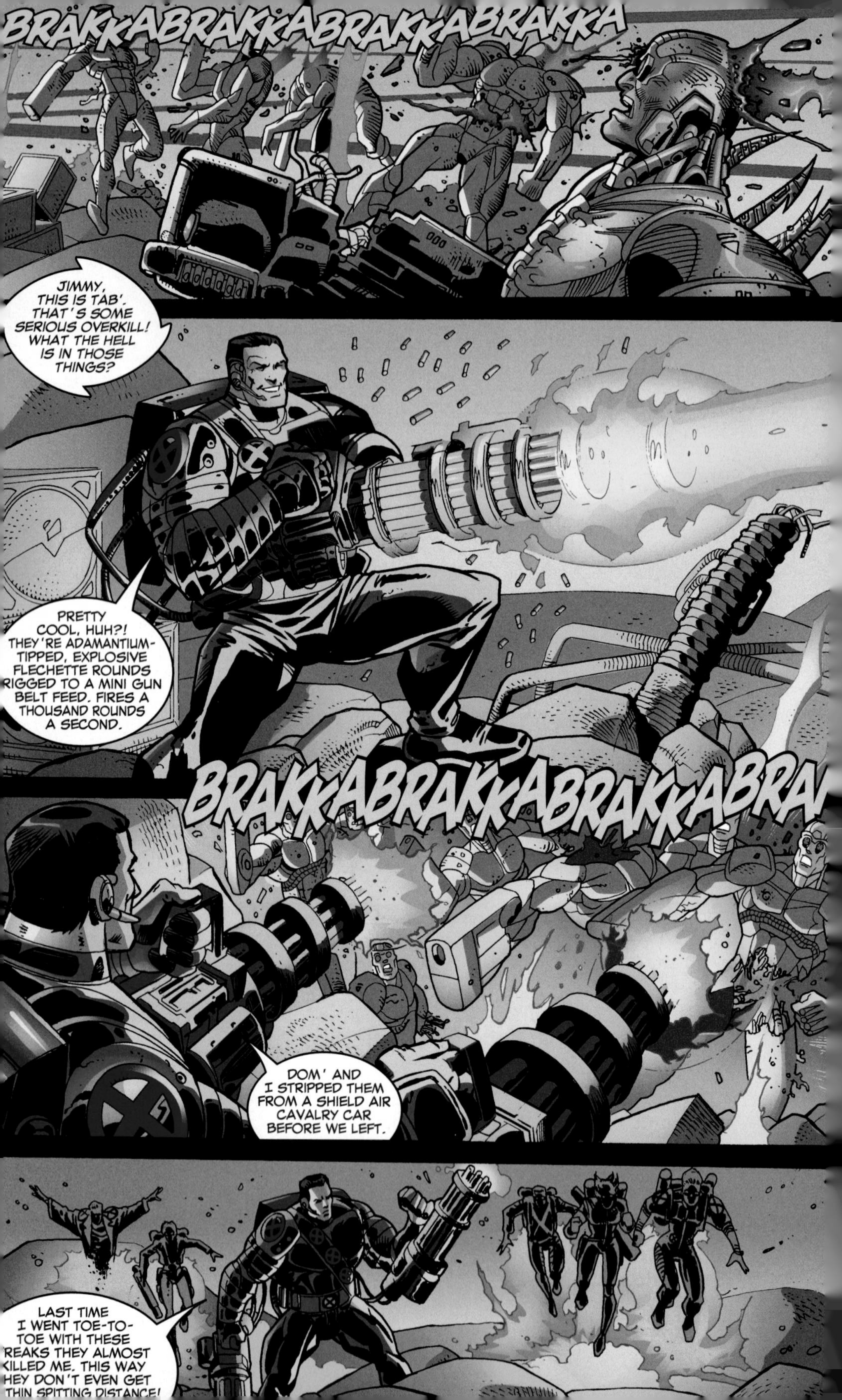

BRAKKABRAKKABRAKKABRAKKA
JIMMY, THIS IS TAB'. THAT'S SOME SERIOUS OVERKILL! WHAT THE HELL IS IN THOSE THINGS?
PRETTY COOL, HUH?! THEY'RE ADAMANTIUM-TIPPED, EXPLOSIVE FLECHETTE ROUNDS RIGGED TO A MINI GUN BELT FEED. FIRES A THOUSAND ROUNDS A SECOND.
BRAKKABRAKKABRAKKABRA
DOM' AND I STRIPPED THEM FROM A SHIELD AIR CAVALRY CAR BEFORE WE LEFT.
LAST TIME I WENT TOE-TO-TOE WITH THESE REAKS THEY ALMOST KILLED ME. THIS WAY HEY DON'T EVEN GET

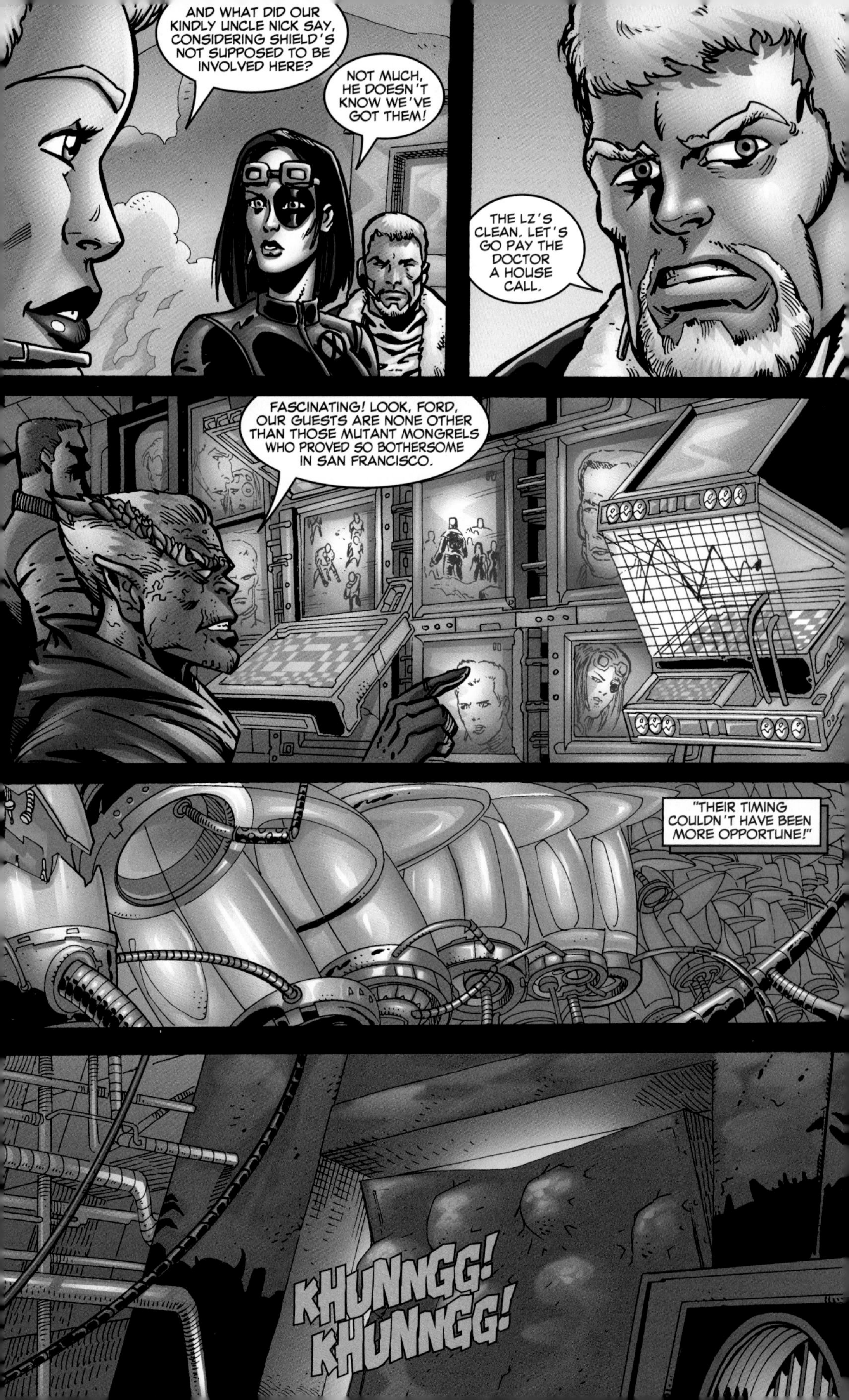
AND WHAT DID OUR KINDLY UNCLE NICK SAY, CONSIDERING SHIELD'S NOT SUPPOSED TO BE INVOLVED HERE?
NOT MUCH, HE DOESN'T KNOW WE'VE GOT THEM!
THE LZ'S CLEAN. LET'S GO PAY THE DOCTOR A HOUSE CALL.
FASCINATING! LOOK, FORD, OUR GUESTS ARE NONE OTHER THAN THOSE MUTANT MONGRELS WHO PROVED SO BOTHERSOME IN SAN FRANCISCO.
"THEIR TIMING COULDN'T HAVE BEEN MORE OPPORTUNE!"
KHUNNGG! KHUNNGG!

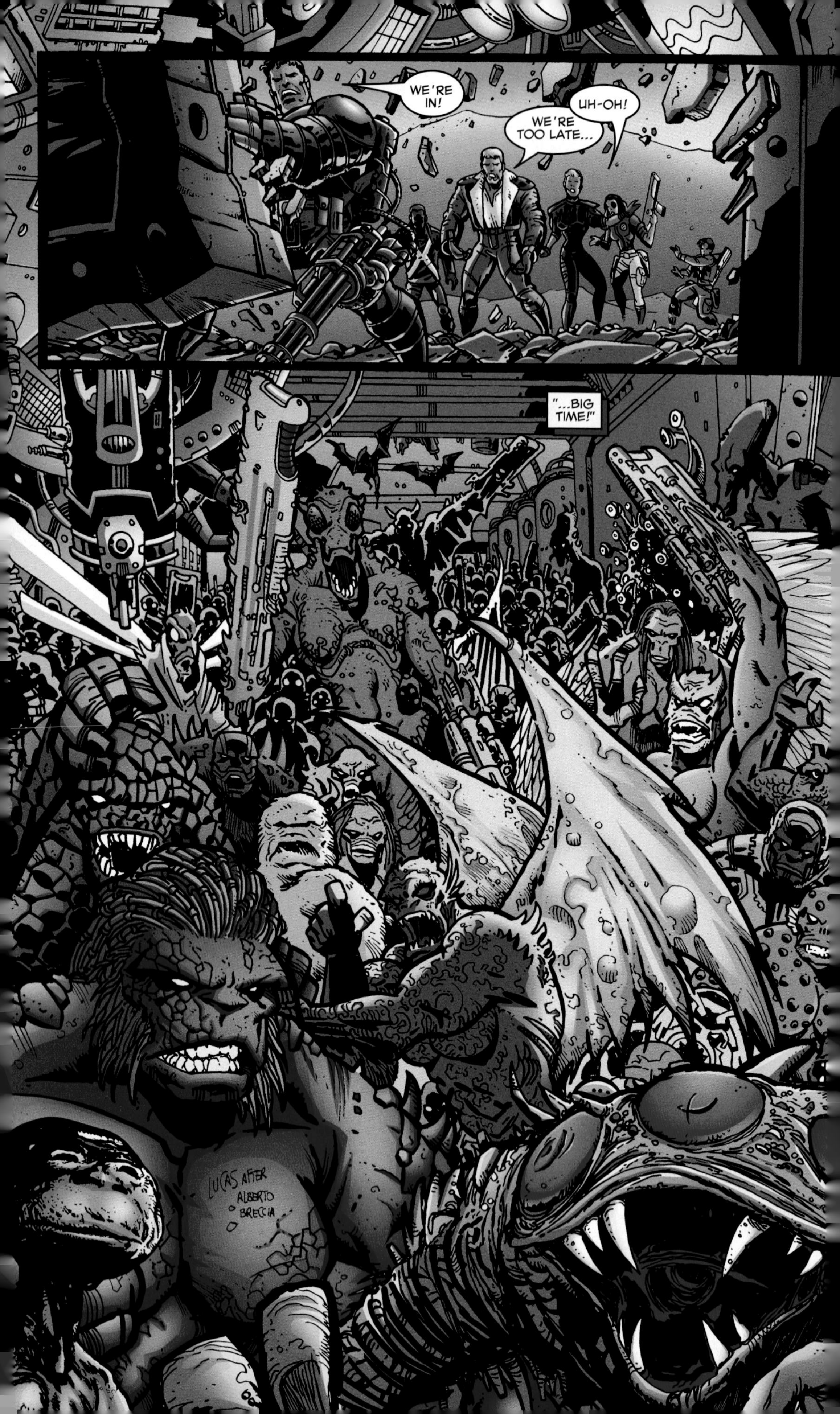
WE'RE IN!
WE'RE TOO LATE...
UH-OH!
"...BIG TIME!"
LUCAS AFTER ALBERTO BRECCIA

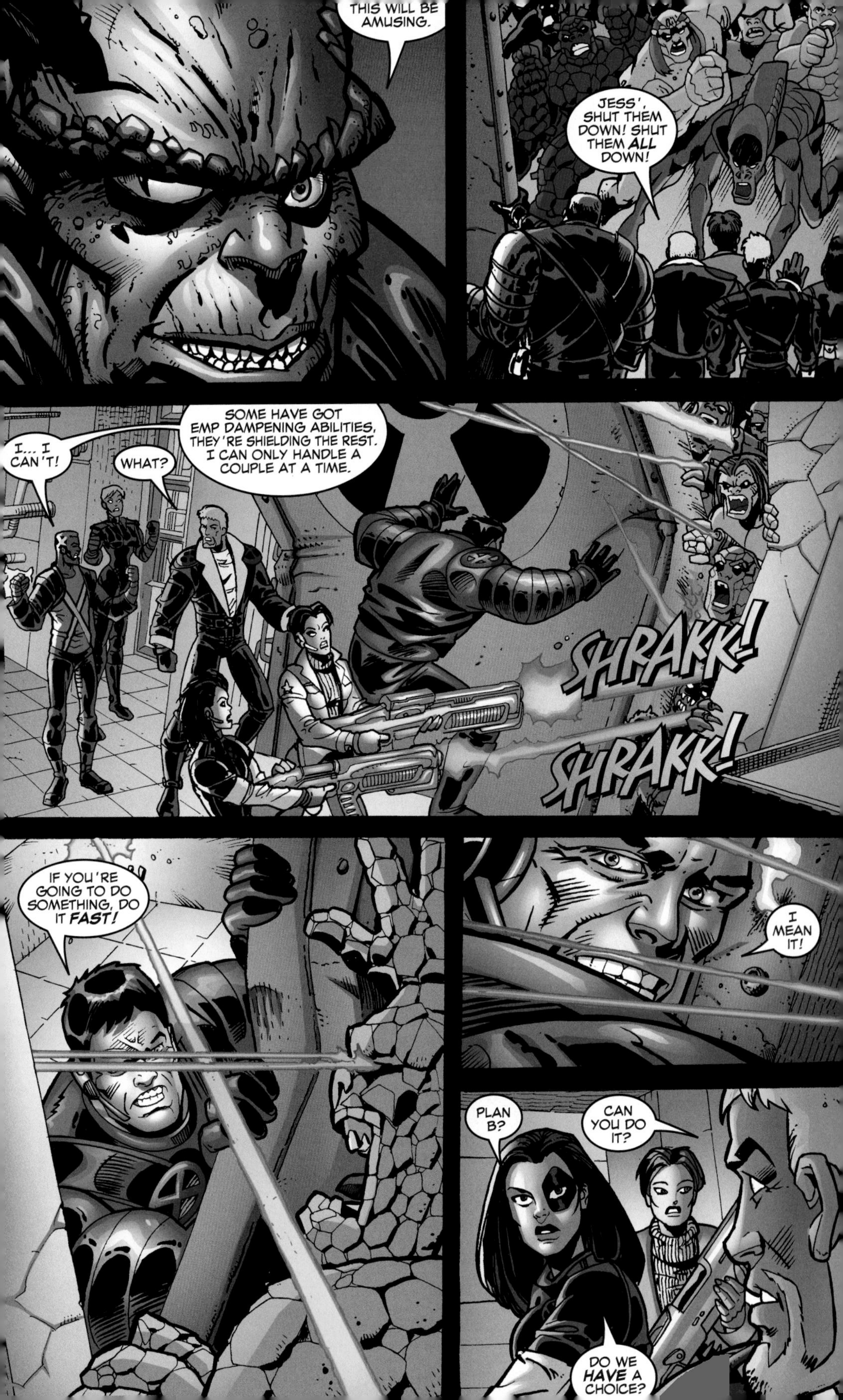
THIS WILL BE AMUSING.
JESS', SHUT THEM DOWN! SHUT THEM **ALL** DOWN!
I... I CAN'T!
WHAT?
SOME HAVE GOT EMP DAMPENING ABILITIES, THEY'RE SHIELDING THE REST. I CAN ONLY HANDLE A COUPLE AT A TIME.
SHRAKK!
SHRAKK!
IF YOU'RE GOING TO DO SOMETHING, DO IT **FAST!**
I MEAN IT!
PLAN B?
CAN YOU DO IT?
DO WE **HAVE** A CHOICE?

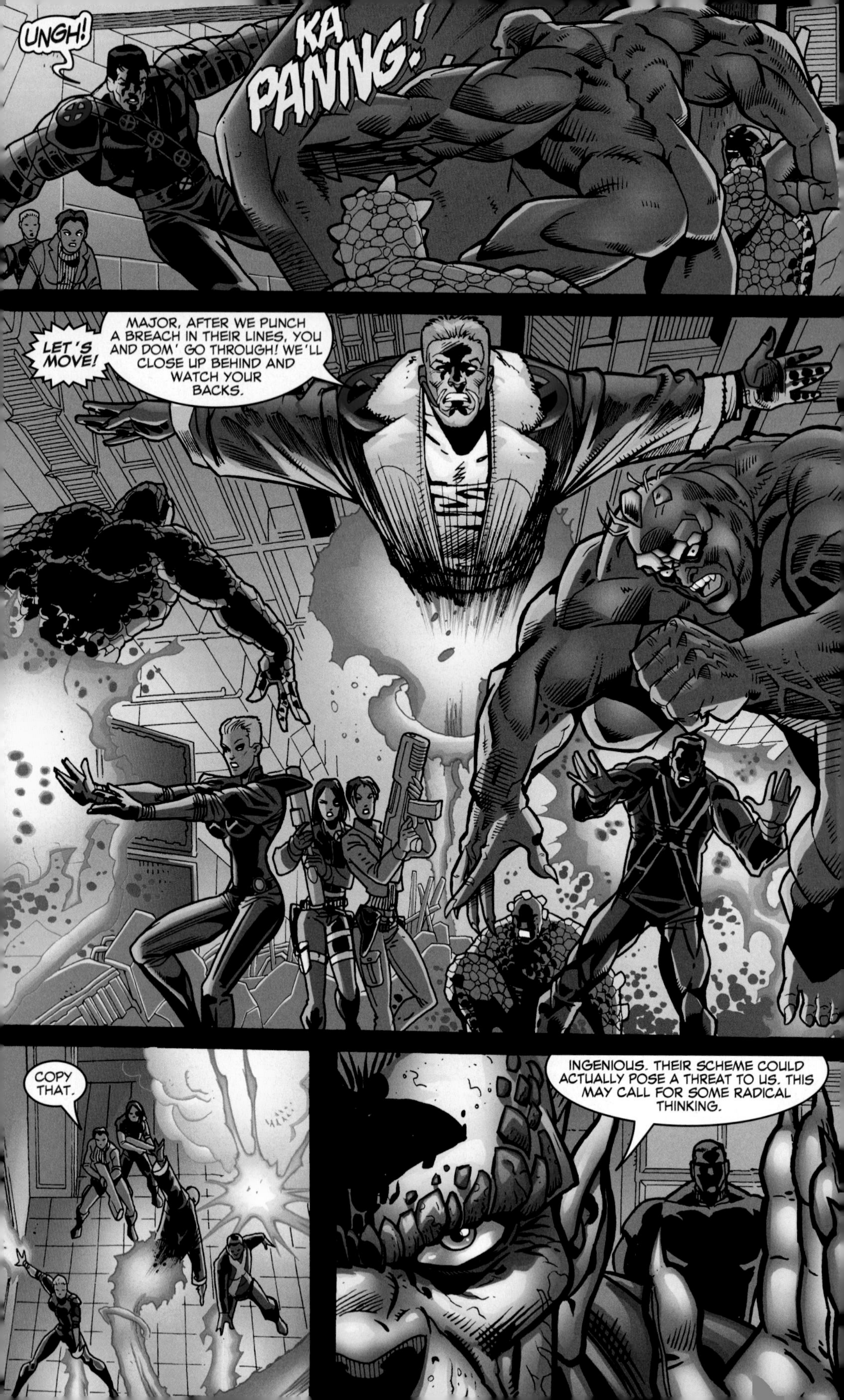
UNGH!
KA PANNG!
LET'S MOVE!
MAJOR, AFTER WE PUNCH A BREACH IN THEIR LINES, YOU AND DOM' GO THROUGH! WE'LL CLOSE UP BEHIND AND WATCH YOUR BACKS.
COPY THAT.
INGENIOUS. THEIR SCHEME COULD ACTUALLY POSE A THREAT TO US. THIS MAY CALL FOR SOME RADICAL THINKING.

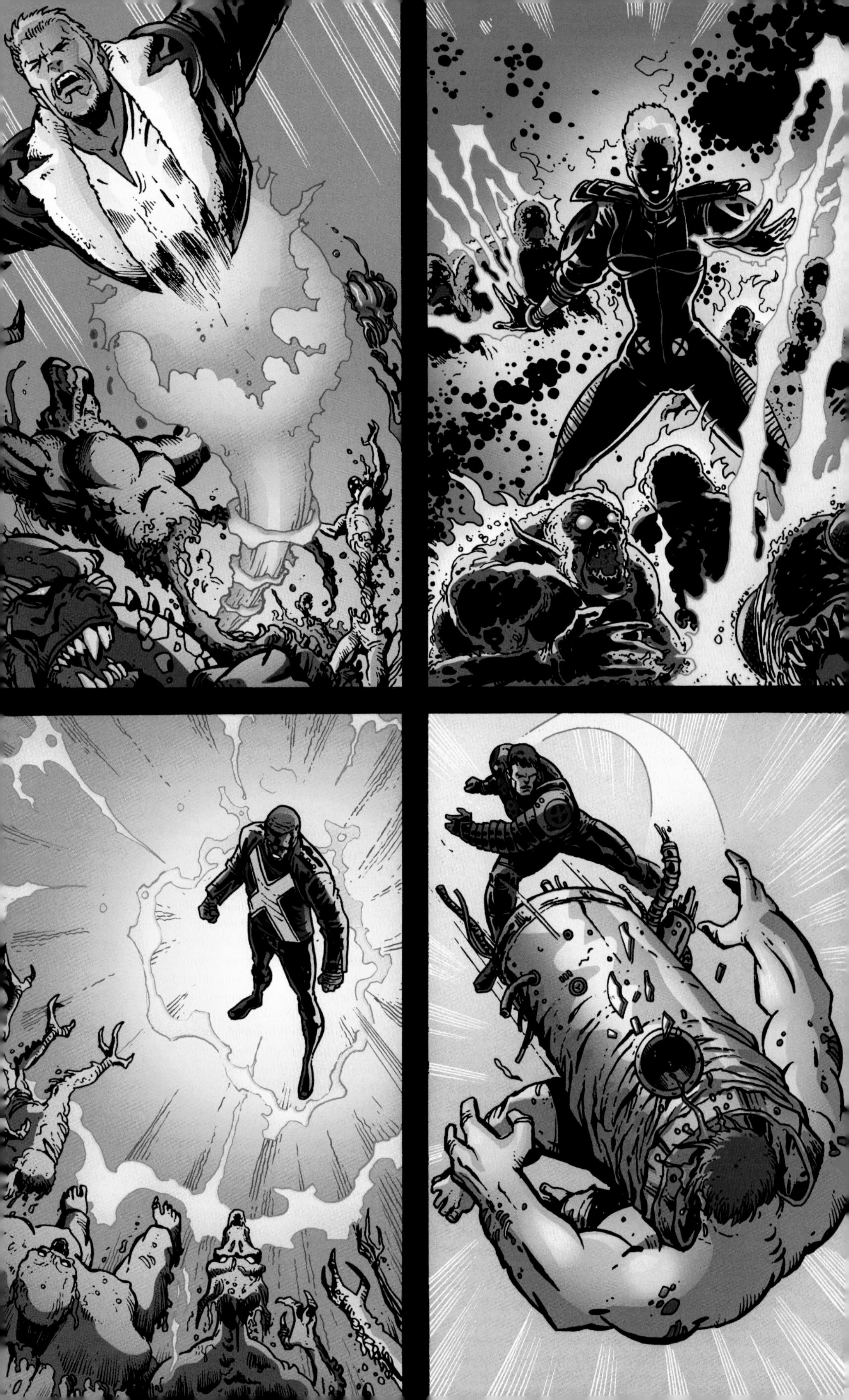

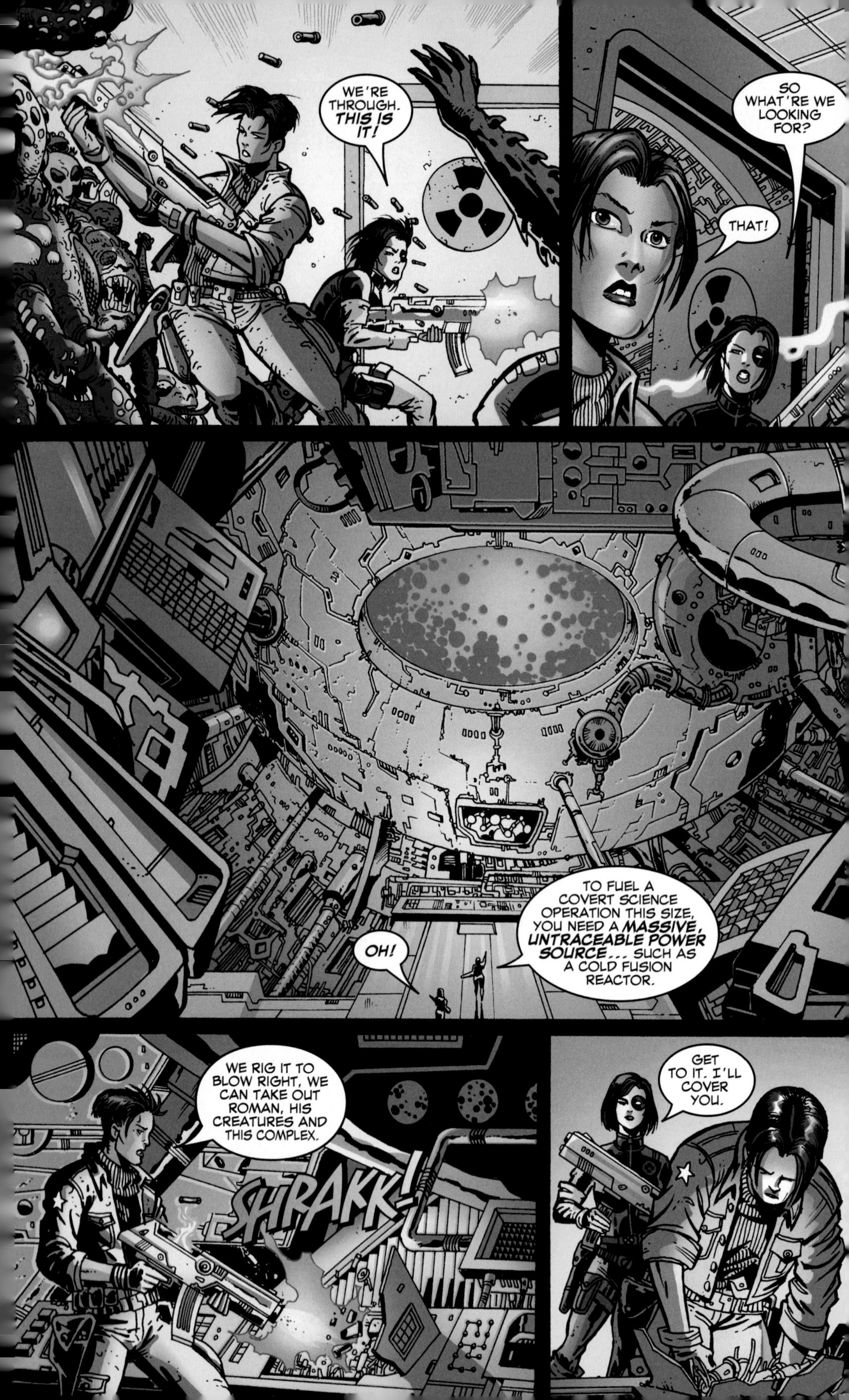

WE'RE THROUGH. ***THIS IS IT!***
SO WHAT'RE WE LOOKING FOR?
THAT!
TO FUEL A COVERT SCIENCE OPERATION THIS SIZE, YOU NEED A ***MASSIVE, UNTRACEABLE POWER SOURCE...*** SUCH AS A COLD FUSION REACTOR.
OH!
WE RIG IT TO BLOW RIGHT, WE CAN TAKE OUT ROMAN, HIS CREATURES AND THIS COMPLEX.
SHRAKK!
GET TO IT. I'LL COVER YOU.

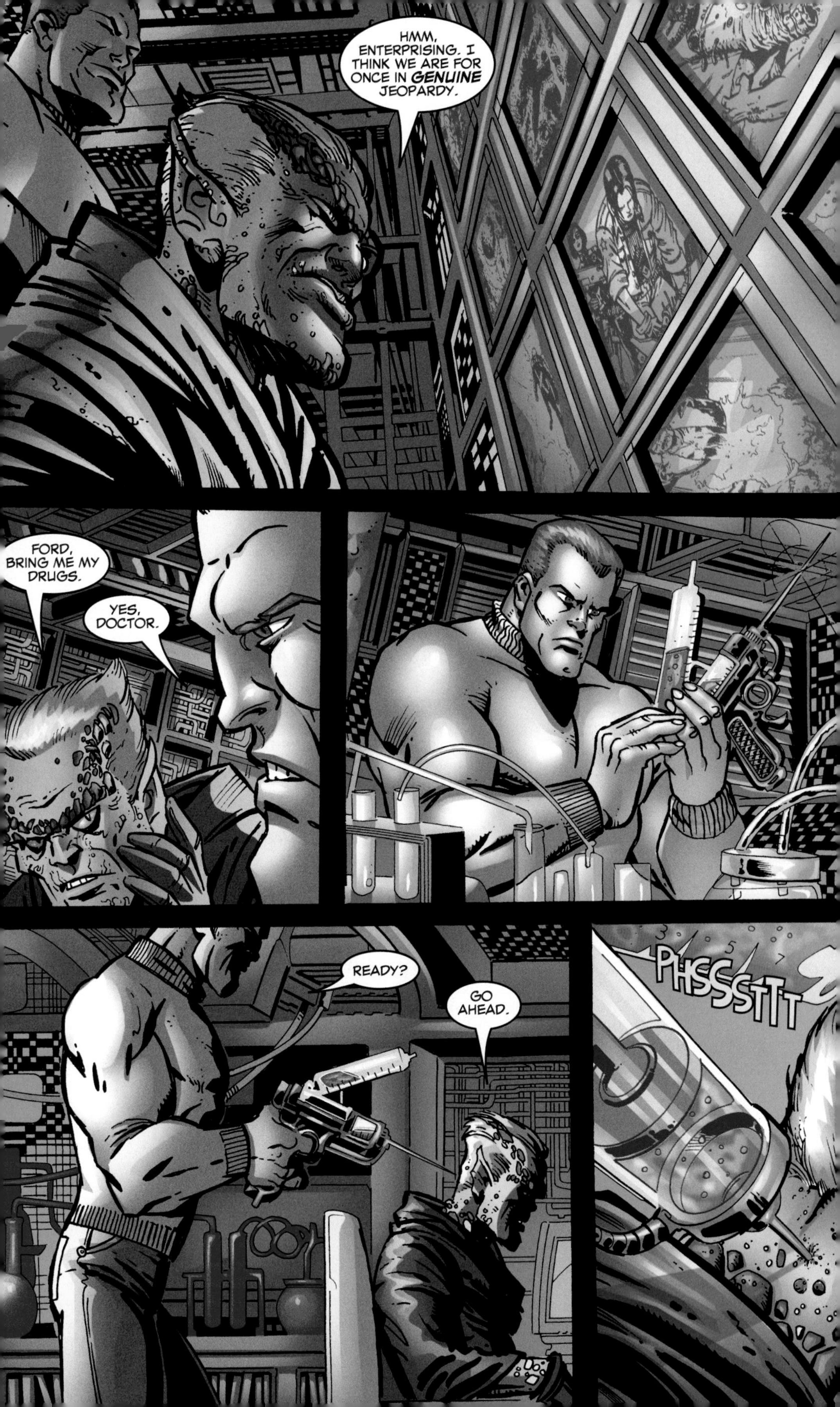

HMM, ENTERPRISING. I THINK WE ARE FOR ONCE IN GENUINE JEOPARDY.
FORD, BRING ME MY DRUGS.
YES, DOCTOR.
READY?
GO AHEAD.
PHSSSTTT

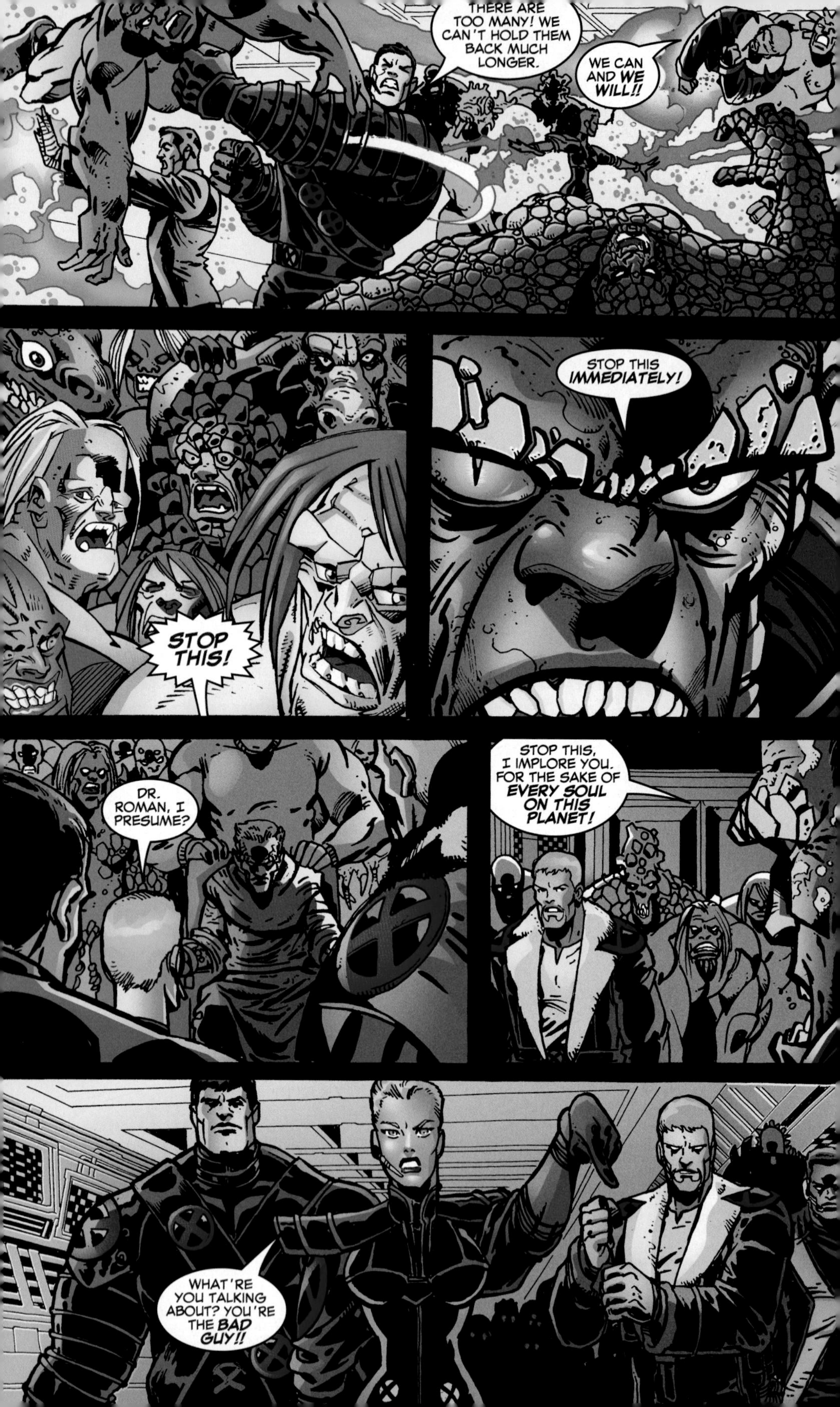
THERE ARE TOO MANY! WE CAN'T HOLD THEM BACK MUCH LONGER.
WE CAN AND WE WILL!!
STOP THIS!
STOP THIS IMMEDIATELY!
DR. ROMAN, I PRESUME?
STOP THIS, I IMPLORE YOU. FOR THE SAKE OF EVERY SOUL ON THIS PLANET!
WHAT'RE YOU TALKING ABOUT? YOU'RE THE BAD GUY!!

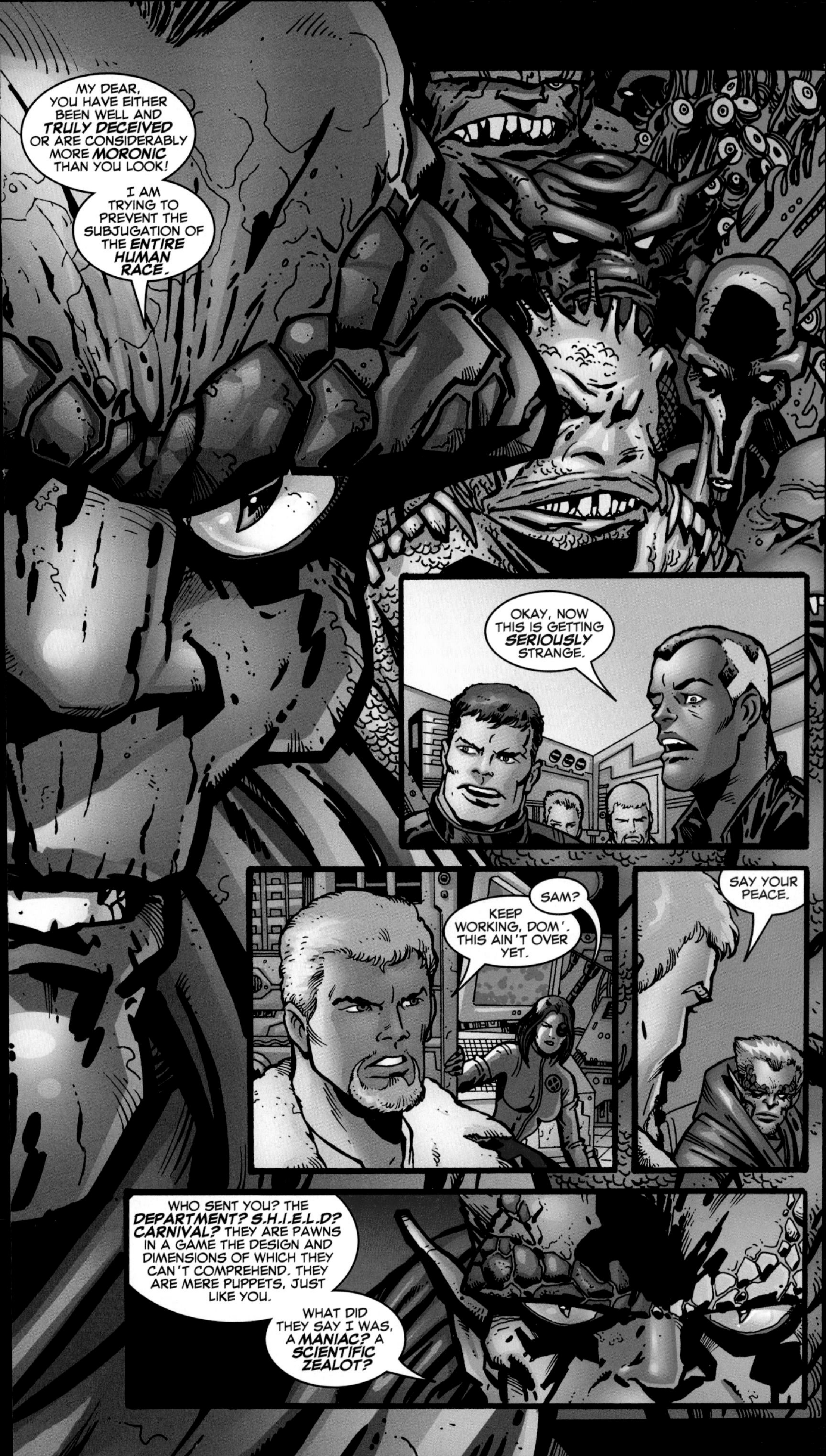
MY DEAR, YOU HAVE EITHER BEEN WELL AND TRULY DECEIVED OR ARE CONSIDERABLY MORE MORONIC THAN YOU LOOK!
I AM TRYING TO PREVENT THE SUBJUGATION OF THE ENTIRE HUMAN RACE.
OKAY, NOW THIS IS GETTING SERIOUSLY STRANGE.
SAM?
KEEP WORKING, DOM'. THIS AIN'T OVER YET.
SAY YOUR PEACE.
WHO SENT YOU? THE DEPARTMENT? S.H.I.E.L.D? CARNIVAL? THEY ARE PAWNS IN A GAME THE DESIGN AND DIMENSIONS OF WHICH THEY CAN'T COMPREHEND. THEY ARE MERE PUPPETS, JUST LIKE YOU.
WHAT DID THEY SAY I WAS, A MANIAC? A SCIENTIFIC ZEALOT?

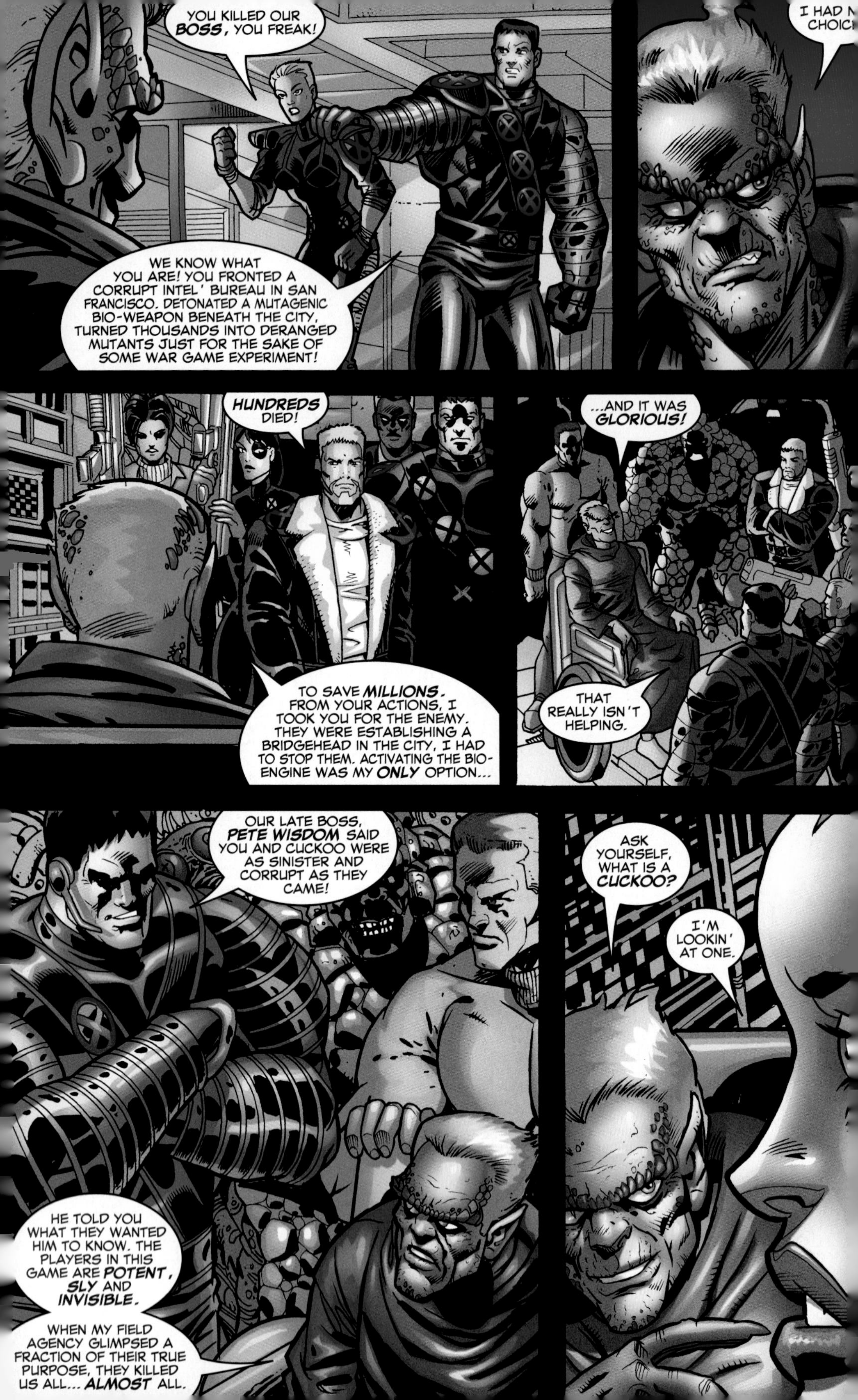
YOU KILLED OUR BOSS, YOU FREAK!
WE KNOW WHAT YOU ARE! YOU FRONTED A CORRUPT INTEL' BUREAU IN SAN FRANCISCO. DETONATED A MUTAGENIC BIO-WEAPON BENEATH THE CITY, TURNED THOUSANDS INTO DERANGED MUTANTS JUST FOR THE SAKE OF SOME WAR GAME EXPERIMENT!
I HAD N CHOIC
HUNDREDS DIED!
TO SAVE MILLIONS. FROM YOUR ACTIONS, I TOOK YOU FOR THE ENEMY. THEY WERE ESTABLISHING A BRIDGEHEAD IN THE CITY, I HAD TO STOP THEM. ACTIVATING THE BIO-ENGINE WAS MY ONLY OPTION...
...AND IT WAS GLORIOUS!
THAT REALLY ISN'T HELPING.
OUR LATE BOSS, PETE WISDOM SAID YOU AND CUCKOO WERE AS SINISTER AND CORRUPT AS THEY CAME!
HE TOLD YOU WHAT THEY WANTED HIM TO KNOW. THE PLAYERS IN THIS GAME ARE POTENT, SLY AND INVISIBLE.
WHEN MY FIELD AGENCY GLIMPSED A FRACTION OF THEIR TRUE PURPOSE, THEY KILLED US ALL... ALMOST ALL.
ASK YOURSELF, WHAT IS A CUCKOO?
I'M LOOKIN' AT ONE.

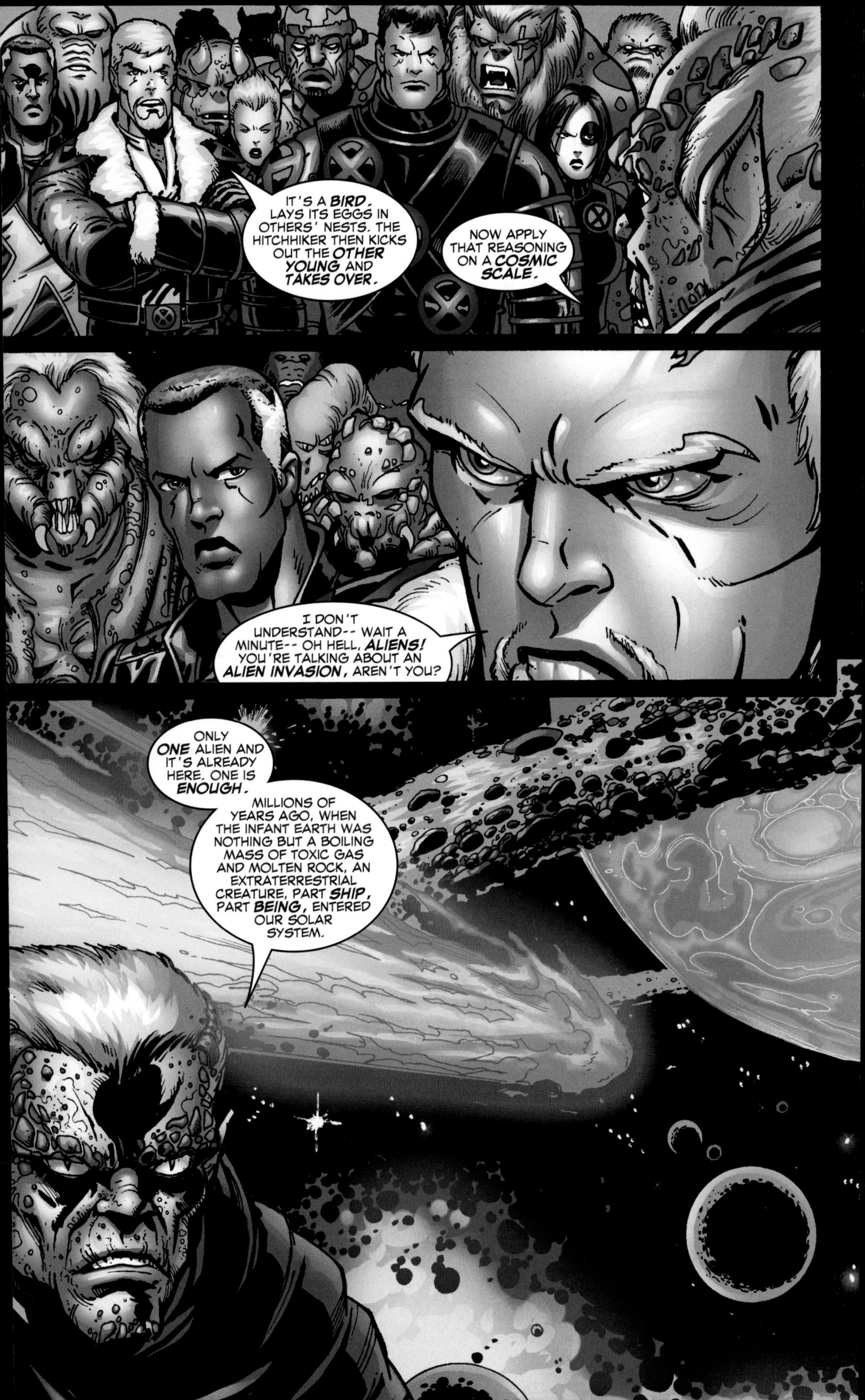
IT'S A BIRD. LAYS ITS EGGS IN OTHERS' NESTS. THE HITCHHIKER THEN KICKS OUT THE OTHER YOUNG AND TAKES OVER.
NOW APPLY THAT REASONING ON A COSMIC SCALE.
I DON'T UNDERSTAND-- WAIT A MINUTE-- OH HELL, ALIENS! YOU'RE TALKING ABOUT AN ALIEN INVASION, AREN'T YOU?
ONLY ONE ALIEN AND IT'S ALREADY HERE. ONE IS ENOUGH.
MILLIONS OF YEARS AGO, WHEN THE INFANT EARTH WAS NOTHING BUT A BOILING MASS OF TOXIC GAS AND MOLTEN ROCK, AN EXTRATERRESTRIAL CREATURE, PART SHIP, PART BEING, ENTERED OUR SOLAR SYSTEM.

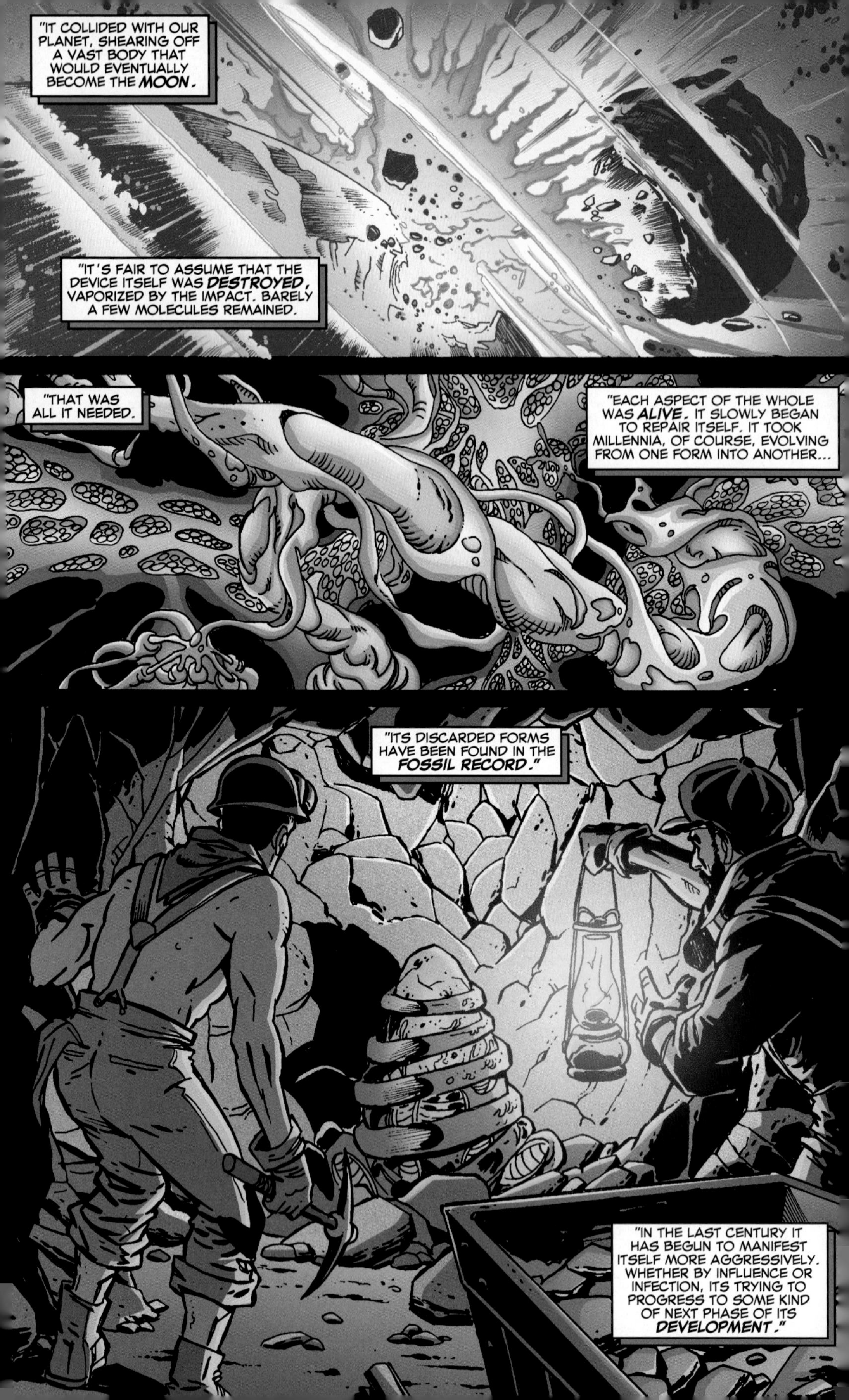
"IT COLLIDED WITH OUR PLANET, SHEARING OFF A VAST BODY THAT WOULD EVENTUALLY BECOME THE MOON.
"IT'S FAIR TO ASSUME THAT THE DEVICE ITSELF WAS DESTROYED, VAPORIZED BY THE IMPACT. BARELY A FEW MOLECULES REMAINED.
"THAT WAS ALL IT NEEDED.
"EACH ASPECT OF THE WHOLE WAS ALIVE. IT SLOWLY BEGAN TO REPAIR ITSELF. IT TOOK MILLENNIA, OF COURSE, EVOLVING FROM ONE FORM INTO ANOTHER...
"ITS DISCARDED FORMS HAVE BEEN FOUND IN THE FOSSIL RECORD."
"IN THE LAST CENTURY IT HAS BEGUN TO MANIFEST ITSELF MORE AGGRESSIVELY. WHETHER BY INFLUENCE OR INFECTION, ITS TRYING TO PROGRESS TO SOME KIND OF NEXT PHASE OF ITS DEVELOPMENT."

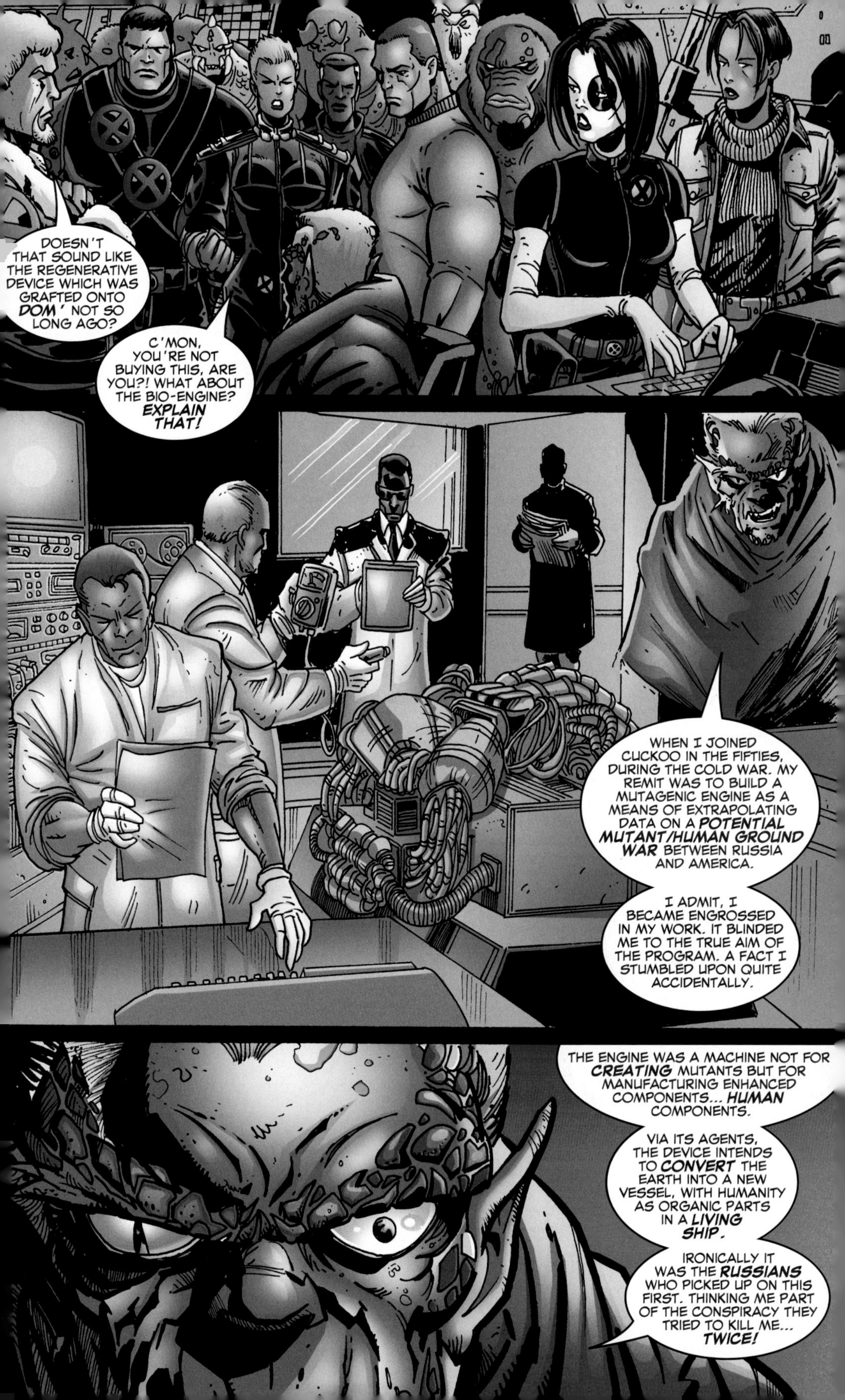

DOESN'T THAT SOUND LIKE THE REGENERATIVE DEVICE WHICH WAS GRAFTED ONTO DOM' NOT SO LONG AGO?
C'MON, YOU'RE NOT BUYING THIS, ARE YOU?! WHAT ABOUT THE BIO-ENGINE? EXPLAIN THAT!
WHEN I JOINED CUCKOO IN THE FIFTIES, DURING THE COLD WAR. MY REMIT WAS TO BUILD A MUTAGENIC ENGINE AS A MEANS OF EXTRAPOLATING DATA ON A POTENTIAL MUTANT/HUMAN GROUND WAR BETWEEN RUSSIA AND AMERICA.
I ADMIT, I BECAME ENGROSSED IN MY WORK. IT BLINDED ME TO THE TRUE AIM OF THE PROGRAM. A FACT I STUMBLED UPON QUITE ACCIDENTALLY.
THE ENGINE WAS A MACHINE NOT FOR CREATING MUTANTS BUT FOR MANUFACTURING ENHANCED COMPONENTS... HUMAN COMPONENTS.
VIA ITS AGENTS, THE DEVICE INTENDS TO CONVERT THE EARTH INTO A NEW VESSEL, WITH HUMANITY AS ORGANIC PARTS IN A LIVING SHIP.
IRONICALLY IT WAS THE RUSSIANS WHO PICKED UP ON THIS FIRST. THINKING ME PART OF THE CONSPIRACY THEY TRIED TO KILL ME... TWICE!

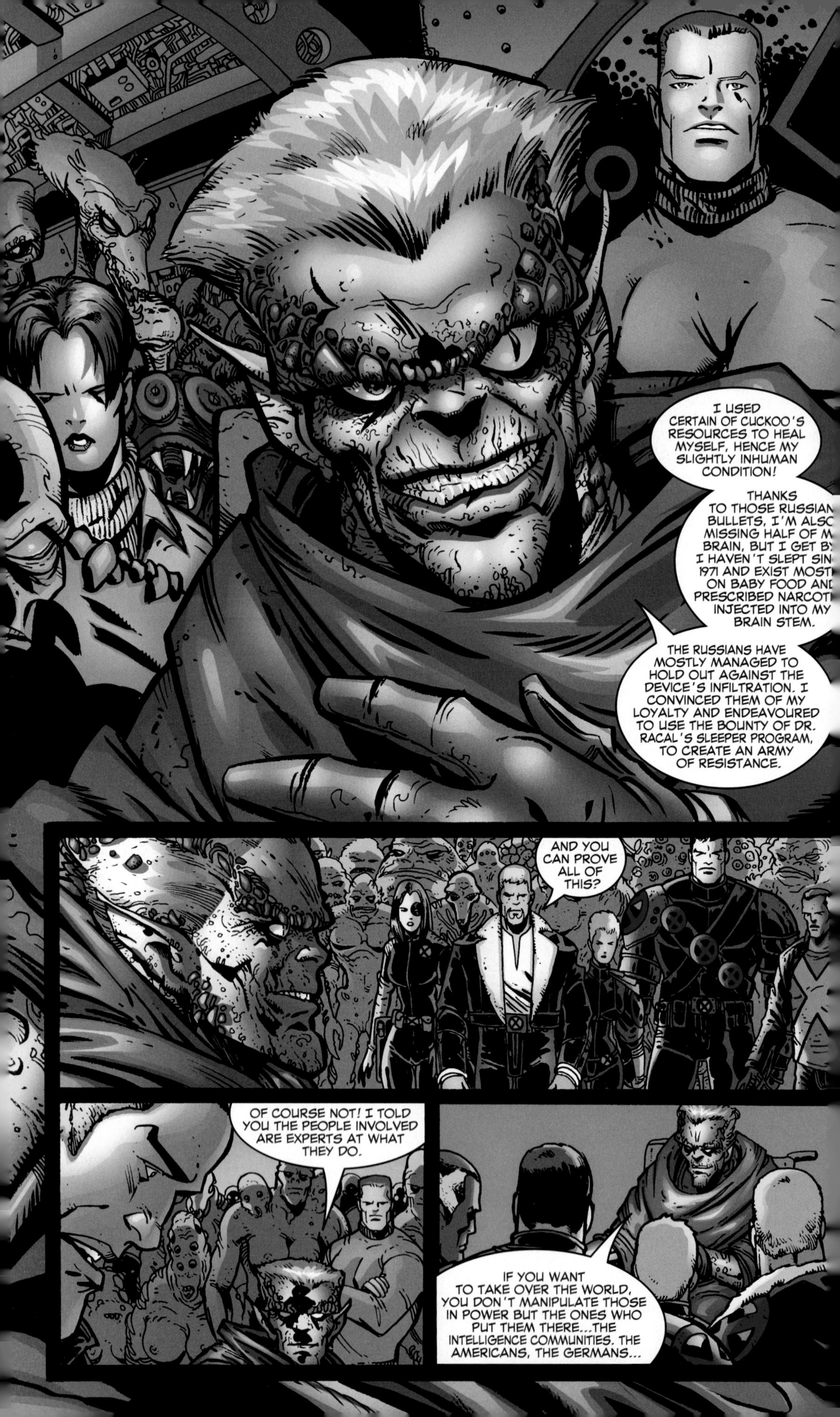
I USED CERTAIN OF CUCKOO'S RESOURCES TO HEAL MYSELF, HENCE MY SLIGHTLY INHUMAN CONDITION!
THANKS TO THOSE RUSSIAN BULLETS, I'M ALSO MISSING HALF OF MY BRAIN, BUT I GET BY. I HAVEN'T SLEPT SINCE 1971 AND EXIST MOSTLY ON BABY FOOD AND PRESCRIBED NARCOTICS INJECTED INTO MY BRAIN STEM.
THE RUSSIANS HAVE MOSTLY MANAGED TO HOLD OUT AGAINST THE DEVICE'S INFILTRATION. I CONVINCED THEM OF MY LOYALTY AND ENDEAVOURED TO USE THE BOUNTY OF DR. RACAL'S SLEEPER PROGRAM, TO CREATE AN ARMY OF RESISTANCE.
AND YOU CAN PROVE ALL OF THIS?
OF COURSE NOT! I TOLD YOU THE PEOPLE INVOLVED ARE EXPERTS AT WHAT THEY DO.
IF YOU WANT TO TAKE OVER THE WORLD, YOU DON'T MANIPULATE THOSE IN POWER BUT THE ONES WHO PUT THEM THERE...THE INTELLIGENCE COMMUNITIES. THE AMERICANS, THE GERMANS...

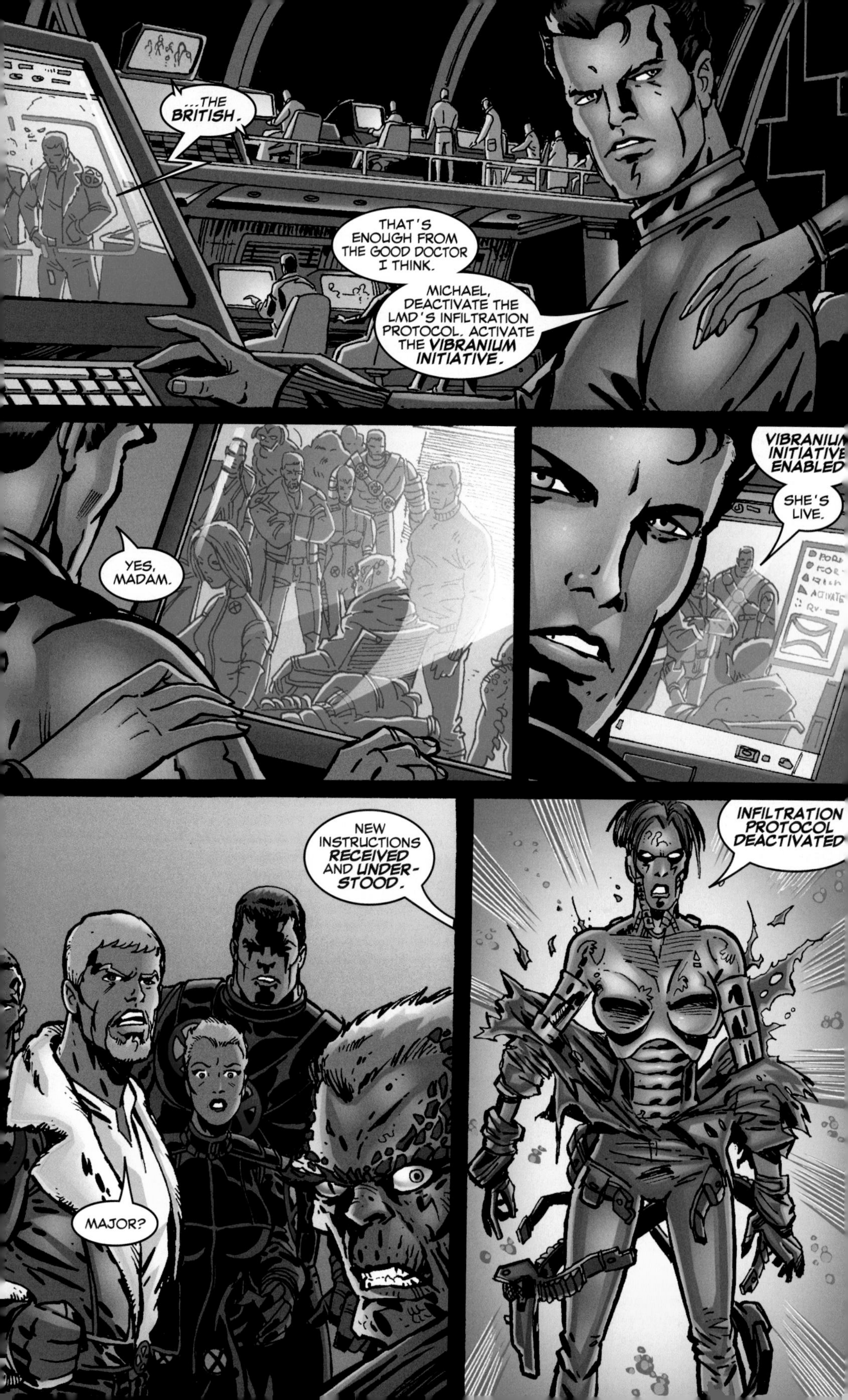
...THE BRITISH.
THAT'S ENOUGH FROM THE GOOD DOCTOR I THINK.
MICHAEL, DEACTIVATE THE LMD'S INFILTRATION PROTOCOL. ACTIVATE THE VIBRANIUM INITIATIVE.
YES, MADAM.
VIBRANIUM INITIATIVE ENABLED.
SHE'S LIVE.
NEW INSTRUCTIONS RECEIVED AND UNDER-STOOD.
MAJOR?
INFILTRATION PROTOCOL DEACTIVATED.

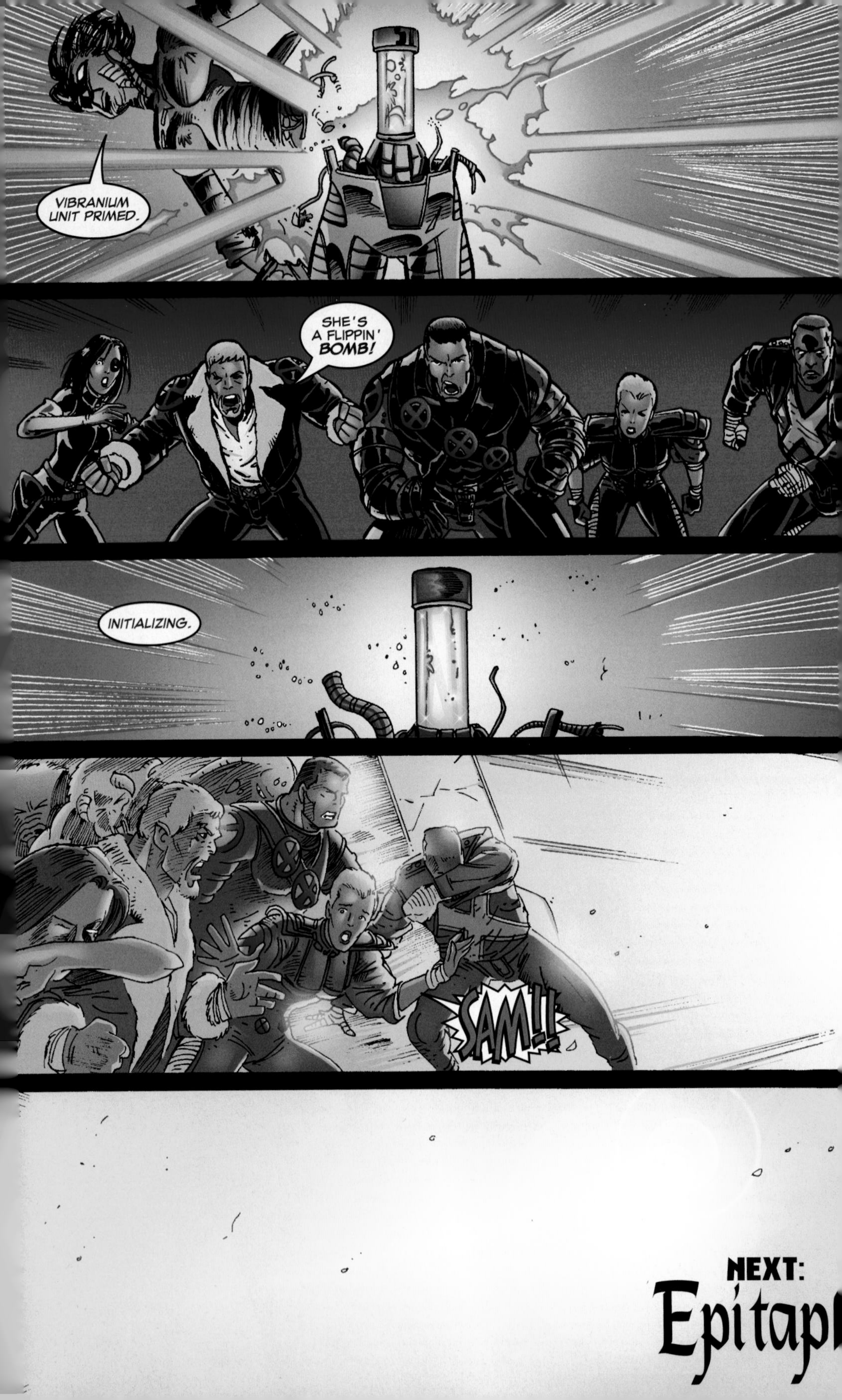
VIBRANIUM UNIT PRIMED.
SHE'S A FLIPPIN' BOMB!
INITIALIZING.
SAM!!
NEXT:
Epitaph

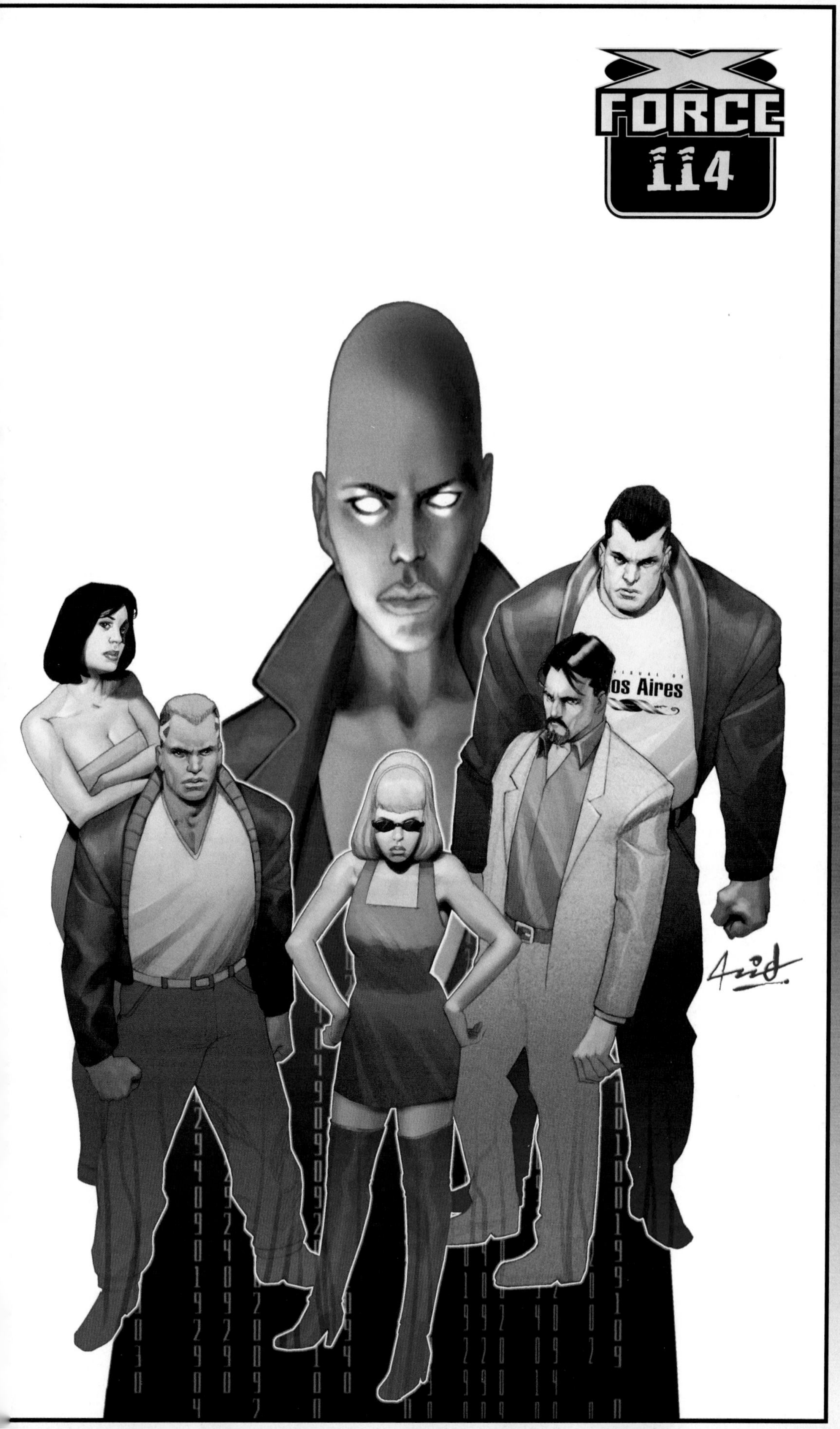
X FORCE
114
os Aires

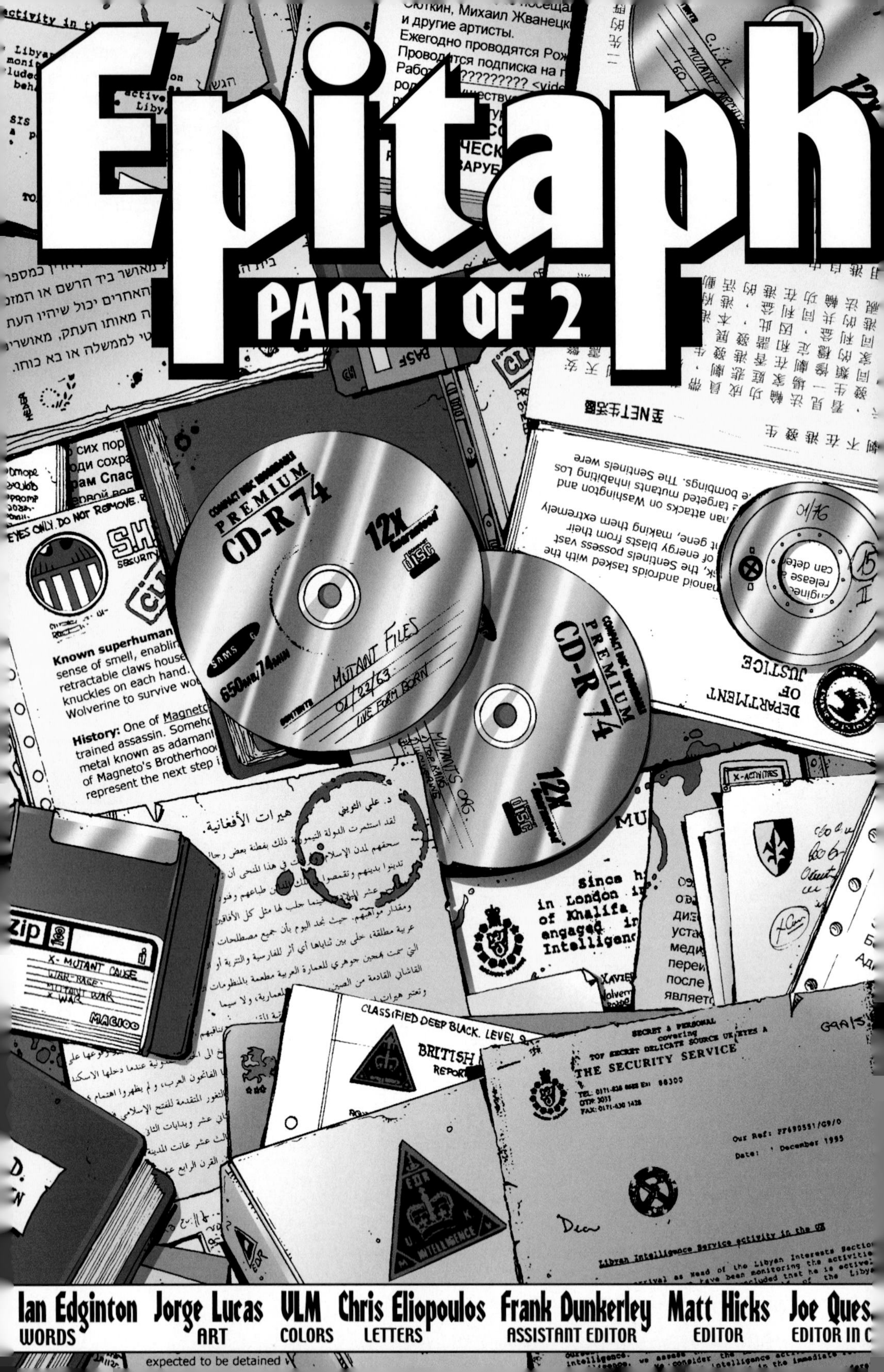
Epitaph
PART 1 OF 2
Ian Edginton WORDS
Jorge Lucas ART
ULM COLORS
Chris Eliopoulos LETTERS
Frank Dunkerley ASSISTANT EDITOR
Matt Hicks EDITOR
Joe Ques... EDITOR IN C...

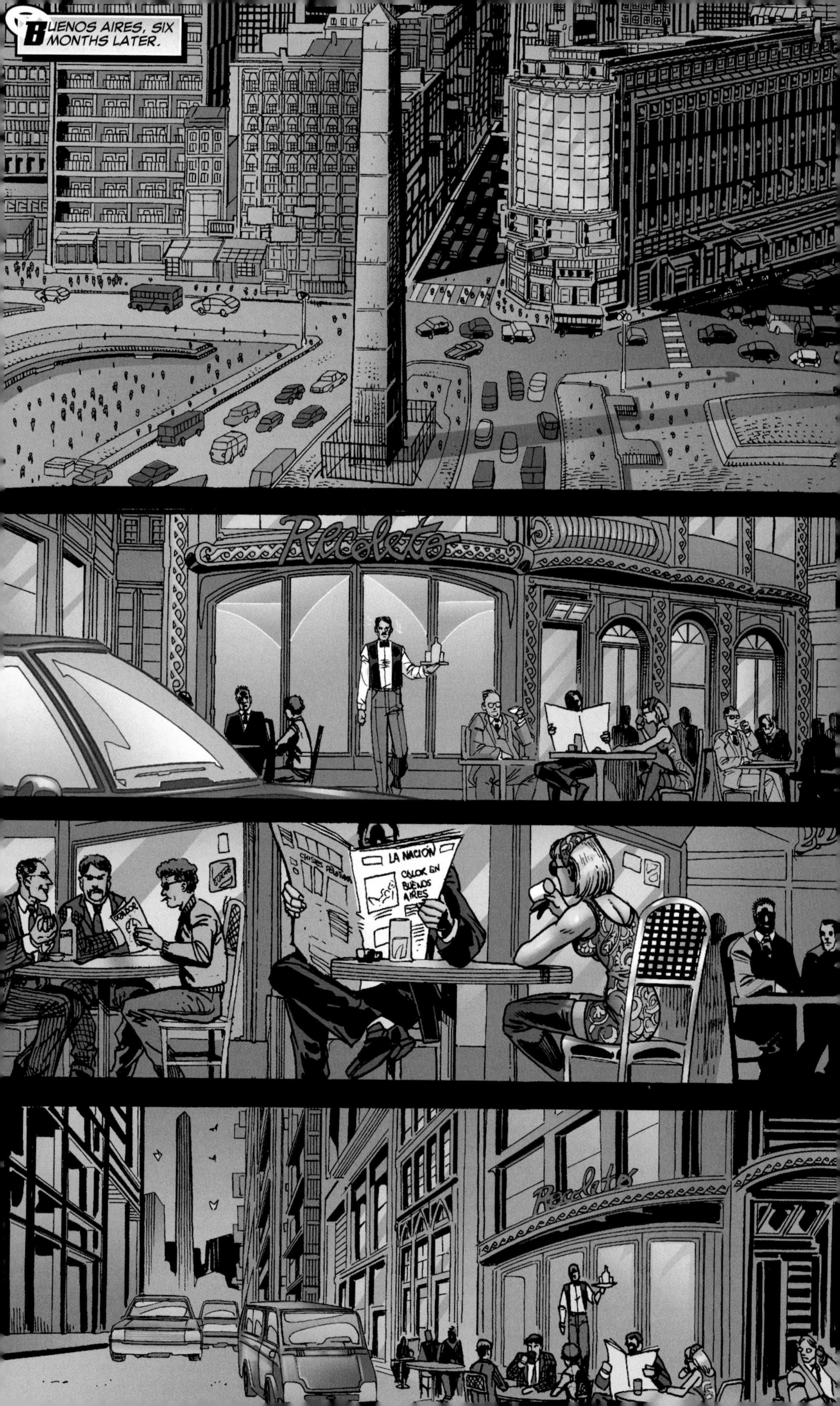
BUENOS AIRES, SIX MONTHS LATER.
Recoleta
LA NACIÓN
CALOR EN BUENOS AIRES

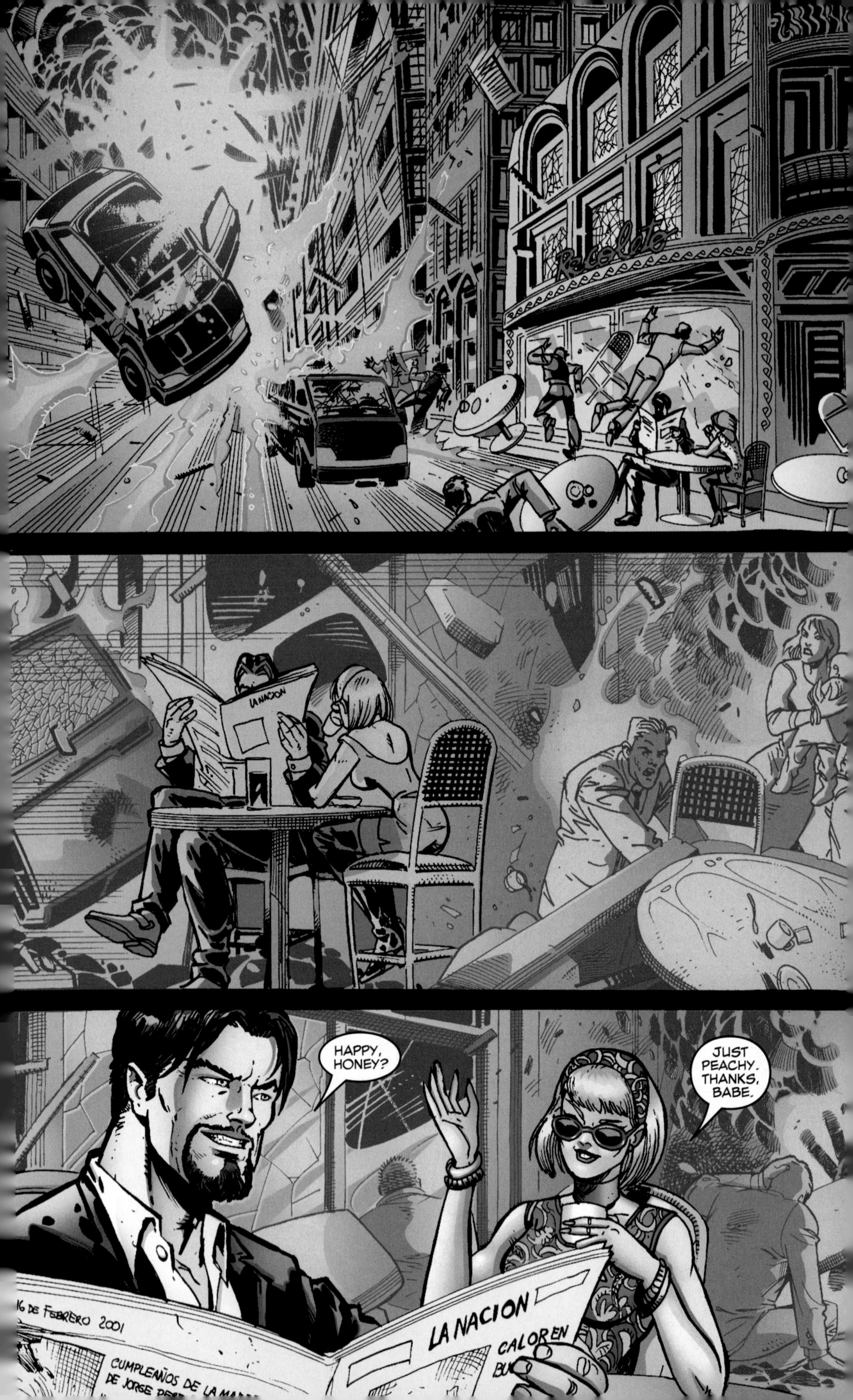
Recoleta
LA NACION
HAPPY, HONEY?
JUST PEACHY. THANKS, BABE.
16 DE FEBRERO 2001
LA NACION
CALOR EN
CUMPLEAÑOS DE LA
DE JORGE

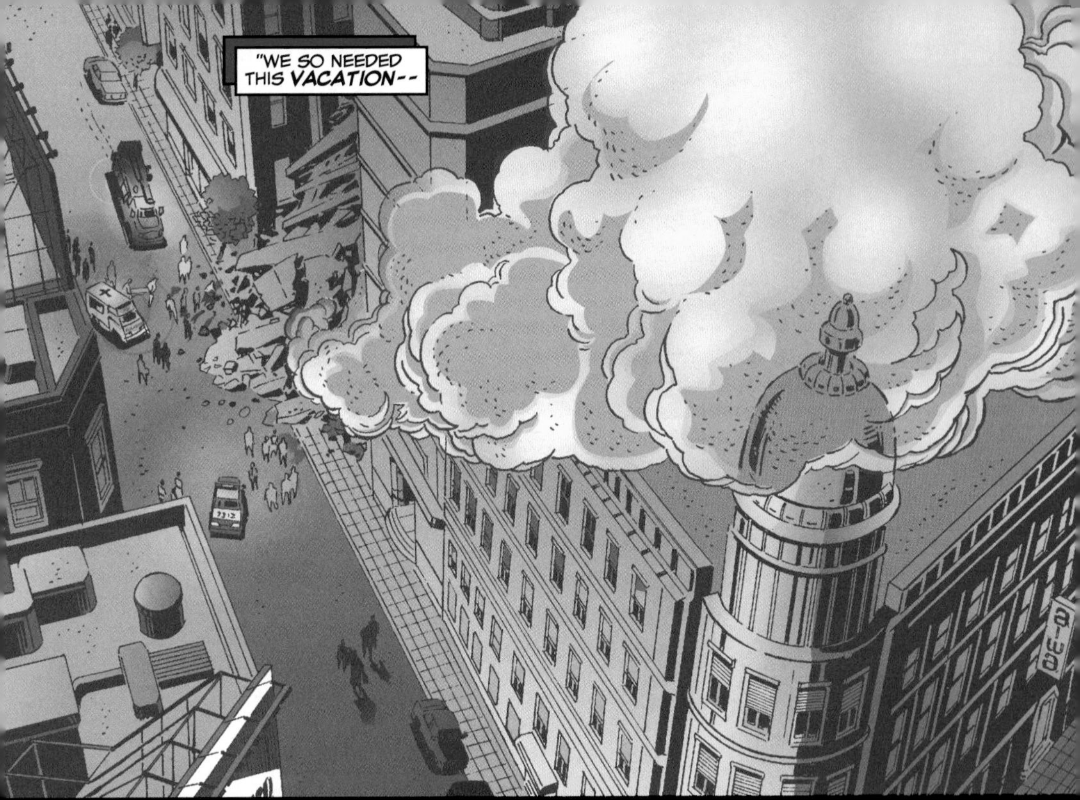

"WE SO NEEDED THIS VACATION--

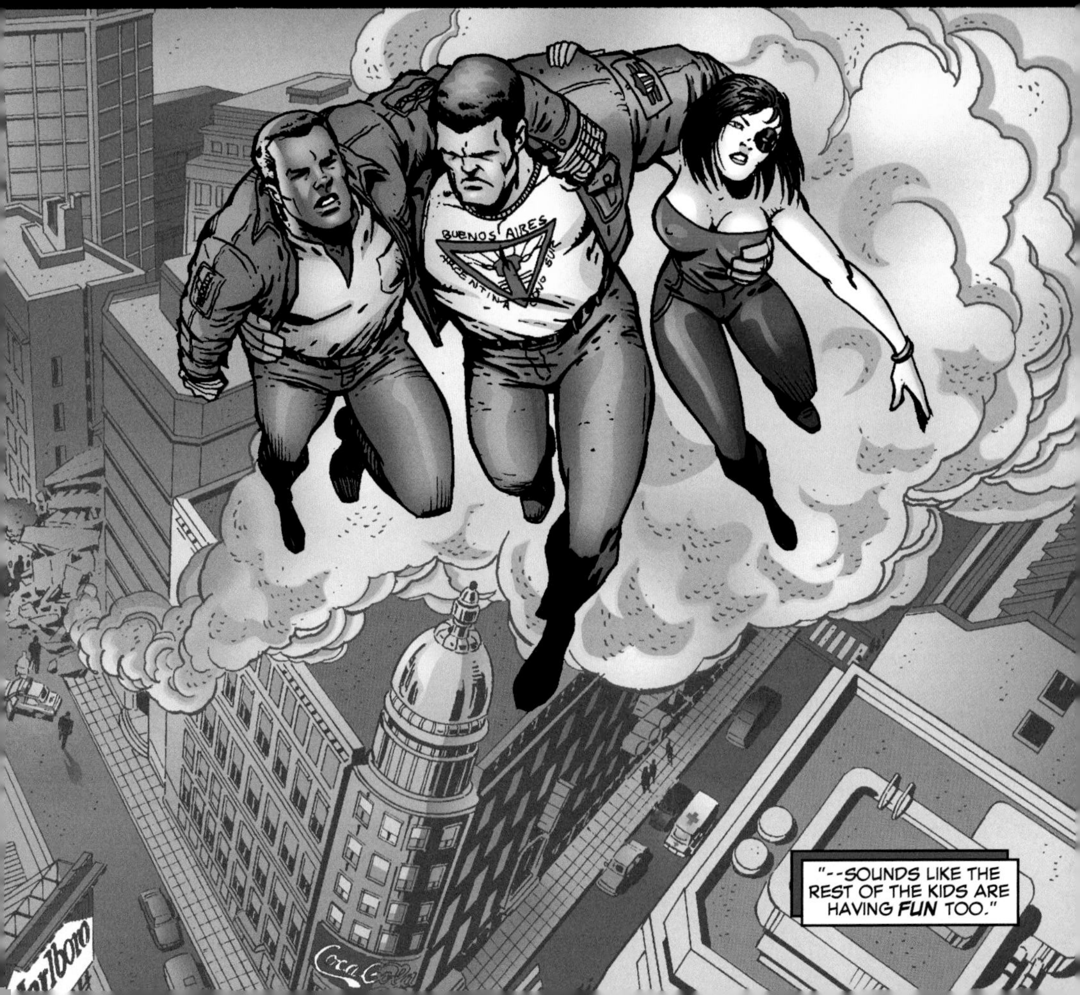

BUENOS AIRES
ARGENTINA
"--SOUNDS LIKE THE REST OF THE KIDS ARE HAVING FUN TOO."

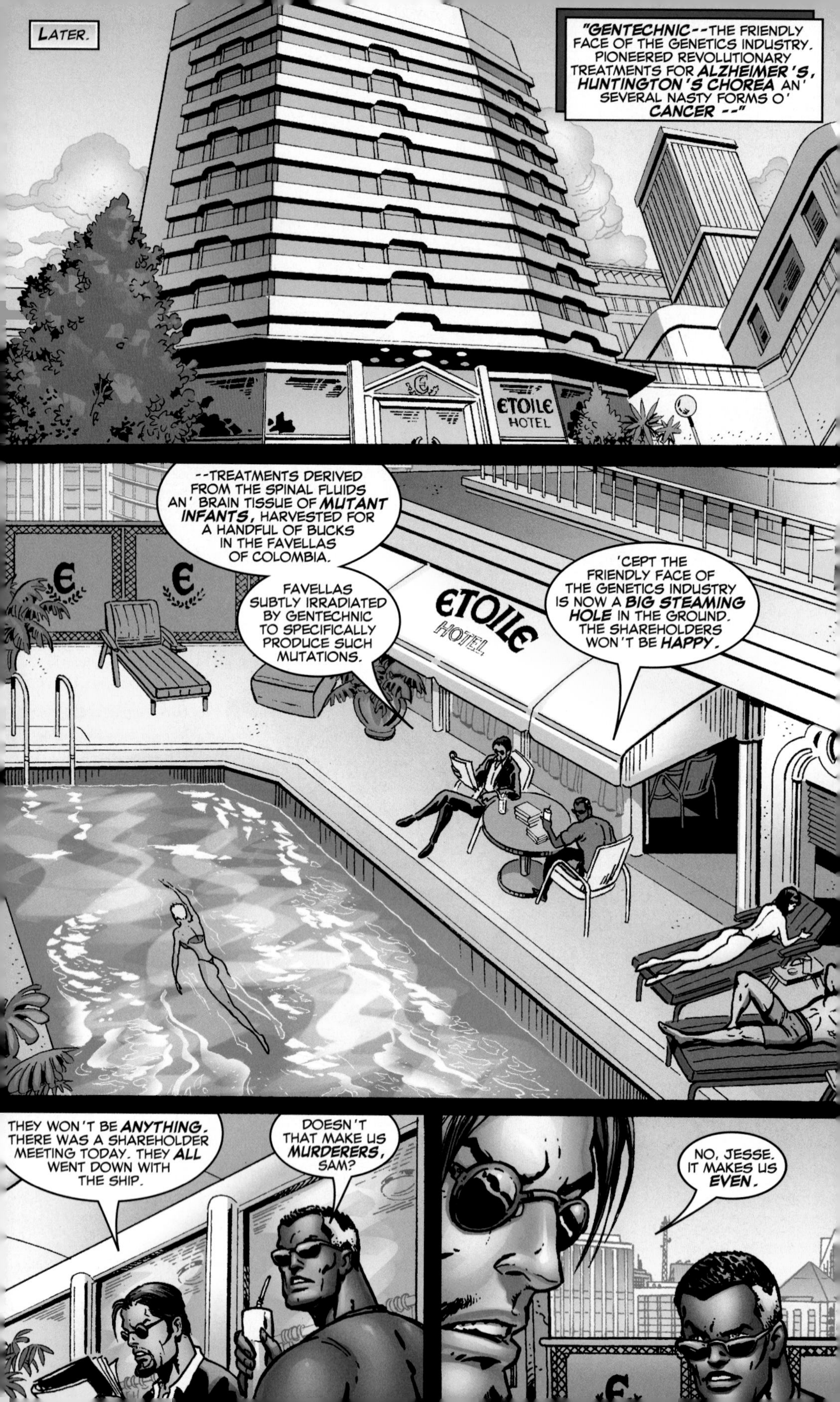
LATER.
"GENTECHNIC--THE FRIENDLY FACE OF THE GENETICS INDUSTRY. PIONEERED REVOLUTIONARY TREATMENTS FOR ALZHEIMER'S, HUNTINGTON'S CHOREA AN' SEVERAL NASTY FORMS O' CANCER--"
ETOILE HOTEL
--TREATMENTS DERIVED FROM THE SPINAL FLUIDS AN' BRAIN TISSUE OF MUTANT INFANTS, HARVESTED FOR A HANDFUL OF BUCKS IN THE FAVELLAS OF COLOMBIA.
FAVELLAS SUBTLY IRRADIATED BY GENTECHNIC TO SPECIFICALLY PRODUCE SUCH MUTATIONS.
ETOILE HOTEL
'CEPT THE FRIENDLY FACE OF THE GENETICS INDUSTRY IS NOW A BIG STEAMING HOLE IN THE GROUND. THE SHAREHOLDERS WON'T BE HAPPY.
THEY WON'T BE ANYTHING. THERE WAS A SHAREHOLDER MEETING TODAY. THEY ALL WENT DOWN WITH THE SHIP.
DOESN'T THAT MAKE US MURDERERS, SAM?
NO, JESSE. IT MAKES US EVEN.

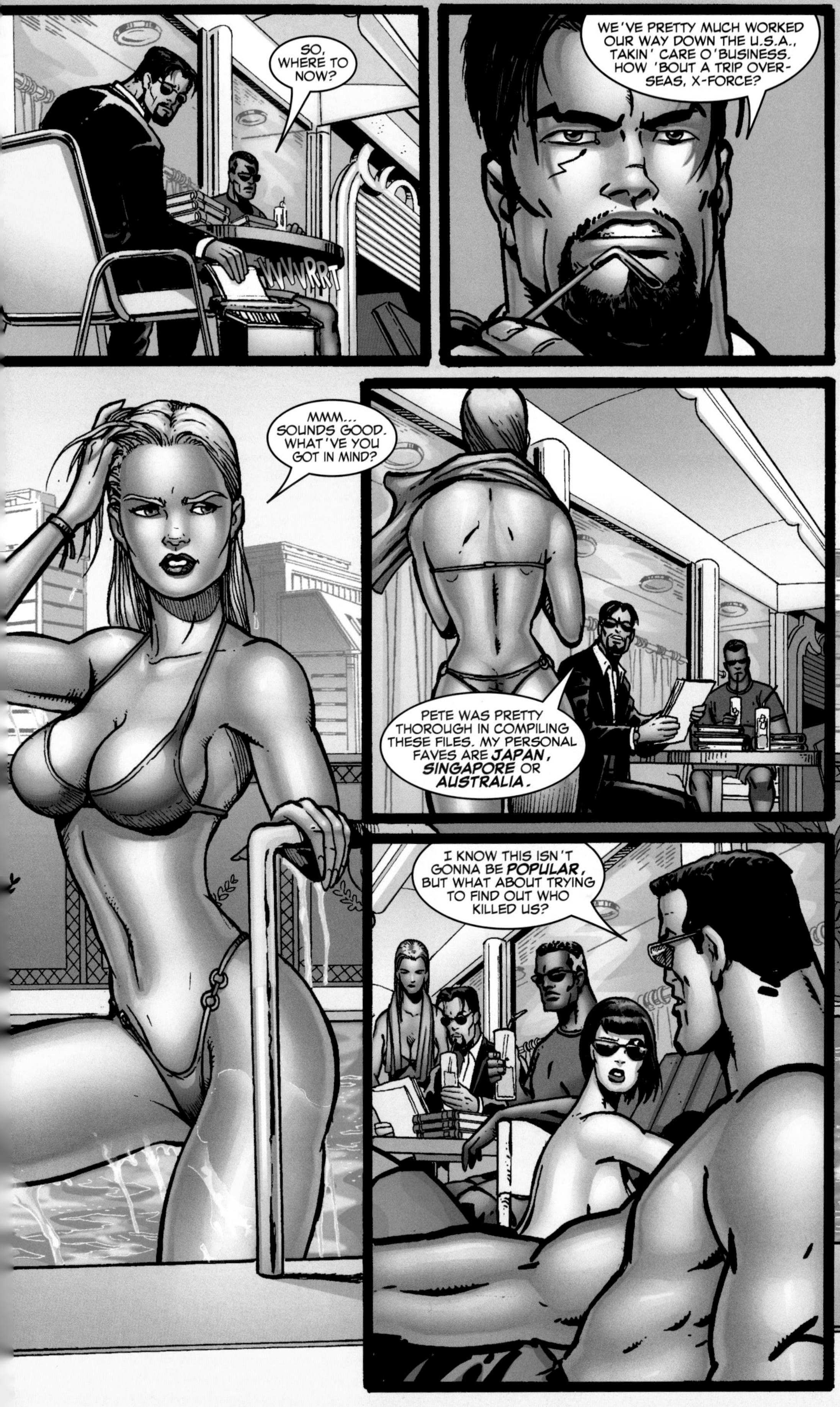
SO, WHERE TO NOW?
VVVVRRRT
WE'VE PRETTY MUCH WORKED OUR WAY DOWN THE U.S.A., TAKIN' CARE O'BUSINESS. HOW 'BOUT A TRIP OVER-SEAS, X-FORCE?
MMM... SOUNDS GOOD. WHAT'VE YOU GOT IN MIND?
PETE WAS PRETTY THOROUGH IN COMPILING THESE FILES. MY PERSONAL FAVES ARE ***JAPAN***, ***SINGAPORE*** OR ***AUSTRALIA***.
I KNOW THIS ISN'T GONNA BE ***POPULAR***, BUT WHAT ABOUT TRYING TO FIND OUT WHO KILLED US?

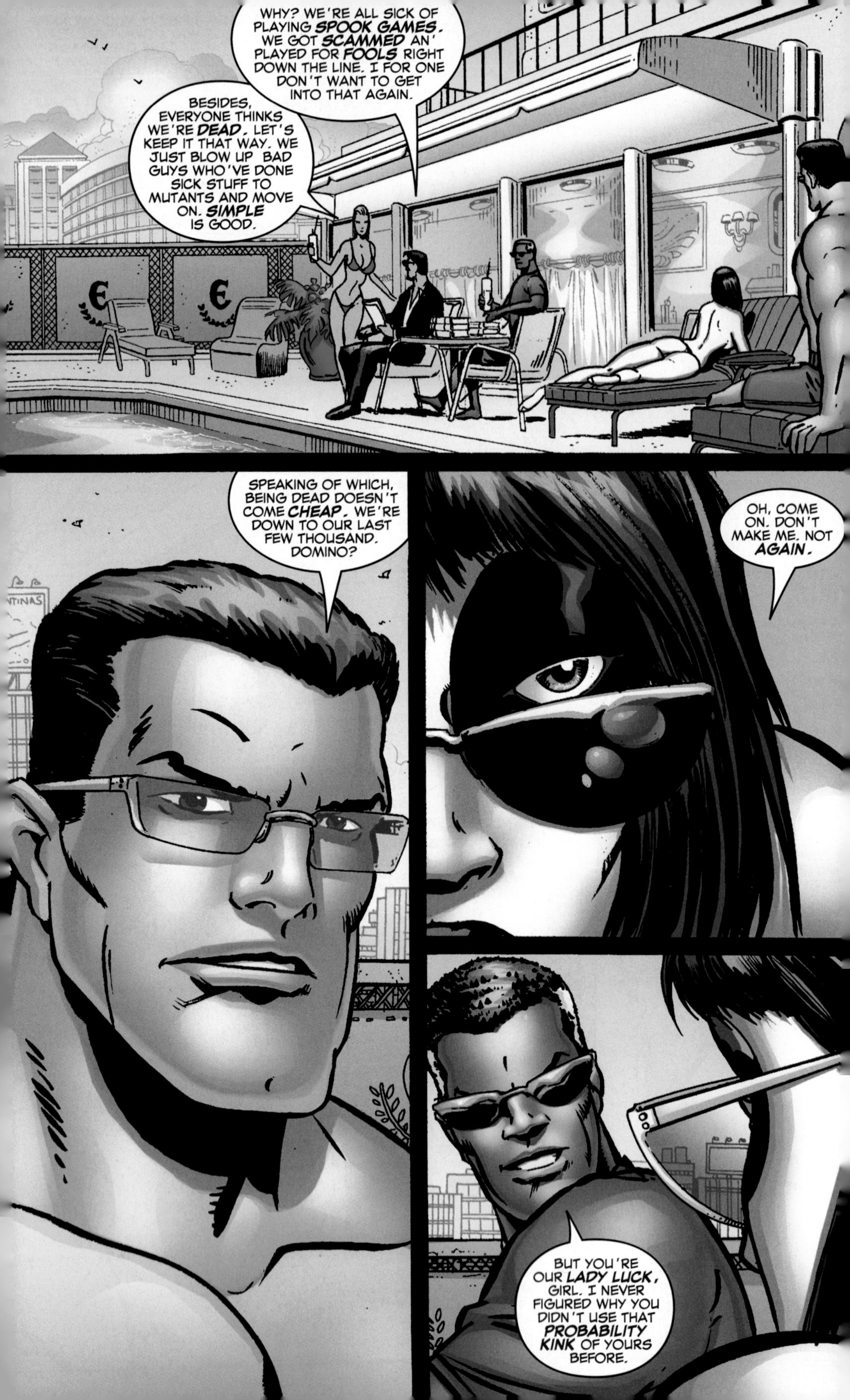
WHY? WE'RE ALL SICK OF PLAYING SPOOK GAMES. WE GOT SCAMMED AN' PLAYED FOR FOOLS RIGHT DOWN THE LINE. I FOR ONE DON'T WANT TO GET INTO THAT AGAIN.
BESIDES, EVERYONE THINKS WE'RE DEAD. LET'S KEEP IT THAT WAY. WE JUST BLOW UP BAD GUYS WHO'VE DONE SICK STUFF TO MUTANTS AND MOVE ON. SIMPLE IS GOOD.
SPEAKING OF WHICH, BEING DEAD DOESN'T COME CHEAP. WE'RE DOWN TO OUR LAST FEW THOUSAND. DOMINO?
OH, COME ON. DON'T MAKE ME. NOT AGAIN.
BUT YOU'RE OUR LADY LUCK, GIRL. I NEVER FIGURED WHY YOU DIDN'T USE THAT PROBABILITY KINK OF YOURS BEFORE.

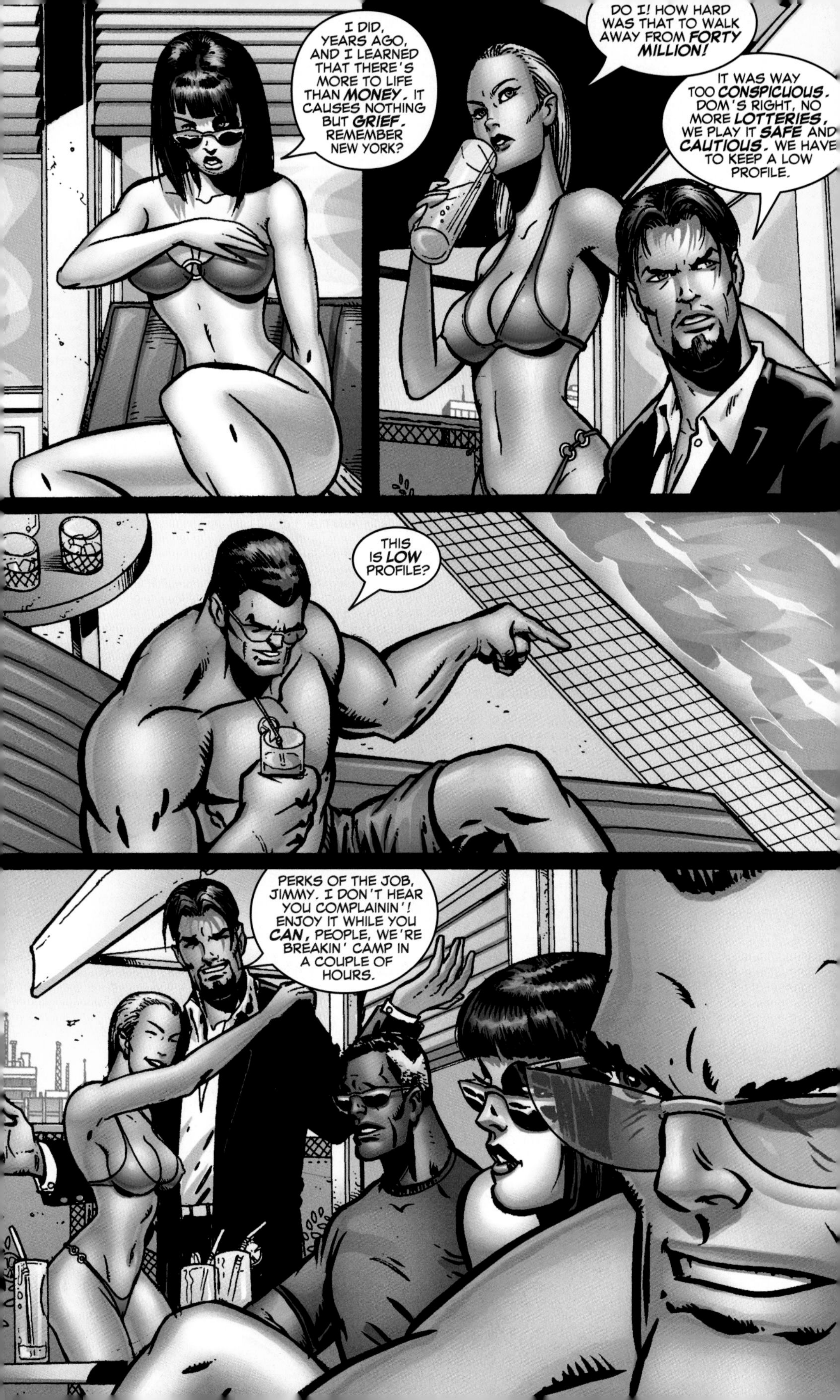
I DID, YEARS AGO, AND I LEARNED THAT THERE'S MORE TO LIFE THAN MONEY. IT CAUSES NOTHING BUT GRIEF. REMEMBER NEW YORK?
DO I! HOW HARD WAS THAT TO WALK AWAY FROM FORTY MILLION!
IT WAS WAY TOO CONSPICUOUS. DOM'S RIGHT, NO MORE LOTTERIES, WE PLAY IT SAFE AND CAUTIOUS. WE HAVE TO KEEP A LOW PROFILE.
THIS IS LOW PROFILE?
PERKS OF THE JOB, JIMMY. I DON'T HEAR YOU COMPLAININ'! ENJOY IT WHILE YOU CAN, PEOPLE, WE'RE BREAKIN' CAMP IN A COUPLE OF HOURS.

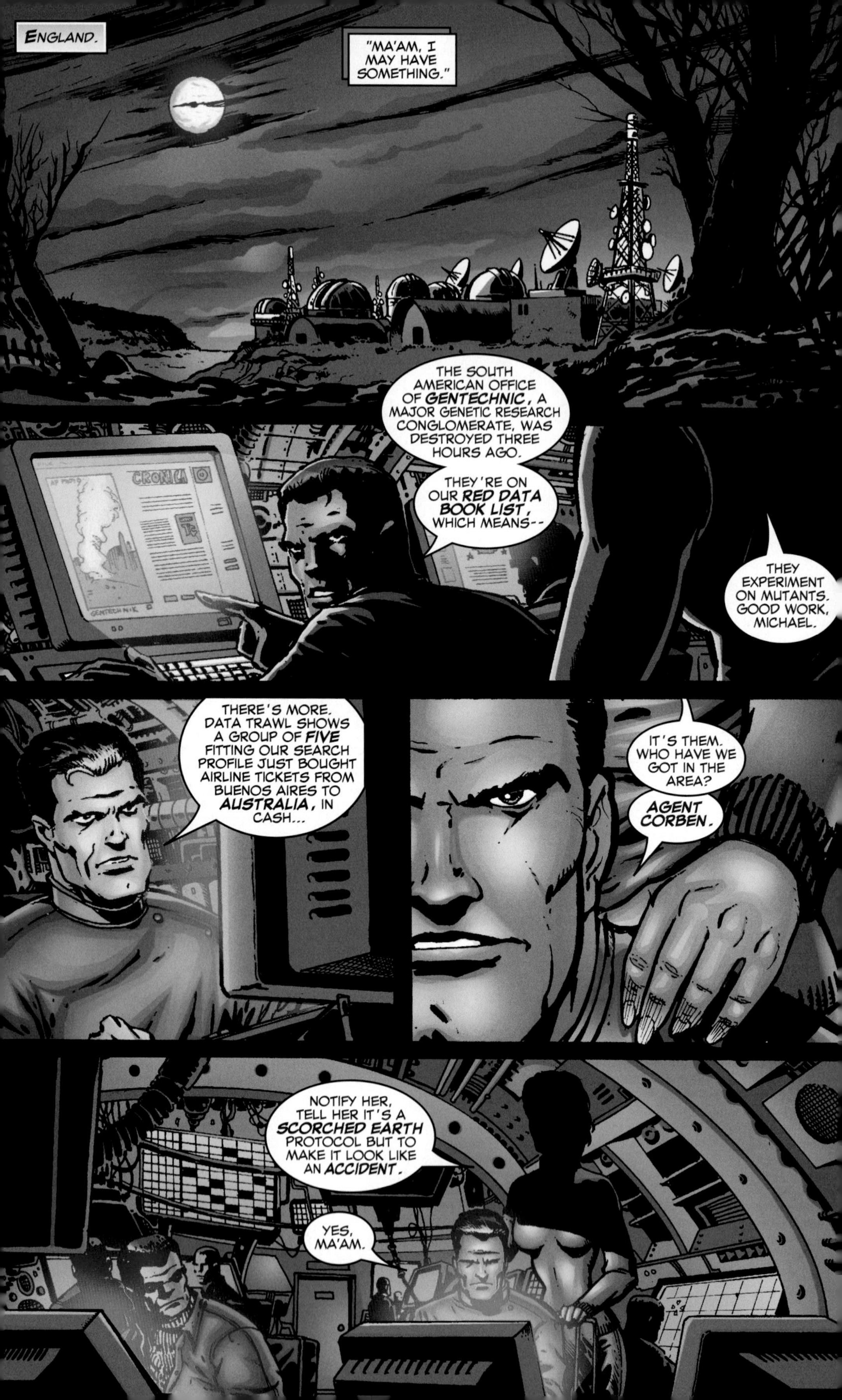
ENGLAND.
"MA'AM, I MAY HAVE SOMETHING."
THE SOUTH AMERICAN OFFICE OF GENTECHNIC, A MAJOR GENETIC RESEARCH CONGLOMERATE, WAS DESTROYED THREE HOURS AGO.
THEY'RE ON OUR RED DATA BOOK LIST, WHICH MEANS--
THEY EXPERIMENT ON MUTANTS. GOOD WORK, MICHAEL.
THERE'S MORE. DATA TRAWL SHOWS A GROUP OF FIVE FITTING OUR SEARCH PROFILE JUST BOUGHT AIRLINE TICKETS FROM BUENOS AIRES TO AUSTRALIA, IN CASH...
IT'S THEM. WHO HAVE WE GOT IN THE AREA?
AGENT CORBEN.
NOTIFY HER, TELL HER IT'S A SCORCHED EARTH PROTOCOL BUT TO MAKE IT LOOK LIKE AN ACCIDENT.
YES, MA'AM.

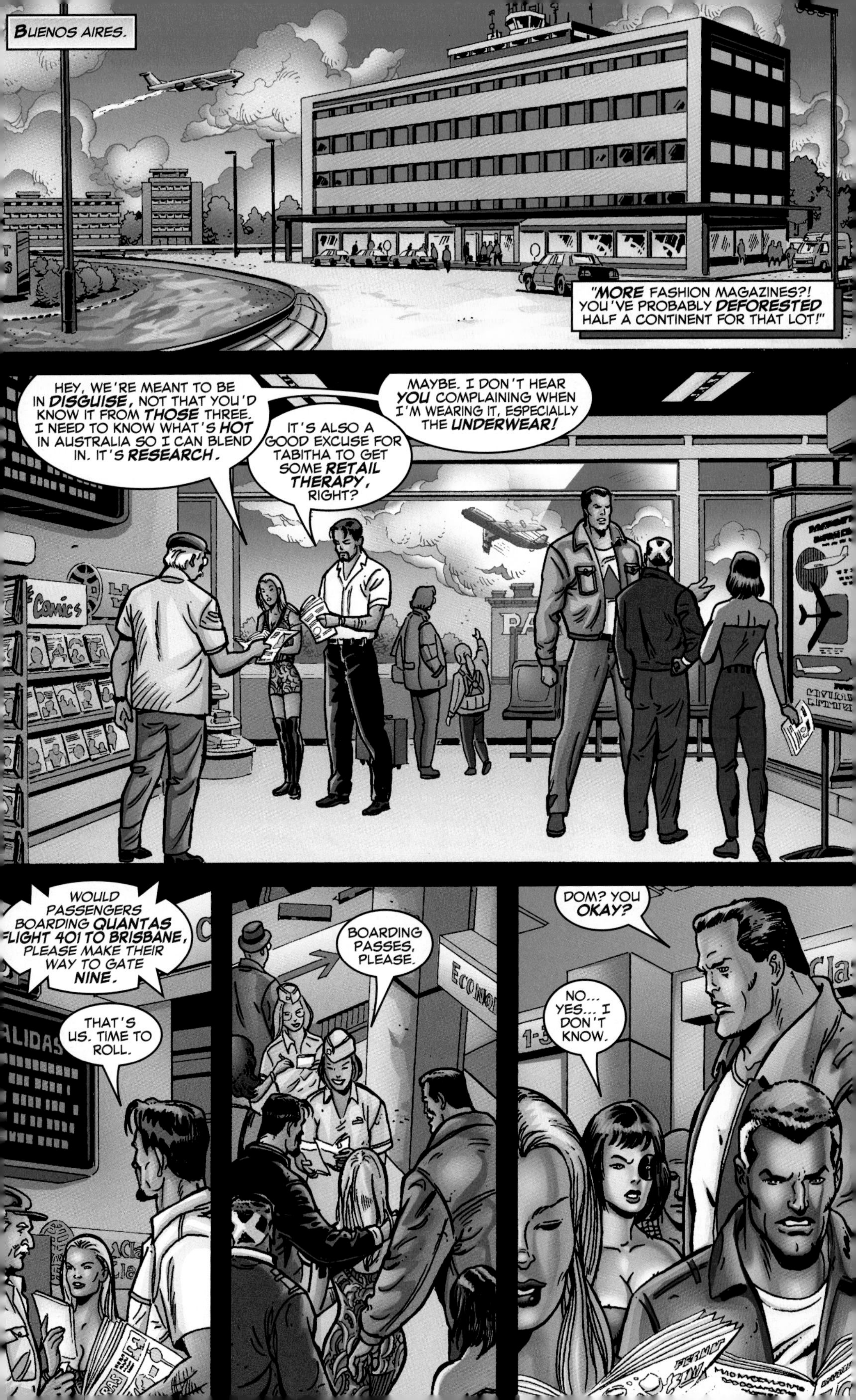
BUENOS AIRES.
"MORE FASHION MAGAZINES?! YOU'VE PROBABLY DEFORESTED HALF A CONTINENT FOR THAT LOT!"
HEY, WE'RE MEANT TO BE IN DISGUISE, NOT THAT YOU'D KNOW IT FROM THOSE THREE. I NEED TO KNOW WHAT'S HOT IN AUSTRALIA SO I CAN BLEND IN. IT'S RESEARCH.
IT'S ALSO A GOOD EXCUSE FOR TABITHA TO GET SOME RETAIL THERAPY, RIGHT?
MAYBE. I DON'T HEAR YOU COMPLAINING WHEN I'M WEARING IT, ESPECIALLY THE UNDERWEAR!
Comics
WOULD PASSENGERS BOARDING QUANTAS FLIGHT 401 TO BRISBANE, PLEASE MAKE THEIR WAY TO GATE NINE.
THAT'S US. TIME TO ROLL.
BOARDING PASSES, PLEASE.
DOM? YOU OKAY?
NO... YES... I DON'T KNOW.

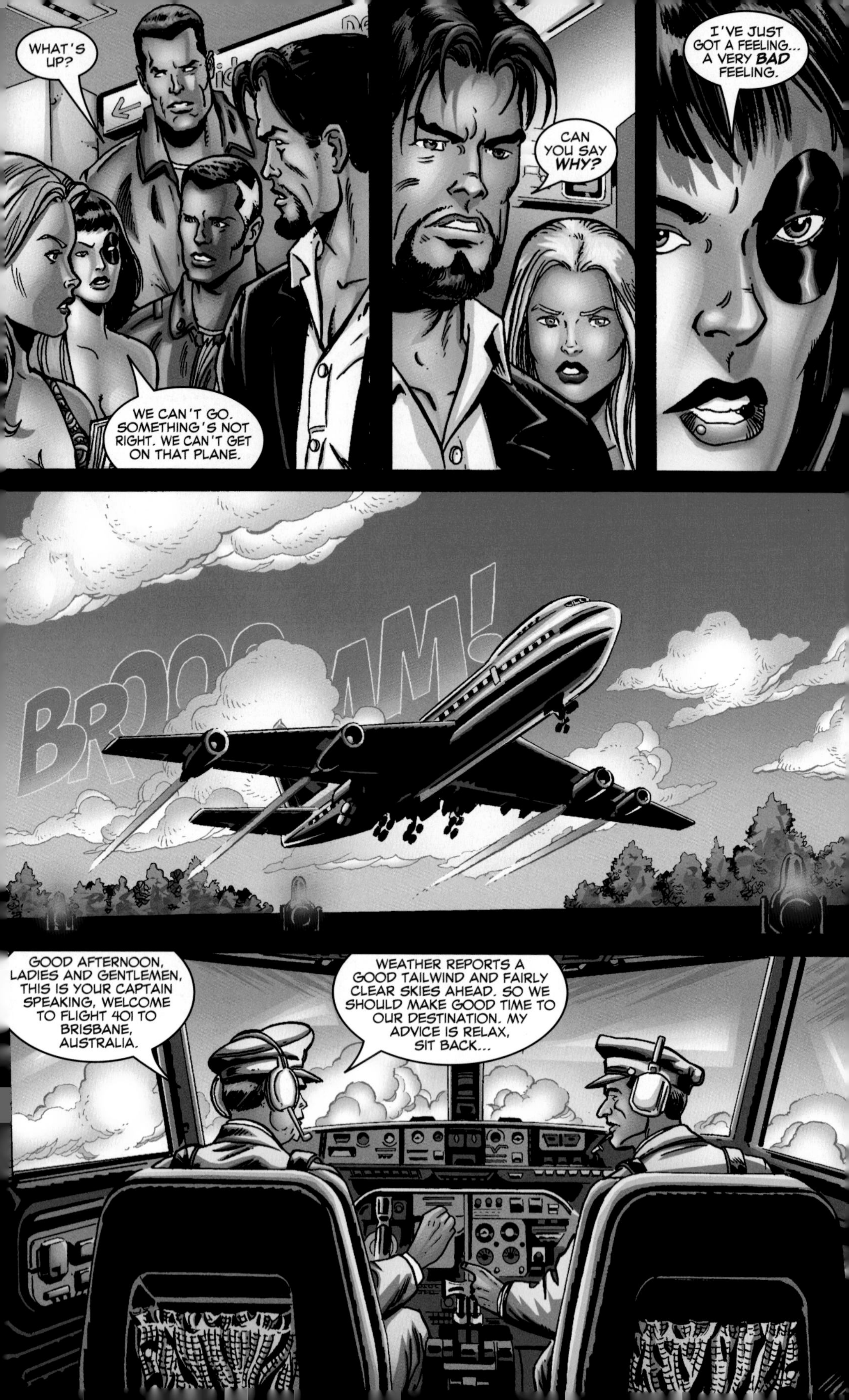
WHAT'S UP?
WE CAN'T GO. SOMETHING'S NOT RIGHT. WE CAN'T GET ON THAT PLANE.
CAN YOU SAY WHY?
I'VE JUST GOT A FEELING... A VERY BAD FEELING.
GOOD AFTERNOON, LADIES AND GENTLEMEN, THIS IS YOUR CAPTAIN SPEAKING, WELCOME TO FLIGHT 401 TO BRISBANE, AUSTRALIA.
WEATHER REPORTS A GOOD TAILWIND AND FAIRLY CLEAR SKIES AHEAD. SO WE SHOULD MAKE GOOD TIME TO OUR DESTINATION. MY ADVICE IS RELAX, SIT BACK...

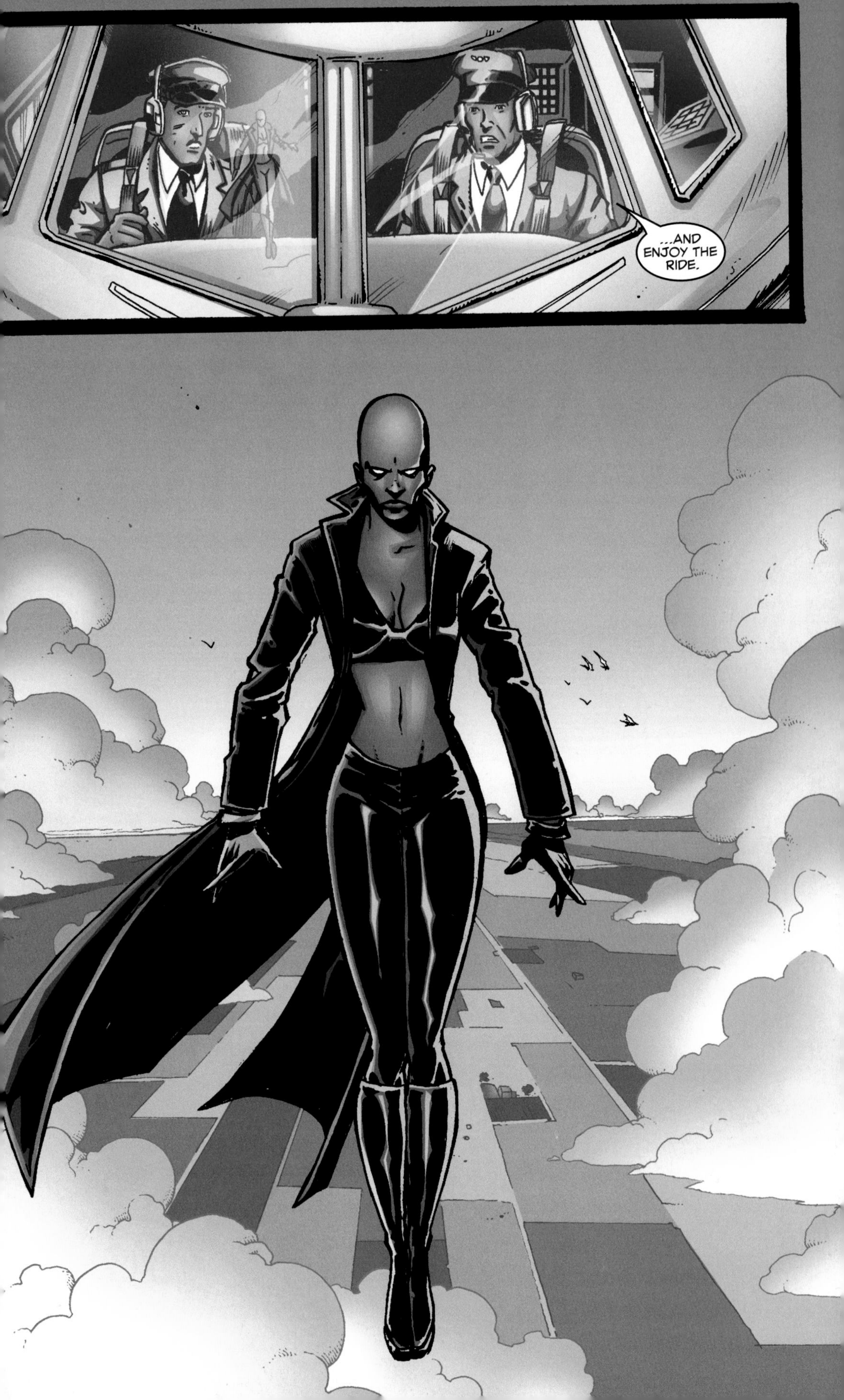
...AND ENJOY THE RIDE.

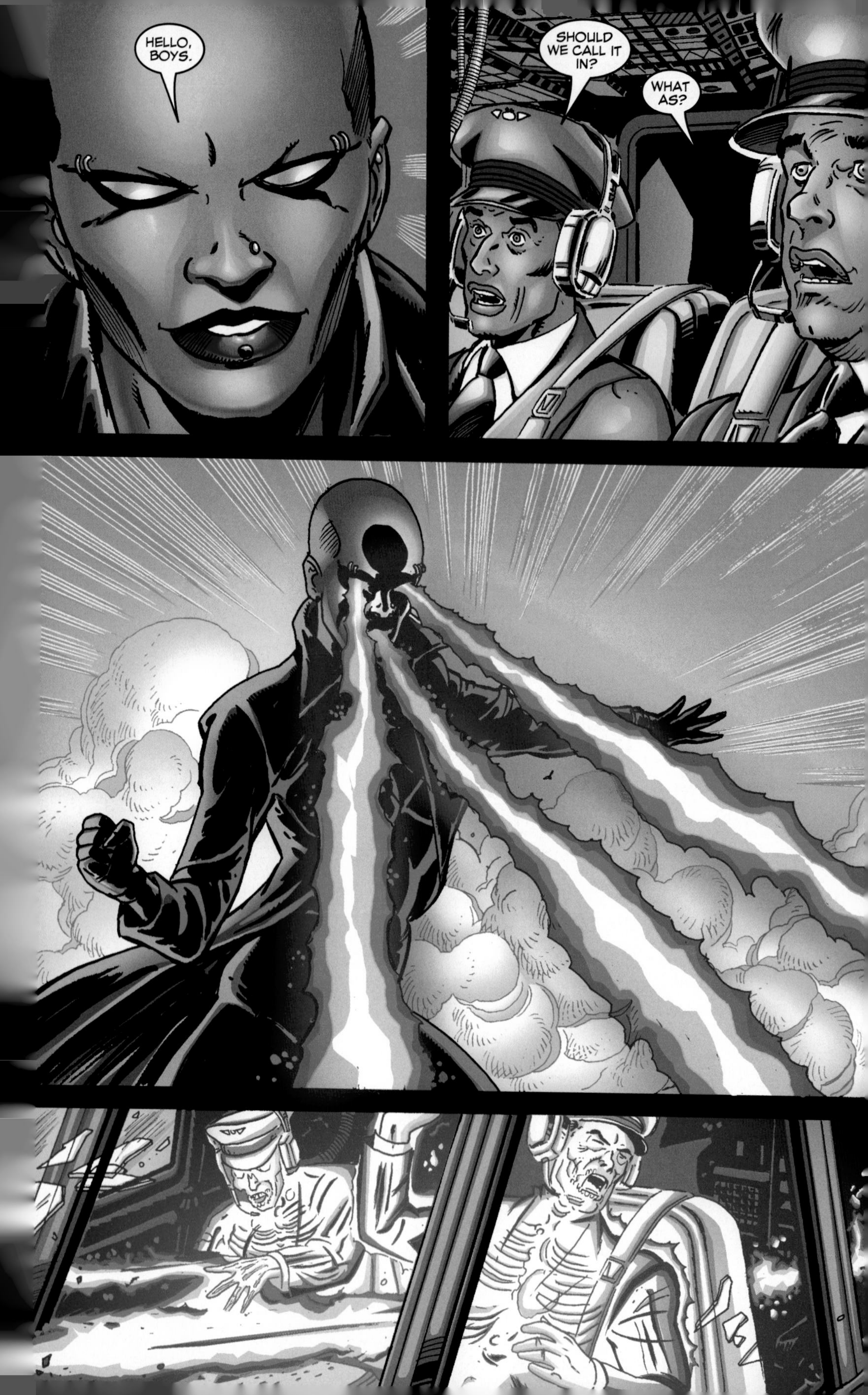
HELLO, BOYS.
SHOULD WE CALL IT IN?
WHAT AS?

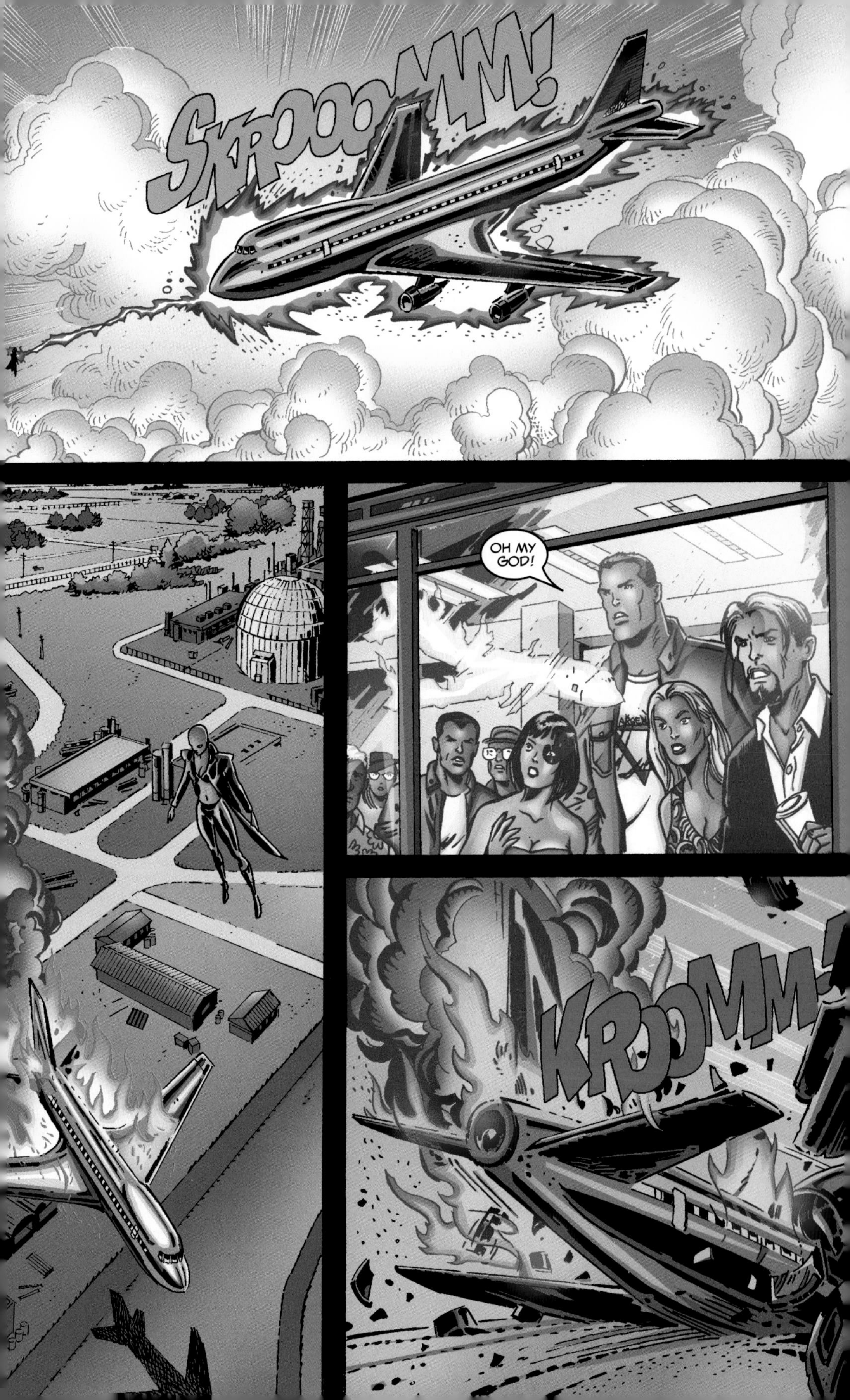
SKROOOMMM!
OH MY GOD!
KROOMM!

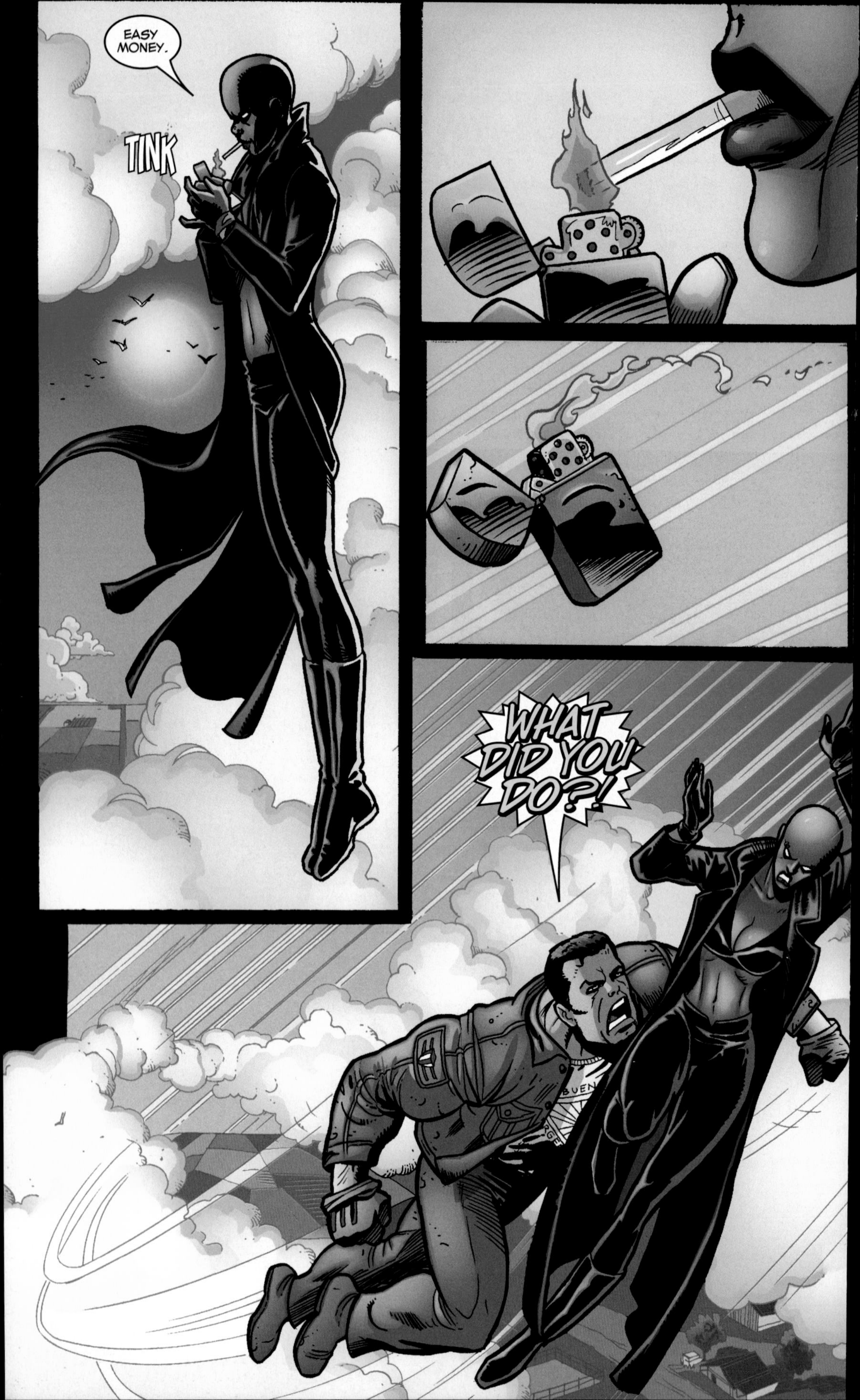
EASY MONEY.
TINK
WHAT DID YOU DO?!

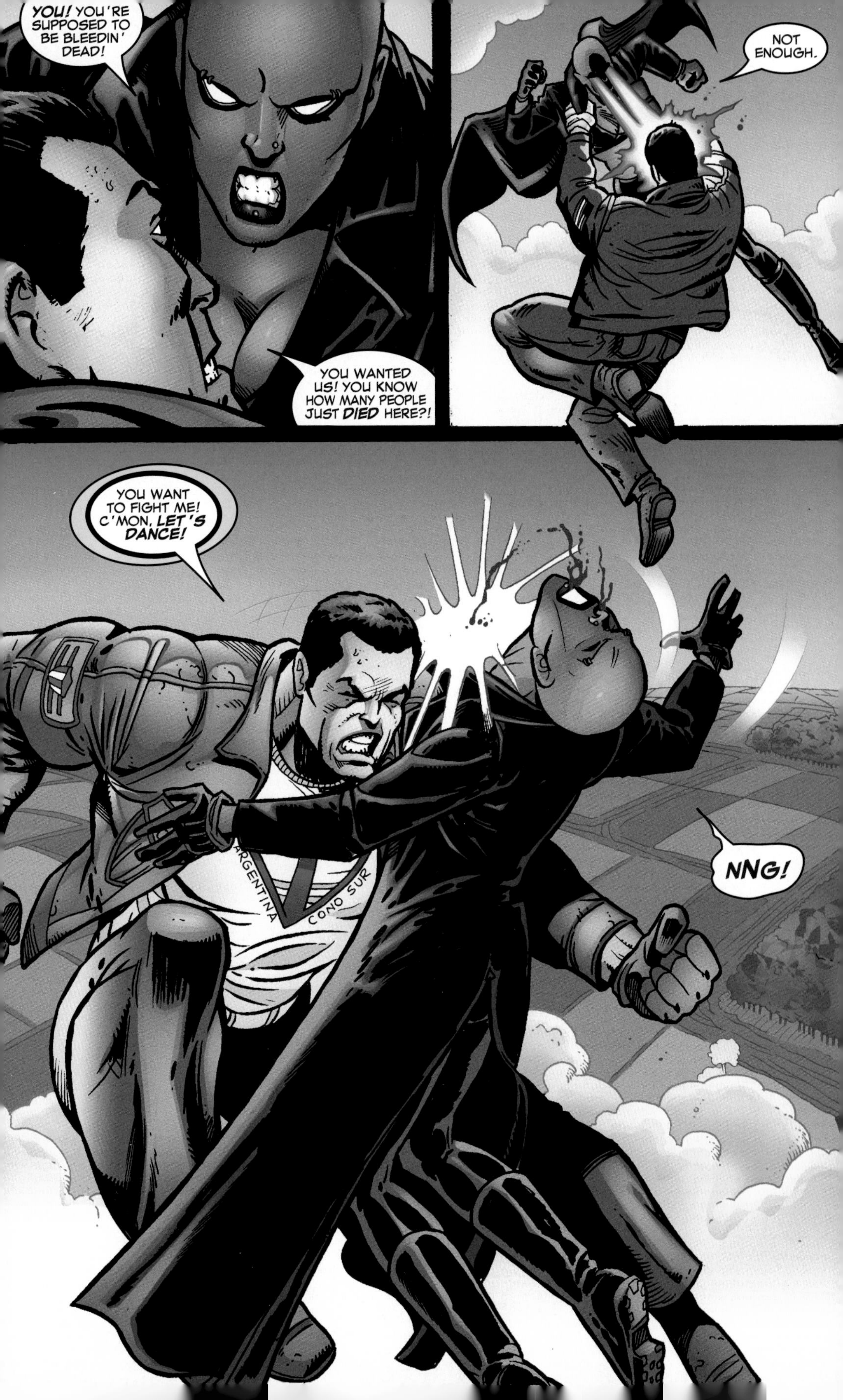
YOU! YOU'RE SUPPOSED TO BE BLEEDIN' DEAD!
YOU WANTED US! YOU KNOW HOW MANY PEOPLE JUST DIED HERE?!
NOT ENOUGH.
YOU WANT TO FIGHT ME! C'MON, LET'S DANCE!
ARGENTINA
CONO SUR
NNG!

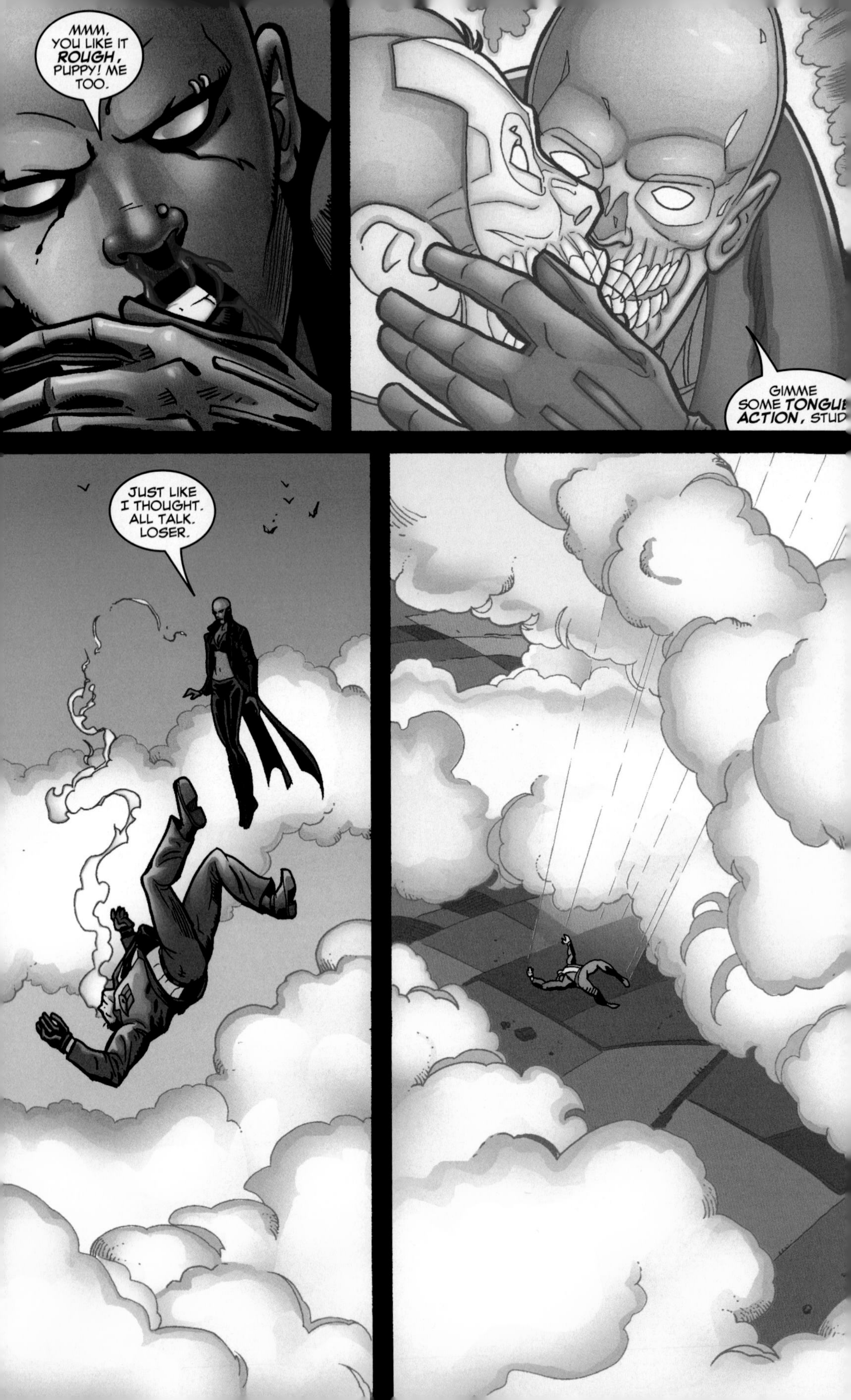
MMM, YOU LIKE IT ROUGH, PUPPY! ME TOO.
GIMME SOME TONGUE ACTION, STUD
JUST LIKE I THOUGHT. ALL TALK. LOSER.

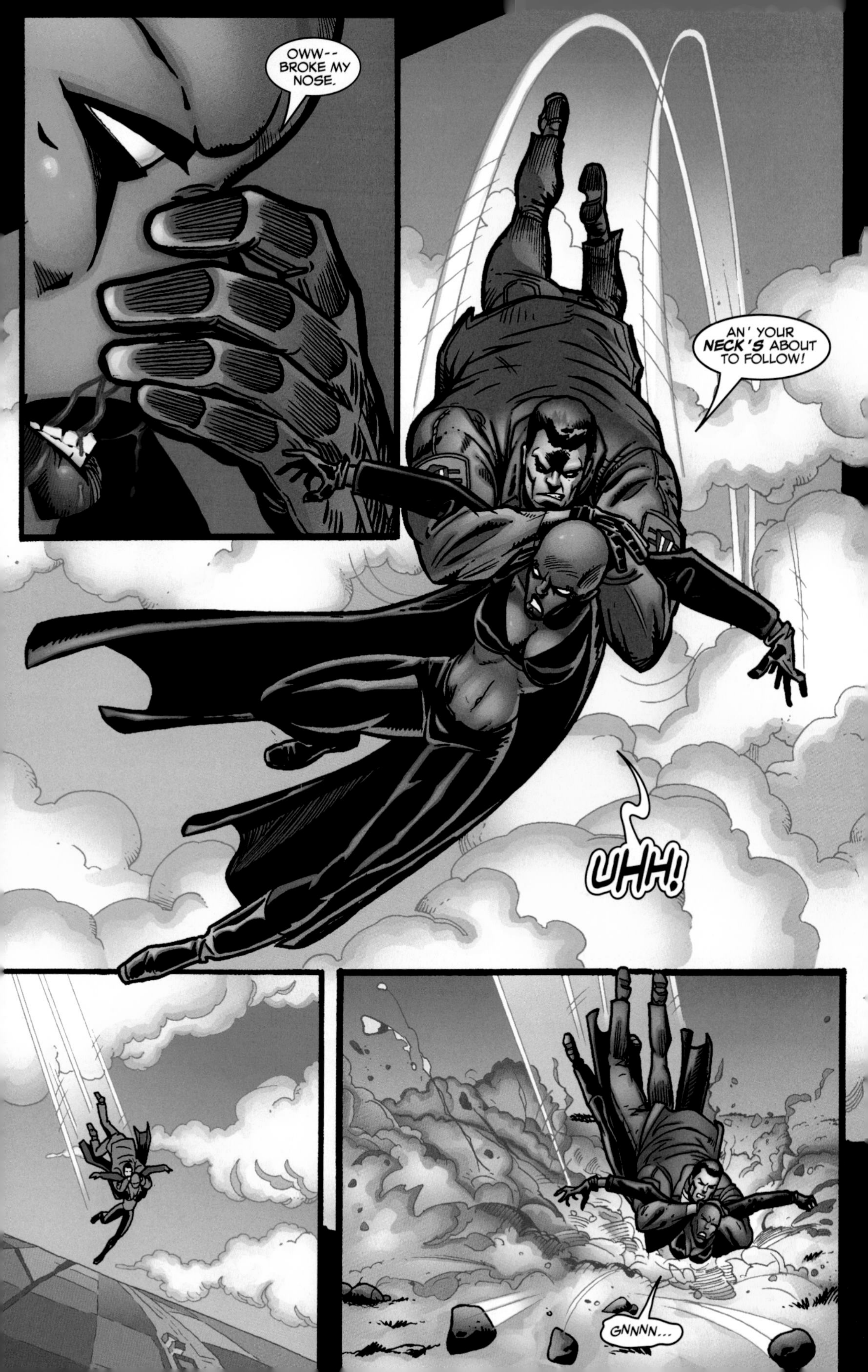
OWW--
BROKE MY
NOSE.
AN' YOUR
NECK'S ABOUT
TO FOLLOW!
UHH!
GNNNN...

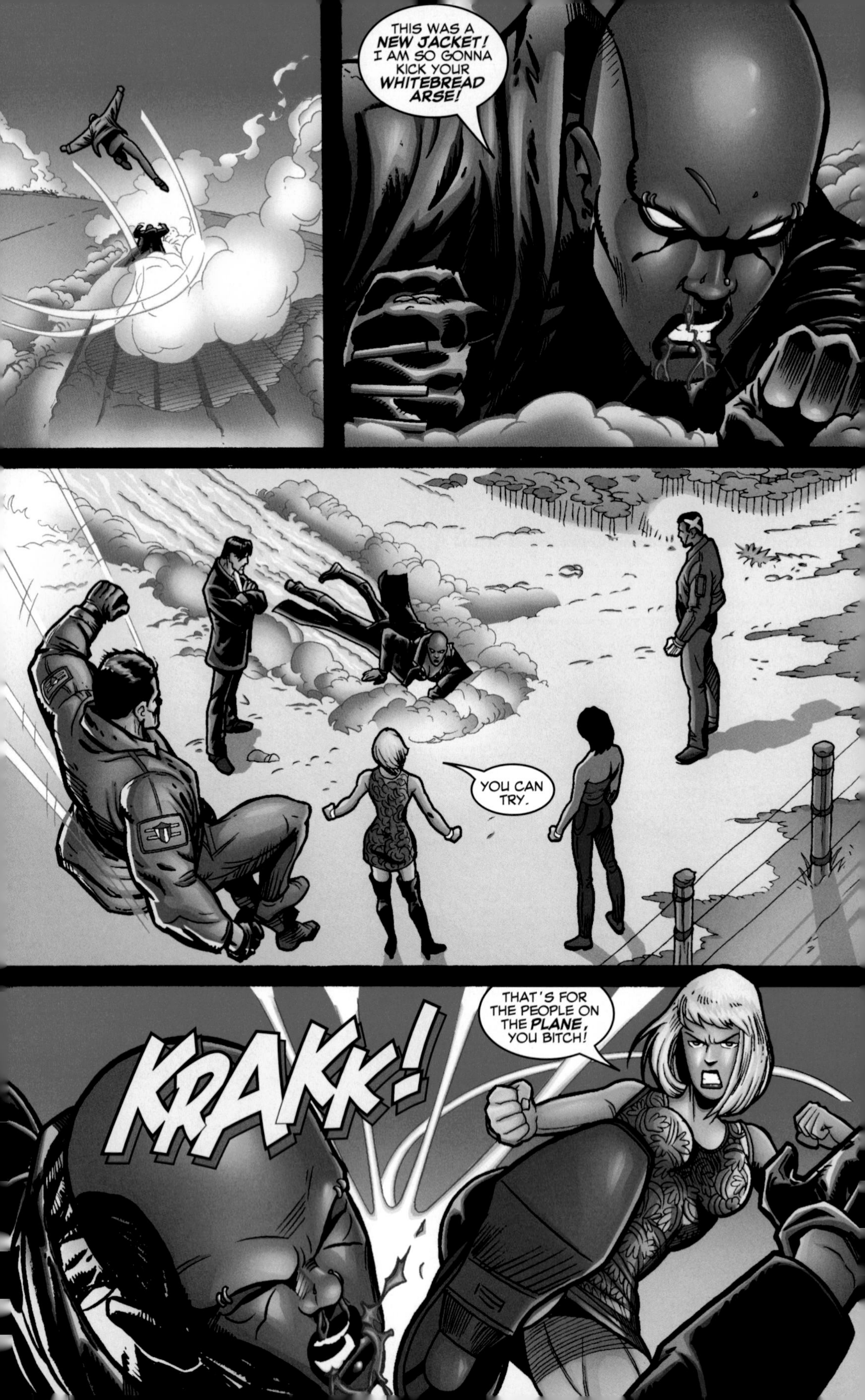
THIS WAS A NEW JACKET! I AM SO GONNA KICK YOUR WHITEBREAD ARSE!
YOU CAN TRY.
KRAKK!
THAT'S FOR THE PEOPLE ON THE PLANE, YOU BITCH!

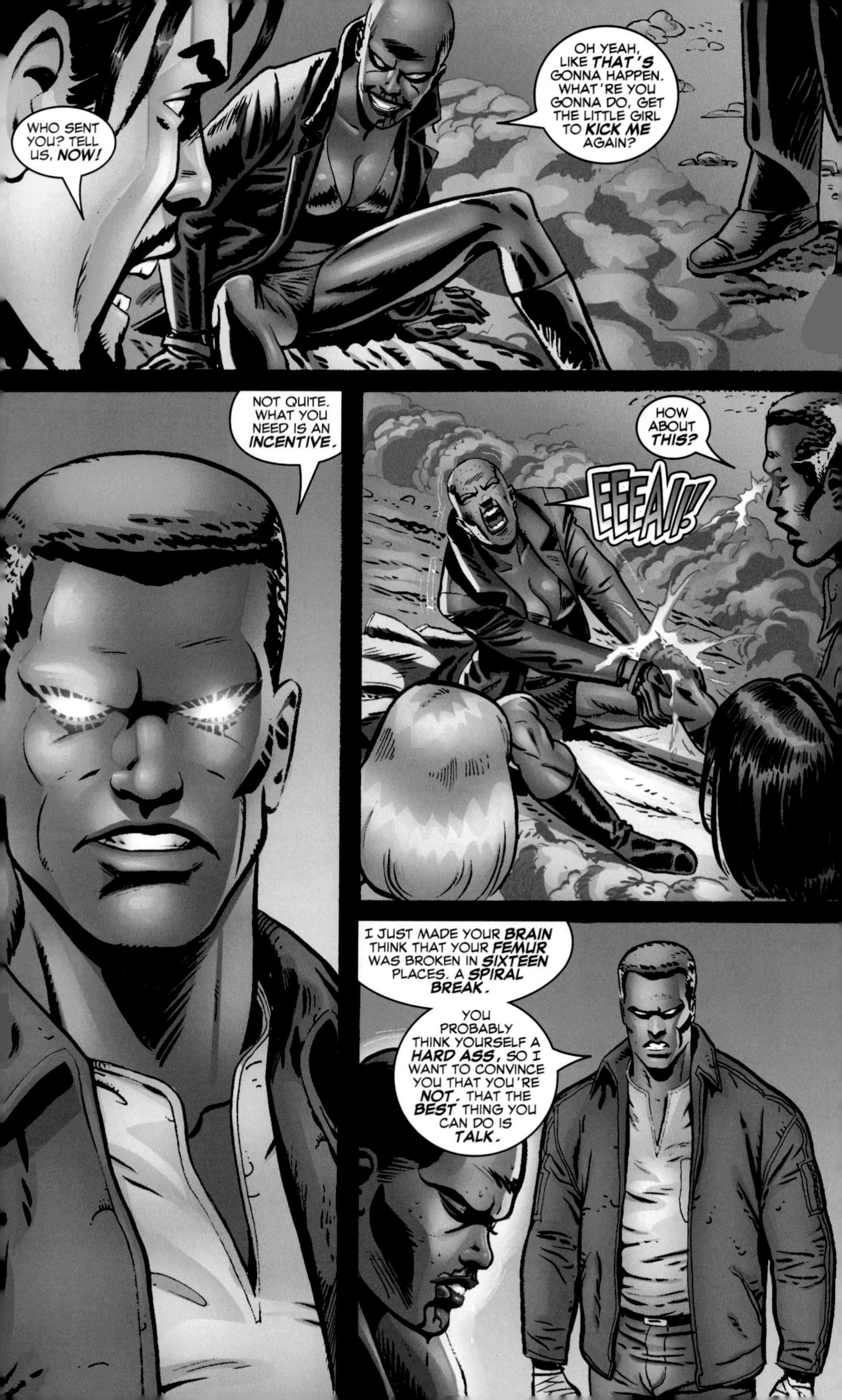
WHO SENT YOU? TELL US, NOW!
OH YEAH, LIKE THAT'S GONNA HAPPEN. WHAT'RE YOU GONNA DO, GET THE LITTLE GIRL TO KICK ME AGAIN?
NOT QUITE. WHAT YOU NEED IS AN INCENTIVE.
HOW ABOUT THIS?
EEEAII!
I JUST MADE YOUR BRAIN THINK THAT YOUR FEMUR WAS BROKEN IN SIXTEEN PLACES. A SPIRAL BREAK.
YOU PROBABLY THINK YOURSELF A HARD ASS, SO I WANT TO CONVINCE YOU THAT YOU'RE NOT. THAT THE BEST THING YOU CAN DO IS TALK.

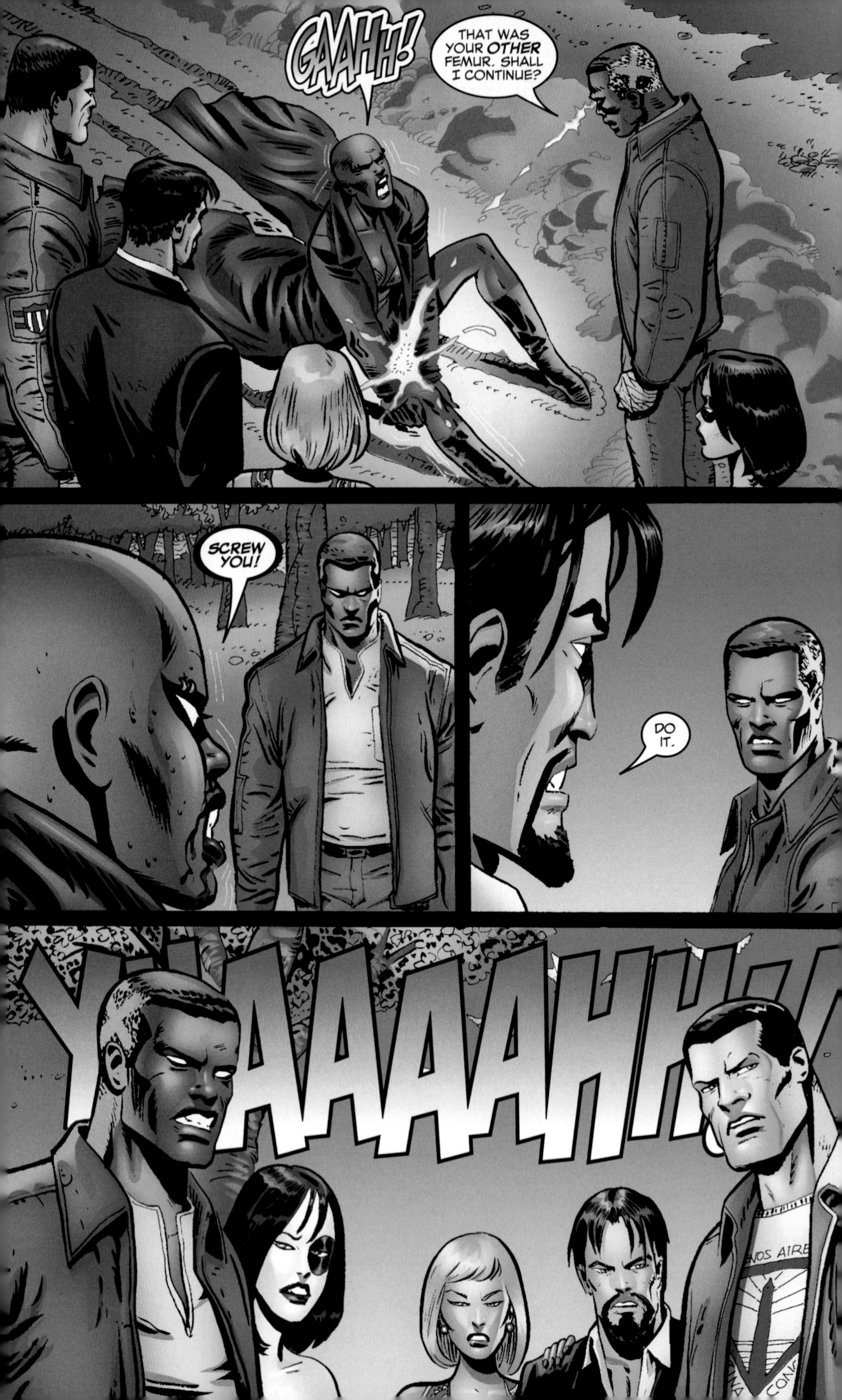
GAAHH!
THAT WAS YOUR OTHER FEMUR. SHALL I CONTINUE?
SCREW YOU!
DO IT.
YAAAAHH

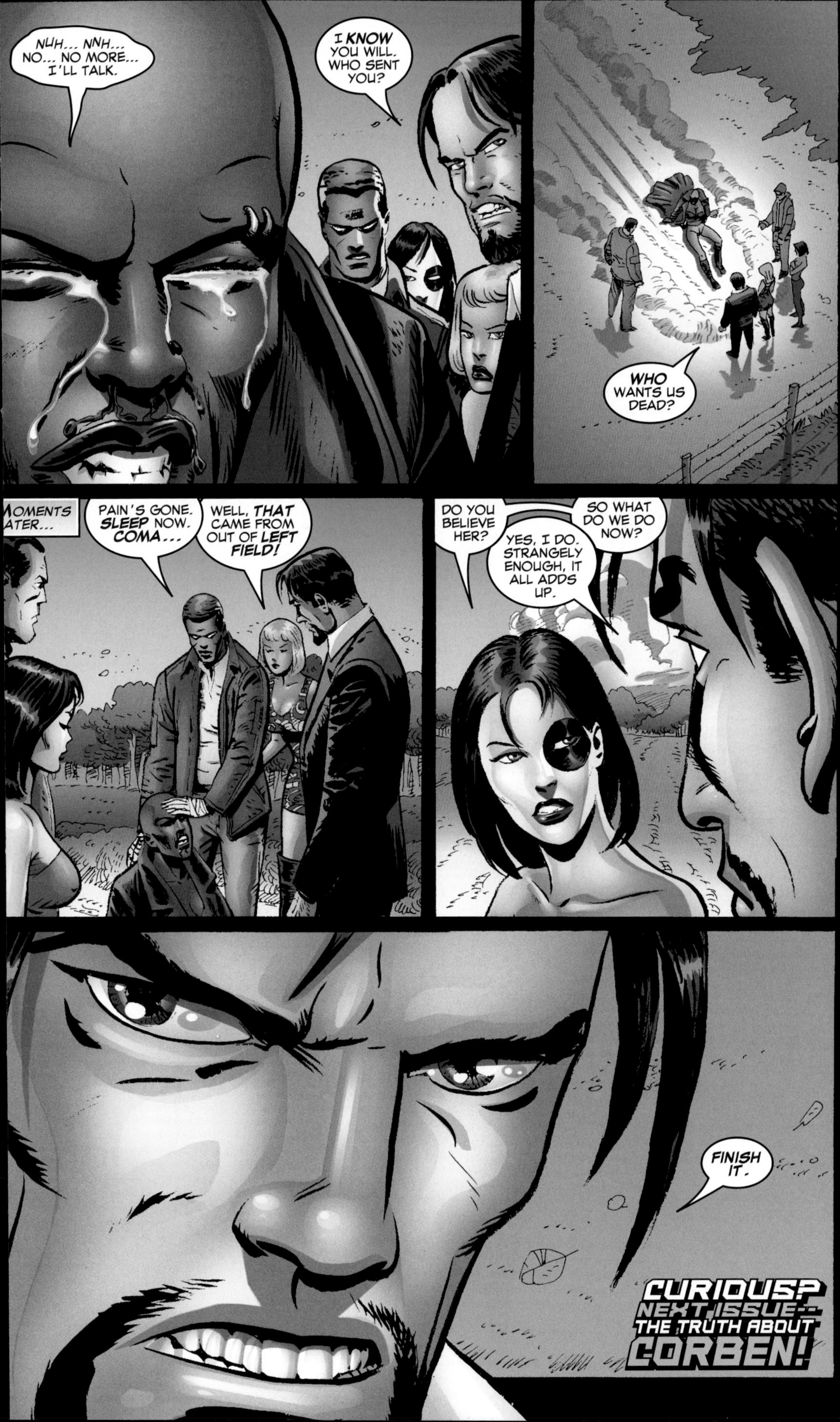
NUH... NNH... NO... NO MORE... I'LL TALK.
I KNOW YOU WILL. WHO SENT YOU?
WHO WANTS US DEAD?
MOMENTS LATER...
PAIN'S GONE. SLEEP NOW. COMA...
WELL, THAT CAME FROM OUT OF LEFT FIELD!
DO YOU BELIEVE HER?
YES, I DO. STRANGELY ENOUGH, IT ALL ADDS UP.
SO WHAT DO WE DO NOW?
FINISH IT.
CURIOUS? NEXT ISSUE-- THE TRUTH ABOUT CORBEN!

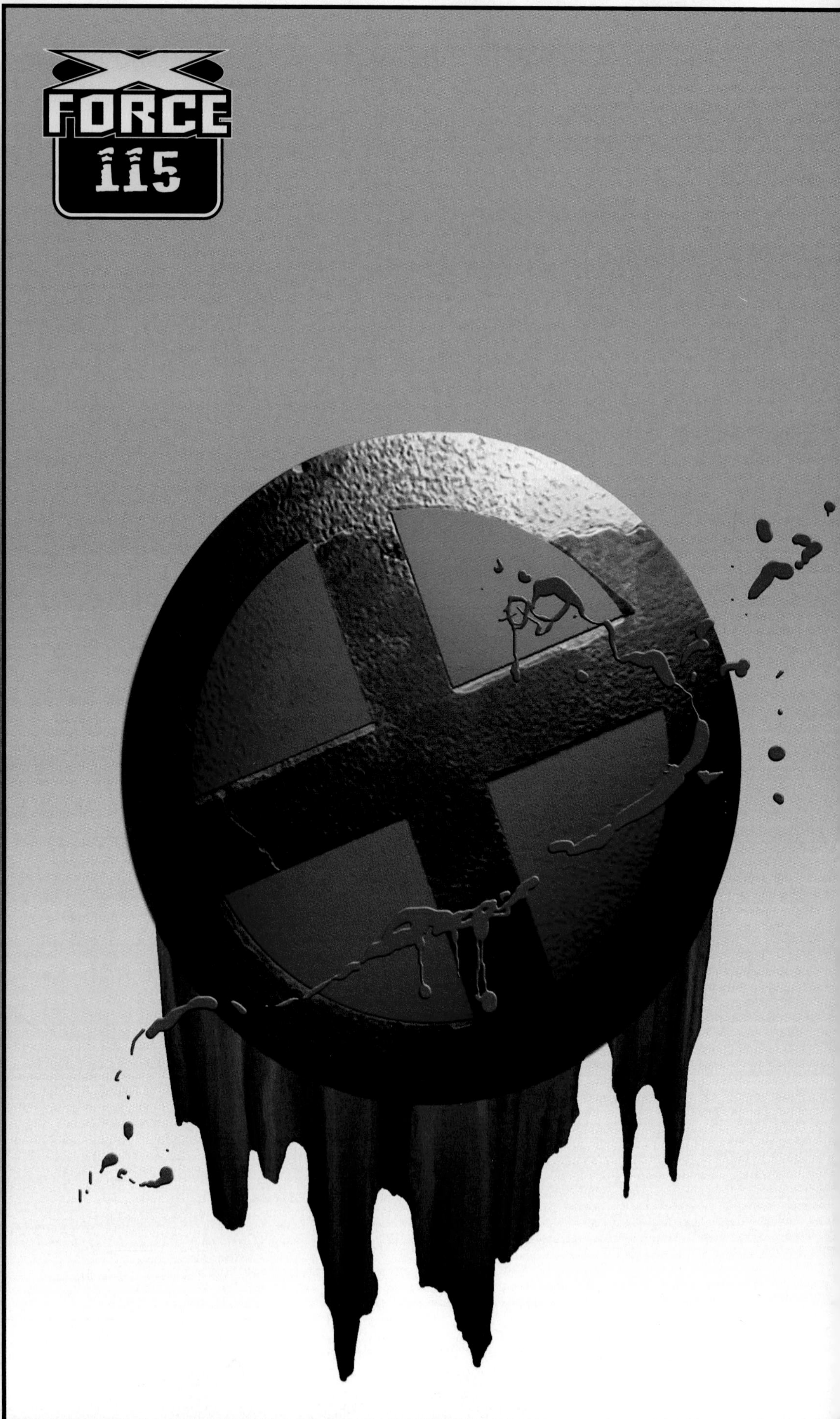
X FORCE
115

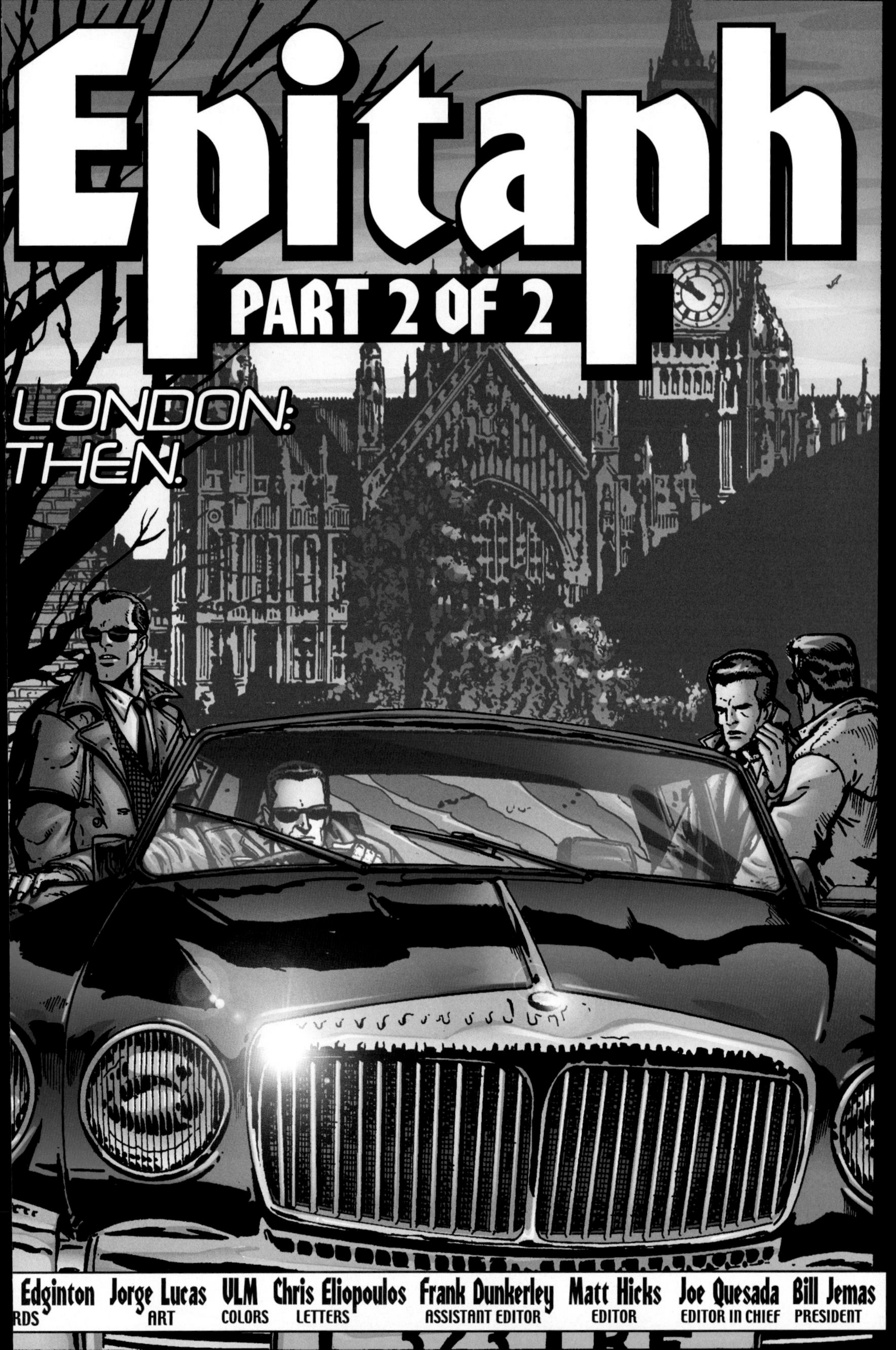

Epitaph
PART 2 OF 2
LONDON:
THEN.
Edginton RDS
Jorge Lucas ART
VLM COLORS
Chris Eliopoulos LETTERS
Frank Dunkerley ASSISTANT EDITOR
Matt Hicks EDITOR
Joe Quesada EDITOR IN CHIEF
Bill Jemas PRESIDENT

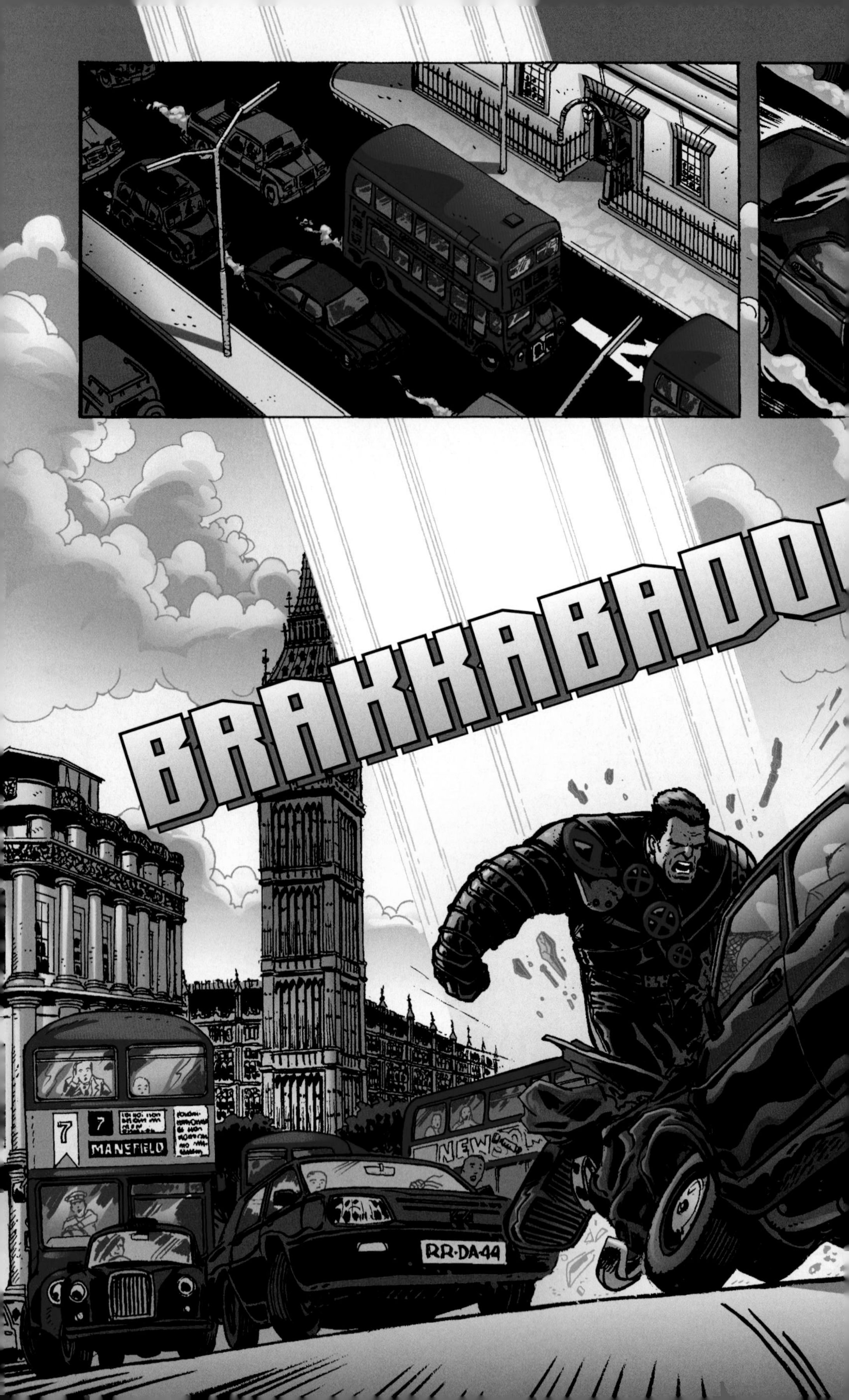
BRAKKABADO
7
7
MANSFIELD
NEWS
RR-DA-44

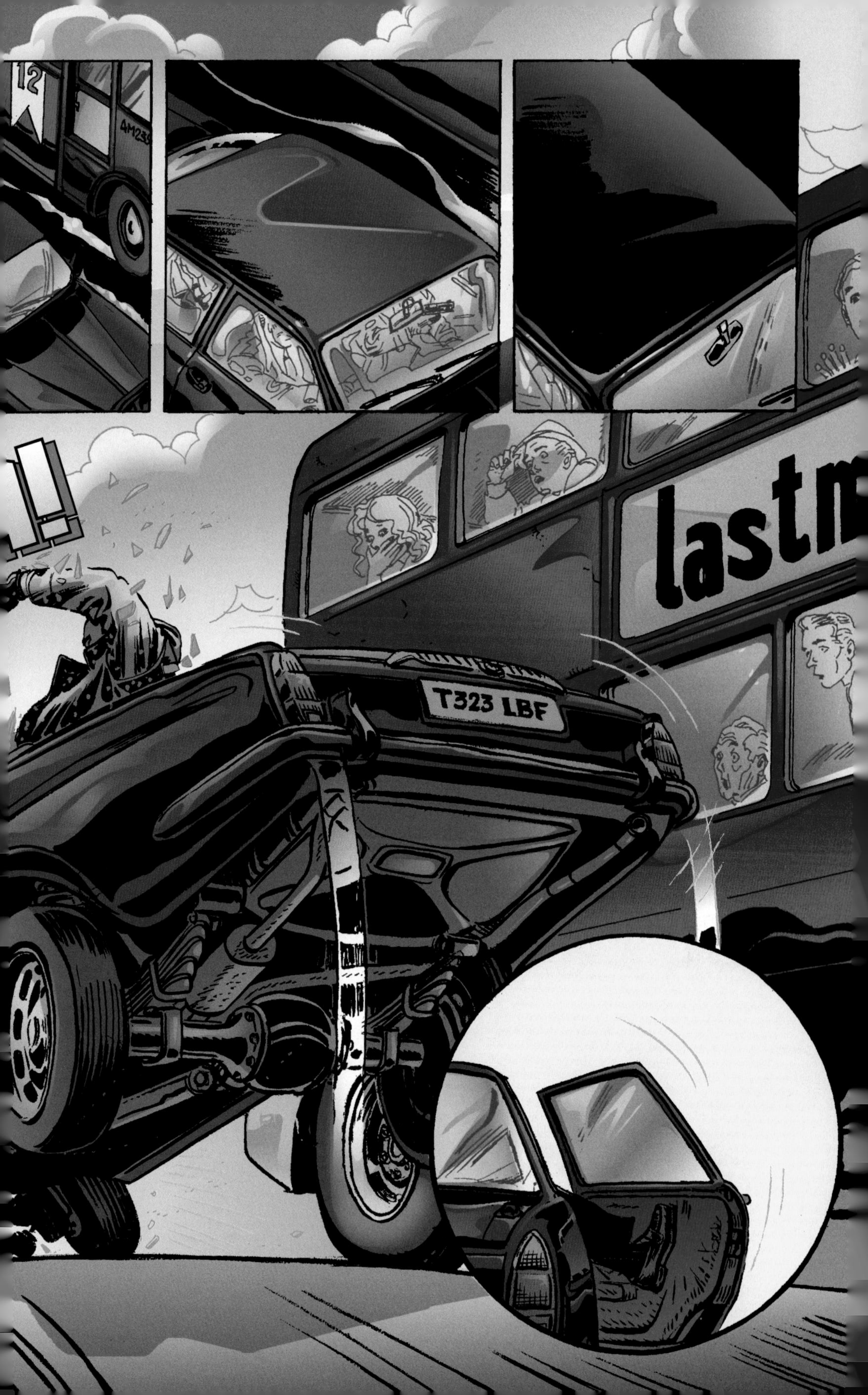

12
!
lastm
T323 LBF

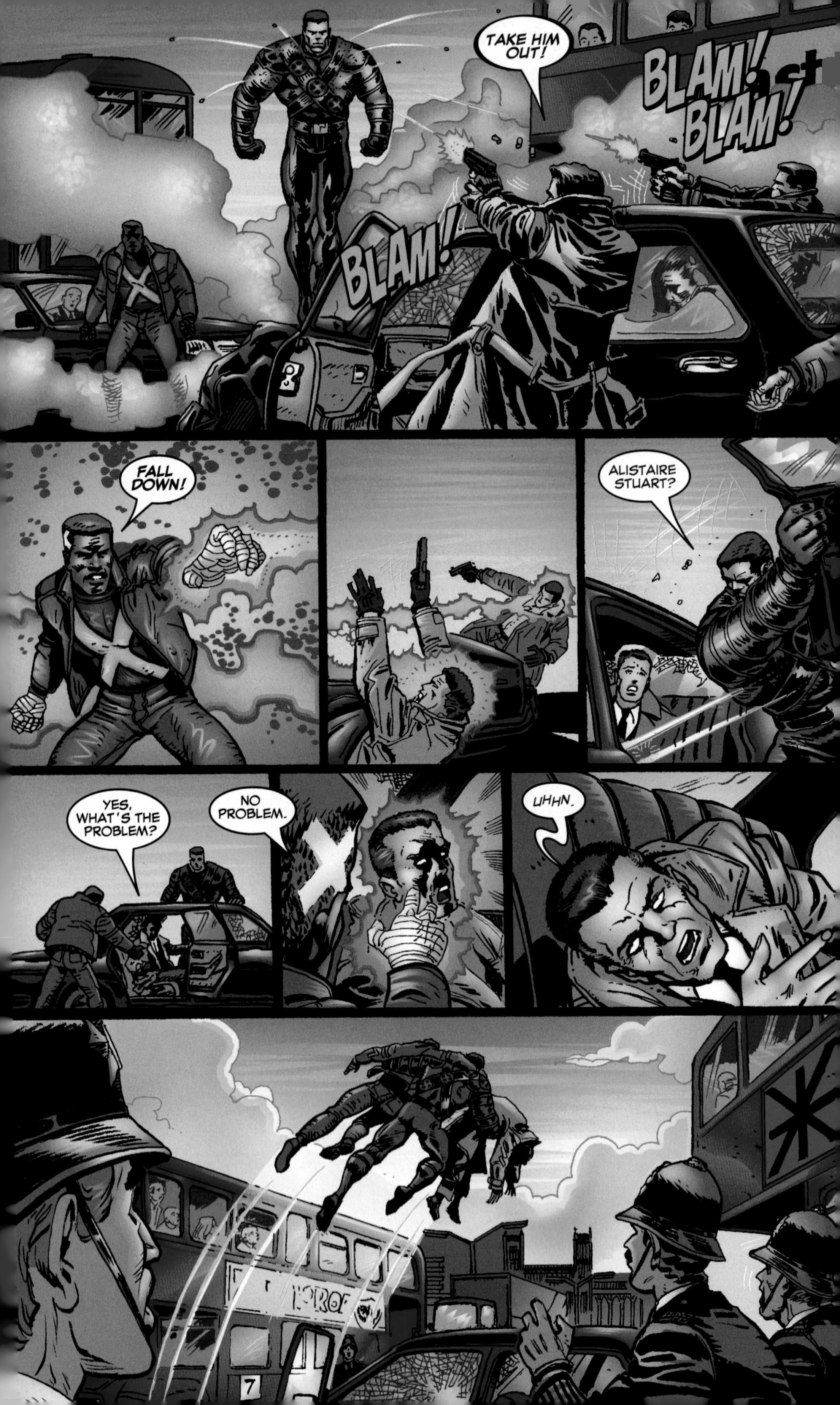
TAKE HIM OUT!
BLAM! BLAM!
BLAM!
FALL DOWN!
ALISTAIRE STUART?
YES, WHAT'S THE PROBLEM?
NO PROBLEM.
UHHN.

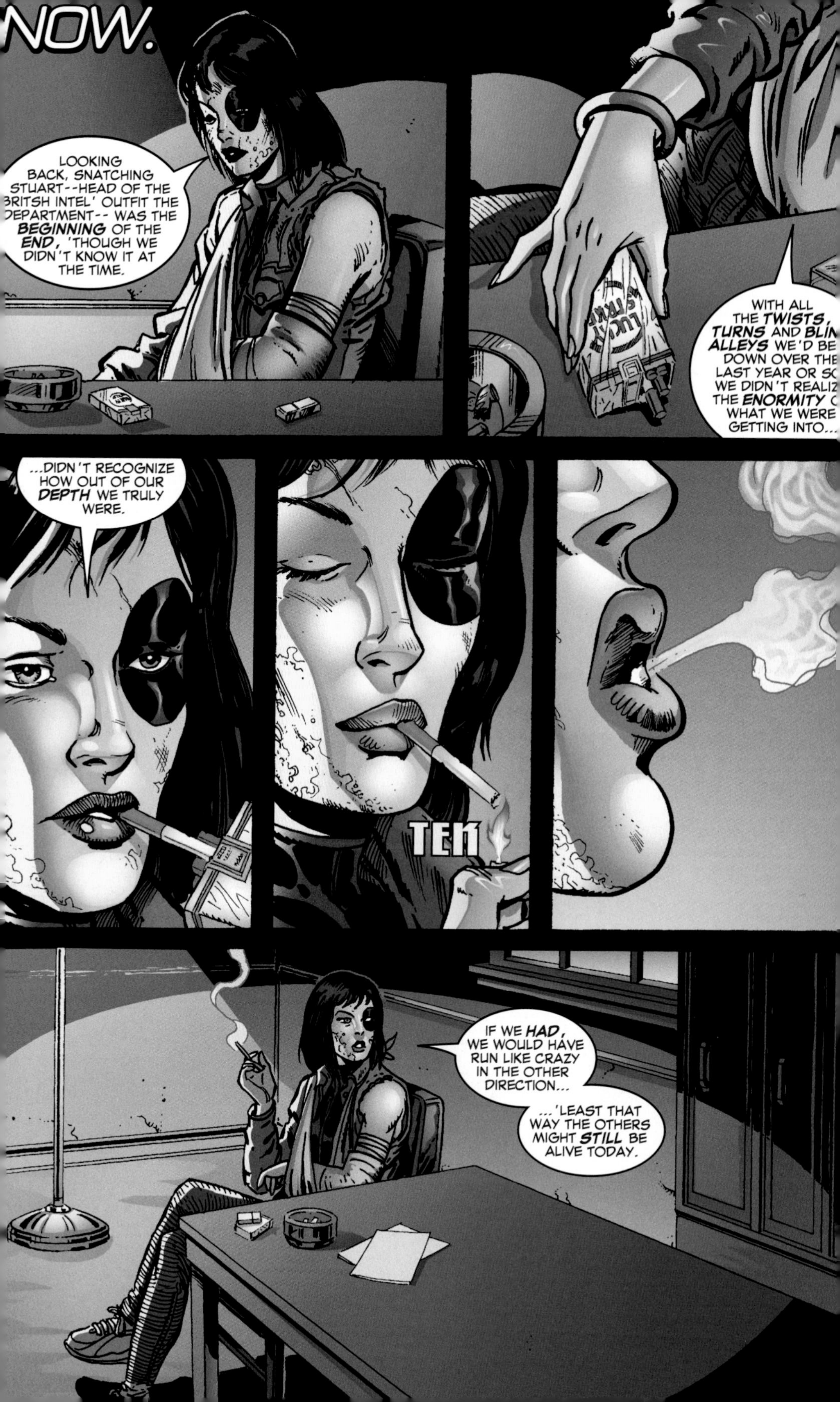
NOW.
LOOKING BACK, SNATCHING STUART--HEAD OF THE BRITSH INTEL' OUTFIT THE DEPARTMENT-- WAS THE BEGINNING OF THE END, 'THOUGH WE DIDN'T KNOW IT AT THE TIME.
WITH ALL THE TWISTS, TURNS AND BLIN ALLEYS WE'D BE DOWN OVER THE LAST YEAR OR SO WE DIDN'T REALIZ THE ENORMITY O WHAT WE WERE GETTING INTO...
...DIDN'T RECOGNIZE HOW OUT OF OUR DEPTH WE TRULY WERE.
TEK
IF WE HAD, WE WOULD HAVE RUN LIKE CRAZY IN THE OTHER DIRECTION...
...'LEAST THAT WAY THE OTHERS MIGHT STILL BE ALIVE TODAY.

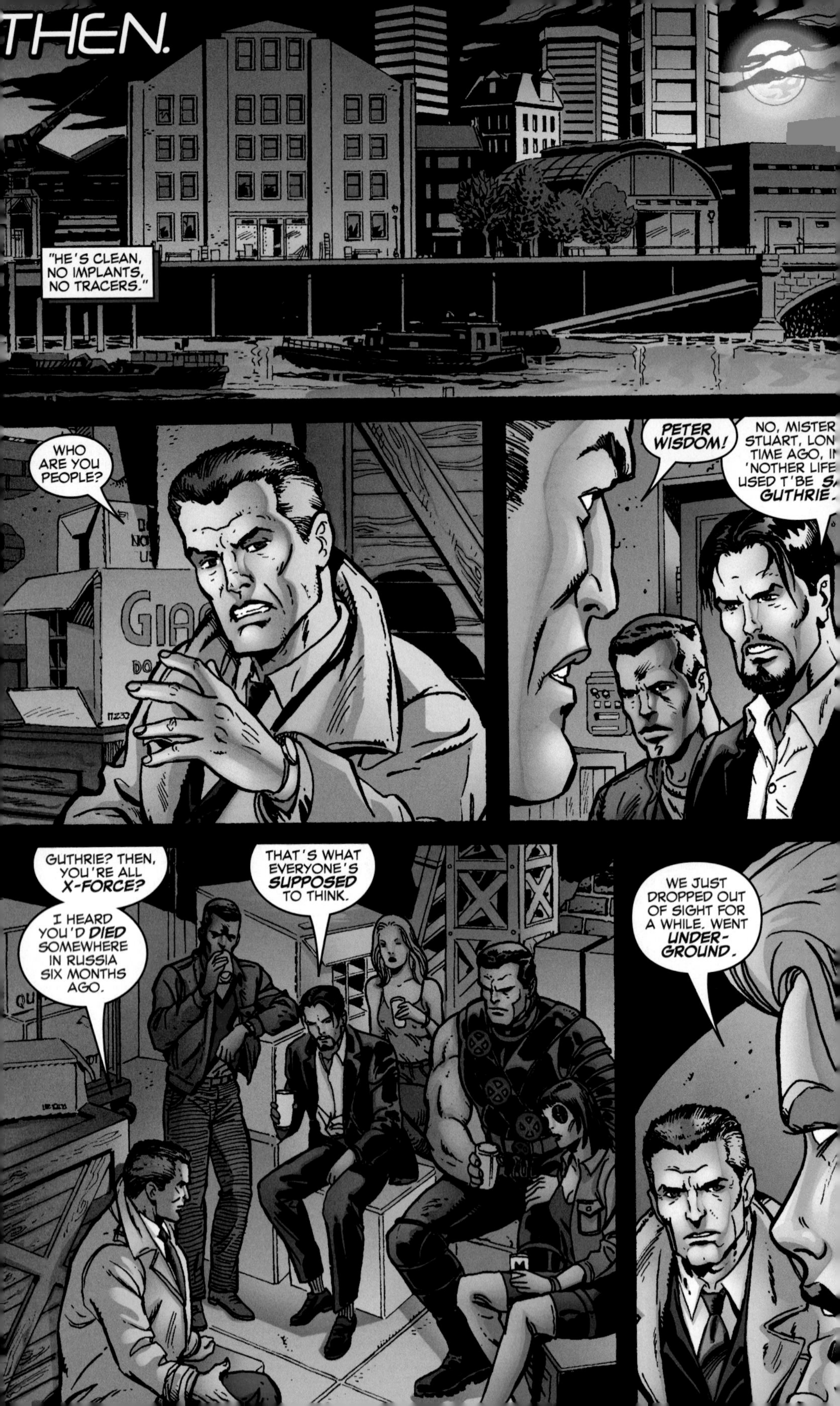

THEN.
"HE'S CLEAN, NO IMPLANTS, NO TRACERS."
WHO ARE YOU PEOPLE?
PETER WISDOM!
NO, MISTER STUART, LON TIME AGO, I 'NOTHER LIFE USED T'BE S GUTHRIE.
GUTHRIE? THEN, YOU'RE ALL X-FORCE?
I HEARD YOU'D DIED SOMEWHERE IN RUSSIA SIX MONTHS AGO.
THAT'S WHAT EVERYONE'S SUPPOSED TO THINK.
WE JUST DROPPED OUT OF SIGHT FOR A WHILE. WENT UNDERGROUND.

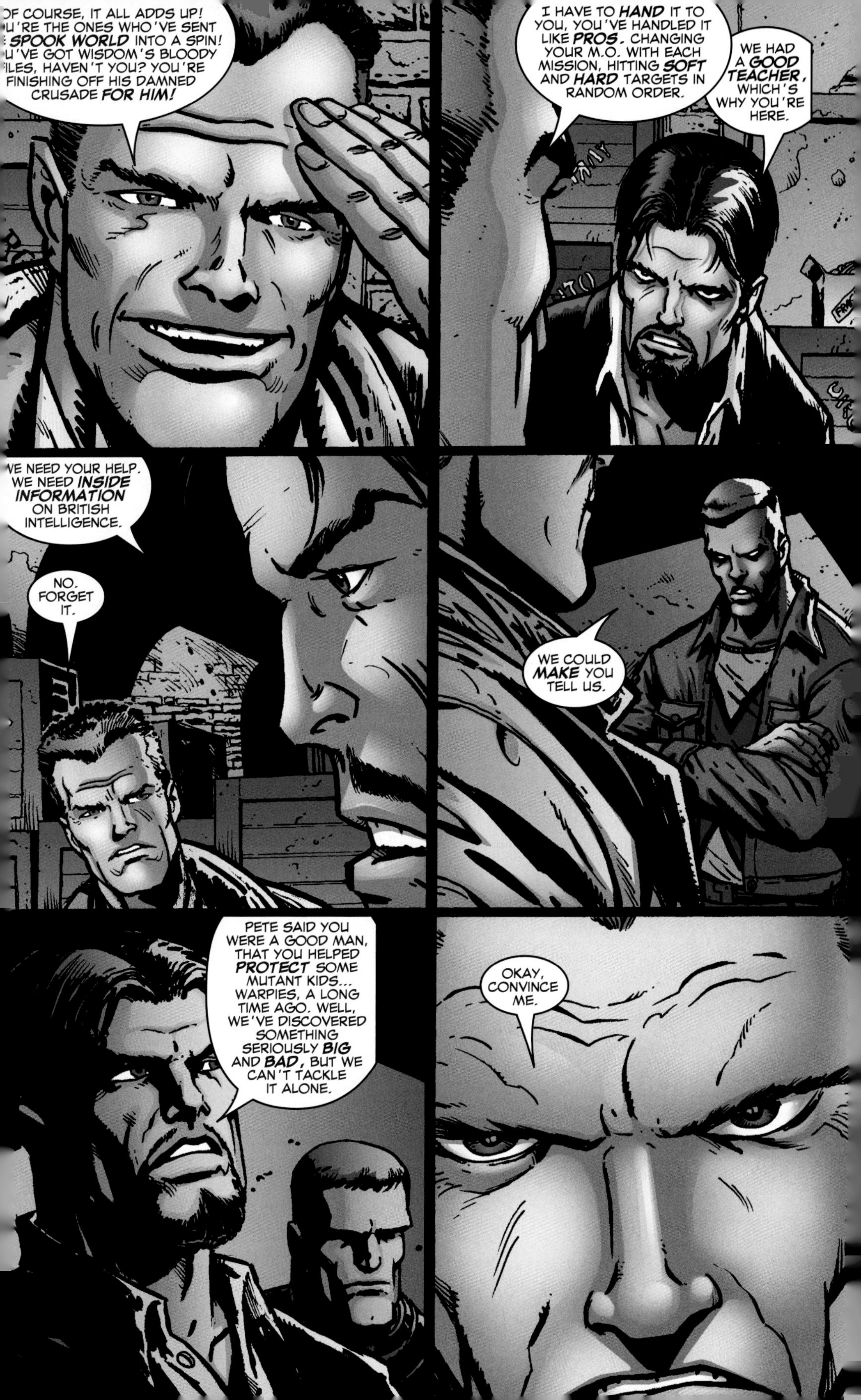
OF COURSE, IT ALL ADDS UP! ...U'RE THE ONES WHO'VE SENT ...SPOOK WORLD INTO A SPIN! ...U'VE GOT WISDOM'S BLOODY ...FILES, HAVEN'T YOU? YOU'RE FINISHING OFF HIS DAMNED CRUSADE FOR HIM!
I HAVE TO HAND IT TO YOU, YOU'VE HANDLED IT LIKE PROS. CHANGING YOUR M.O. WITH EACH MISSION, HITTING SOFT AND HARD TARGETS IN RANDOM ORDER.
WE HAD A GOOD TEACHER, WHICH'S WHY YOU'RE HERE.
...E NEED YOUR HELP. WE NEED INSIDE INFORMATION ON BRITISH INTELLIGENCE.
NO. FORGET IT.
WE COULD MAKE YOU TELL US.
PETE SAID YOU WERE A GOOD MAN, THAT YOU HELPED PROTECT SOME MUTANT KIDS... WARPIES, A LONG TIME AGO. WELL, WE'VE DISCOVERED SOMETHING SERIOUSLY BIG AND BAD, BUT WE CAN'T TACKLE IT ALONE.
OKAY, CONVINCE ME.

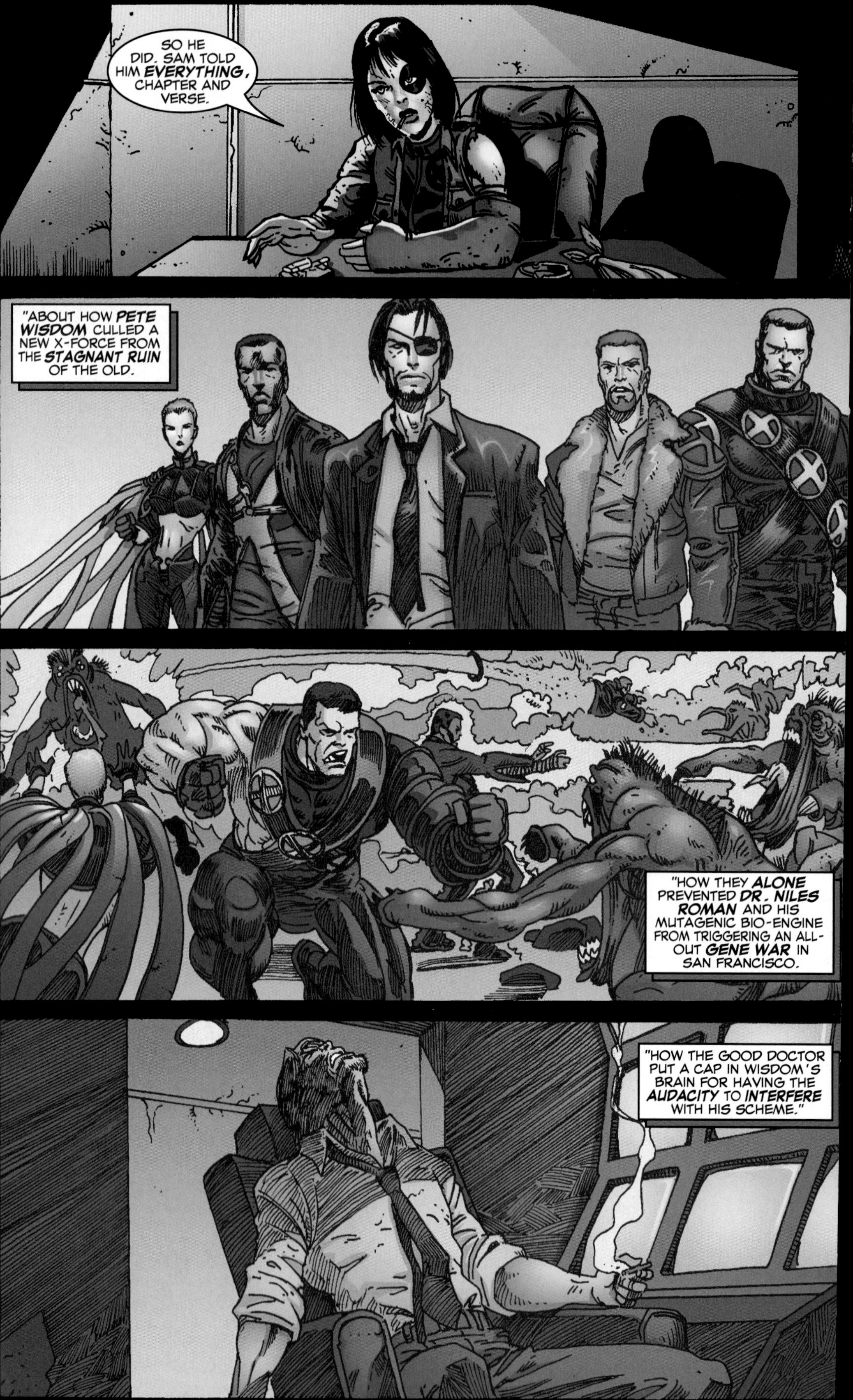
SO HE DID. SAM TOLD HIM EVERYTHING, CHAPTER AND VERSE.
"ABOUT HOW PETE WISDOM CULLED A NEW X-FORCE FROM THE STAGNANT RUIN OF THE OLD.
"HOW THEY ALONE PREVENTED DR. NILES ROMAN AND HIS MUTAGENIC BIO-ENGINE FROM TRIGGERING AN ALL-OUT GENE WAR IN SAN FRANCISCO.
"HOW THE GOOD DOCTOR PUT A CAP IN WISDOM'S BRAIN FOR HAVING THE AUDACITY TO INTERFERE WITH HIS SCHEME."

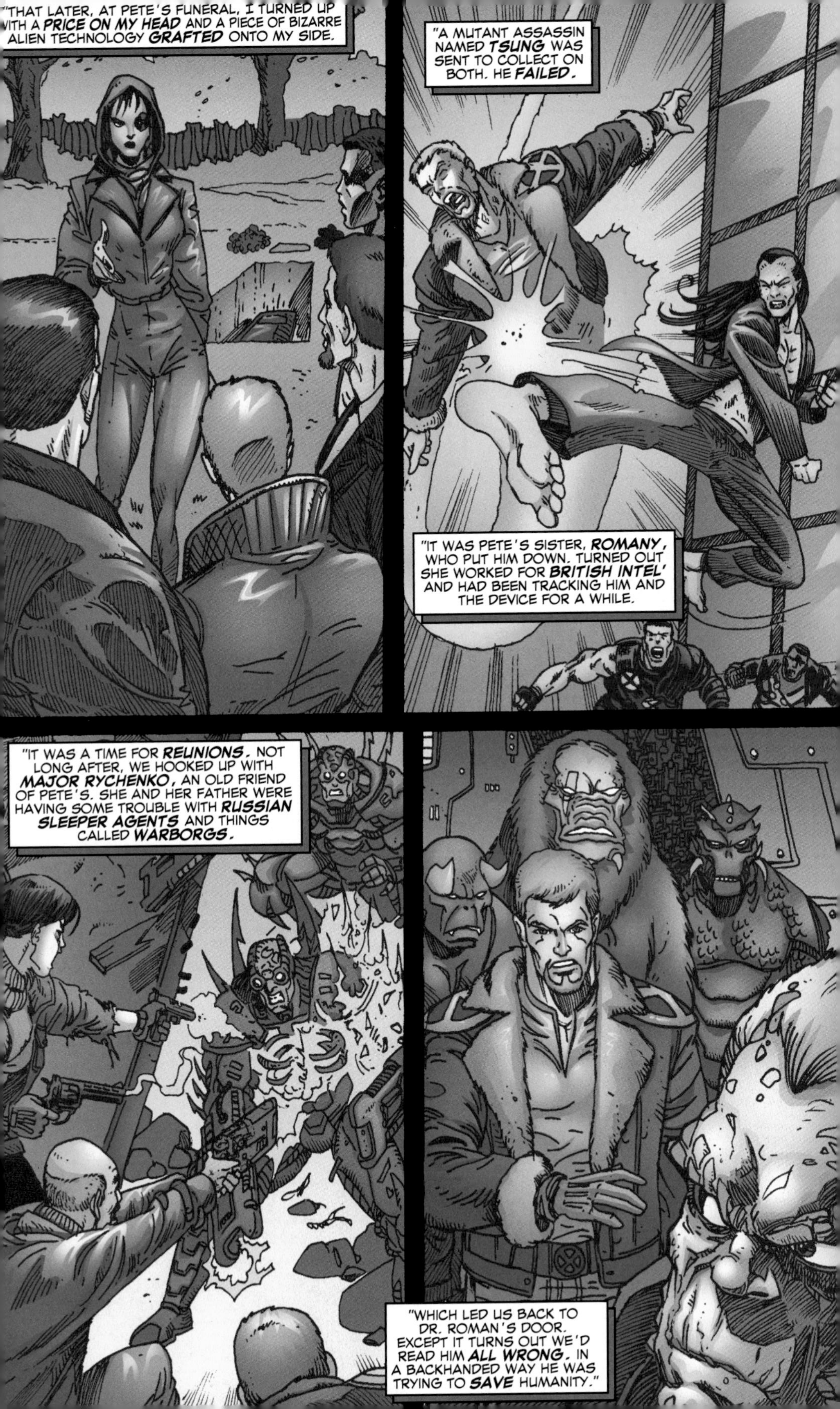
"THAT LATER, AT PETE'S FUNERAL, I TURNED UP WITH A PRICE ON MY HEAD AND A PIECE OF BIZARRE ALIEN TECHNOLOGY GRAFTED ONTO MY SIDE.
"A MUTANT ASSASSIN NAMED TSUNG WAS SENT TO COLLECT ON BOTH. HE FAILED.
"IT WAS PETE'S SISTER, ROMANY, WHO PUT HIM DOWN. TURNED OUT SHE WORKED FOR BRITISH INTEL' AND HAD BEEN TRACKING HIM AND THE DEVICE FOR A WHILE.
"IT WAS A TIME FOR REUNIONS. NOT LONG AFTER, WE HOOKED UP WITH MAJOR RYCHENKO, AN OLD FRIEND OF PETE'S. SHE AND HER FATHER WERE HAVING SOME TROUBLE WITH RUSSIAN SLEEPER AGENTS AND THINGS CALLED WARBORGS.
"WHICH LED US BACK TO DR. ROMAN'S DOOR. EXCEPT IT TURNS OUT WE'D READ HIM ALL WRONG. IN A BACKHANDED WAY HE WAS TRYING TO SAVE HUMANITY."

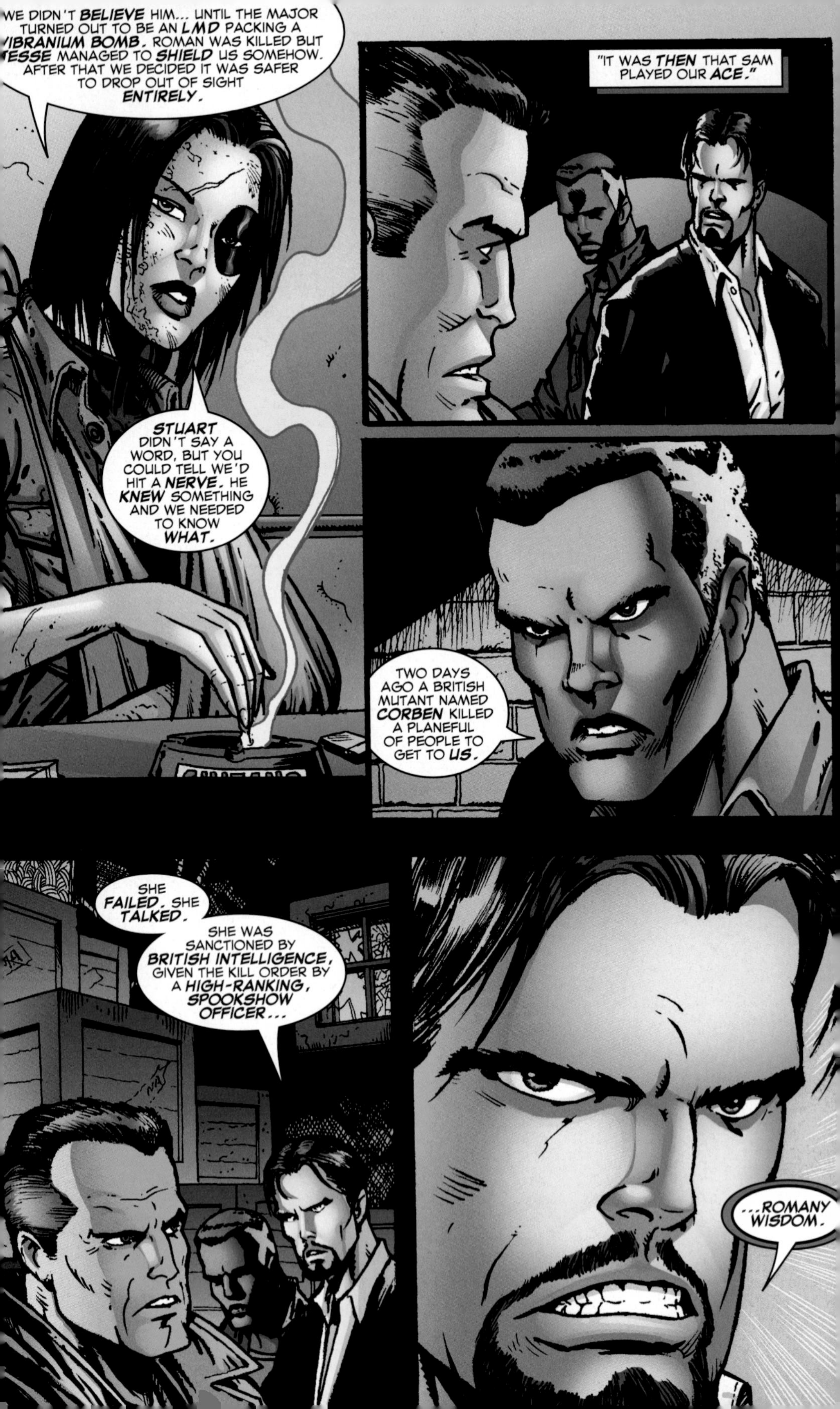
WE DIDN'T BELIEVE HIM... UNTIL THE MAJOR TURNED OUT TO BE AN LMD PACKING A VIBRANIUM BOMB. ROMAN WAS KILLED BUT JESSE MANAGED TO SHIELD US SOMEHOW. AFTER THAT WE DECIDED IT WAS SAFER TO DROP OUT OF SIGHT ENTIRELY.
STUART DIDN'T SAY A WORD, BUT YOU COULD TELL WE'D HIT A NERVE. HE KNEW SOMETHING AND WE NEEDED TO KNOW WHAT.
"IT WAS THEN THAT SAM PLAYED OUR ACE."
TWO DAYS AGO A BRITISH MUTANT NAMED CORBEN KILLED A PLANEFUL OF PEOPLE TO GET TO US.
SHE FAILED. SHE TALKED.
SHE WAS SANCTIONED BY BRITISH INTELLIGENCE, GIVEN THE KILL ORDER BY A HIGH-RANKING, SPOOKSHOW OFFICER...
...ROMANY WISDOM.

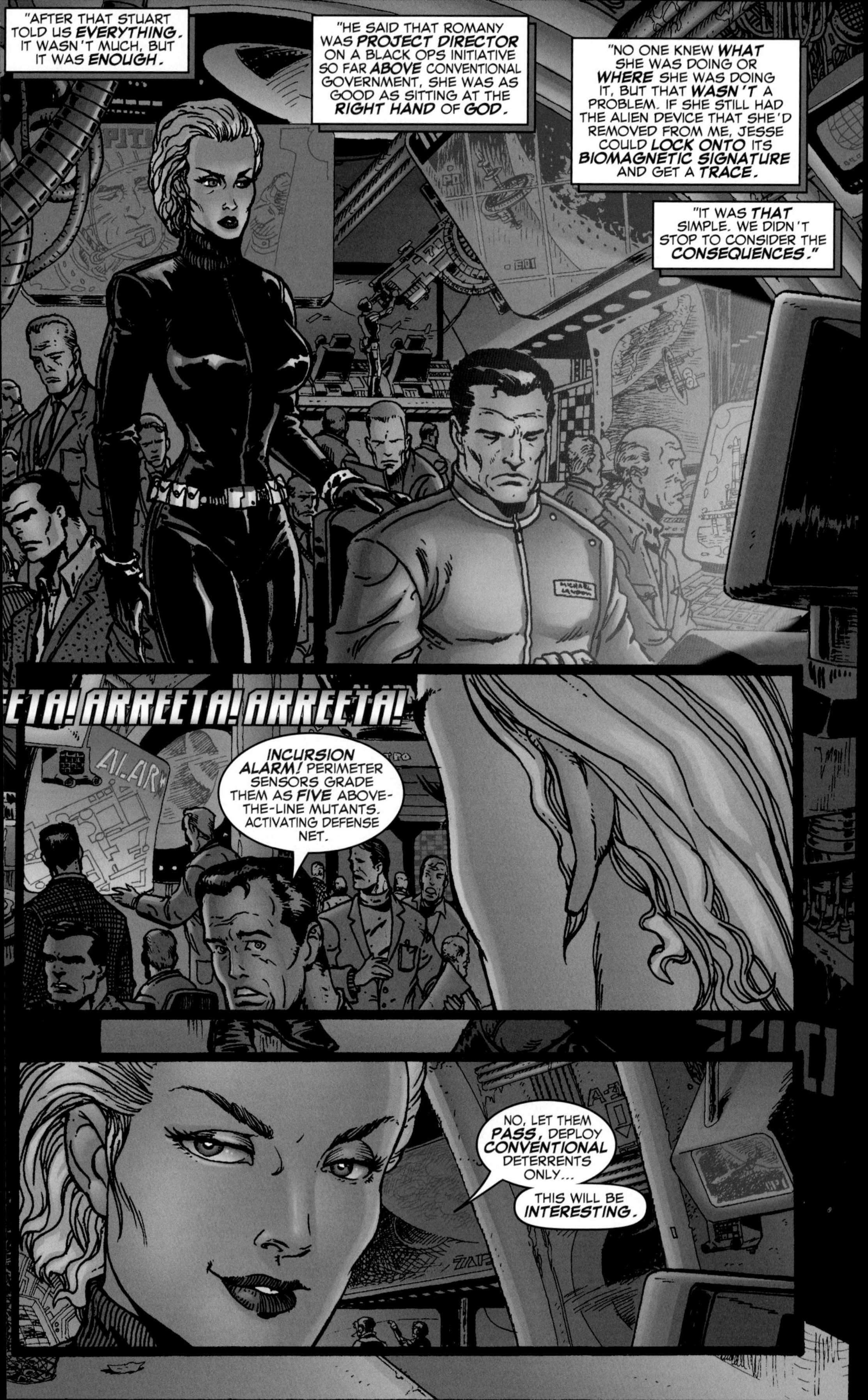
"AFTER THAT STUART TOLD US EVERYTHING. IT WASN'T MUCH, BUT IT WAS ENOUGH.
"HE SAID THAT ROMANY WAS PROJECT DIRECTOR ON A BLACK OPS INITIATIVE SO FAR ABOVE CONVENTIONAL GOVERNMENT, SHE WAS AS GOOD AS SITTING AT THE RIGHT HAND OF GOD.
"NO ONE KNEW WHAT SHE WAS DOING OR WHERE SHE WAS DOING IT, BUT THAT WASN'T A PROBLEM. IF SHE STILL HAD THE ALIEN DEVICE THAT SHE'D REMOVED FROM ME, JESSE COULD LOCK ONTO ITS BIOMAGNETIC SIGNATURE AND GET A TRACE.
"IT WAS THAT SIMPLE. WE DIDN'T STOP TO CONSIDER THE CONSEQUENCES."
EETA! ARREETA! ARREETA!
INCURSION ALARM! PERIMETER SENSORS GRADE THEM AS FIVE ABOVE-THE-LINE MUTANTS. ACTIVATING DEFENSE NET.
NO, LET THEM PASS, DEPLOY CONVENTIONAL DETERRENTS ONLY...
THIS WILL BE INTERESTING.

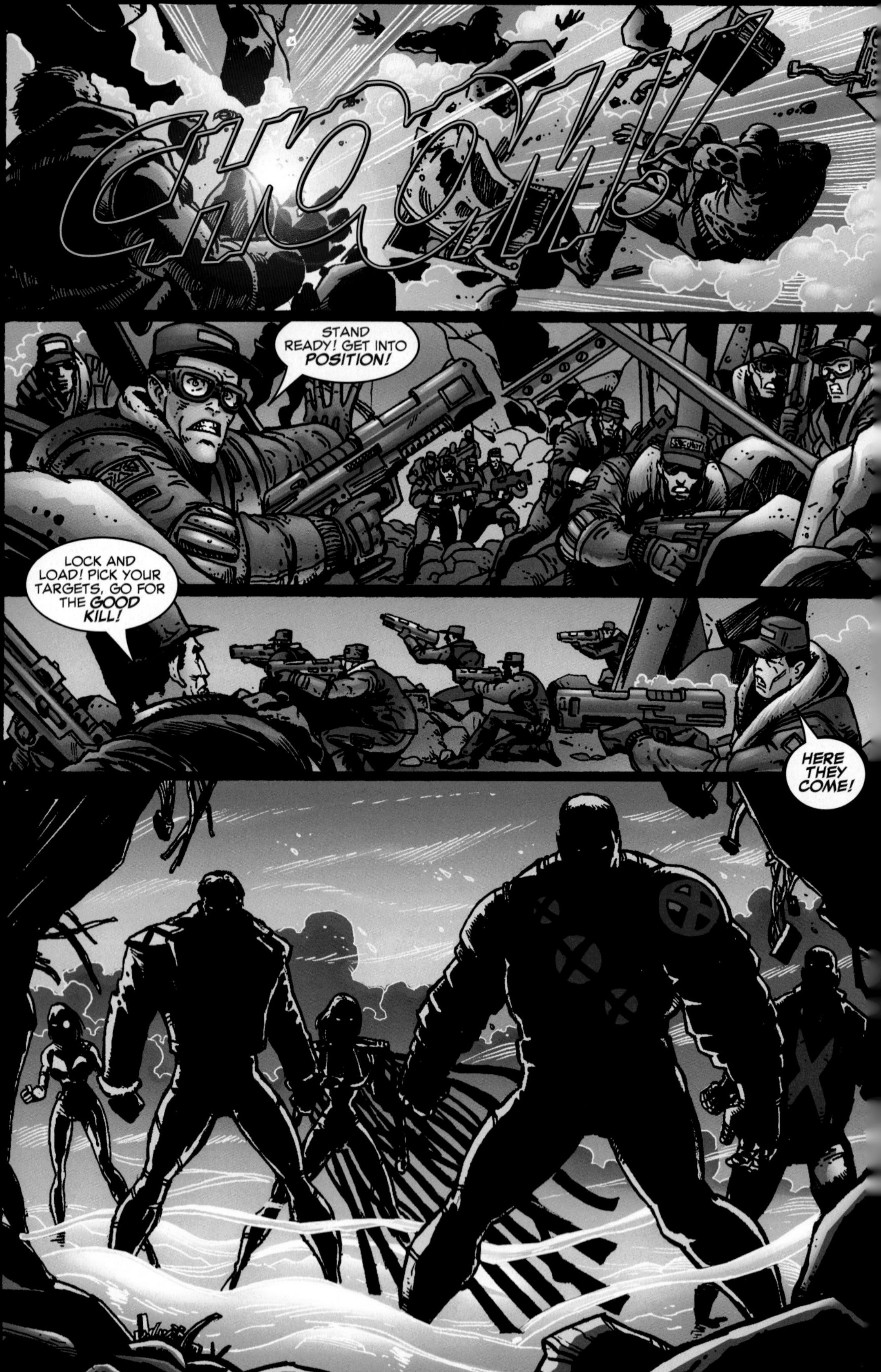
CHOOM!
STAND READY! GET INTO POSITION!
LOCK AND LOAD! PICK YOUR TARGETS, GO FOR THE GOOD KILL!
HERE THEY COME!

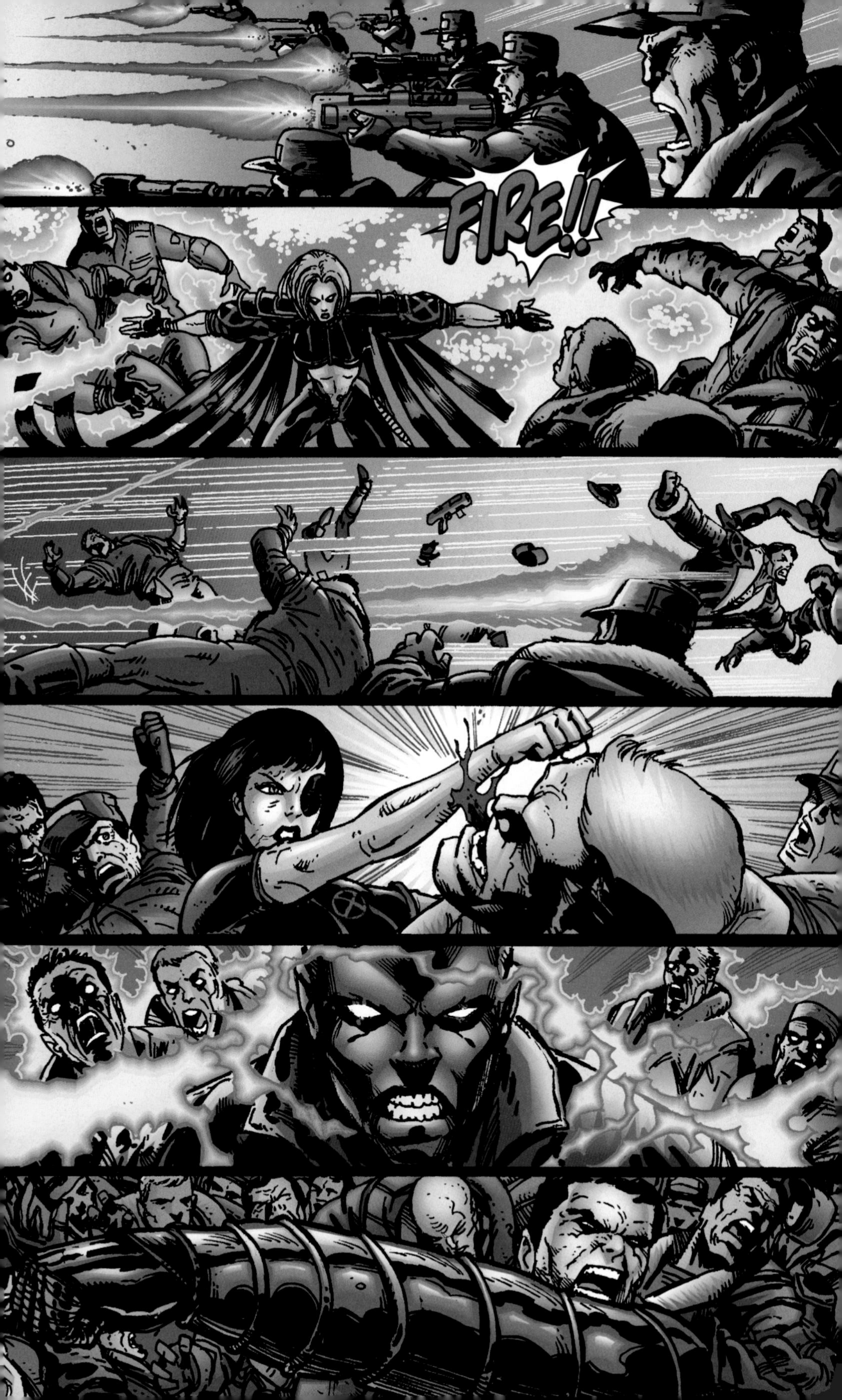
FIRE!!

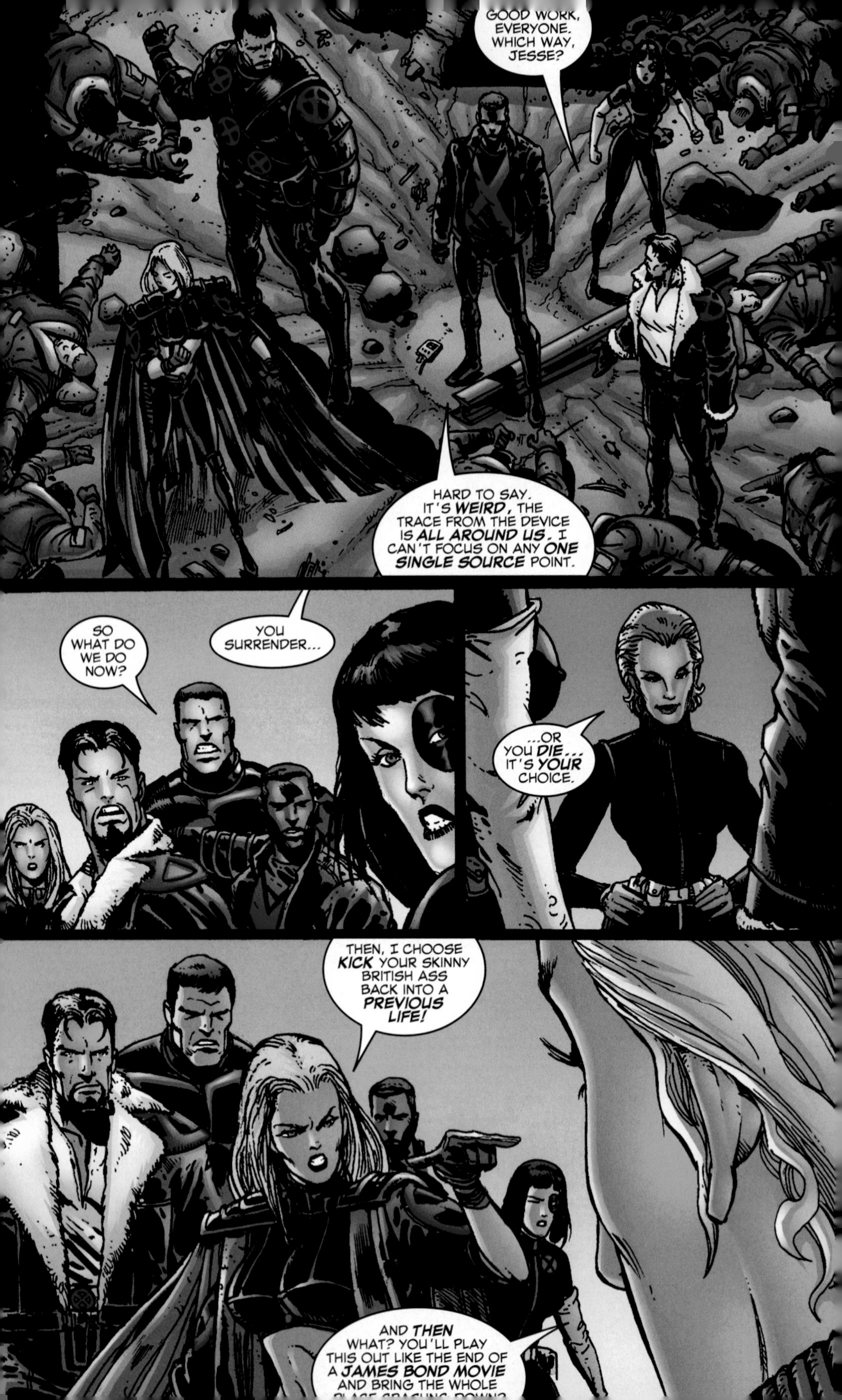
GOOD WORK, EVERYONE. WHICH WAY, JESSE?
HARD TO SAY. IT'S WEIRD, THE TRACE FROM THE DEVICE IS ALL AROUND US. I CAN'T FOCUS ON ANY ONE SINGLE SOURCE POINT.
SO WHAT DO WE DO NOW?
YOU SURRENDER...
...OR YOU DIE... IT'S YOUR CHOICE.
THEN, I CHOOSE KICK YOUR SKINNY BRITISH ASS BACK INTO A PREVIOUS LIFE!
AND THEN WHAT? YOU'LL PLAY THIS OUT LIKE THE END OF A JAMES BOND MOVIE AND BRING THE WHOLE

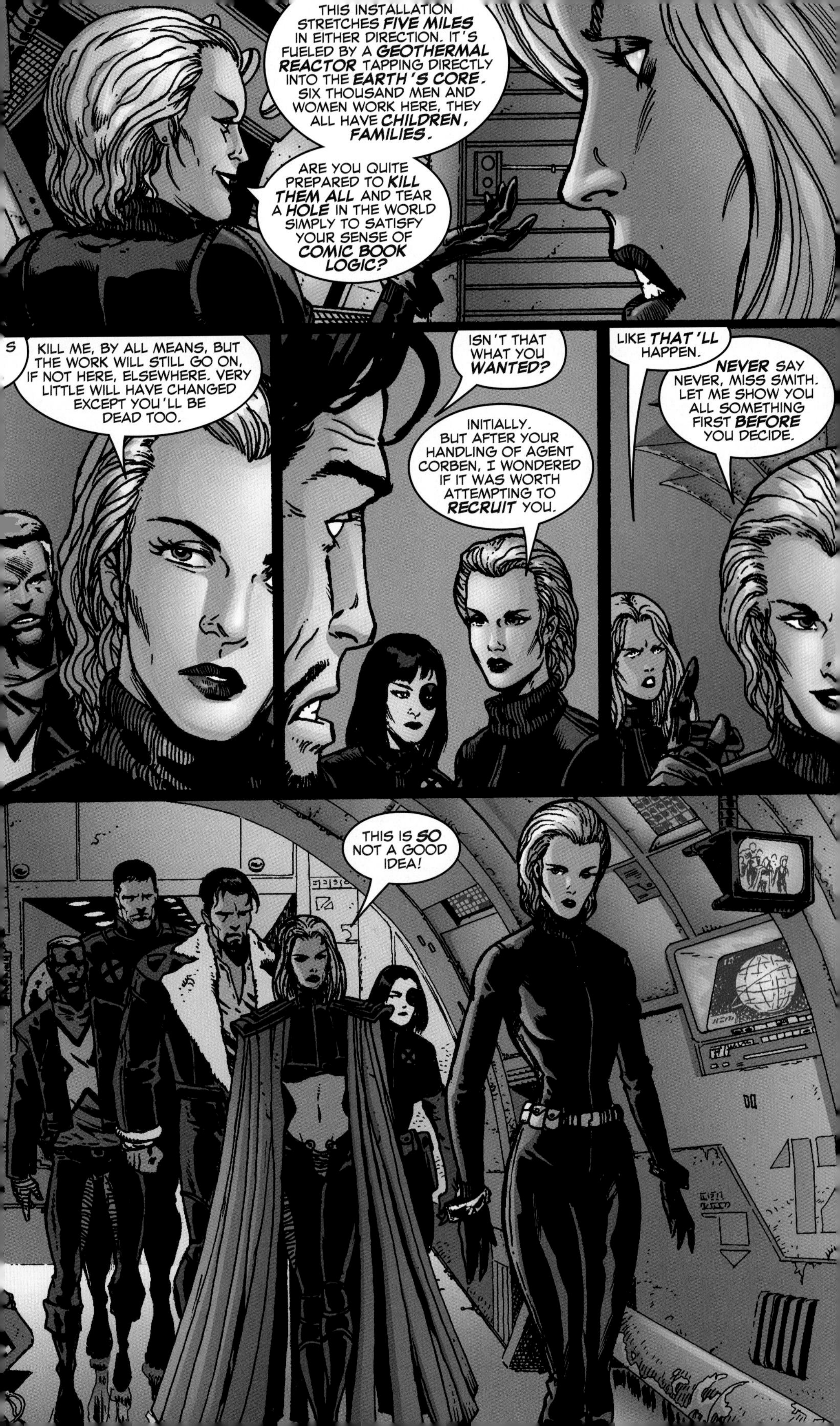

THIS INSTALLATION STRETCHES **FIVE MILES** IN EITHER DIRECTION. IT'S FUELED BY A **GEOTHERMAL REACTOR** TAPPING DIRECTLY INTO THE **EARTH'S CORE**. SIX THOUSAND MEN AND WOMEN WORK HERE, THEY ALL HAVE **CHILDREN**, **FAMILIES**.
ARE YOU QUITE PREPARED TO **KILL THEM ALL** AND TEAR A **HOLE** IN THE WORLD SIMPLY TO SATISFY YOUR SENSE OF **COMIC BOOK LOGIC?**
KILL ME, BY ALL MEANS, BUT THE WORK WILL STILL GO ON, IF NOT HERE, ELSEWHERE. VERY LITTLE WILL HAVE CHANGED EXCEPT YOU'LL BE DEAD TOO.
ISN'T THAT WHAT YOU **WANTED?**
INITIALLY. BUT AFTER YOUR HANDLING OF AGENT CORBEN, I WONDERED IF IT WAS WORTH ATTEMPTING TO **RECRUIT** YOU.
LIKE **THAT'LL** HAPPEN.
NEVER SAY NEVER, MISS SMITH. LET ME SHOW YOU ALL SOMETHING FIRST **BEFORE** YOU DECIDE.
THIS IS **SO** NOT A GOOD IDEA!

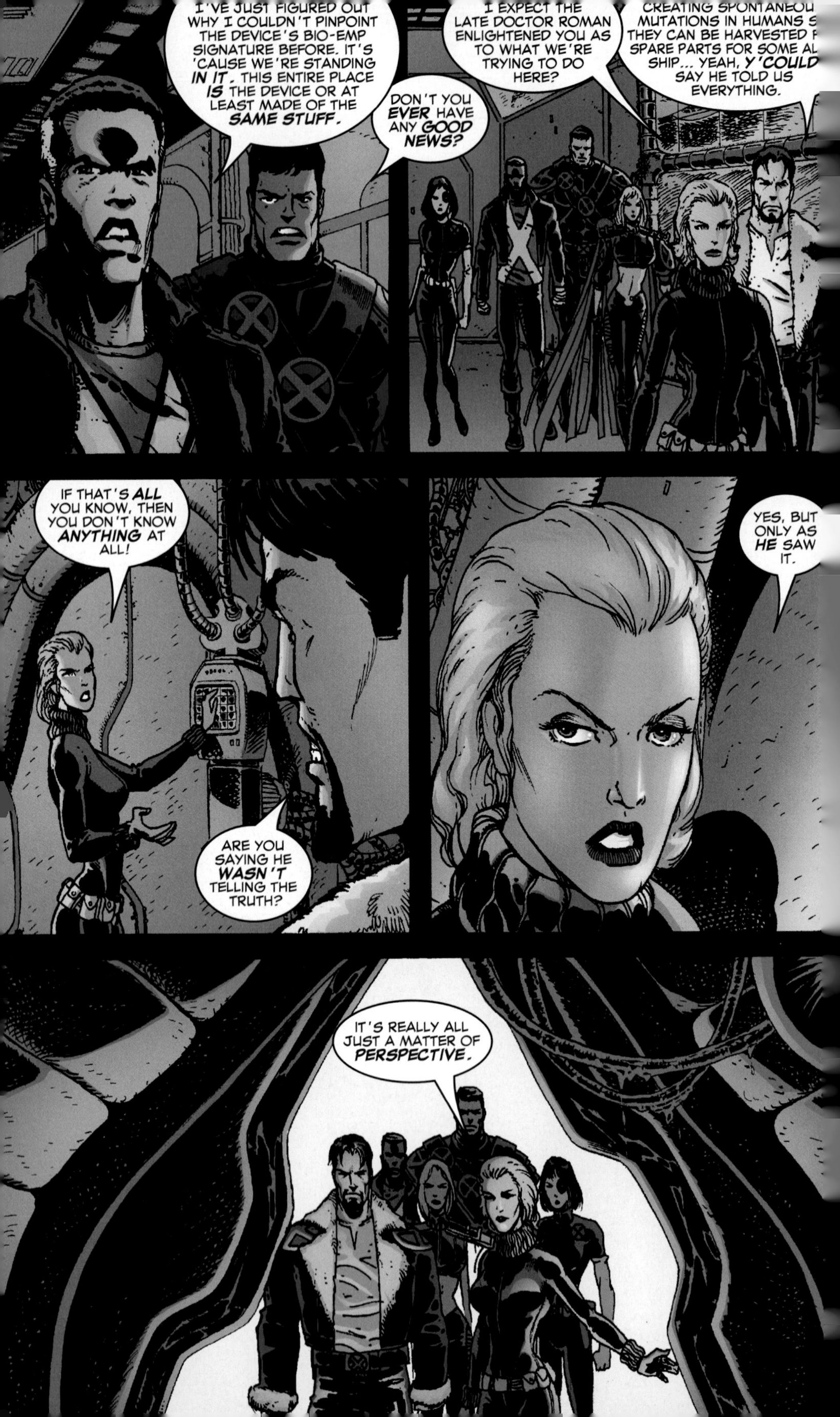
I'VE JUST FIGURED OUT WHY I COULDN'T PINPOINT THE DEVICE'S BIO-EMP SIGNATURE BEFORE. IT'S 'CAUSE WE'RE STANDING IN IT. THIS ENTIRE PLACE IS THE DEVICE OR AT LEAST MADE OF THE SAME STUFF.
DON'T YOU EVER HAVE ANY GOOD NEWS?
I EXPECT THE LATE DOCTOR ROMAN ENLIGHTENED YOU AS TO WHAT WE'RE TRYING TO DO HERE?
CREATING SPONTANEOU MUTATIONS IN HUMANS S THEY CAN BE HARVESTED F SPARE PARTS FOR SOME AL SHIP... YEAH, Y'COULD SAY HE TOLD US EVERYTHING.
IF THAT'S ALL YOU KNOW, THEN YOU DON'T KNOW ANYTHING AT ALL!
ARE YOU SAYING HE WASN'T TELLING THE TRUTH?
YES, BUT ONLY AS HE SAW IT.
IT'S REALLY ALL JUST A MATTER OF PERSPECTIVE.

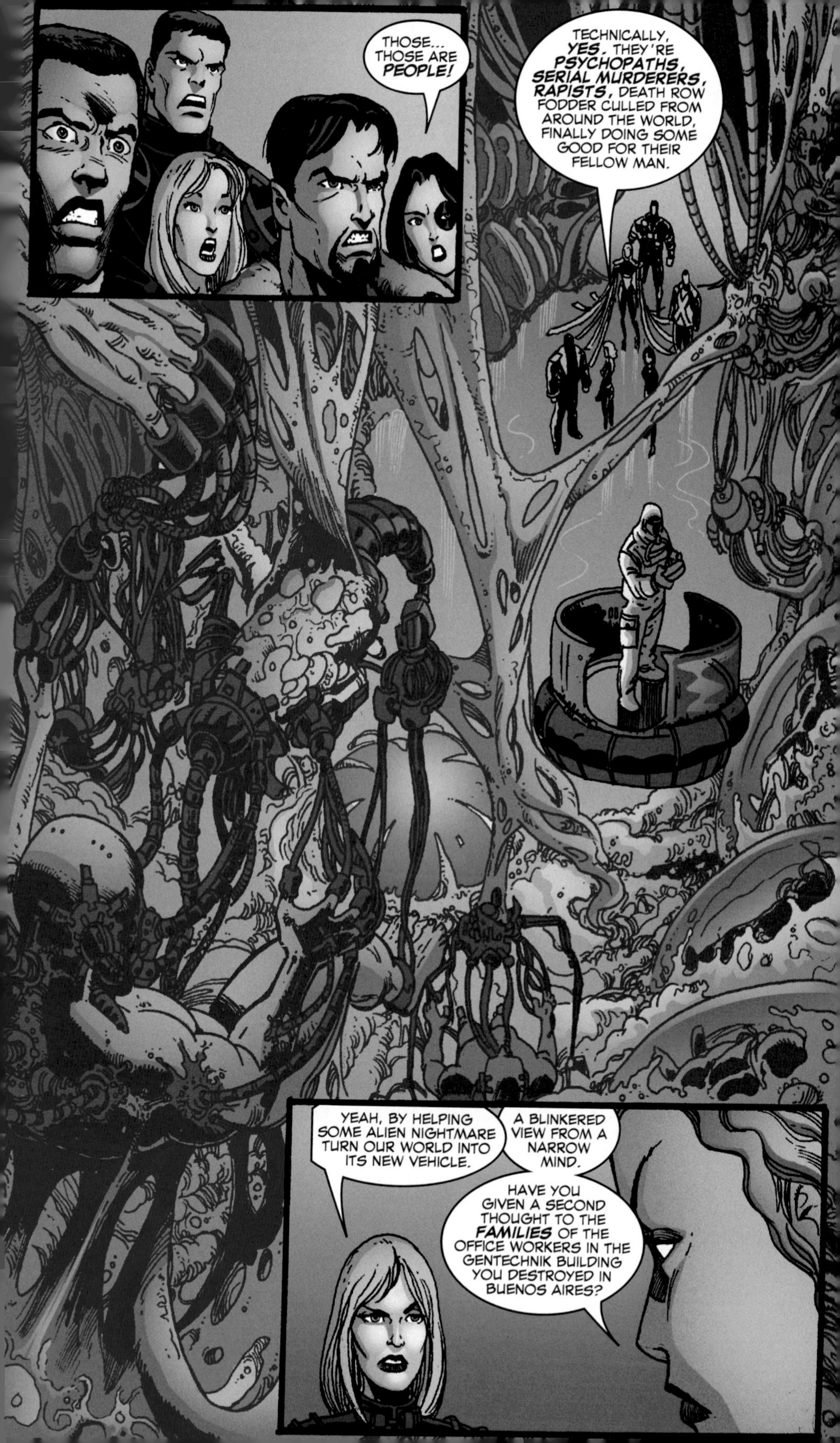
THOSE... THOSE ARE PEOPLE!
TECHNICALLY, YES. THEY'RE PSYCHOPATHS, SERIAL MURDERERS, RAPISTS, DEATH ROW FODDER CULLED FROM AROUND THE WORLD, FINALLY DOING SOME GOOD FOR THEIR FELLOW MAN.
YEAH, BY HELPING SOME ALIEN NIGHTMARE TURN OUR WORLD INTO ITS NEW VEHICLE.
A BLINKERED VIEW FROM A NARROW MIND.
HAVE YOU GIVEN A SECOND THOUGHT TO THE FAMILIES OF THE OFFICE WORKERS IN THE GENTECHNIK BUILDING YOU DESTROYED IN BUENOS AIRES?

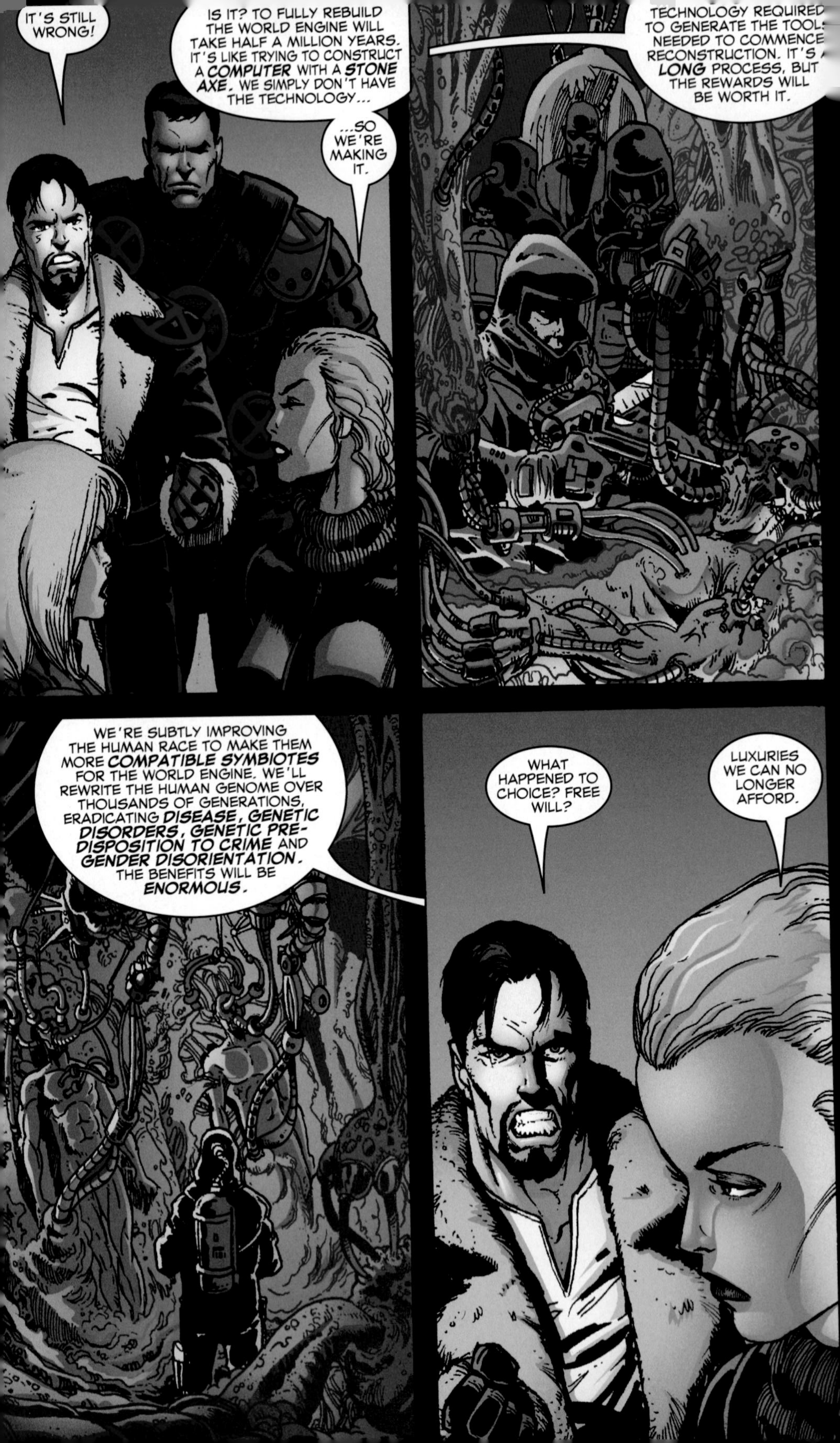
IT'S STILL WRONG!
IS IT? TO FULLY REBUILD THE WORLD ENGINE WILL TAKE HALF A MILLION YEARS. IT'S LIKE TRYING TO CONSTRUCT A COMPUTER WITH A STONE AXE. WE SIMPLY DON'T HAVE THE TECHNOLOGY...
...SO WE'RE MAKING IT.
TECHNOLOGY REQUIRED TO GENERATE THE TOOLS NEEDED TO COMMENCE RECONSTRUCTION. IT'S A LONG PROCESS, BUT THE REWARDS WILL BE WORTH IT.
WE'RE SUBTLY IMPROVING THE HUMAN RACE TO MAKE THEM MORE COMPATIBLE SYMBIOTES FOR THE WORLD ENGINE. WE'LL REWRITE THE HUMAN GENOME OVER THOUSANDS OF GENERATIONS, ERADICATING DISEASE, GENETIC DISORDERS, GENETIC PRE-DISPOSITION TO CRIME AND GENDER DISORIENTATION. THE BENEFITS WILL BE ENORMOUS.
WHAT HAPPENED TO CHOICE? FREE WILL?
LUXURIES WE CAN NO LONGER AFFORD.

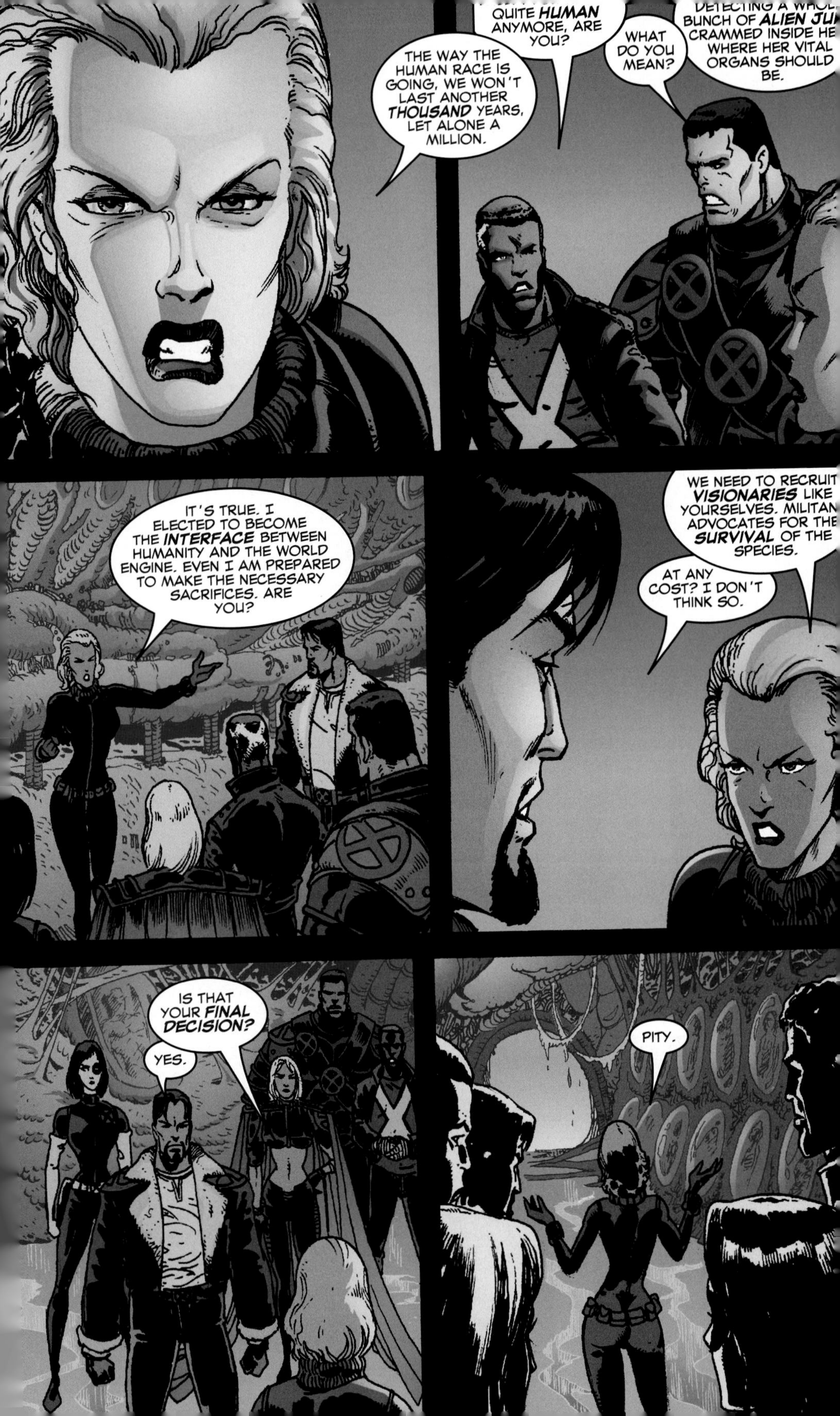
THE WAY THE HUMAN RACE IS GOING, WE WON'T LAST ANOTHER THOUSAND YEARS, LET ALONE A MILLION.
QUITE HUMAN ANYMORE, ARE YOU?
WHAT DO YOU MEAN?
BUNCH OF ALIEN JU CRAMMED INSIDE HE WHERE HER VITAL ORGANS SHOULD BE.
IT'S TRUE. I ELECTED TO BECOME THE INTERFACE BETWEEN HUMANITY AND THE WORLD ENGINE. EVEN I AM PREPARED TO MAKE THE NECESSARY SACRIFICES. ARE YOU?
WE NEED TO RECRUIT VISIONARIES LIKE YOURSELVES. MILITAN ADVOCATES FOR THE SURVIVAL OF THE SPECIES.
AT ANY COST? I DON'T THINK SO.
IS THAT YOUR FINAL DECISION?
YES.
PITY.

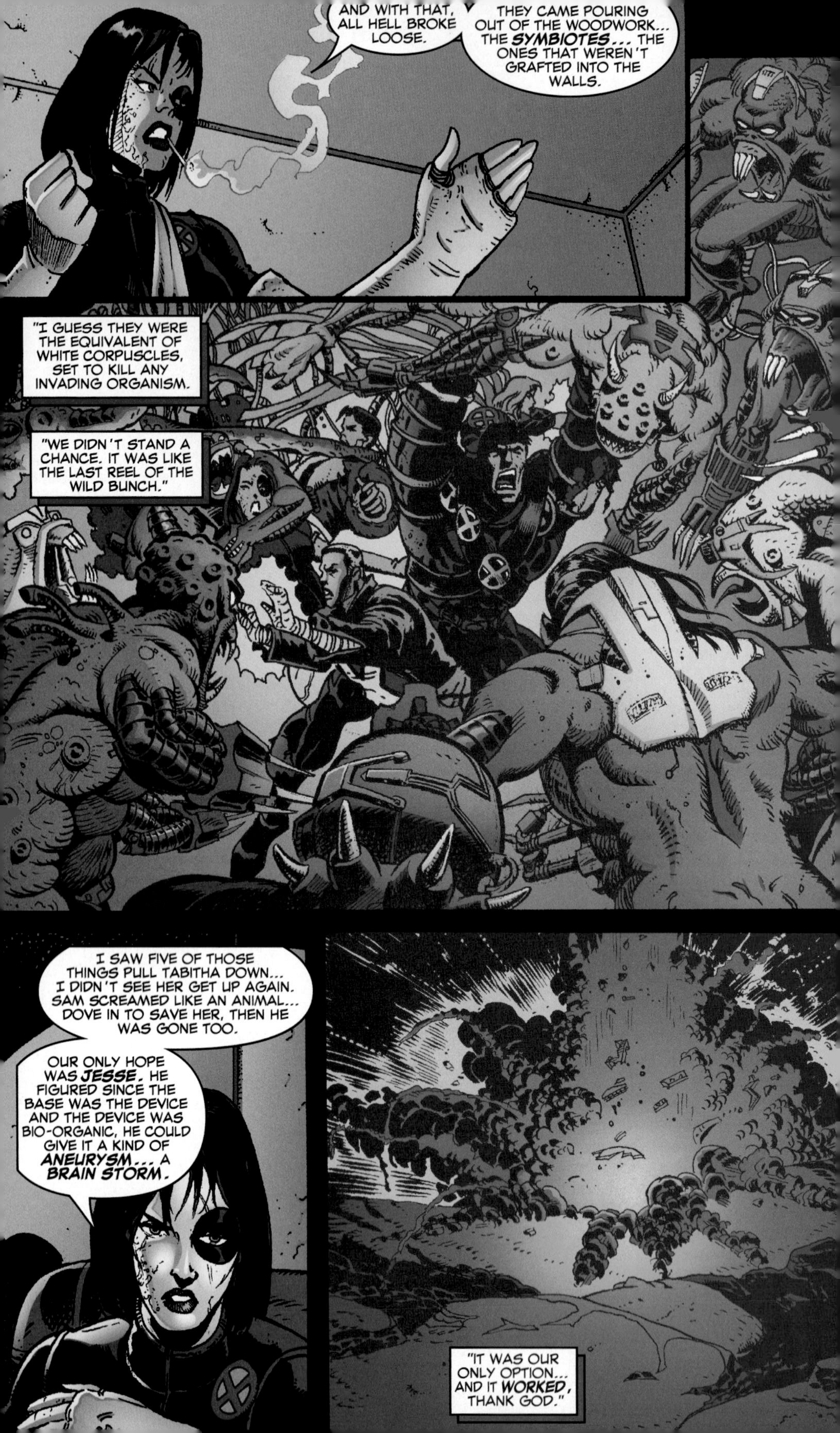
AND WITH THAT, ALL HELL BROKE LOOSE.
THEY CAME POURING OUT OF THE WOODWORK... THE SYMBIOTES... THE ONES THAT WEREN'T GRAFTED INTO THE WALLS.
"I GUESS THEY WERE THE EQUIVALENT OF WHITE CORPUSCLES, SET TO KILL ANY INVADING ORGANISM.
"WE DIDN'T STAND A CHANCE. IT WAS LIKE THE LAST REEL OF THE WILD BUNCH."
I SAW FIVE OF THOSE THINGS PULL TABITHA DOWN... I DIDN'T SEE HER GET UP AGAIN. SAM SCREAMED LIKE AN ANIMAL... DOVE IN TO SAVE HER, THEN HE WAS GONE TOO.
OUR ONLY HOPE WAS JESSE. HE FIGURED SINCE THE BASE WAS THE DEVICE AND THE DEVICE WAS BIO-ORGANIC, HE COULD GIVE IT A KIND OF ANEURYSM... A BRAIN STORM.
"IT WAS OUR ONLY OPTION... AND IT WORKED, THANK GOD."

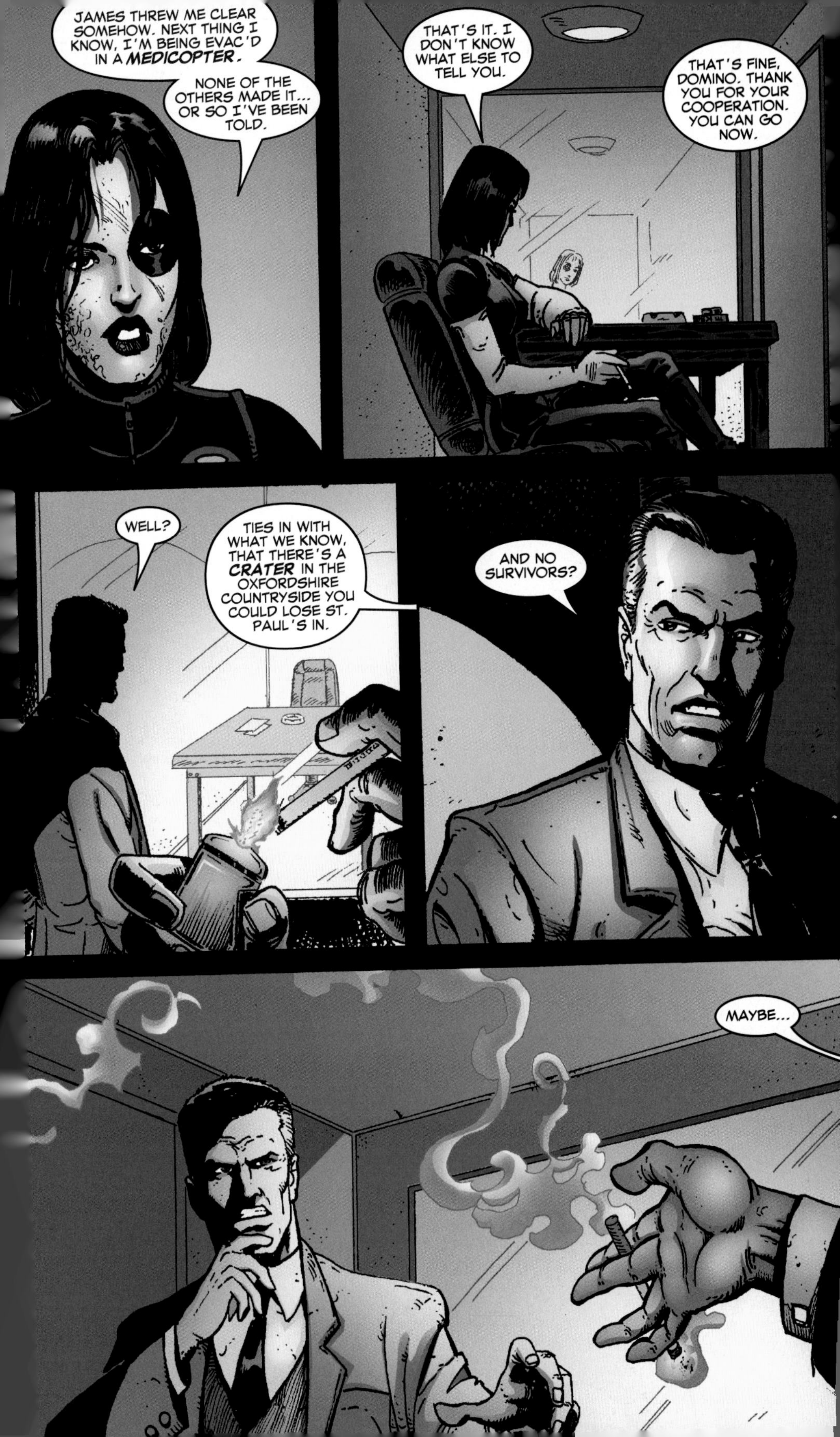
JAMES THREW ME CLEAR SOMEHOW. NEXT THING I KNOW, I'M BEING EVAC'D IN A MEDICOPTER.
NONE OF THE OTHERS MADE IT... OR SO I'VE BEEN TOLD.
THAT'S IT. I DON'T KNOW WHAT ELSE TO TELL YOU.
THAT'S FINE, DOMINO. THANK YOU FOR YOUR COOPERATION. YOU CAN GO NOW.
WELL?
TIES IN WITH WHAT WE KNOW, THAT THERE'S A CRATER IN THE OXFORDSHIRE COUNTRYSIDE YOU COULD LOSE ST. PAUL'S IN.
AND NO SURVIVORS?
MAYBE...

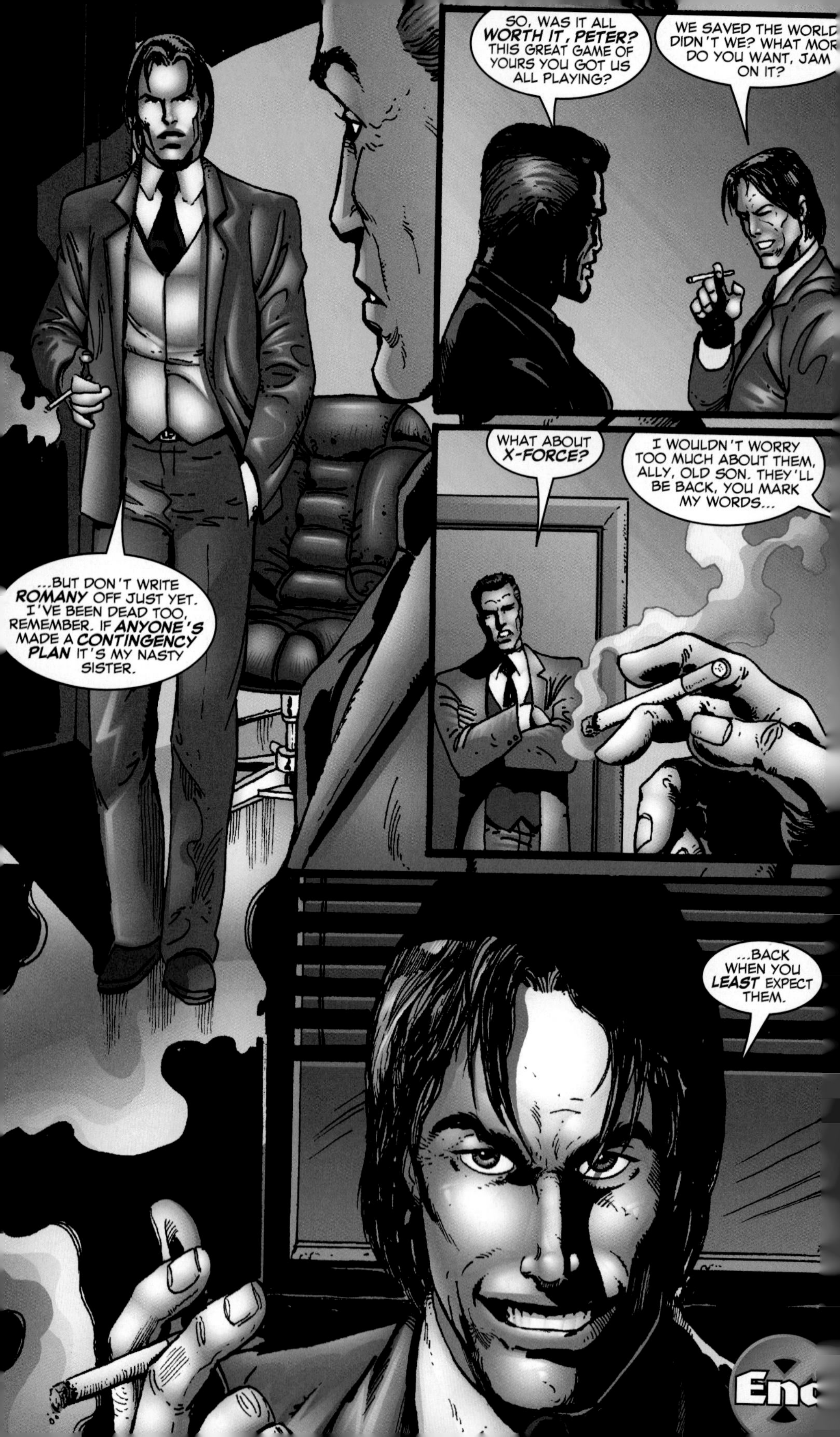
...BUT DON'T WRITE ROMANY OFF JUST YET. I'VE BEEN DEAD TOO, REMEMBER. IF ANYONE'S MADE A CONTINGENCY PLAN IT'S MY NASTY SISTER.
SO, WAS IT ALL WORTH IT, PETER? THIS GREAT GAME OF YOURS YOU GOT US ALL PLAYING?
WE SAVED THE WORLD DIDN'T WE? WHAT MOR DO YOU WANT, JAM ON IT?
WHAT ABOUT X-FORCE?
I WOULDN'T WORRY TOO MUCH ABOUT THEM, ALLY, OLD SON. THEY'LL BE BACK, YOU MARK MY WORDS...
...BACK WHEN YOU LEAST EXPECT THEM.

You may be asking yourself what makes X-FORCE #102 so special that it would demand this extra 'Rough Cut' edition? The answer is, just about everything!

X-FORCE #102 marked the beginning of a brand new era in the direction of the X-books' middle children. Warren Ellis, one of the most twisted and respected minds in comic books today, had come on board the junior X-titles for an experiment named Counter-X. It would be his job to creatively redirect three X-books— GENERATION X, X-MAN, and X-FORCE. Each would be unique but connected in thematic ways. It would be Warren's job to dramatically alter the face of one of Marvel's longest running mutant titles— X-FORCE.

Inside this 'Rough Cut' you'll get to peek behind the wall of madness, the mind of Warren Ellis. This book contains the actual plot for X-FORCE #102, straight from the editor's desk to your hands.

By Warren's side would be Whilce Portacio, a penciler who had not stepped inside the mighty halls of Marvel since his amazing run on UNCANNY X-MEN nearly a decade ago. Here Whilce would finally make his triumphant return to the X-MEN family. His commitment to take X-FORCE to unprecedented highs was the force that drove this book over the top.

And when you see his untouched pencils inside these pages you'll understand why this book demanded a 'Rough Cut' version.

Which leads us to the reason this book was even possible. The process we used to complete this first part of the Counter-X experiment was key in its success. Normally, the process of putting a comic book together is always the same. The penciler finishes a page and then sends it off to an inker who inks over the actual pencils. This did not happen on X-FORCE #102. When Whilce finished a page on this book, he scanned the pencils into his computer, and e-mailed that file off to his inker, Gerry Alanguilan. Gerry then printed that page onto artboard, using light blue ink, and proceeded to ink over the top of that art board printout. A technique that, at Marvel at least, had never been used before. Pretty wild stuff, and a process that not only saved time, but allowed for all of the original pencils of the issue to remain intact.

So here it is, laid out bare before you. It's a special chance to take a peek under the hood to see what makes this baby run. We hope you agree that X-Force #102 is a phenomenal book, and worthy of a closer look.

- Jason Liebig, Editor

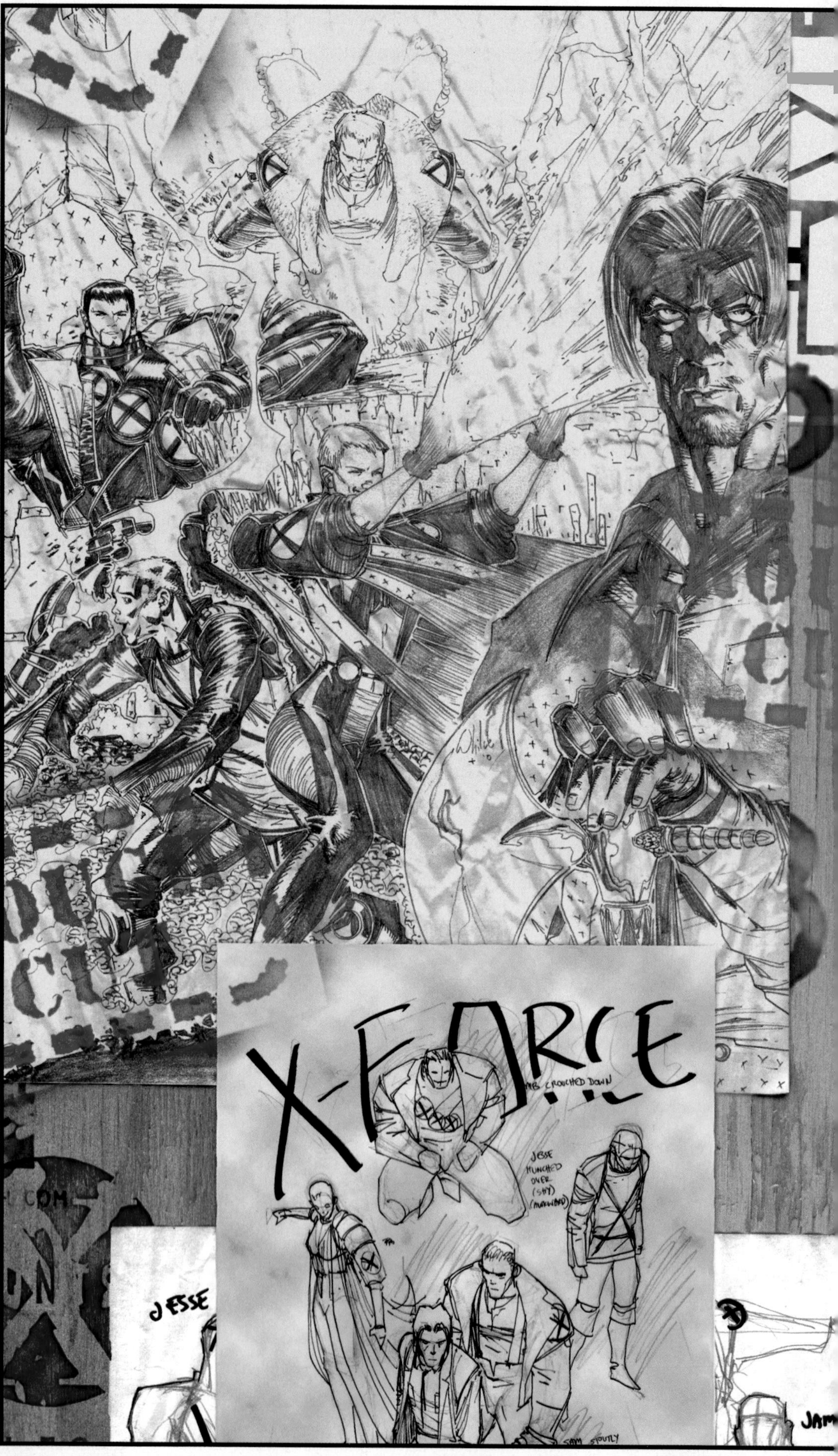

X-FORCE
MB CROUCHED DOWN
JESSE HUNCHED OVER (SHY) (AWKWARD)
JESSE
SAM STOUTLY

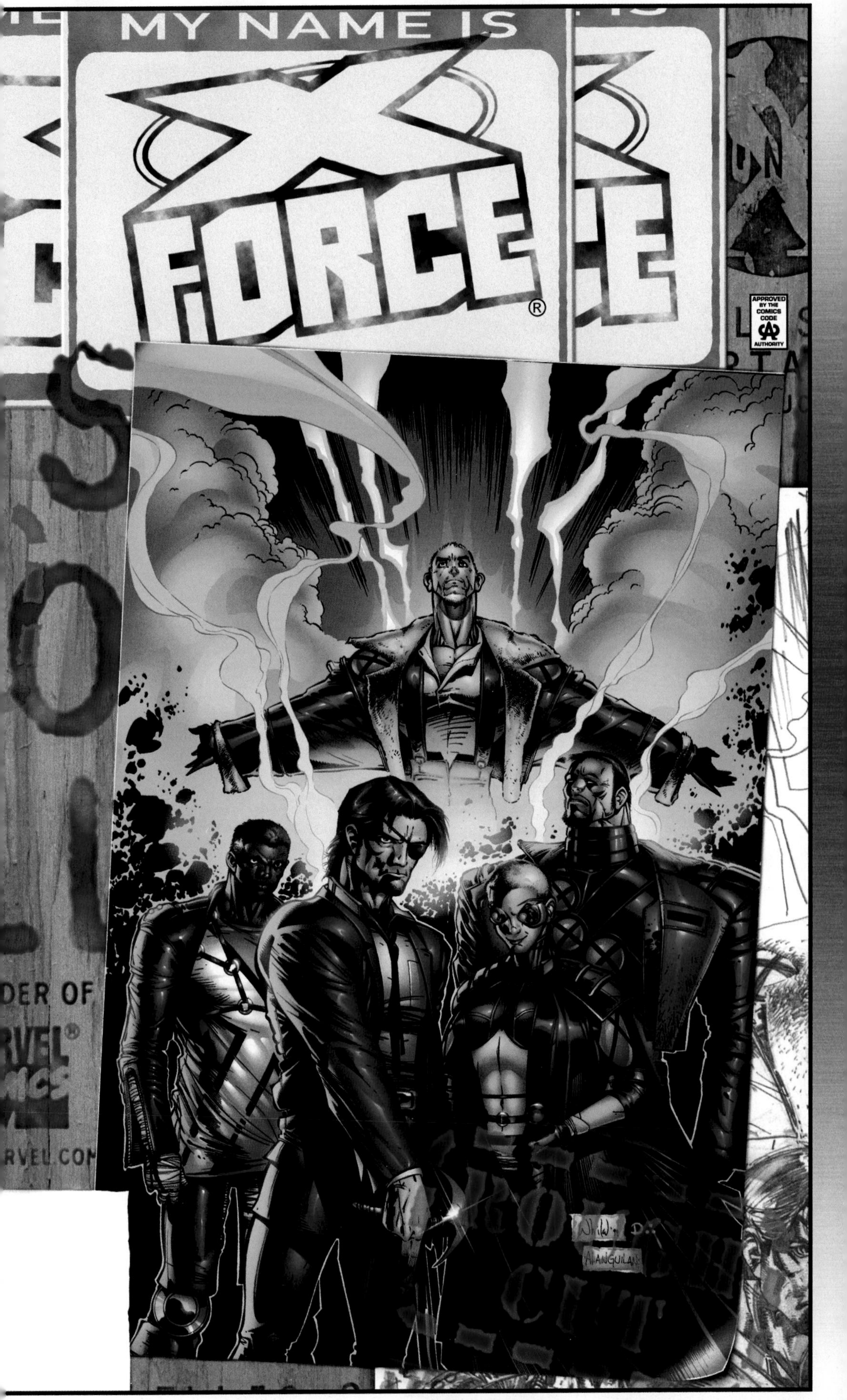
MY NAME IS
X-FORCE
APPROVED BY THE COMICS CODE AUTHORITY
DER OF
RVEL
RVEL.COM

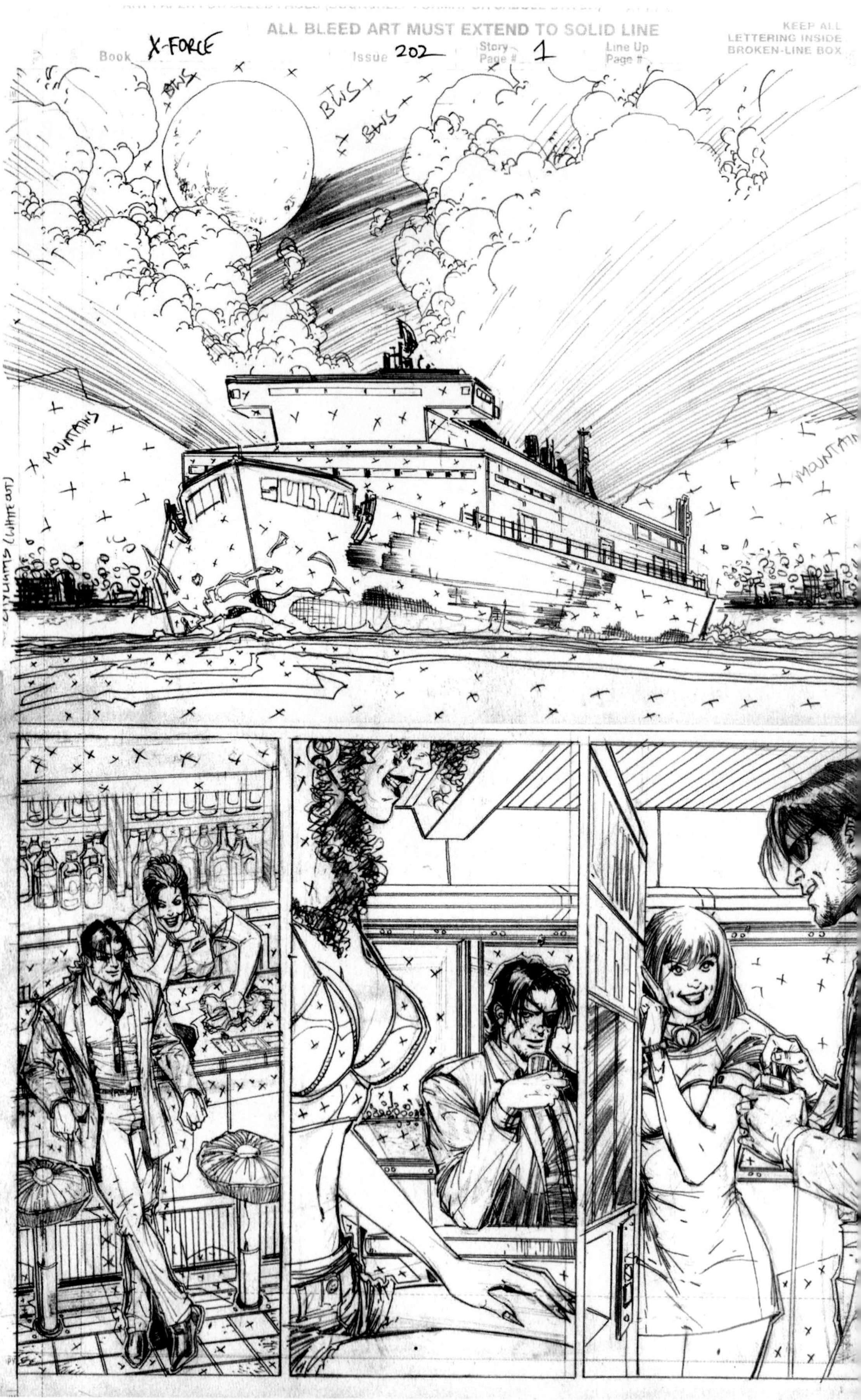
ALL BLEED ART MUST EXTEND TO SOLID LINE
KEEP ALL LETTERING INSIDE BROKEN-LINE BOX
Book X-FORCE
Issue 202
Story Page # 1
Line Up Page #
BWS
BWS
BWS
MOUNTAINS
MOUNTAINS
SULYA
CITYLIGHTS (WHITE OUT)

COLOR NIGHT SKY WITH STARS

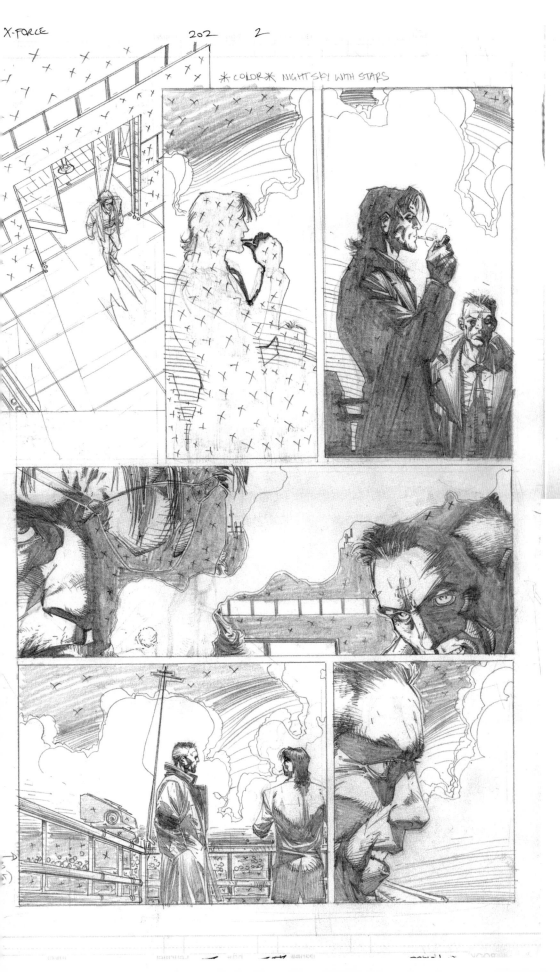

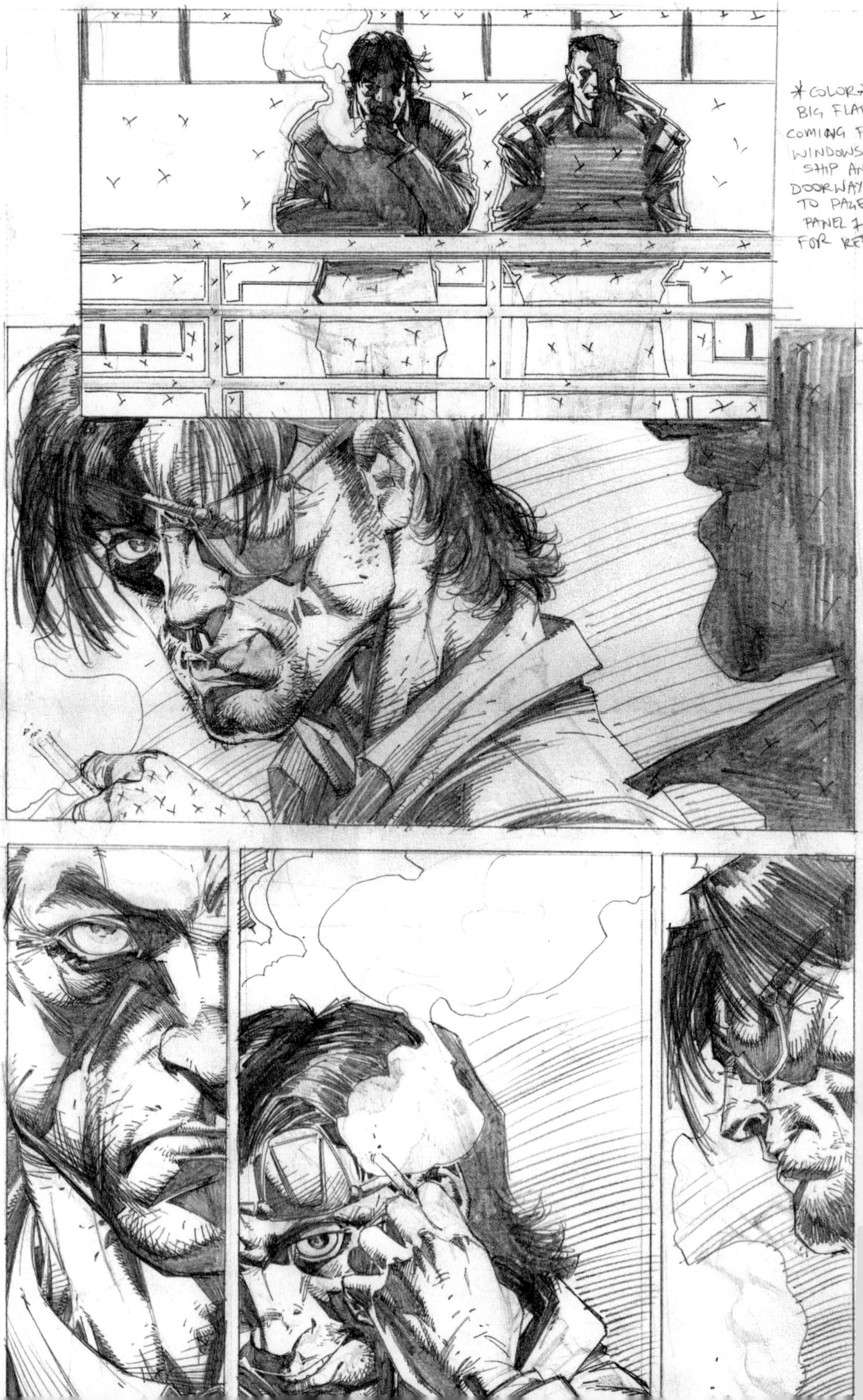

COLOR
BIG FLA
COMING F
WINDOWS
SHIP AN
DOORWAY
TO PAGE
PANEL 7
FOR REF

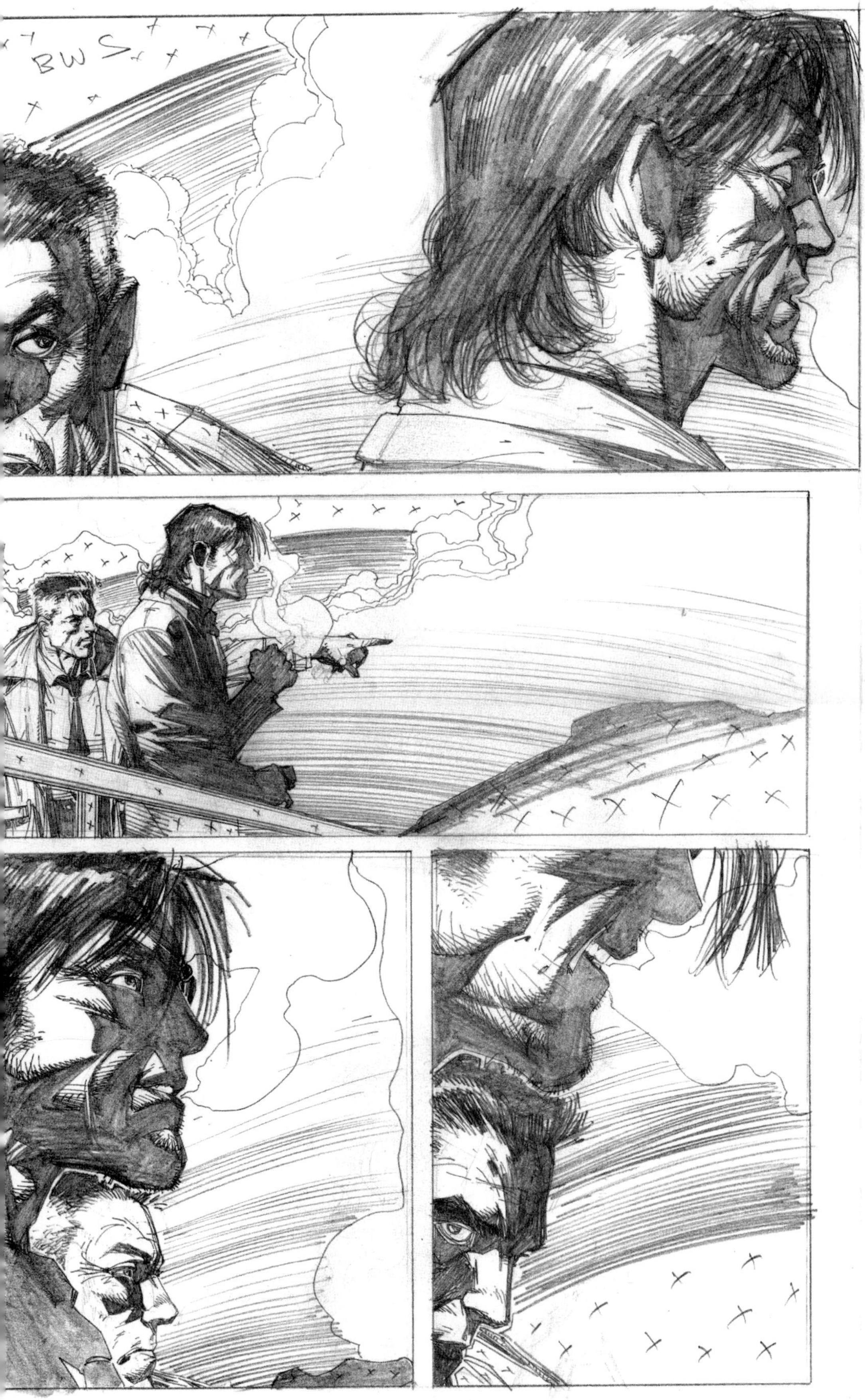
BWS

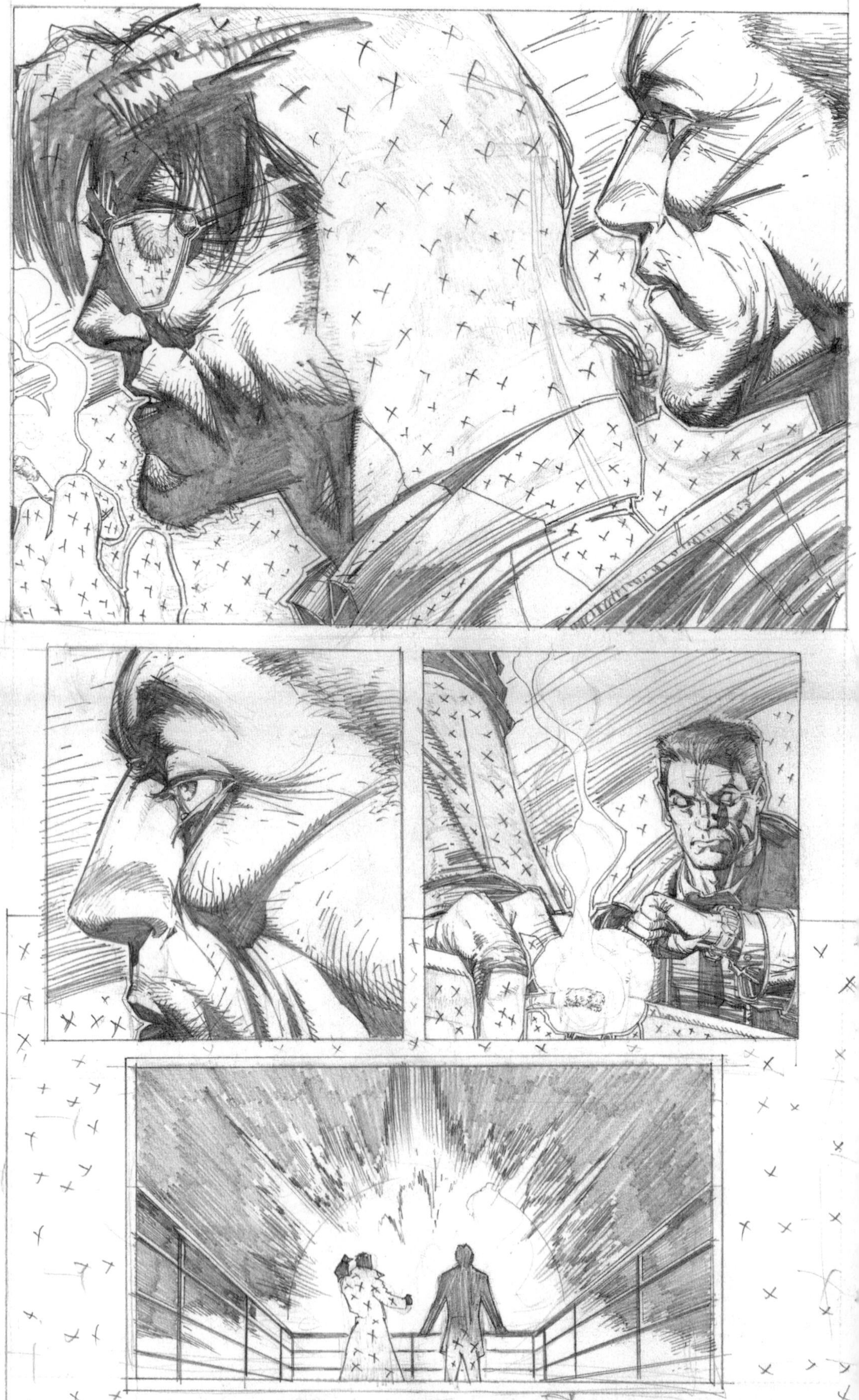

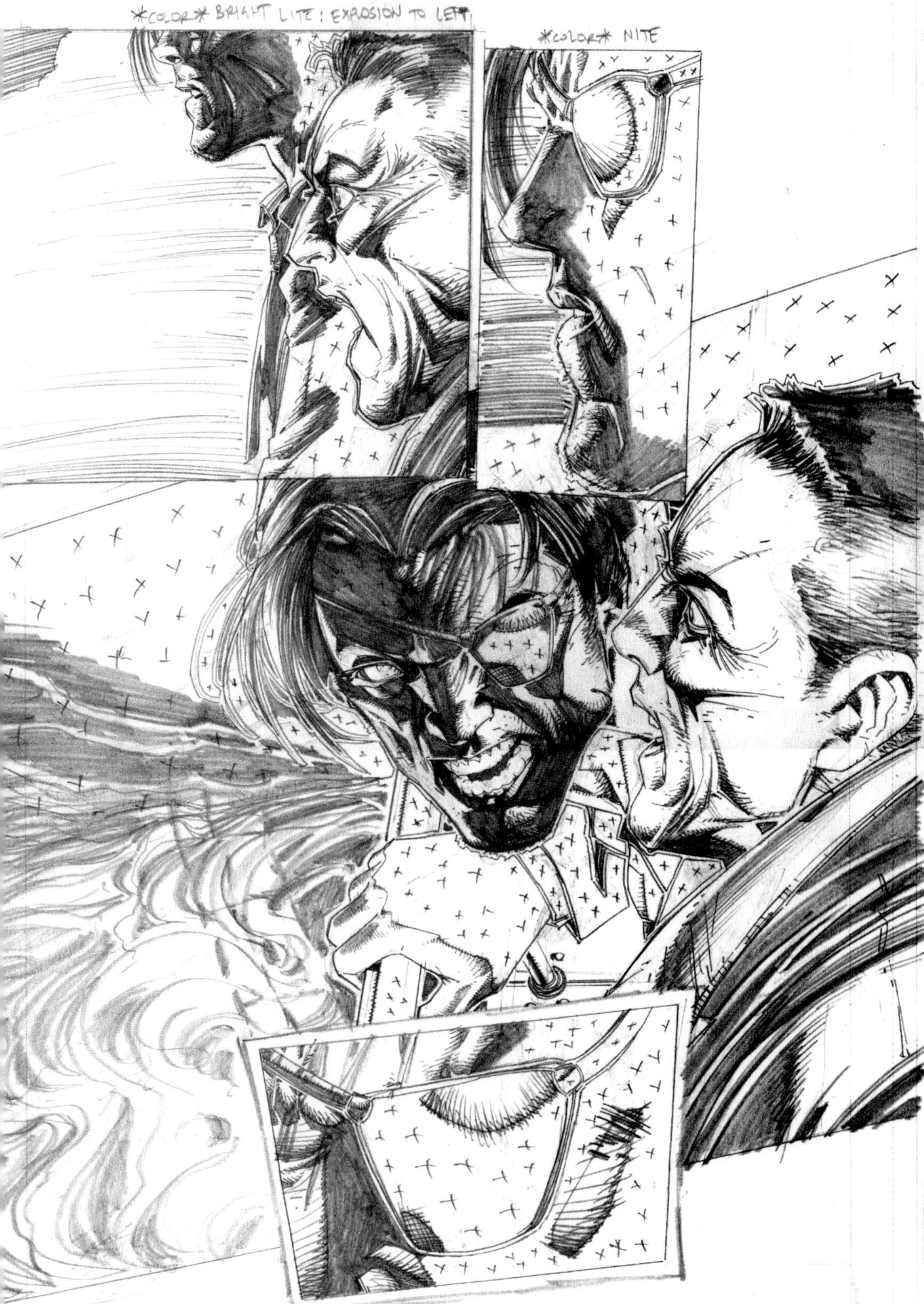
COLOR BRIGHT LITE: EXPLOSION TO LEFT
COLOR NITE

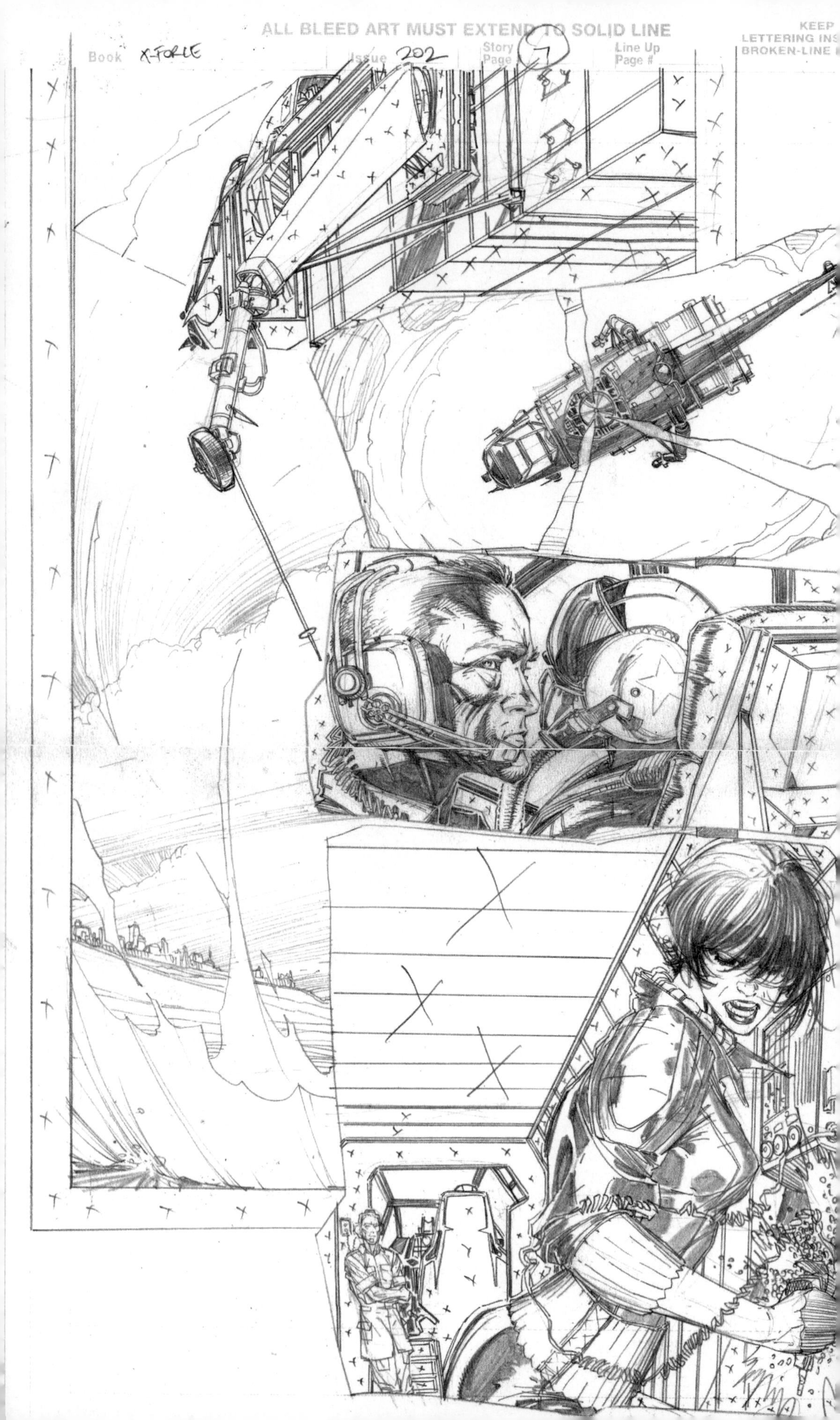
ALL BLEED ART MUST EXTEND TO SOLID LINE
Book X-FORCE
Issue 202
Story Page 7
Line Up Page #
KEEP
LETTERING INS
BROKEN-LINE

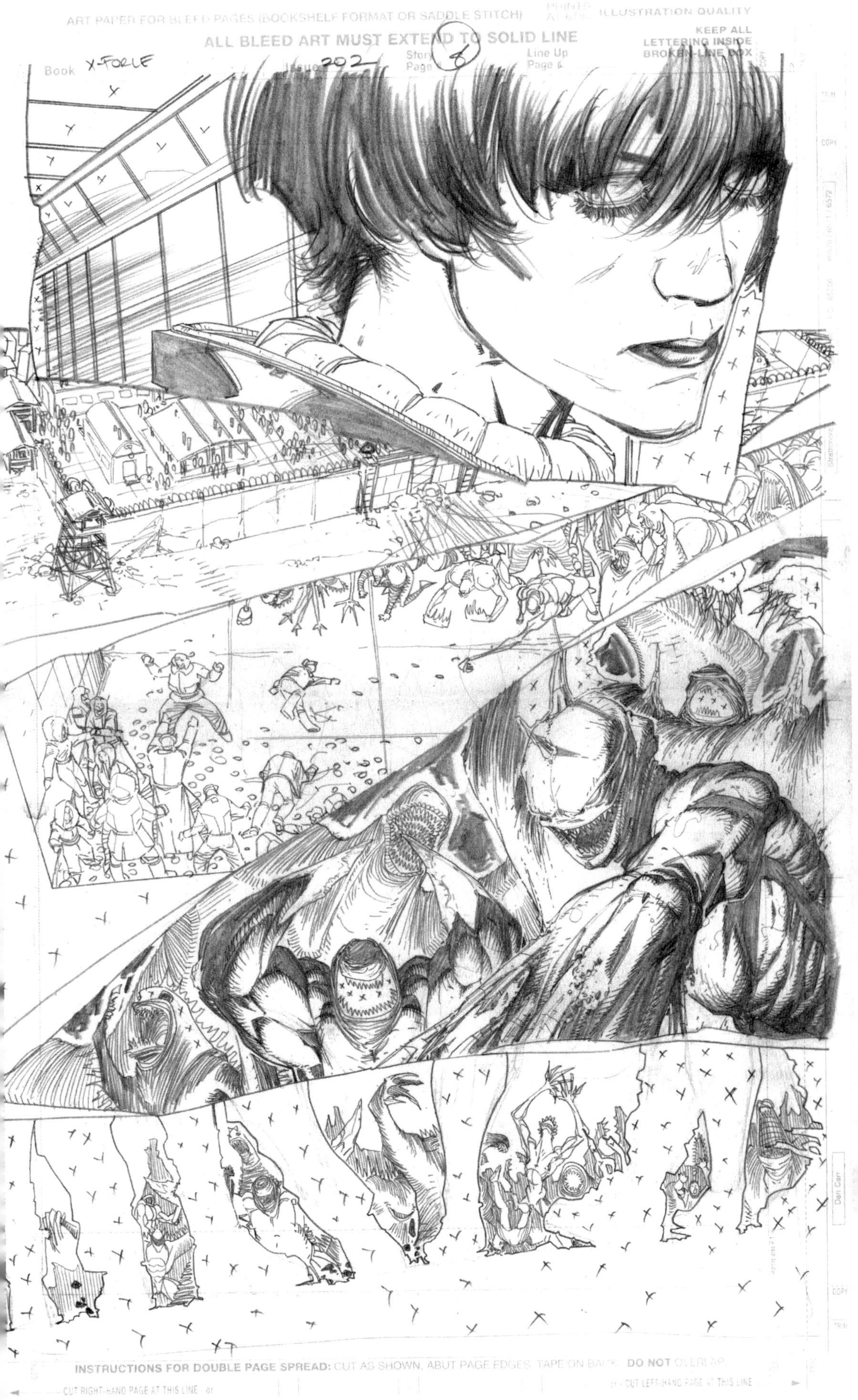
ART PAPER FOR BLEED PAGES (BOOKSHELF FORMAT OR SADDLE STITCH)
ILLUSTRATION QUALITY
ALL BLEED ART MUST EXTEND TO SOLID LINE
KEEP ALL LETTERING INSIDE BROKEN-LINE BOX
Book X-FORCE
Issue 202
Story Page 8
Line Up Page
INSTRUCTIONS FOR DOUBLE PAGE SPREAD: CUT AS SHOWN. ABUT PAGE EDGES. TAPE ON BACK. DO NOT OVERLAP
CUT RIGHT-HAND PAGE AT THIS LINE
CUT LEFT-HAND PAGE AT THIS LINE

Book | Issue | Story Page # 9 | Line Up Page # | BROKEN-LINE BOX

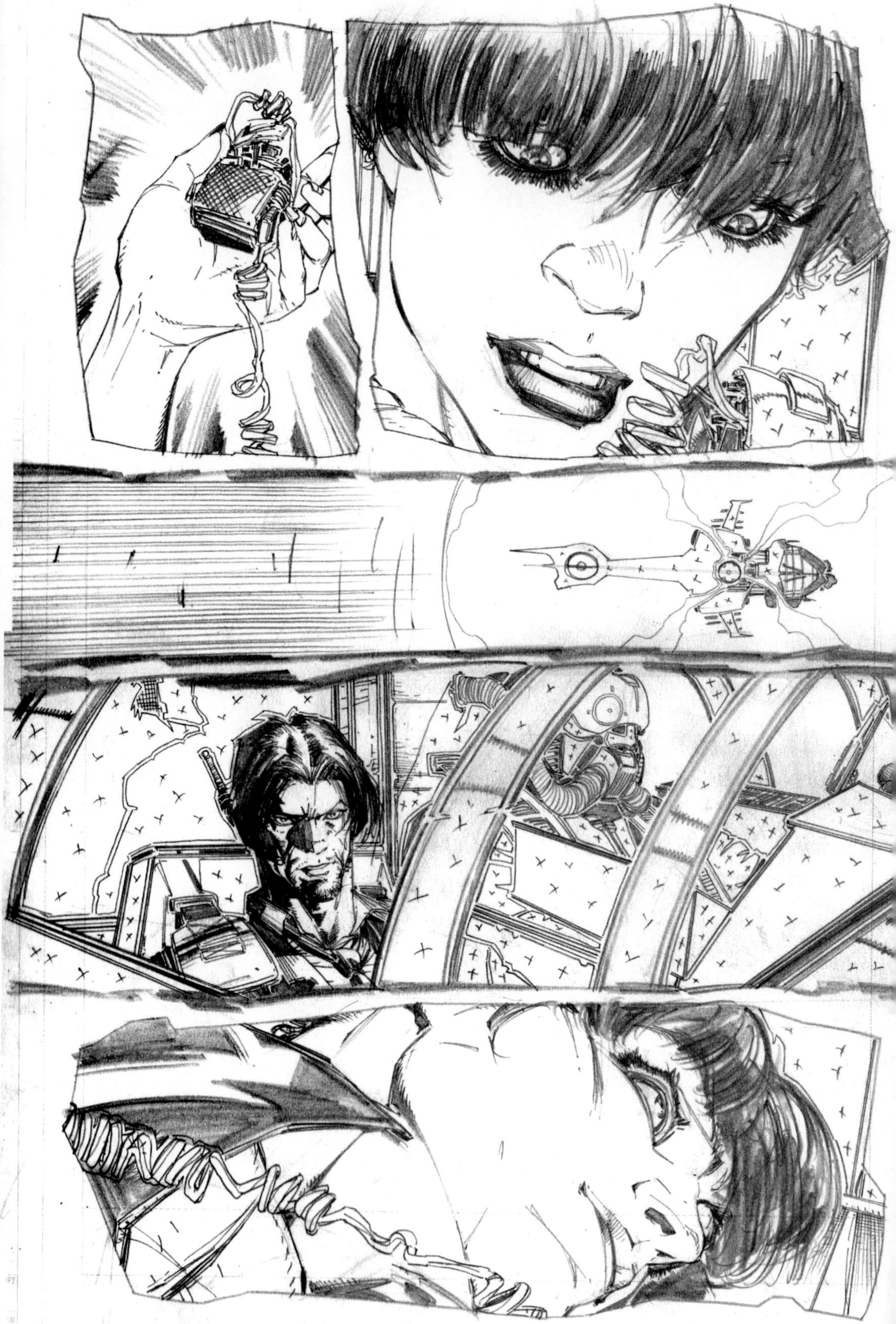

INSTRUCTIONS FOR DOUBLE PAGE SPREAD: CUT AS SHOWN. ABUT PAGE EDGES. TAPE ON BACK. DO NOT OVERLAP.

CUT RIGHT HAND PAGE AT THIS LINE - or

or - CUT LEFT-HAND PAGE AT THIS LINE

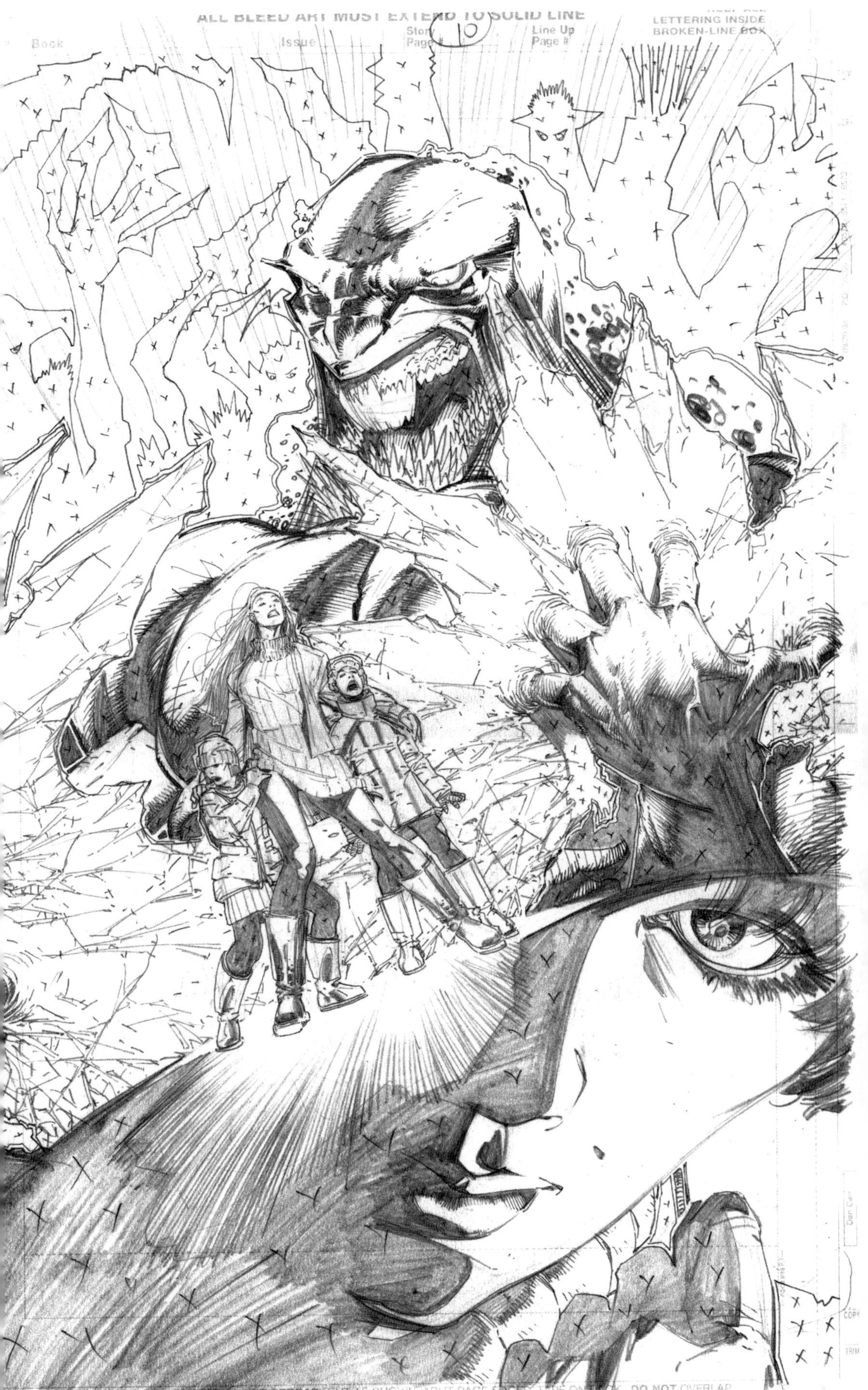
ALL BLEED ART MUST EXTEND TO SOLID LINE
Book
Issue
Story Page # 10
Line Up Page #
LETTERING INSIDE BROKEN-LINE BOX
INSTRUCTIONS FOR DOUBLE PAGE SPREAD: CUT AS SHOWN, ABUT PAGE EDGES, TAPE ON BACK. DO NOT OVERLAP

ART PAPER FOR BLEED PAGES (BOOKSHELF FORMAT OR SADDLE STITCH)
ALL BLEED ART MUST EXTEND TO SOLID LINE
PRINTS AT 67% ILLUSTRATION QUALITY
KEEP ALL LETTERING INSIDE BROKEN-LINE BOX

Book X-FORCE   Issue 102   Story Page 13   Line Up Page #

ALL BLEED ART MUST EXTEND TO SOLID LINE

Book X-FORCE Issue 102 Story Page # 15 Line Up Page #

KEEP ALL LETTERING INSIDE BROKEN LINE BOX

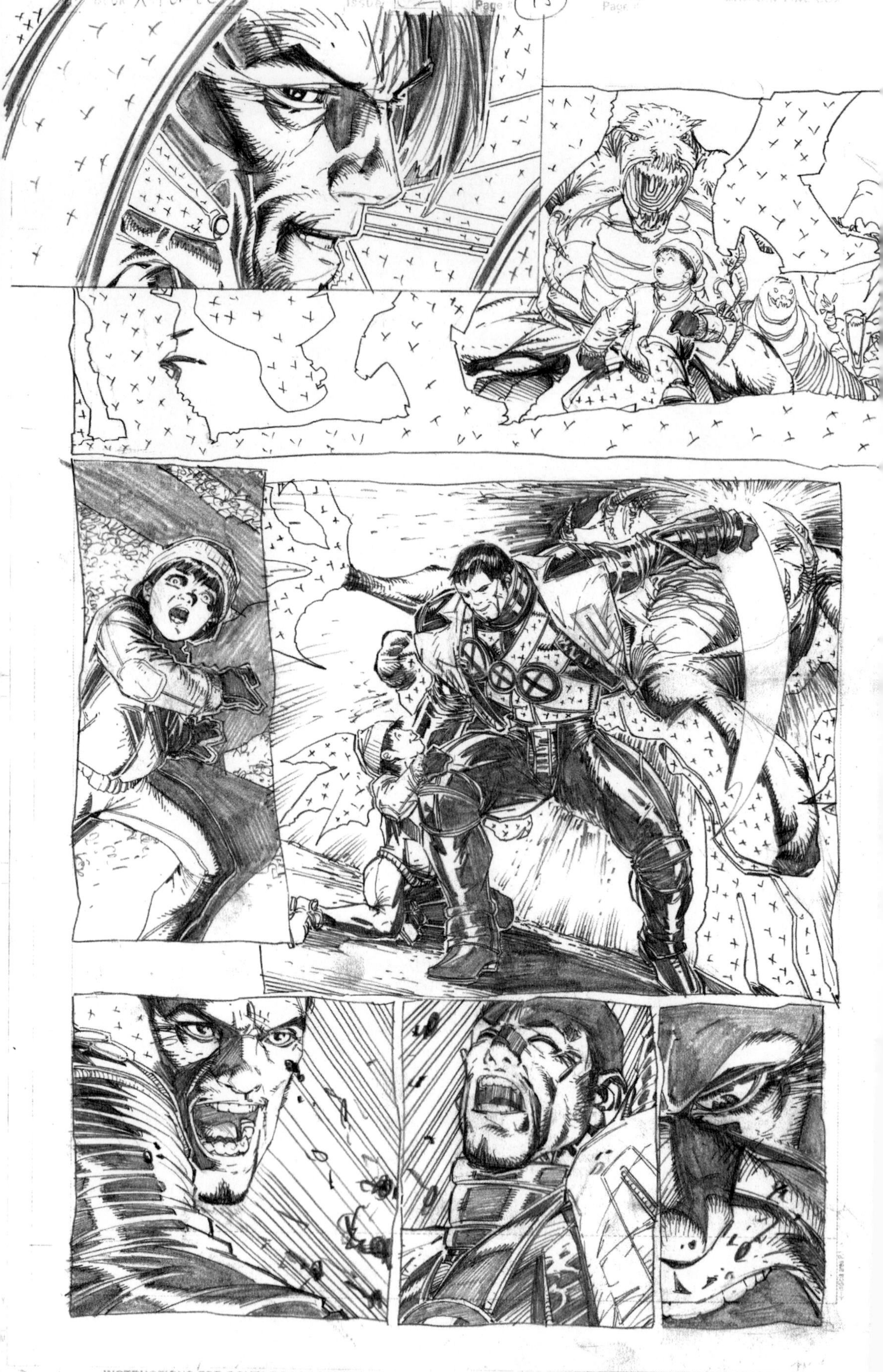

INSTRUCTIONS FOR DOUBLE PAGE SPREAD: CUT AS SHOWN, ABUT PAGE EDGES, TAPE ON BACK. **DO NOT** OVERLAP.

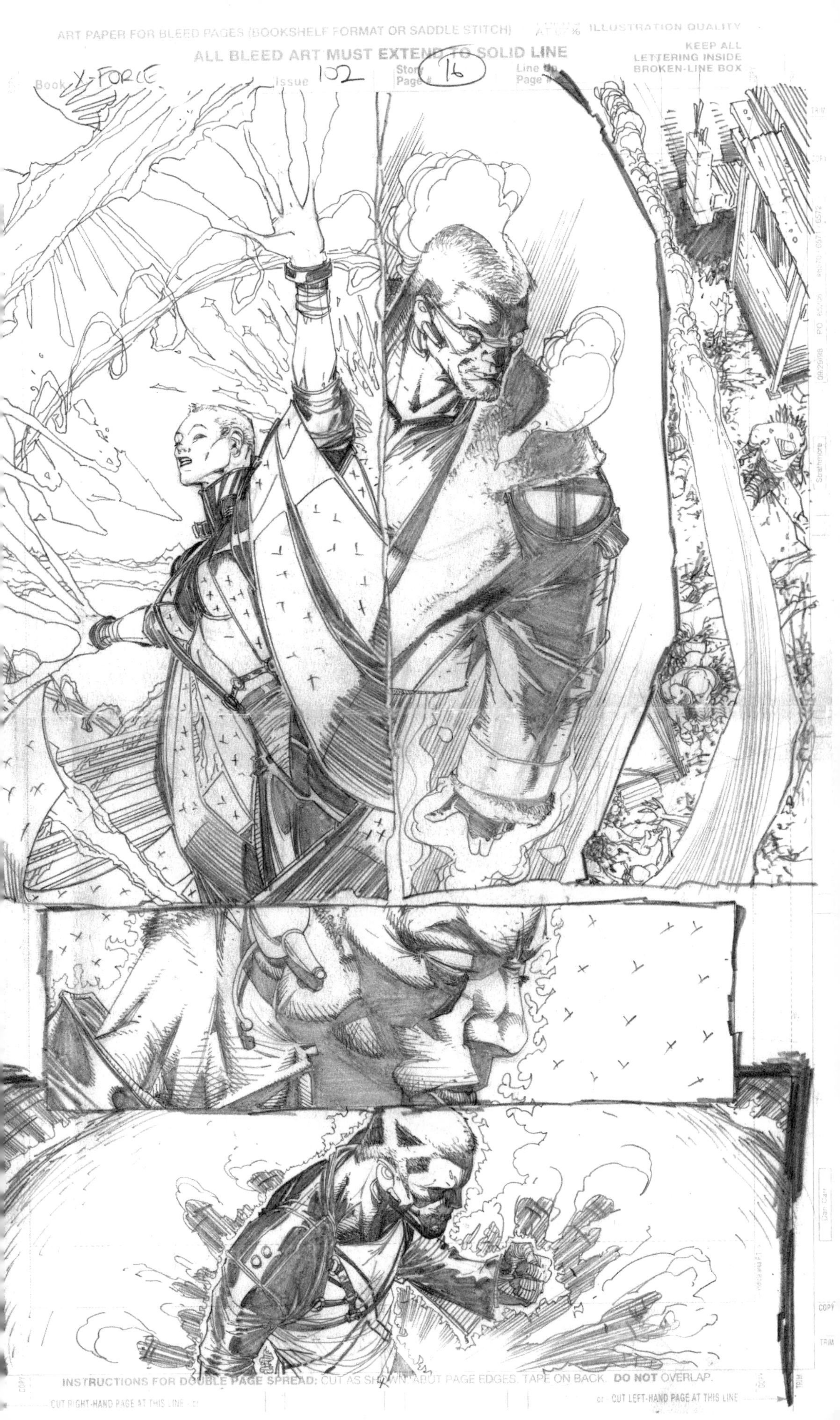
ART PAPER FOR BLEED PAGES (BOOKSHELF FORMAT OR SADDLE STITCH)
ILLUSTRATION QUALITY
ALL BLEED ART MUST EXTEND TO SOLID LINE
KEEP ALL LETTERING INSIDE BROKEN-LINE BOX
Book X-FORCE
Issue 102
Story Page # 16
Line Up Page #
INSTRUCTIONS FOR DOUBLE PAGE SPREAD: CUT AS SHOWN. ABUT PAGE EDGES, TAPE ON BACK. DO NOT OVERLAP.
CUT RIGHT-HAND PAGE AT THIS LINE
CUT LEFT-HAND PAGE AT THIS LINE

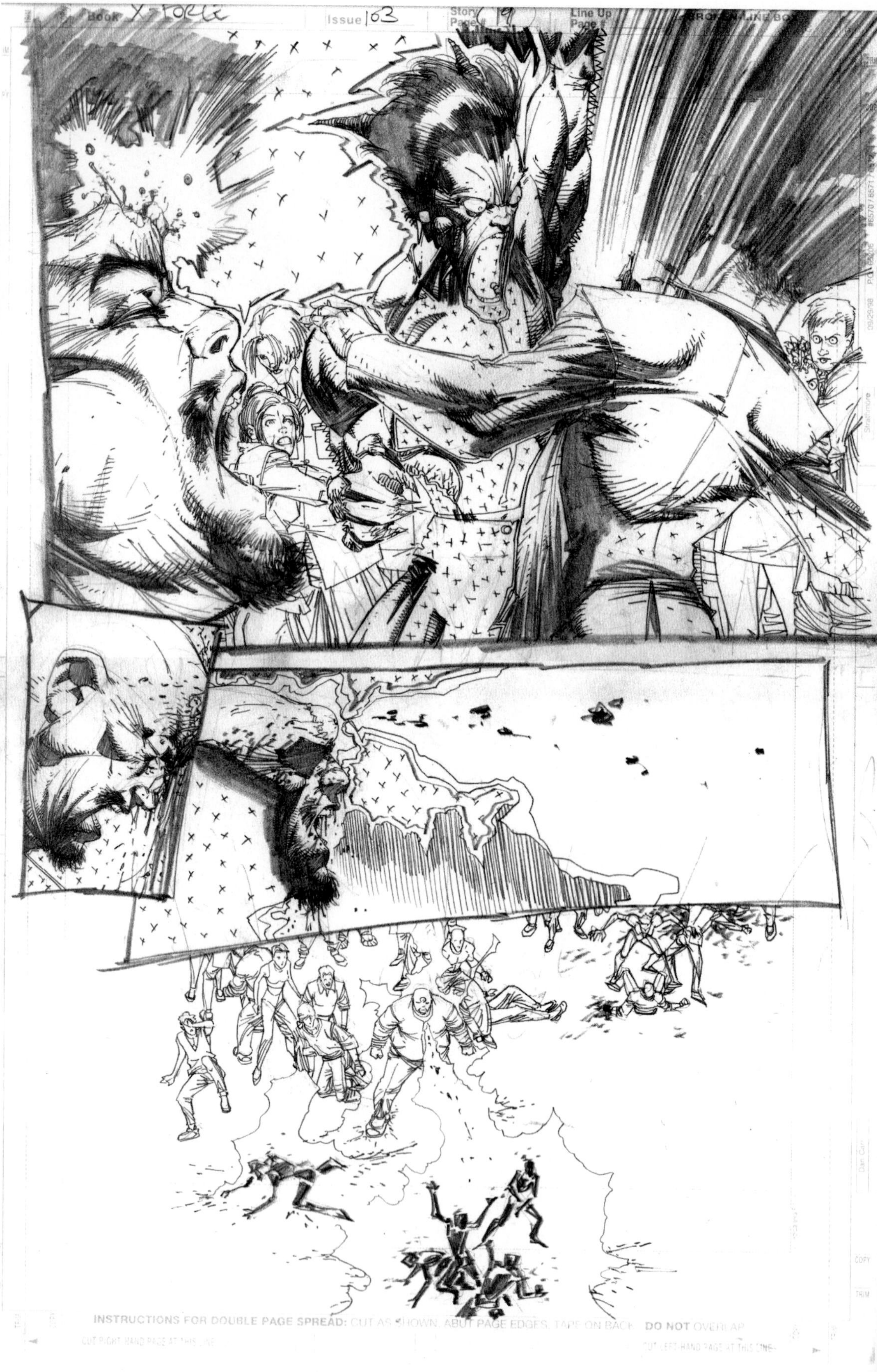
Book X-Force
Issue 103
Story Page # 19
Line Up Page #
INSTRUCTIONS FOR DOUBLE PAGE SPREAD: CUT AS SHOWN, ABUT PAGE EDGES, TAPE ON BACK. DO NOT OVERLAP
CUT RIGHT-HAND PAGE AT THIS LINE
CUT LEFT-HAND PAGE AT THIS LINE

ALL BLEED ART MUST EXTEND TO SOLID LINE

KEEP ALL LETTERING INSIDE BROKEN-LINE BOX

Book X-FORCE Issue 102 Story Page # 20 Line Up Page #

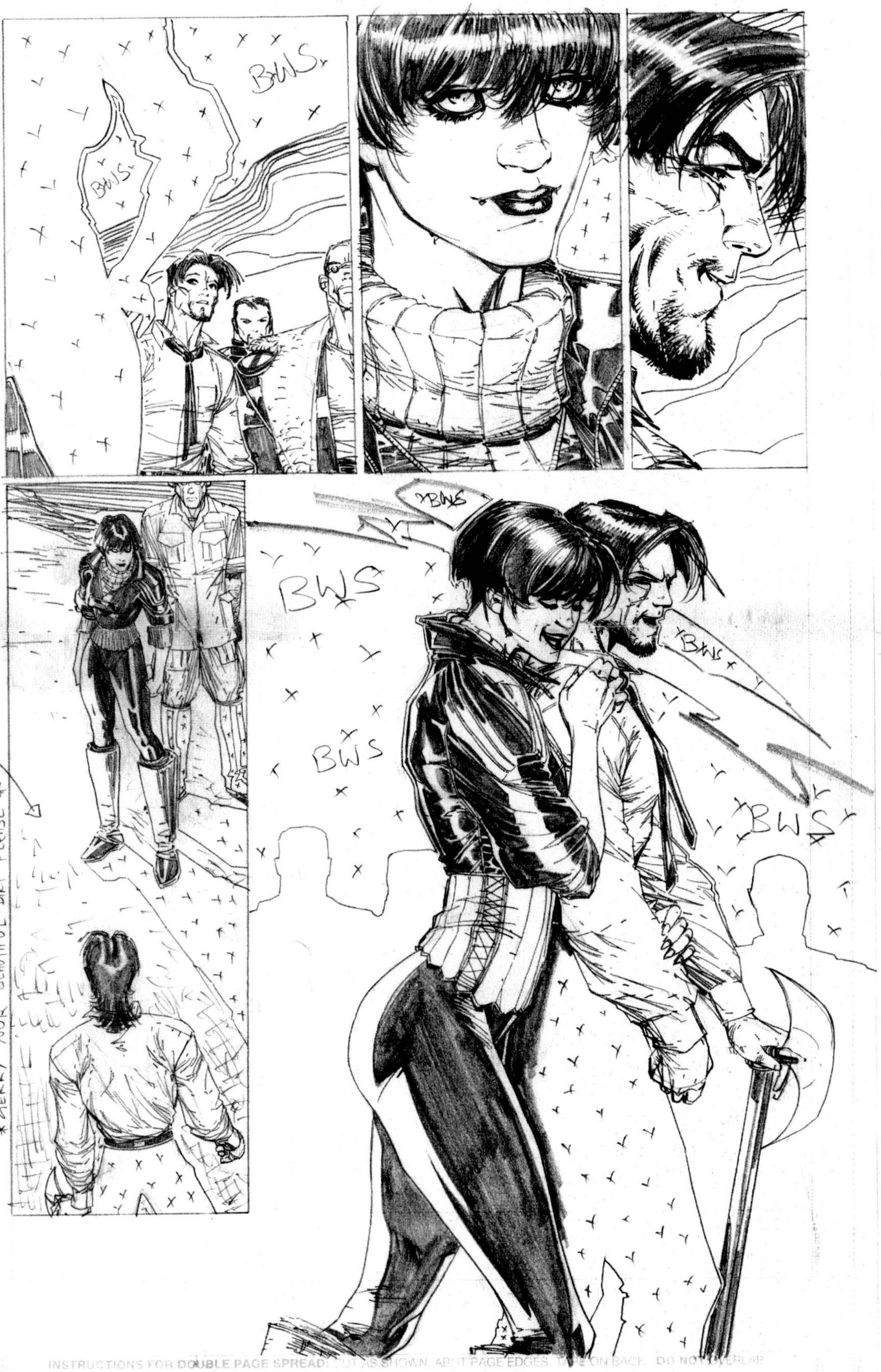
BWS
BWS
BWS
BWS
BWS
BWS
BWS
GERRY YOUR BEAUTIFUL DIRT PLEASE

INSTRUCTIONS FOR DOUBLE PAGE SPREAD: CUT AS SHOWN, ABUT PAGE EDGES, TAPE ON BACK. DO NOT OVERLAP

CUT RIGHT-HAND PAGE AT THIS LINE

CUT LEFT-HAND PAGE AT THIS LINE

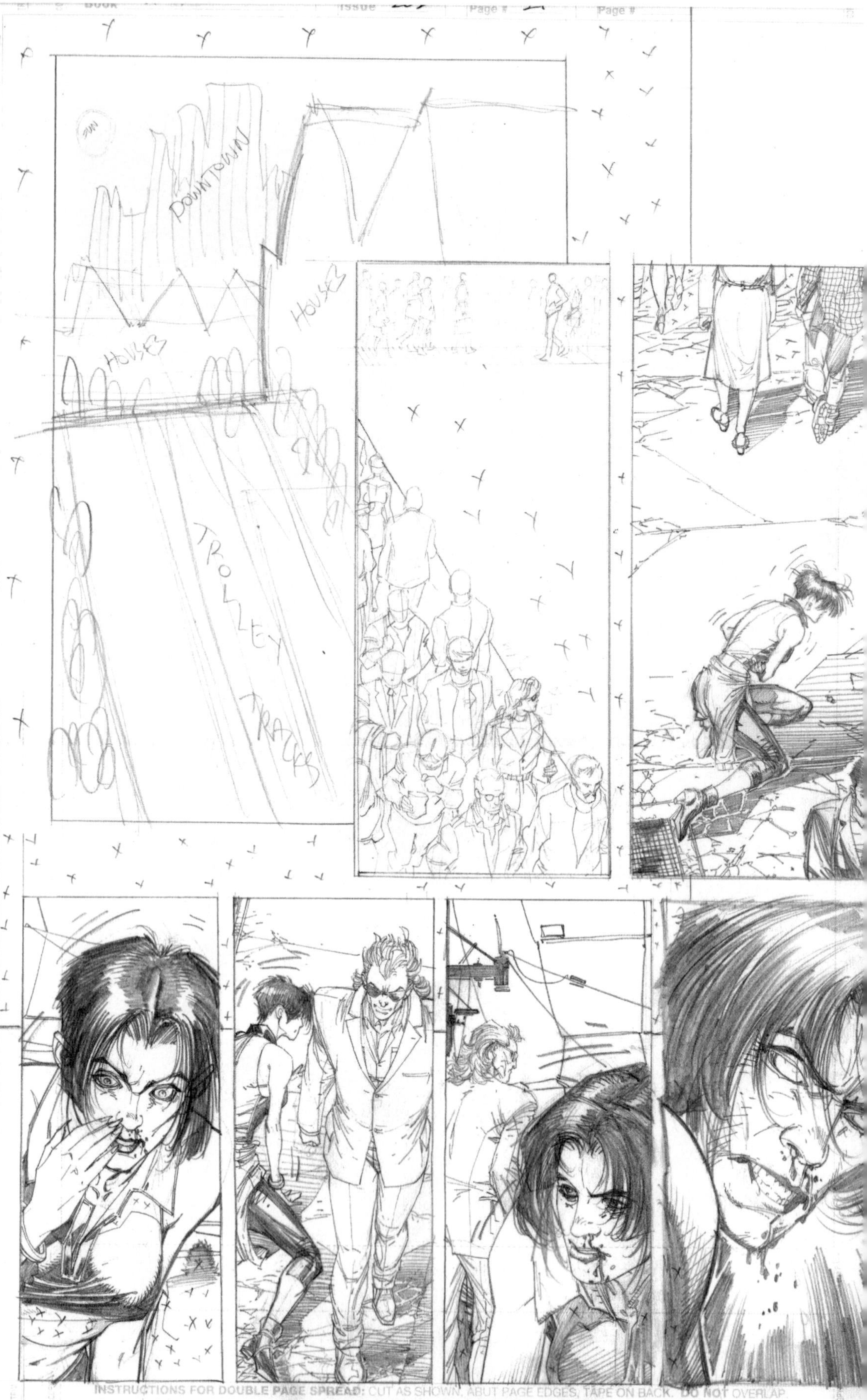
SUN
DOWNTOWN
HOUSES
HOUSES
TROLLEY
TRACKS

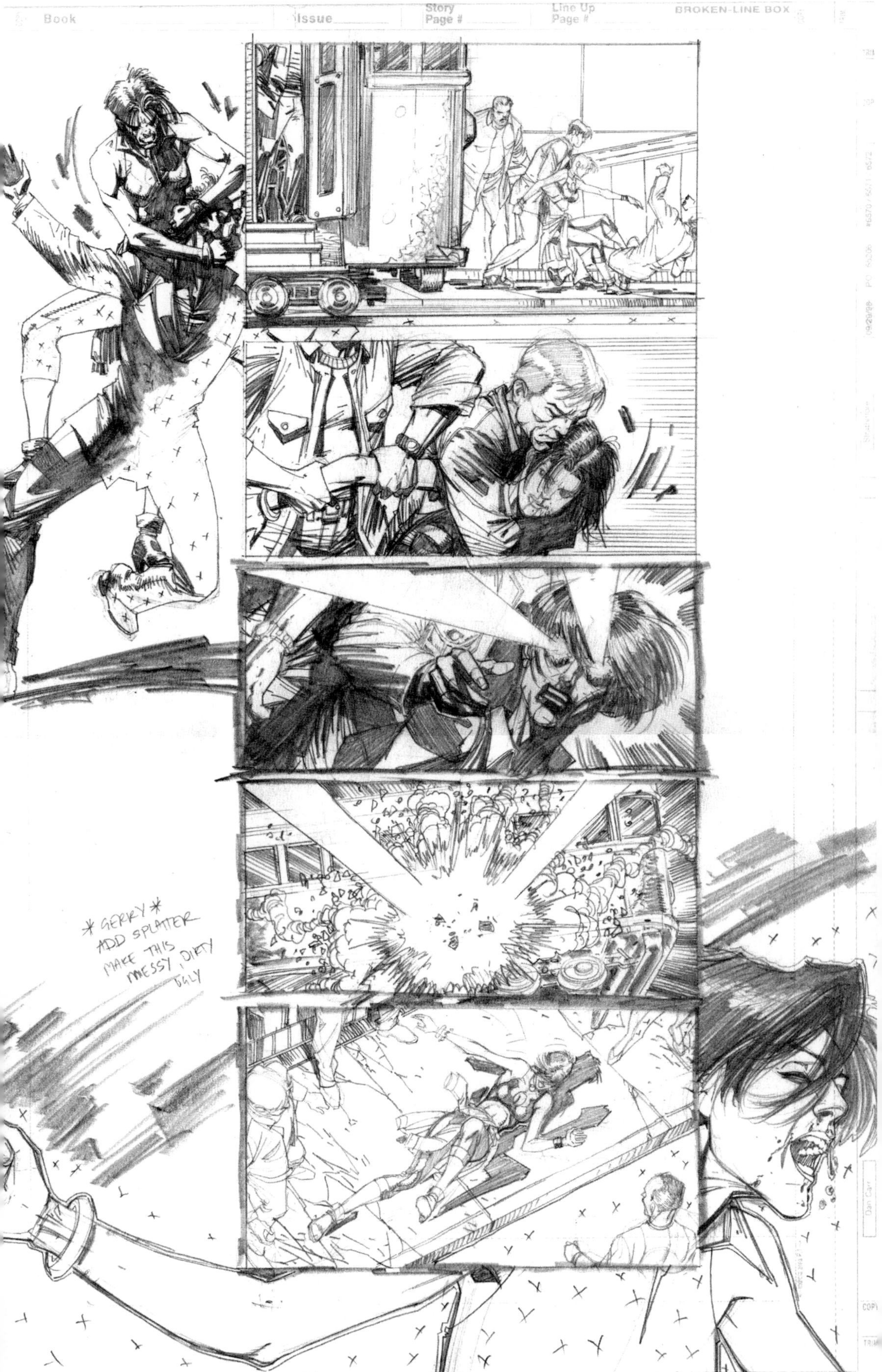
Book
Issue
Story Page #
Line Up Page #
BROKEN-LINE BOX
GERRY
ADD SPLATTER
MAKE THIS
MESSY, DIRTY
UGLY
DO NOT OVERLAP
CUT RIGHT-HAND PAGE AT THIS LINE
CUT LEFT-HAND PAGE AT THIS LINE

X-FORCE #102 PLOT

GAMES WITHOUT FRONTIERS

ONE of FOUR

plot

WARREN ELLIS

PREMISE:

X-FORCE are the flipside of the attempt to integrate the new mutant race into mainstream humanity: a proactive strikeforce that holds humanity to task for its secret crimes.

GAMES WITHOUT FRONTIERS is about how deep the hate goes.

There was an intelligence office devoted to analysing, advising on and reacting to "the mutant threat" as far back as the 1950's. It was called Cuckoo. Like the RAND Corporation, they were a hawkish, spooky unit who saw suffering and horror in terms of numbers and tables. Like the RAND Corporation, they demanded some visceral data from which to make their cold equations. And they didn't have the data they wanted for what became, by 1955, their central concerns -- making projections on a theoretical mutant-human ground war. They just didn't have the examples to hand.

So they decided to make the examples. They caused to have constructed a bioreactor: a device that beamed signals into nearby mutant genetic structures, signals that caused the mutant elements of the genome to mutate further, and to send very specific chemical signals to the brain. This device would have led to both full and latent mutants becoming very aggressively enhanced, and lethally hostile towards normal humans. It would, in effect, have forced interspecies war.

Cuckoo's permission to test was withdrawn at the last second by an administration increasingly nervous about backfire. The CIA had just, infamously, attempted to release LSD gas into San Francisco. Triggering a small contained civil war just for numbers... well, not right now. Cuckoo were ordered to destroy the bioreactor.

Cuckoo was disgusted. But not defeated. That tarnished and dubious CIA team in San Francisco were seconded to supervise the "destruction" of the bioreactor. A lie. It was buried

under San Francisco, set to standby, equipped with a disposable motion trigger. A fully-deniable configuration -- we just buried it to safely get rid of it, sir, we didn't realise that any number of things could have set it off, that its ageing trigger mechanism might become susceptible to seismic activity, or heavy building work aboveground, or any one of a dozen other things.

Cuckoo sat quietly down to wait. Sooner or later, it would get its data.

PAGES ONE to SIX

OPEN ON: A FERRY, travelling dark waters at night. Make this a page-wide shot, whacked out to bleed at top, left and right... a touch of the old Cinemascope and all that...

DISPLAY LETT;   PROLOGUE: Six Months Ago

CUT TO: the brightly lit BAR, we find PETE WISDOM, dressed in the usual (black double-breasted suit, white shirt, loosened black tie), buying a drink from an attentive BARMAID. An adjacent window shows the dark sea, night sky. He smiles at her. Pete Wisdom sports a black EYE-PATCH over his left eye, these days... (REF: EXCALIBUR 86-103)

BARMAID;   OH, YOUR POOR EYE. WHAT HAPPENED?

CUT TO: Pete sitting at a table with a shot of whisky; a pretty GIRL looks across at him from the next table. He looks across, raises an eyebrow. You can almost hear the Homer Simpson voiceover: Mmmm, pretty...

GIRL;   HELLO.

GIRL;   NEVER SEEN ANYONE WITH AN EYEPATCH BEFORE.

GIRL;   I KIND OF LIKE IT.

CUT TO: later, another WOMAN stands leaning against a wall smiling at him as he works a cigarette machine.

WOMAN;   IT'S... MANLY.

WOMAN;   HOW DID IT HAPPEN?

PETE;   WELL, I TELL YOU, I'M NEVER GOING TO BLOODY DAGESTAN AGAIN...

Later: Pete wanders out through a glass double-door onto the deck, smiling quietly to himself --

(no dialogue)

-- lights himself a cigarette in the dark with a Zippo, as he approaches the edge of the boat --

(no dialogue)

-- and the flame illuminates someone else out there. A tall man, in his thirties, short army haircut, heavy grey trenchcoat, patrician, tired eyes. ALISTAIRE STUART. (REF: EXCALIBUR 97-100 approx.)

STUART; HELLO, MR WISDOM.

Pete draws on his cigarette, making the end glow hotly -- not about to let it show that he's been surprised.

PETE; ALISTAIRE STUART.

PETE; I HAVEN'T SEEN YOU SINCE BLACK AIR RAN ITS TERMINAL PHASE IN LONDON.

They stand side by side at the edge of the ferry, at the railings, looking out at the dark. In the distance, the lights of a shoreline burn.

PETE; DIDN'T YOU GO OFF TO RUN THE OFFICE THAT REPLACED BLACK AIR'S REMIT?

STUART; THE DEPARTMENT. YES.

PETE; WELL, THEN, CALL ME WEIRD, BUT WHAT'S THE HEAD OF THE DEPARTMENT, WITH PERSONAL HELICOPTERS AND JETS AND ALL THAT DOING ON A MIDNIGHT FERRY OUT OF HARWICH?

Stuart in profile, looking out, stone-faced. There's trouble ahead.

STUART; WAITING TO HAVE A WORD WITH YOU, MR WISDOM.

Flip the angle, so we're looking at them both from a point that is actually several feet off the boat, out in the water.

PETE; CALL ME PETE, ALLY OLD SON. CALL ME PETE.

STUART; YOU'RE UP TO SOMETHING, MR WISDOM. AND I DON'T LIKE IT.

Pete turns and looks at the older man, smiling, cigarette in hand.

PETE; ME? I DON'T WORK IN INTEL ANYMORE, ALLY. AND I DON'T RUN WITH AN X-TEAM ANYMORE.

PETE; I'M WHAT YOU MIGHT CALL SEMI-RETIRED.

PETE; YOU KNOW. CONDO IN FLORIDA. NICE BUNGALOW IN CORNWALL. EYESIGHT'S GOING. GOT A WOMAN WHO COMES IN TO WASH ME EVERY SECOND THURSDAY.

Stuart favours Pete with his gaze for the first time. It is an unsettling look, the harsh glare of Authority and superiority. Pete draws on his cigarette smilingly, ignoring it.

STUART; YOU'RE FULL OF IT, PETE.

Pete then does something very odd. He flips up his eyepatch --

-- and scratches idly under the very intact, fully working eye it reveals.

STUART; I THOUGHT YOU LOST THAT EYE.

PETE; ALLY, OLD MATE, THIS IS THE EYEPATCH OF LOVE. BEST THING I EVER INVESTED IN. GIVES ME THE MUTANT POWER OF BEING HORRIBLY SEXY.

Pete replaces the eyepatch, smiling as he looks out to sea.

STUART; I KNOW WHAT HAPPENED TO YOU IN DAGESTAN. YOU'VE BEEN SPOTTED IN GENOSHA. AND TOKYO. HELSINKI. WASHINGTON DC.

Portrait of Pete as he exhales, looking nowhere in particular, cigarette glowing in his hand in the night.

PETE; DAGESTAN WAS A TERRIBLE MISUNDERSTANDING. AND I LIKE TO TRAVEL A LOT.

PETE; IF YOU'D BEEN BORN IN THE SCRAG-END OF LONDON INSTEAD OF IN SOME COUNTRY PILE WITH A SILVER SPOON DOWN YOUR GOB, YOU TOO WOULD WANT TO SPEND A LOT OF TIME

AWAY FROM HOME.

Stuart points out at the dwindling lights of shore, eyeing Pete like he was a bomb-throwing anar-
chist or something.

STUART;
YOU DON'T LIKE ENGLAND, MR WISDOM?

STUART;
BE CAREFUL. WE'RE STILL IN BRITISH WATERS.
THAT'S THE ENGLISH SHORELINE OUT THERE,
GOOD OLD ESSEX...

Pete draws on his cigarette, tight-lipped, eyes burning.

PETE;
I DON'T PARTICULARLY LIKE ANYWHERE, ALLY.

PETE;
EVERYWHERE I GO IS FULL OF SECRETS AND LIES,
YOU SEE.

PETE;
MAYBE IT'S JUST MY DODGY CHOICE OF HOLIDAY
DESTINATIONS, BUT EVERYWHERE I GO, THERE'S
CORRUPTION, AND SCUM, AND OTHER THINGS
THAT GET ON MY WICK.

Pete roughly indicates where Stuart was pointing, with his cigarette.

PETE;
I MEAN, BLOODY ESSEX THERE. YOU KNOW
WHAT'S JUST UP THE ROAD FROM HARWICH?

STUART;
THERE'S AN OLD GOVERNMENT NUCLEAR
BUNKER IN THE VICINITY. WOULD'VE BEEN
COMMAND AND CONTROL IN THE EVENT OF
WORLD WAR THREE. IT'S A TOURIST ATTRACTION
NOW.

Stuart turns and looks at Pete sharply; but now Pete has the upper hand. His turn to ignore
Stuart, smiling. Sinister.

PETE;
RIGHT. AND EAST OF THAT, RIGHT ON THE
COAST, IS BRITISH INTEL'S PRIMARY DISSECTION
LAB.

STUART;
EXCUSE ME?

PETE;
IT STARTED OUT AS PART OF THE EASY TIGER
PROGRAM. THEY DISSECTED MARTIANS HERE IN
1899, KICKING OFF A HUNDRED YEARS OF CUTTING
UP ALIENS FOR FUN AND PROFIT.

PETE;
BLACK AIR USED IT TO DISSECT THE WARPIES.

PETE;
REMEMBER THE WARPIES? POOR LITTLE BUGGERS
MUTATED BY ALL THAT REALITY-STRUCTURE
DAMAGE.

PETE;
COURSE YOU DO. YOU HELPED RESCUE A LOT OF
THEM FROM SOME BAD GUY, DIDN'T YOU?

PETE;
YOU'D THINK SOMEONE WHO RESCUED
DEFENSELESS MUTANT CHILDREN AND NOW RUNS
BRITAIN'S SINGLE PARANORMAL RESPONSE
OFFICE WOULD BE AWARE OF WHERE THEY DIED,
AND SHUT IT DOWN.

PETE;
WOULDNT YOU?

PETE;
IN FACT, YOU'D THINK THAT PERSON WOULD BE
AWARE OF WHAT STILL GOES ON THERE.

PETE;
WHAT'S THE TIME?

Stuart, nonplussed, reflexively goes for his watch.

PETE;
MIDNIGHT.

And suddenly, out in the dark, on the coastline, there's a huge explosion.

PETE;
OOOPS. I THINK YOUR DISSECTION LAB
ACCIDENTALLY BLEW UP.

Stuart turns on Pete, seething.

STUART;
THAT, WISDOM, WAS A TERRORIST ACT.

PETE;
BUGGER ME, WAS IT REALLY?

Red light flashes in Pete's eye. Stuart's forgotten what he's dealing with -- a MUTANT.

PETE;
YOU PEOPLE -- THE WORLD INTEL COMMUNITY --
ARE NOT BEHAVING PROPERLY. YOU ARE
PERPETRATING DISGUSTING CRIMES AGAINST
HUMANITY --

PETE; -- AND I AM PERSONALLY OFFENDED BY THE CRIMES AGAINST MUTANT HUMANITY, WHICH ARE COMMITTED WITH ABANDON.

PETE; BE ADVISED; THERE ARE A LOT OF PEOPLE LIKE ME OUT THERE IN THE DARK.

Close on Pete --

PETE; AND WE'RE KEEPING AN EYE ON YOU.

PAGES SEVEN to SEVENTEEN

OPEN ON: Desolate RUSSIAN terrain, broken by a large black HELICOPTER hanging in the chill air, and the sense of a grey CITY, breaking the horizon....

DISPLAY LETT; TODAY:

Close in on the HELICOPTER, then INSIDE:

To find a PILOT, a skinny ageing man called KOROLYEV in fatigues, and an attractive woman in her early forties called VALENTINA, who is slamming the mike of a field radio against the side of the long cargo area that takes up the bulk of the chopper's long fuselage.

VALENTINA; DAMNIT!

VALENTINA; MOSCOW WILL GIVE US NOTHING!

KOROLYEV; BUT THEY HAVE TO -- YOU TOLD THEM WHAT'S LOOSE IN 53 --

VALENTINA; THEY SAY, SCIENCE CITY 53 STILL DOES NOT OFFICIALLY EXIST, EVEN OVER A DECADE AFTER COMMUNISM. HOW CAN WE BE SEEN TO COMMIT FORCES TO A CITY THAT DOES NOT EXIST, IS NOT ON MAPS?

VALENTINA; PILOT -- BRING US BACK ACROSS THE CITY. WATCH FOR GROUND-TO-AIR ATTACK.

KOROLYEV; SO WHAT NOW?

VALENTINA; WE WATCH THIS REPRODUCE AND ADVANCE UNTIL EVERYONE IN THE CITY IS DEAD, AND THEN UNTIL EVERYONE IN THE PROVINCE IS DEAD, AND

SO ON UNTIL SOMEONE NOTICES OR UNTIL WE'RE ALL DEAD.

We advance on SCIENCE CITY 53, a grey pre-fab concrete hell of a city within grey walls. These places were built quickly and cheaply during the post-war Soviet regime as hothouses for scientists. They would live here, work here, reproduce here, teach here, die here.

We close in; to see the city overrun by... things. At first glance, you'd think them robots -- weird symmetrical designed shapes, all of them the same size and shape. But the longer we look, we realise -- the damned things are made out of MEAT, and their awful cutting weapons made from bone. They hack with serrated bone blades, jab with bone bayonets, shoot off bone and tendon missiles though gas-driven launchers or electromagnetic drivers powered by eel-like organs... (think the specialisation of creatures in STARSHIP TROOPERS).

The men, women and children of Science City 53 are being driven to the walls and savaged to death. Horrible.

INT. HELICOPTER

The FIELD RADIO crackles to life.

FROM RADIO; VALENTINA?

Valentina, baffled;

VALENTINA; WHO IS THIS?

FROM RADIO; PETE WISDOM. YOU CALLED FOR HELP. THE OLD SPOOKS NETWORK.

VALENTINA; THAT WAS BARELY TWELVE HOURS AGO! WHEN THE SPORE FIRST WENT CRITICAL!

CUT TO: A BLACK STEALTH HELICOPTER blasting low across Russian scrubland terrain.

INT. BLACK HELICOPTER: PETE WISDOM in his usual black suit, no eyepatch, speaking quickly and tensely into a radio mike. Behind him, one darkened figure we can't quite make out...

PETE; SOMEONE OWED ME A FAVOR. AND I'VE BROUGHT FRIENDS. DO YOU HAVE A CONTAINMENT OP IN PROGRESS?

INT. VALENTINA'S COPTER: ,

VALENTINA; WE HAVE NOTHING! WE DESPERATELY NEED HELP!

FROM RADIO: THEN TELL ME NOW: WHAT'VE WE GOT? WHAT ARE THEY?

VALENTINA; MEATSPORE STORMTROOPERS.

CUT TO: the horror in the City as we do the into dump -- keep the eye moving while we explain the scene's plot.

note for dialogue phase: if dialogue is in voice-over, as in the following, then don't box it up as a caption with inverted commas. In this kind of action comic, caption boxes can distance us from what's going on. Keep them pure -- just speech balloons and pictures. Therefore, just mark these up as VOICE (NO TAIL); tailless balloons.

VALENTINA; YOU MIGHT CALL THEM CELLULAR AUTOMATA -- ROBOT SOLDIERS THAT JUST HAPPEN TO BE MADE OUT OF FLESH AND BLOOD. TWO FUNCTIONS; TO KILL, AND TO BUILD MORE OF THEMSELVES.

VALENTINA; THEY'RE NOT ALIVE IN ANY TRUE SENSE; NO MIND, JUST A MEDIUM FOR HOLDING INSTRUCTIONS, BRAIN-TISSUE WRAPPED AROUND A SIMPLE COMPUTER PROCESSOR.

VALENTINA; WE STOLE THE PROCESS FROM CUCKOO, AN AMERICAN INTELLIGENCE OFFICE, IN 1953. SCIENCE CITY 23 WAS REDIRECTED INTO OTHER RESEARCH IN '61, AND...

CUT back to PETE, lighting a cigarette. Keep it moving. Fast cuts.

PETE; ...AND SOMETHING SET IT OFF. WHAT?

INT. VALENTINA'S COPTER

VALENTINA; ALL THE CUCKOO INNOVATIONS SEEM STRANGELY UNSTABLE, DESPITE OUR IMPROVEMENT OF THE PROCESSES INVOLVED. THEY WERE A GOOD THIRTY YEARS AHEAD OF THEIR TIME, BUT STILL...

VALENTINA; ... CAN YOU HELP?

INT. BLACK HELICOPTER

PETE; PETE WISDOM TO ALL POINTS. LET'S BRING THIS ONE HOME.

PETE; SAM; DEATH FROM ABOVE.

CUT TO: At high altitude -- SAM GUTHRIE headed down through the upper reaches of the air, through clouds on a ballistic trajectory straight for the ground. Wearing an earpiece/mike radio headset.

SAM; HARD IN WHERE THE CONCENTRATION IS, AT DEAD CENTER; UNDERSTOOD.

FROM HEADSET; YOU KNOW, I'VE BEEN THINKING... MAYBE YOU SHOULD START CALLING ME "PROFESSOR W."

Pete turns to the back of the chopper -- and there, as the lighting changes, are TABITHA SMITH, JIM PROUDSTAR and JESSE BEDLAM. All wearing communications headsets.

PETE; TABBY; DOWN ON THE GROUND WHEN WE'RE IN CLOSE ENOUGH.

PETE; JIM; YOU'RE JESSE'S DELIVERY SYSTEM. SAM'S MAKING YOUR MARK -- DROP HIM IN IT.

JESSE; HE DIDN'T MEAN DROP. HE DIDN'T.

PETE;

SAM GUTHRIE, WHERE ARE YOU? TIME'S TICKING AWAY HERE.

CUT TO: A dizzying shot from behind Sam, of Science City 53 bulging into view in front of him, very close now, he moving very fast, protection field sparking and blurring with the velocity acting on it...

SAM;

INCOMING.

A clutch of meatspore troopers look up --

-- and Sam hits the center of the city like an A-bomb --

-- impact shockwaves vaporising the nearby buildings --

-- and smashing all the troopers in the center of the city to wet bits.

As the smoke clears ---

-- the BLACK HELICOPTER is seen sweeping towards the city --

-- PROUDSTAR and BEDLAM dive out of the chopper's side, the former hanging onto the latter --

-- shooting down and under the advancing chopper --

-- Bedlam dropped in the steaming crater of ground zero, Proudstar going on to overshoot the area. Sam Guthrie's still there, standing up, surveying the damage.

JESSE;

DEATH FROM ABOVE.

SAM;

SOMETHING LIKE THAT. WHICH WAY YOU HEADED, JESSE?

Jesse points off to his left.

JESSE;

I'M GOING TO WORK FROM HERE. PETE WANTS YOU TO WORK THE PERIMETER WITH JIM AND TABBY. TRY TO SAVE ANYONE WHO'S SURVIVED HERE THIS LONG.

SAM;

DONE.

JESSE;

PETE, THIS IS JESSE; GET THE CHOPPER THE HELL OUTSIDE THE CITY ONCE YOU'VE PUT TABBY DOWN. I'M GOING TO BE PUTTING OUT A SERIOUS ELECTRONIC DISRUPTION FIELD HERE.

FROM HEADSET;

THAT'S WHAT YOU WERE HIRED FOR. GIVE US TEN SECONDS AND THEN GIVE IT SOME, MY SON.

CUT TO: TABITHA SMITH at the city edge, just inside the wall, dropping from the black helicopter.

FROM HEADSET;

OKAY. I'VE GOT YOU AT FOUR O'CLOCK, JIM PROUDSTAR AT 8 O'CLOCK AND SAM AT 12. YOU EACH COVER A THIRD OF THE CITY PERIMETER.

FROM HEADSET;

PUSH THE TROOPERS BACK IN AND SAVE THEM THAT NEED SAVING.

TABBY;

THAT'S THE JOB DESCRIPTION, BOSS.

She lands like a cat, and immediately starts setting off her eye-burning little plasma bombs in hot sparking sweeps in the air....

TABBY;

SAVE THEM THAT NEED SAVING.

Troopers advance on her. She grows still and silent, concentrating;

CUT TO: PETE WISDOM, obviously watching from the chopper window;

PETE;

REMEMBER HOW I TAUGHT YOU TO DO IT. SHARPEN YOUR MIND. DRAW FOCUS ON THE PLASMA BOMBS YOU GENERATE, MAKE THEM CLEAR AND BRIGHT IN YOUR MIND...

...and now we see how her powers have come on in six months. A brilliant spray of fireworks gives way to a spread of harsh explosions; multiple hot blasts that blow her assailants apart.

PETE, from chopper, smiling out the window;

PETE;

TABITHA SMITH, I AM BLOODY IMPRESSED. NICE ONE.

Tabby allows herself a lop-sided smile.

TABBY;   "CHEERS."

CUT TO: civilian men and women and children, ordinary poor people, rushing down down cold grey concrete streets, away from the advancing morass of meatspore killers, being cut down one by one as they slow down, fall, are overtaken....

...and then JAMES PROUDSTAR lands between them.

Makes sure the civilians are behind him --

-- and then lashes out with one fast massive arm, ripping the lead soldiers apart.

Blow after blow, smashing the soldiers, driving them back, back...

CUT TO: TABBY doing the same.

CUT TO: SAM doing the same.

CUT TO: JESSE BEDLAM, concentrating.

JESSE;   HERE WE GO --

And a visible expanding disc of JESSE BEDLAM SPECIAL EFFECT -- a fractal colour-hold rush -- emanates out from him...

...booming across the city streets and houses --

-- and every soldier in its orbit DETONATES, its control chip exploding as Jesse's disruptor field hits it.

Therefore, as Tabby, Sam and James hold the soldiers back, the wave hits the soldiers from behind --

-- and in seconds, the city is quiet.

CUT TO: PETE WISDOM

PETE;   AND THAT'S A WRAP. TAKE ME DOWN, PILOT.

PAGES EIGHTEEN to TWENTY

LATER: X-FORCE gather around the BLACK HELICOPTER, which is parked in dry scrubland just outside the city.

PETE WISDOM is emerging slowly from the back of the chopper; we note now that he is walking

In the background, the other chopper puts down, a few hundred yards away.

PETE;   WHERE NOW, MY X-MEN?

SAM;   SAN FRANCISCO. WE GOT REAL COMFORTABLE THERE, LAST YEAR.

PETE;   SAN FRANCISCO IT IS.

JESSE;   YOU KNOW YOU CAN'T SMOKE IN CALIFORNIAN BARS NOW, MR W?

PETE;   LET'S GO TO MOROCCO.

TABBY;   YOU SAID SAN FRANCISCO.

PETE;   I LIED.

Tabby reaches for Pete's throat. He starts laughing.

PETE;   OKAY, OKAY, WE'RE GOING TO SAN FRANCISCO....

PETE;   ...BUT NOT YET.

PETE;   WE'VE ONLY DONE HALF OUR JOB HERE.

TABBY;   OH, MAN...

PETE;   COME ON. THIS IS WHAT YOU SIGNED UP FOR.

PETE;   YOU WANTED A REAL JOB, A REAL ROLE TO PLAY; THIS IS IT.

PETE;   THIS IS THE UNDERSIDE OF THE WORLD HERE; THE SECRET THINGS IN THE DARK, THE UNKNOWN CRIMES AGAINST HUMANITY THAT JUMP UP TO BITE US ALL ON THE BUTT WHEN WE LEAST EXPECT IT.

PETE;   WE'RE THE UNDERSIDE OF THE WORLD. MUTANTS. THIS IS WHAT YOU WANTED TO DO -- TO SHOW 'EM ALL THAT WE DO THE JOBS WORTH DOING.

PETE;   WHAT WAS IT YOU SAID TO ME, JESSE? TO HELL WITH XAVIER'S FAIRY-DUST BULL ABOUT INTEGRATION? LET'S JUST SHOW 'EM BY

PETE; JOB AIN'T DONE YET. I WANT TO KNOW WHAT CUCKOO WAS, THAT IT DESIGNED A "SPORE" THAT CLONES INSANE MEAT ROBOTS AT FACTORY SPEED.

VALENTINA walks up.

VALENTINA; WE STILL HAVE THE ARCHIVES; OR DID, ANYWAY, BEFORE THE SPORE ERUPTED.

VALENTINA; PROVIDED IT'S STILL INTACT, ALL THE INFORMATION WE HAVE IS YOURS.

PETE; WON'T THAT CAUSE TROUBLE IN MOSCOW?

VALENTINA; EITHER WE PAY YOU IN INFORMATION OR YOU INVOICE YELTSIN FOR MANY ROUBLES LIKE GOOD WESTERNERS. THEY WILL LOVE US FOR THIS.

VALENTINA; HELL, THEY'LL JUST BE GRATEFUL WE DID NOT GIVE YOU A NUCLEAR MISSILE OR TWO AS A BONUS.

She takes a good look at Pete, and then takes his arm, giving him support, paying him lots of attention...

VALENTINA; OH, NOW LOOK AT YOU, PETE... YOUR POOR LEG...

PAGE TWENTY-ONE to TWENTY-TWO

OPEN ON: SAN FRANCISCO. Give me a nice big picture of a bit of San Francisco -- not the Golden Gate, but a residential district; a few shops, a lot of those beautiful houses, a tram coming up the hill....

DISPLAY LETT;   TODAY: SAN FRANCISCO

MOVE IN on the image; pedestrians, cars going by. People.

A woman stops, there on the steep San Franciscan street. Shivers, as if there were a sudden chill in the air. Something's wrong. She touches her fingers to her nose.

Her nose is bleeding.

A young man walks past, oblivious to her. She turns to look at him, looks at the back of his head as he goes past.

And her eyes shine.

She goes for him. Literally leaps on him, her fingernails gouging into his skin. he shrieks, flails, doesn't know what's happening to him --

-- and then she breaks his neck.

Bystanders struggle to pull her off him. The tram clangs past.

Her eyes burn.

And as she's pulled away, that's it, flashpoint -- she jerks her head to the side, as if to glare at her "attackers" --

-- and EYEBEAMS ignite from her wide eyes, just missing the nearest person, but slashing through and destroying the passing tram.

As it falls over in smoking halves, bodies tumbling out of it, she falls onto her back, in the midst of what looks like an epileptic fit, blood streaming from her nose...

TO BE CONTINUED

Whilce Portacio   Pencils

Warren Ellis   Plot

Comicraft's
John Roshell   Cover Design

Dan Carr &
Sue Crespi   Production

Christine Slusarz   Manufacturing

Jason Liebig   Editor

Lysa Hawkins   Assistant Editor

Bob Harras   Editor in Chief